SECTION OF LITIGATION

Discovery Problems
and their
Solutions

Paul W. Grimm · Charles S. Fax · Paul Mark Sandler

Defending Liberty
Pursuing Justice

Cover design by ABA Publishing

08 07 06 05 04   5 4 3 2 1

Library of Congress Cataloging-in-Publication Data

Fax, Charles S., 1948-
Discovery problems and their solutions / Charles S. Fax, Paul W. Grimm, Paul M. Sandler, authors.
    p. cm.
    Includes index.
    ISBN 1-59031-347-X
    1. Discovery (Law)—United States. I. Grimm, Paul W., 1951- II. Sandler, Paul Mark. III. Title.
KF8900.F29 2004
347.73'72—dc22   2004023405

Contents

Dedication

For our wives: Lynne Grimm, Michele Weil, and Peggy Sandler; and our children: John, Samantha, and Gia Grimm, Joanna and Ben Fax, and Douglas and David Sandler.

Acknowledgments

We could not have written this book without the generous assistance of friends, colleagues, and assistants.

Foremost, we offer our special gratitude to our editor, Christopher Lutz of Steptoe and Johnson, and the ABA Litigation Section's book publishing committee.

We further owe a debt of gratitude to the following attorneys and staff of Shapiro Sher Guinot & Sandler: Robert B. Levin, Eric R. Harlan, Erin E. Johnson, John J. Leidig, Colleen D. Lorenzen, and Kathleen L. Pollard; and the following attorneys from the chambers of the Honorable Paul W. Grimm: Jackie Badders and Claudia Diamond.

Foreword

Discovery is the inescapable, enduring feature of modern civil litigation. Since 1960, the United States civil justice system has witnessed a litigation explosion and trial implosion. The number of cases has skyrocketed, but the number of trials has declined—both proportionately and, in federal court, absolutely.[1] As Chief Judge William G. Young of the District of Massachusetts has eloquently encapsulated the vanishing trial phenomenon: "The American jury system is withering away."[2]

Putting aside all other issues raised by the vanishing trial phenomenon, it clearly accentuates the critical importance of discovery. Parties evaluate cases, and make judgments about settlement value and other disposition techniques, in light of the evidence gathered in discovery. Effective discovery is crucial.

This book teaches effective discovery. Judge Grimm and Messrs. Fax and Sandler interweave practical advice with salient case law and keen observations honed by decades of experience. They examine in detail the many nettlesome problems presented by discovery, including electronic discovery, in light of the strictures imposed by the Federal Rules of Civil Procedure.

H. L. Mencken once wrote "For every complex problem there is an answer that is clear, simple, and wrong." There is no single, clear, simple answer to the complex issues raised by discovery, especially in

---

1. *See* AMERICAN COLLEGE OF TRIAL LAWYERS, THE "VANISHING TRIAL:" THE COLLEGE, THE PROFESSION, THE CIVIL JUSTICE SYSTEM at § I, pp. 5-10 (October 2004); Marc Galanter, *The Vanishing Trial: An Examination of Trials and Related Matters in Federal and State Courts*, 1 THE JOURNAL OF EMPIRICAL LEGAL STUDIES, No. 3 (Nov. 2004); Thomas H. Cohen & Steven K. Smith, *Civil Trial Cases and Verdicts in Large Counties, 2001*, BUREAU OF JUSTICE STATISTICS BULLETIN at 9, Table 10 (U.S. Department of Justice, April 2004).

2. Hon. William G. Young, *An Open Letter to U.S. District Court Judges*, THE FEDERAL LAWYER 30, 31 (July 2003).

this era of spoliation. Parties engaged in discovery seek not merely to find documentary evidence but rather to find evidence that documents have been destroyed. But there are effective, straightforward approaches to discovery and to addressing spoliation issues. This book deftly captures them. This volume is an invaluable resource for discovery techniques and for associated motion practice.

Gregory P. Joseph
New York, New York
October 2004

Introduction

Much has been written about courtroom advocacy in civil trials and appeals in the federal courts, but far less commentary is available on pretrial discovery and, in particular, the disputes that arise in discovery. The dearth of writing on this topic is a problem, because it does not accurately reflect what litigators actually do. Lawyers and clients today devote enormous time, effort, and expense to discovery. More often than not, discovery, and not trial, is the central battleground of a case. Most civil lawsuits in federal court end before trial, either by pretrial settlement or on dispositive motion. In either case, the fruits of discovery can be critical to the outcome. The need for analytical and strategic guidance on problems in discovery is heightened by the fact that much of it is handled by relatively inexperienced lawyers and, in the case of document production, legal assistants.

This book is written to address that need. It describes the problems that civil litigators encounter most frequently in pretrial discovery and presents suggestions and strategies for solving these problems. Following a background discussion on the scope and types of discovery, discovery problems are presented as hypotheticals (many of which the authors have encountered in their experience), followed by a discussion that includes the law and helpful practice tips.

OVERVIEW

Rules 26-37 and Rule 45 of the Federal Rules of Civil Procedure, which embrace pretrial discovery, were meant to simplify and rationalize civil litigation by emphasizing reciprocal pretrial disclosure. The framers of the rules thought that cases would more likely settle or be resolved by dispositive motion if each side had a thorough pretrial understanding of its adversary's case. Of course, as the world has become more complex, the discovery rules have themselves become more complex. Amidst the complications, two truths have emerged: First, anyone who aspires to be a competent civil litigator must master the rules of pretrial discovery. Second, that process takes time and experience.

Originally adopted in 1938, the discovery provisions of the Federal Rules of Civil Procedure remained largely unchanged until 1970, when the belief that discovery was being abused triggered the first wave of significant amendments. There were additional amendments in 1980 and again in 1983 (it was then that Rule 26(b) was amended to empower the court to limit the frequency and extent of discovery methods). In 1993, despite concerted opposition from the bar, the United States Supreme Court approved extensive amendments to Rule 26, including the crucial feature of mandatory initial disclosures. Yet another series of amendments was adopted in 2000, incorporating, among other changes, a uniform national standard for mandatory disclosures.

Generally speaking, attorneys have at their disposal the following discovery instruments under the Federal Rules of Civil Procedure:

1. Written interrogatories (Rule 33);
2. Production of documents and things and entry upon land for inspection and other purposes (Rule 34);
3. The issuance of subpoenas (Rule 45);
4. Physical and mental examinations (Rule 35);
5. Depositions upon written questions (Rule 31);
6. Oral depositions (Rule 30); and
7. Request for admissions and genuineness of documents (Rule 36).

Appendix A contains the current (2004) version of the discovery rules, that is, Rules 26-37 and Rule 45. The following summary, which identifies only key elements of the rules, obviously is not a substitute for reading and understanding each rule. In addition—and this is a crucial point—the rules cannot be fully understood without consulting each United States District Court's complementary *local* rules on discovery. They, too, are required reading for a federal litigator, but are beyond the scope of this text except as used in a number of examples for illustrative purposes. Finally, practitioners who are accustomed to relying on state rules should take care to note the differences in interpretation between the state courts and the federal courts, even when the language of a particular rule is identical or similar.

RULE 26: GENERAL PROVISIONS GOVERNING DISCOVERY; DUTY OF DISCLOSURE

Rule 26 is central to all discovery. It should be consulted at the outset of litigation and whenever a specific discovery device is being used. Rule 26(a) identifies three distinct types of discovery disclosures. The first, "initial disclosures," is addressed in Rule 26(a)(1). This rule requires disclosure of certain information to the other side at the start of the lawsuit and before any adverse request for discovery. The required information includes the name, telephone number and address of individuals likely to have discoverable information; copies (or a description by category and location) of documents in the possession, custody or control of the party; and a computation of any category of damages claimed by the disclosing party.

The 2000 changes to the discovery rules rescinded the power of the district courts to adopt local rules that "opted out" of the Rule 26(a)(1) initial disclosures. As some courts had in fact opted out, this change greatly expanded the number of cases in which disclosures must be made. Additionally, the 2000 changes narrowed the scope of initial disclosures to information in each category that the disclosing party "may use" to support its claims or defenses. Previously, disclosure was required of information applicable to each topic covered by the rule even if the disclosing party did not intend to rely on such information in its case, and even if the information might be harmful to the disclosing party.

The second of the Rule 26 disclosures, spelled out in subsection (a)(2)(B), requires each party to disclose the identity of any expert it may use as a witness, as well as a statement of the expert's opinions, data, and other information considered in forming his or her opinions; exhibits that support the opinion; the expert's qualifications and publications; the rate of compensation of the expert and a list of other cases in which the expert has participated for at least the preceding four years. The deadline for expert disclosures is usually set forth in a scheduling order adopted by the court.

The third of the disclosures, set forth in Rule 26(a)(3), requires specific "pretrial disclosures." Each party must disclose the address and telephone number of witnesses intended to be called at trial and identify deposition excerpts intended to be offered in lieu of trial testimony, as well as documents and exhibits that may be introduced or used at trial. Unless otherwise ordered by the court, these disclosures must be made not later than 30 days before trial.

Rule 37(c) puts teeth into the Rule 26(a) mandatory disclosures by precluding a party that failed to make them from using, at trial or in support of any motion, information that should have been disclosed but was not, unless there was substantial justification for failing to make the disclosure or the failure was harmless.

After describing required disclosures, Rule 26 defines the scope of adversary discovery. Rule 26(b)(1) provides that discovery embraces any matter not privileged that is relevant to the claims or defenses raised in the pleadings even if it does not constitute admissible evidence. This language was added in 2000 to narrow the scope of discovery from the previous standard, which permitted discovery of any unprivileged information relevant to the "subject matter" of the litigation—not just the claims and defenses. Even as limited, however, the scope of permissible discovery remains broad.

Rule 26(b)(2) establishes a key discovery management tool that is too frequently overlooked. It allows the court, on its own initiative or upon motion of a party, to limit discovery if it determines, after employing a multi-factor cost/benefit analysis, that the discovery sought would be too cumulative, expensive or burdensome.

Rule 26(b)(3) provides that trial preparation materials are not discoverable except upon a showing that the party seeking such discovery has substantial need of the materials in preparing for trial and is unable, without undue hardship, to obtain a substantial equivalent of the materials by other means. The rule further provides that in ordering discovery of such materials, the court must still protect against disclosure of the mental impressions, conclusions, opinions or legal theories of an attorney or other representative of a party concerning the litigation. In sum, Rule 26(b)(3) codifies the "work product" objection to discovery.

Rule 26(b)(4) authorizes depositions and other discovery of experts.

Rule 26(b)(5) provides that if a party claiming privilege or work product withholds information that is otherwise discoverable, it must describe the nature of the document or communication withheld to enable the other party to assess the applicability of the privilege or protection.

Rule 26(c) authorizes the issuance of protective orders to limit discovery, with the proviso that the movant must certify that it has conferred with the adverse party in an effort to resolve the dispute, or has at least attempted to do so. The prevailing party in such dispute is entitled to seek an award of expenses.

Rule 26(d) governs the timing and sequence of discovery. Generally, a party may not seek discovery before the parties have conferred as required by Rule 26(f), but once discovery is initiated, it may be conducted in any sequence, and it is not grounds for delay of one party's discovery that an adverse party is conducting discovery.

Rule 26(e) sets forth the predicates for mandatory supplementation of disclosures and discovery responses. A party is under a duty to supplement at appropriate intervals its disclosures and prior responses to interrogatories, requests for production of documents, and requests for admissions. Experts are required to supplement their reports and responses to depositions by the time the party's pretrial disclosures under Rule 26(a)(3) are due.

Rule 26(f) sets forth the general requirement for a pre-discovery conference among counsel to discuss the issues in the case and potential for settlement, and to endeavor to develop a discovery plan.

Finally, Rule 26(g) mandates that an attorney of record or, in the case of an unrepresented party, the party itself, sign all disclosures, discovery requests, responses, and objections. That signature certifies that the disclosure is complete and correct as of the date made and that the discovery request, response, or objection conforms to the rules and is not interposed for an improper purpose. Rule 26(g)(3) provides for sanctions if the rule is violated.

RULE 27: DEPOSITIONS BEFORE ACTION OR PENDING APPEAL

A person who wants to perpetuate testimony before suit has been initiated may file a verified petition in the United States District Court stating (a) that the petitioner expects to be a party to an action, (b) that the petitioner is presently unable to bring the action, (c) the subject matter of the expected action, (d) the facts that the petitioner desires to establish by the proposed testimony, (e) the names of the persons the petitioner expects will be adverse parties, (f) the names and addresses of the persons to be examined and the substance of the testimony that petitioner expects to elicit, and (g) a request for an order authorizing the deposition(s) of such persons. Notice must be given to potential adverse parties. This procedure is also available for cases on appeal as to evidence needed to perpetuate the record for use in the event of further fact-finding proceedings.

RULE 28: PERSONS BEFORE WHOM DEPOSITIONS MAY BE TAKEN

A deposition in the United States must be taken before an officer authorized to administer oaths and take testimony. A deposition abroad may be taken pursuant to any applicable treaty, convention or letter of request, or upon notice before a person authorized to administer oaths or commissioned by the court.

RULE 29: STIPULATIONS REGARDING DISCOVERY PROCEDURE

Parties may stipulate regarding discovery procedures. Federal and local rules and pretrial orders cannot be avoided or changed, however, absent court order.

RULE 30: DEPOSITIONS UPON ORAL EXAMINATION

Rule 30(a) establishes when an oral deposition may be taken—with and without leave of court. Rule 30(b) sets forth the notice requirements for an oral deposition ("reasonable notice" if documents are not sought, 30 days' notice if documents are sought) as well as the methods of recording the deposition and the mechanism for production of documents and things at a deposition (referring the proponent to Rule 34).

Rule 30(b)(6) allows a party to name as the deponent an entity, as distinct from an individual. In that case, the requesting party must designate with reasonable particularity the matters for which the examination is requested. The entity so named must designate one or more officers, directors or agents on its behalf and may set forth for each person designated the matters about which the person will testify. The designee's testimony is not limited to his or her personal knowledge of the topics identified in the notice of deposition, but includes information "known or reasonably available" to the designating organization. Rule 32(a)(2) states that the deposition of a Rule 30(b)(6) designee may be used at trial by an adverse party for "any purpose."

Rule 30(c) sets forth the procedures for taking a deposition, administration of the oath, and making objections. Rule 30(d) provides that objections to questions must be stated concisely and in a non-argumentative and non-suggestive fashion. Instructions not to answer may be given only when necessary to preserve a privilege or enforce a limitation directed by the court, or to present a motion to terminate a deposition for abusive or bad faith conduct under Rule 30(d)(4). Rule 30(d)(2) limits the deposition of an individual party or witness to one day of seven hours. However, the court must allow additional time consistent with Rule 26(b)(2) if needed for fair examination of the deponent. Under Rule 30(d)(3), if counsel conducts himself or herself in an improper fashion, frustrates the fair examination of a deponent or interposes impediments or delays, the court may impose sanctions, including the reasonable costs and attorneys' fees incurred by any parties as a result of the misconduct.

Rule 30(e) provides that, if requested by the deponent or a party before completion of the deposition, the deponent shall have 30 days after being notified by the officer that the transcript or recording is available in which to review it, and if there are any changes in form or substance, to sign a statement reciting such changes and the reasons for making them.

RULE 31: DEPOSITIONS UPON WRITTEN QUESTIONS

Parties that want to take a deposition upon written questions shall serve them upon every other party. An adverse party may then serve cross-questions and the initiating party may serve redirect questions. Copies of the notice and all questions served are delivered by the party seeking the deposition to the officer designated in the notice; that officer then proceeds to take the deposition of the witness and prepares, certifies, and files or mails the deposition, attaching a copy of the notice and the questions received by the officer.

RULE 32: USE OF DEPOSITIONS IN COURT PROCEEDINGS

The deposition of an adverse party and its Rule 30(b)(6) designee may be used for any purpose. The deposition of a witness may be used for any purpose if the witness is dead; more than 100 miles from the place of trial or out of the country; unable to attend because of age, illness or infirmity; or due to other exceptional circumstances. The deposition of a party or witness may also be used to contradict or impeach the trial testimony of that person. However, the deposition of a party cannot be used against that party if it was served with notice of the deposition less than 11 days before its commencement and he or she filed a motion for protective order promptly upon receiving such notice (which motion remained pending at the time of the deposition). Objections to the competency of a witness or the relevance or materiality of testimony are not waived for failure to make them during the deposition unless the ground(s) for the objection could have been obviated if stated at that time.

RULE 33: INTERROGATORIES TO PARTIES

Rule 33(a) provides for the issuance of interrogatories. There may not be more than 25 interrogatories unless the court allows or the parties so stipulate. Absent leave of court or stipulation, interrogatories may not be served before the time specified in Rule 26(d) (generally, until after the parties have conferred to evaluate the case and settlement possibilities and plan discovery). Rule 33(b) sets forth the procedure for answers and objections to interrogatories. Rule 33(b)(4) states that a failure to state with specificity all grounds for objection to an interrogatory waives the unstated objection unless the court later permits it for good cause shown. Rule 33(c) allows for the use of interrogatory answers as evidence at trial to the extent permitted by the rules of evidence. Rule 33(d) provides for the option to produce business records in lieu of a narrative answer to an interrogatory where such answer may be derived from the business records of the party upon whom the interrogatory has been served, and the burden of retrieving that information from the records is substantially the same for both parties.

RULE 34: PRODUCTION OF DOCUMENTS AND THINGS AND ENTRY UPON LAND FOR INSPECTION AND OTHER PURPOSES

Responses to requests for production are due 30 days after service. The response shall address each request, either permitting inspection or objecting and stating the reasons for the objection. The party making production must produce the documents in the form in which they are kept in the usual course of business; alternatively, documents may be organized and labeled to correspond with the categories in the request. A non-party can be compelled to produce documents as provided in Rule 45.

RULE 35: PHYSICAL AND MENTAL EXAMINATIONS OF PERSONS

The court may order a party to submit to a physical or mental examination when such condition is in controversy. The order can be made only upon a motion for good cause shown and upon notice to the person to be examined and to all parties.

RULE 36: REQUESTS FOR ADMISSION

A party may serve an unlimited number of requests for admissions or genuineness of documents. Each matter for which an admission is requested shall be stated separately. If the request seeks admission that a document is genuine, it must be attached unless it has already been produced or made available for inspection. A matter is deemed admitted unless a response to the request is served within 30 days, subject to an agreement or order modifying the time limit. When an objection is made, the grounds must be stated. Lack of knowledge is not an acceptable response unless it is accompanied by a statement that reasonable inquiry has been made.

A party who has requested admissions may move to determine the sufficiency of the responses. Admissions are deemed conclusive absent court order permitting withdrawal or amendment of the admission.

RULE 37: FAILURE TO MAKE DISCLOSURE OR COOPERATE IN DISCOVERY: SANCTIONS

Rule 37(a) provides that a party may move to compel disclosure and for sanctions if another party fails to make disclosure required by Rule 26(a), answer a question under Rule 30 or 31, fails to make a designation under Rule 30(b)(6) or Rule 31(a), fails to answer an interrogatory under Rule 33, or fails to respond to a document request under Rule 34.

A Rule 37 motion must certify that the movant, in good faith, has conferred or attempted to confer with the party not making the disclosure or response in an effort to secure the information without court action. The court may order the party or deponent whose conduct necessitated the motion, or the attorney advising the conduct that necessitated the motion, or both of them, to pay the moving party its reasonable expenses incurred in making the motion, including attorneys' fees, unless the court determines that the opposing party's nondisclosure, response or objection was substantially justified or that other circumstances make an award of expenses unjust.

Rule 37(a)(3) contains the extremely important, but often overlooked, requirement that an incomplete or evasive discovery disclosure, response or answer, whether to written discovery or a deposition question, is deemed to be a failure to disclose, respond or answer.

Rule 37(b) provides for sanctions for failure to be sworn or answer a question at deposition after being ordered to do so by the court. It also permits a court to impose sweeping, and potentially case-determinative, sanctions against a party that refuses to obey an order directing discovery. The sanctions include: ordering that certain facts be taken as established at trial; refusing to allow the disobedient party to support or oppose designated claims at trial; striking pleadings or parts thereof; staying or dismissing the action; and rendering a default judgment.

Under Rule 37(c), absent substantial justification or a showing that the violation is harmless, the failure of a party to disclose information required by Rule 26(a) or 26(e)(1), or to amend a prior response to discovery as required by Rule 26(e)(2), bars that party from using as evidence at trial any witness or information not so disclosed. Rule 37(d) permits the imposition of sanctions against a party that fails to attend its own deposition or to answer interrogatories or document production requests, and Rule 37(g) establishes sanctions that may be issued against a party or attorney who fails to participate in good faith in the development and submission of a discovery plan as required by Rule 26(f).

RULE 45: SUBPOENA

When seeking disclosure of testimony or documents from persons who are not parties, a party may obtain and serve a subpoena pursuant to Rule 45. Generally, a subpoena is valid if served and returnable within the district of the court that has issued it, or if served anywhere outside the district within 100 miles of the place where the deposition or trial is to occur. A subpoena may be valid if served under other circumstances identified in the rule, as well. A subpoena commanding the production of documents and things, or for the inspection of a premises prior to trial, must be served on all parties to the litigation, as well as to the person or entity ordered to make the production. Rule 45(c) establishes procedures to protect non-parties from abusive subpoenas.

With this summary of the rules' basic discovery features in mind, we now proceed to actual discovery problems and their solutions.

Section 1

Interrogatories, Document Requests, Requests for Admission and Motions for Mental and Physical Examinations

Interrogatories, Document Requests, Requests for Admission and Motions for Mental and Physical Examinations

1

OVERVIEW

Frequently relegated to new associates, interrogatories and requests for production of documents often get too little attention in planning the case. Properly used, they provide a framework for thorough pretrial discovery. Identification of witnesses and key documents during the early stages of litigation is indispensable for effective preparation. Likewise, contention interrogatories that require opposing parties to support or respond to contentions in pleadings help everyone understand what is really at stake. They are a way to frame the issues for summary judgment, depositions, settlement, and trial.

Drafting and responding to requests for production of documents can also pose numerous complex problems—among other things, a lawyer must be familiar with the need for and use of privilege logs and the special challenges of electronic discovery.

The chapters that follow discuss all of these issues.

1. FRAMING PROPER INTERROGATORIES

In a diversity action, the plaintiff, a corporation that owned several office buildings, alleged that the defendant breached a contract to provide janitorial services to the buildings by providing insufficient staff, failing to train them properly, and neglecting to dust and vacuum offices adequately. Faced with these claims, the defendant posed the following interrogatories, among others, to plaintiff:

1. State your date of birth, office and home addresses and telephone numbers, and social security number.
2. If this lawsuit involves an accident, provide all of the details of the accident.
3. If you are claiming medical injury or lost employment as a result of the accident, please. [*sic*]
4. If this is a breach of contract action, do you maintain that the contract that was breached was a written contract?
5. If so, identify the contract by date and substance, and attach a copy of the contract to your answers to these interrogatories.

6. Explain in detail each provision of the contract that you maintain was breached, and state every other fact on which you base your claim.

7. Identify all witnesses whom you intend to call at the trial in this case, including name, home and business address and telephone number, and a summary of the testimony that you expect each witness to give.

In response to these interrogatories, the plaintiff filed a motion to strike and/or for a protective order that they need not be answered; defendant filed a motion to compel answers.[1] How should the court rule?

Comment: As with all other modes of discovery, written interrogatories under Rule 33 have their strengths and limitations. They are excellent for discovering quantitative information such as damages; the identity and whereabouts of persons with discoverable information; the identity and opinions of experts; the specific contentions of the adverse party and their bases; technical or statistical data; and insurance information. *See generally,* "Q: Is This Any Way to Write an Interrogatory? A: You Bet It Is," *Litigation Magazine,* Summer 1993 (ABA); *Jayne H. Lee, Inc. v. Flagstaff Indus. Corp.,* 173 F.R.D. 651, 652 (D. Md. 1997) (Interrogatories are effective in identifying persons with knowledge of facts, as well as facts supporting contentions in pleadings; they yield admissions and information potentially useful for impeachment; they assist in pinning down expert witnesses; they may help identify documents; and they may be used as evidentiary facts under Rule 56 to support or oppose a summary judgment motion). *See Friedlander v. Roberts,* No. 98 Civ. 1684, 2000 WL 1772611, at *1 (S.D.N.Y. Nov. 21, 2000) (discussing interrogatories as a helpful discovery technique).

Interrogatories are less effective in obtaining narrative information meant to exhaust all of the knowledge of the respondent on a given issue and lock him into a position that precludes him from changing his story later, or exposes him to impeachment if he does so. Questions seeking this type of information may be useful, nonetheless, in serving as templates for further probing at deposition.

---

1. Note that counsel should always check the local district court rules before filing a motion for protective order, to compel or for sanctions, to determine whether such rules require the parties to attempt to resolve their dispute—and so certify to the court—before seeking its intervention. *See* chapter 5, *infra.*

Following the 1993 and 2000 amendments to Rule 26 to include mandatory disclosures under new Rule 26(a)(1), (a)(2), and (a)(3), certain categories of interrogatories need no longer be asked in cases in which the mandatory disclosure rules apply. Rule 26(a)(1) ("Required Disclosures: Methods to Discover Additional Material") requires disclosure of (a) the identities of persons who are likely to have discoverable information supportive of the responding party's claims or defenses; (b) documents that support a party's claims or defenses; (c) damages; and (d) insurance. That disclosure requirement is waived only in eight narrow categories of lawsuits.[2] Rule 26(a)(2) ("Disclosure of Expert Testimony") requires that the identity of the responding party's testimonial expert be disclosed, together with a written report of all findings. Rule 26(a)(3) ("Pretrial Disclosures") provides for disclosure of all anticipated witnesses and exhibits of the responding party, and in the case of testimony by deposition, a designation of the pertinent section of the deposition. *See generally, Hilt v. SFC Inc.*, 170 F.R.D. 182 (D. Kan. 1997) (discussing interplay between Rules 33 and 34 on the one hand, and the mandatory disclosures under Rule 26(a) on the other).

With these considerations in mind, there are two ways of evaluating an interrogatory—legal propriety and effectiveness. An interrogatory may be legally unobjectionable but ineffective nonetheless. That is, the question may be framed so broadly and imprecisely that the respondent can answer in a way that is incomplete, open-ended, and unhelpful—and neither exhausts the respondent's knowledge on a subject nor locks him into a position. Likewise, an interrogatory may be effective (that is, it is stated simply and coherently, addresses one point only, and seeks precise information; *see generally*, discussion of conciseness and brevity in interrogatories, *Lawrence v. First Kansas Bank & Trust Co.,* 169 F.R.D. 657, 662 (D. Kan. 1996)), but it may be legally objectionable. These standards obviously overlap *(see, e.g., Capacchione v. Charlotte-Mecklenburg Schs.*, 182 F.R.D. 486, 491 (W.D.N.C. 1998)), but they can also be examined separately.

---

2. (i) An action for review on an administrative record; (ii) a petition for habeas corpus or other proceeding to challenge a criminal conviction or sentence; (iii) an action brought without counsel by a person in custody of the United States, a state, or a state subdivision; (iv) an action to enforce or quash an administrative summons or subpoena; (v) an action by the United States to recover benefit payments; (vi) an action by the United States to collect on a student loan guaranteed by the United States; (vii) a proceeding ancillary to proceedings in other courts; and (viii) an action to enforce an arbitration award. Rule 26(a)(1)(E)

For example, consider the interrogatory: "If you contend that the parties had a meeting on January 5th of last year, describe the substance of the meeting." This is a legally permissible question, assuming that the meeting is relevant to a claim or defense or that disclosure of its contents appears reasonably calculated to lead to the discovery of admissible evidence. *See* Rule 26(b)(1). The question would also be effective if it sought to determine only whether the respondent contended that a meeting occurred.

The interrogatory may otherwise be ineffective, however, particularly as a tool for obtaining all pertinent information regarding the substance of the meeting. The question can be answered in a general way that does not reveal much. (For example: "Answer: The substance of the meeting concerned your inadequate performance of the cleaning contract, which you admitted.") To be sure, the interrogating party may file a motion to compel, but that is time-consuming and expensive, and a court may simply say that a vague question merits only a vague answer. In at least one district, relying on a local rule, courts have held that information that is more readily communicated during deposition need not be provided by interrogatory answer. *Morgan v. City of New York*, 2002 WL 1808233 (S.D.N.Y. 2002); *Madanes v. Madanes*, 186 F.R.D. 279 (S.D.N.Y. 1999). As a practical matter, the principal use for an interrogatory like the meeting inquiry under consideration may be to help counsel for the interrogating party prepare for subsequent follow-up questions at deposition.

In the building cleaning example, the first two interrogatories are effective, in that they are simple and coherent and seek to elicit specific information, but they are objectionable in this case because it is a breach of contract action brought by a corporation—and questions 1 and 2 have nothing to do with that. In fact, it is clear that these are form interrogatories used by counsel with little or no thought. Courts frown on the use of form interrogatories that obviously bear no relevance to the case at hand and often strike them for that reason. *Dollar v. Long Mfg. NC Inc.*, 561 F.2d 613, *reh'g den.*, 565 F.2d 163 (5th Cir. 1977), *cert. den.*, 435 U.S. 996 (1978); *Blank v. Ronson Corp.*, 97 F.R.D. 744 (S.D.N.Y. 1983); *SCM Societa Commerciale S.P.A, v. Indus. & Commercial Research Corp*, 72 F.R.D. 110 (N.D. Tex. 1976). This is not to say that form interrogatories are never useful. To the contrary, in framing interrogatories, a practitioner should consult the pertinent local rules, which frequently contain form interrogatories.[3] The point is simply that each interrogatory posed should be germane.

Interrogatory 3 above is objectionable because it too has nothing to do with the case. It is also objectionable, as well as ineffective, because it is not a complete sentence. The law is clear that a respondent need not be a mind reader and bears no obligation under the Rules to fill in the missing blanks or construe an incoherent question in a coherent manner. *Rucker v. Wabash R. Co.*, 418 F.2d 146 (7th Cir. 1969); *Tsangarakis v. Panama S.S. Co.*, 41 F.R.D. 219 (E.D. Pa. 1966).

Interrogatory 4 is proper and effective but a poor question nonetheless because it would elicit very little information; given the presumptive limit of 25 interrogatories, the interrogator should make every question count. Here, interrogatory 4 could easily be eliminated by reframing interrogatory 5 as follows: "If you contend that the contract breached was in writing, please identify such writing by stating its date and all signatories thereto." Interrogatory 5, however, also directs the respondent to attach a copy of the document to his answers. Rule 33 does not allow for that. *Hickman v. Taylor*, 329 U.S. 495 (1947); *Miller v. Doctor's Gen. Hosp.*, 76 F.R.D. 136 (W.D. Okla. 1977); *Evans v. Local Union 2127, Int'l Broh. of Elec. Workers*, 313 F. Supp. 1354 (N.D. Ga. 1969); *Lee v. Elec. Prod. Co.*, 37 F.R.D. 42 (N.D. Ohio 1963). In fact, that aspect of the instruction is inconsistent with Rule 33(d), which gives the *respondent* the *option* of allowing reasonable access to business records if the other elements of the rule are satisfied (*see* chapter 6, *infra*). A better-drafted version of question 5 would give the respondent a choice between stating the substance of the contract or allowing access to (or producing) a copy. But even that seems unnecessary, when a simple document production request (the number of which is not capped in the federal rules, although it may be by local rule, *see* chapter 8, *infra*) could seek production of any written contract, the breach of which, so plaintiff asserts, gave rise to the claim.

Suppose the defendant in the example objected to interrogatory 6 on three grounds: First, that the first part calls for a legal opinion; second, that the second part is too broad; and third, that it is a compound question consisting of two discrete interrogatories? Which of these objections might be sustained?

---

3. Appendix C contains form interrogatories approved by the United States District Court for the District of Maryland (as Appendix D to its local rules) that are illustrative of the types of interrogatories approved in other districts.

The first objection is groundless. Interrogatories may seek discovery of the legal position of an adverse party as it relates to the facts alleged. Rule 33(c), Fed. R. Civ. P. "An interrogatory otherwise proper is not necessarily objectionable merely because an answer to the interrogatory involves an opinion or contention that relates to fact or the application of law to fact . . ."; *but see* Advisory Committee Notes on 1970 Amendment to Subdivision (b) (re-lettered Subdivision (c) in the 1993 Amendments): "[I]nterrogatories may not extend to issues of 'pure law,' i.e., legal issues unrelated to the facts of the case, *cf.* 8A *Fed. Prac. & Proc. Civ. 2d* § 2167, Wright, Miller & Marcus; *United States v. Maryland & Va. Milk Producers Assn., Inc.*, 22 F.R.D. 300 (D.D.C. 1958).")"; *see also Towner v. Med James, Inc.*, 1995 WL 477700 (D. Kan., Aug. 9, 1995); *Abbott v. U.S.*, 177 F.R.D. 92, 93 (N.D.N.Y. 1997).

The second objection is well taken; questions that ask for "all facts" are generally considered overly broad and unduly burdensome. *Hiskett v. Wal-Mart Stores, Inc.*, 180 F.R.D. 403 (D. Kan. 1998); *see also Bradley v. Val-Mejias*, 2001 WL 1249339 (D. Kan., Oct. 9, 2001), which approved the phraseology "[S]tate in detail your factual version of how the occurrence complained of in your Complaint took place," as distinguished from "State each and every fact . . . ," which was disapproved, the distinction being that the former language sought only material or principal facts, whereas the latter sought "all" facts.

Finally, the third objection may or may not be valid, depending on whether the second half of the interrogatory exceeds the 25-question limit.

Whether or not it is objectionable, interrogatory 6 is not well written. If the drafter wants identification of those provisions of the contract that the plaintiff claims were breached, the interrogatory should state as much, as simply as possible—for example, "Please identify each provision of the contract that you maintain was breached." If the drafter wants the respondent to explain the manner in which each such provision of the contract allegedly was breached, then the question should be, "As to each section of the contract that you maintain was breached, please describe the breach, including the date on and manner in which it occurred."

Note also that interrogatory 6 is *not* objectionable because it asks about the plaintiff's contentions and the bases for them. Rule 33(c), Fed. R. Civ. P.; *Steil v. Humana Kansas City, Inc.*, 197 F.R.D. 445, 446 (D. Kan. 2000); *Capacchione v. Charlotte-Mecklenburg Schs,*, 182 F.R.D. 486, 489 (W.D.N.C.

1998); *Towner v. Med James, Inc.*, *supra*; *see Mack v. W.R. Grace & Co.*, 578 F. Supp. 626, 638 (N.D. Ga. 1983). Contention interrogatories are both proper and effective. Respondent's counsel (who probably will draft the answers) is often motivated to provide a strong and thorough exposition of the basis for his client's claim to magnify its importance in the eyes of the adverse party.

Occasionally, when a contention interrogatory is posed early in a case, the responding party may object on the ground that the question is premature and an answer should await a later stage of discovery when the respondent has more information. Some courts have upheld such objection. Note to 1970 amendment of Rule 33(b), 48 F.R.D. at 524; *McCarthy v. PaineWebber Group, Inc.*, 168 F.R.D. 448 (D. Conn. 1996); *B. Braun Med,, Inc. v. Abbott Labs., Inc.*, 155 F.R.D. 525 (E.D. Pa. 1994); *Leumi Fin. Corp. v. Hartford Acc. & Indem. Co.*, 295 F. Supp. 539, 543 (S.D.N.Y. 1969). The more logical rule, however, is that the question should stand and the respondent should answer as much as possible, and then supplement the answer if and when additional responsive information is obtained. *In re One Bankcorp Sec. Litig.*, 134 F.R.D. 4, 7-8 (D. Me. 1991); *see also* "Q: Is This Any Way to Write an Interrogatory? A: You Bet It Is," *Litigation Magazine*, Summer 1993 (ABA); Rule 26(e)(2) (requiring supplementation of interrogatory responses "if the party learns that the response is in some material respect incomplete or incorrect and if the additional or corrective information has not otherwise been made known to the other parties during the discovery process or in writing").

Finally, barring a local rule that permits such a question (such as Local Rule 33.3 in the Southern District of New York), interrogatory 7 is objectionable because it invades attorney work product. The selection of witnesses lies at the core of the attorney's preparation for trial—and may not even be determined by the attorney until shortly before the trial. The question can be rendered unobjectionable, however, by simply using the language in Rule 26(a)(1)(A): "Identify the name, and if known, the address and telephone number of each individual likely to have discoverable information. . . ." The key distinction between these two questions is that the former asks the respondent to disclose his attorney's views about those he may call as witnesses, whereas the latter simply asks for the identity of persons with knowledge of the facts.

Practice Tip

Each interrogatory should address one subject only, should be stated clearly and simply, and, by its phraseology, should call for a complete answer that contains no ambiguity. Contention interrogatories and other interrogatories that call for a narrative answer should ask for all "material" facts, rather than "each and every fact" or "all facts."

2. INTERROGATORIES—NUMEROSITY: PARTS AND SUBPARTS

An inmate in the custody of a state prison system, assisted by a fellow convict who happened to be a former attorney, filed a pro se civil action in state court against various prison personnel and state officials, alleging violation of his civil rights under federal law. With his complaint, the plaintiff served 25 interrogatories directed to all defendants (the rules of civil procedure in that state set no limits on the timing or number of interrogatories). Interrogatories 3 through 25 were unexceptional questions that did not require complex or multipart answers.

Interrogatory No. 1, however, read: "For each defendant, state your full name, employment history for the last ten years including jobs held, dates when such jobs were held, titles in such jobs, title of current position, responsibilities of current position and person to whom you report in your current position, and identify all allegations of physical brutality brought against you at any time, including dates, names of complaining persons, nature of complaint and disposition."

Interrogatory No. 2 read: "With respect to the incident involving the plaintiff that occurred at the state penitentiary on January 15th of this year, identify: (a) all prison personnel who witnessed the incident; (b) all prison inmates who witnessed the incident; (c) all written or taped witness statements concerning the incident; (d) all written reports concerning the incident; and (e) all administrative actions taken subsequent and in relation to the incident."

After service of the complaint, the defendants timely removed the case to federal court pursuant to 28 U.S.C. § 1443 and filed an answer together with a motion for a protective order.[1] The motion argued that the defendants should not be required to answer any of the interrogatories because (i) they were filed in advance of the party conference mandated by Rule 26(f), and (ii) taking the subparts into account, the interrogatories exceeded 25 in number, in violation of the provision of Rule 33(a) limiting parties to 25 interrogatories "including all discrete subparts" absent leave of court or stipulation of the parties. (The federal district court to which the case was removed did not have a local rule that varied the 25 interrogatory rule.)

The pro se plaintiff responded that the defendants, who were respon-

---

1. *See* chapter 1, note 1, *supra*.

sible for the removal, should not be allowed to object to discovery procedures that were proper when the case was filed. He also argued that the interrogatories were timely filed under Rules 26(d) and 26(a)(1)(E); that the number of interrogatories, inclusive of "all discrete subparts," did not exceed 25; that even if the presumptive limitation had been exceeded, defendants were at least required to answer the first 25 interrogatories; and finally, that the court should allow additional interrogatories if it concluded that the pending interrogatories exceeded the number presumptively allowed. How should the court rule?

Comment: The matter of timing can be dispensed with easily. Rule 26(d) says: "Except in categories of proceedings exempted from initial disclosure under Rule 26(a)(1)(E) . . . a party may not seek discovery from any source before the parties have conferred as required by Rule 26(f)." Rule 26(a)(1)(E), in turn, states: "The following categories of proceedings are exempt from initial disclosure under Rule 26(a)(1): . . . (iii) an action brought without counsel by a person in custody of the United States, a state, or a state subdivision." This is such a case. Accordingly, the interrogatories are timely filed in federal court.

The question of the number of interrogatories is more difficult, although one thing is clear: The prisoner is wrong when he argues that even after removal to federal court, the state rules on numerosity should govern because the case originated there. The Advisory Committee Notes to the 1993 amendments to Rule 33 are explicit about this: "When a case with outstanding interrogatories exceeding the number permitted by this rule is removed to federal court, the interrogating party must seek leave allowing the additional interrogatories, specify which twenty-five are to be answered, or resubmit interrogatories that comply with the rule. . . . See Rule 81(c), providing that these rules govern procedures after removal."

The meaning of "all discrete subparts," however, and whether certain types of "subparts" count as separate questions in evaluating compliance with the limit of 25, is much less clear. The Advisory Committee Notes say: "Parties cannot evade this presumptive limitation through the device of joining as 'subparts' questions that seek information about discrete separate subjects. However, a question asking about communications of a particular type should be treated as a single interrogatory even though it requests that the time, place, persons present, and contents be stated separately for each such communication." Advisory Committee Note, 146 F.R.D. 401 at 675-76. A leading commentator has put it thus: "'[I]t would appear that an interrogatory containing subparts directed at eliciting details concerning the common theme should be considered a single question, although the breadth of an area inquired about may be disputable. On the other hand, an interrogatory with subparts inquiring into discrete areas is more likely to be counted as more than one for purposes of the limitation.' 8A Charles A. Wright, Arthur R. Miller, and Richard L. Marcus, Federal Practice and Procedure § 2168.1 at 261 (2d ed. 1994)." *Cf. Williams v. Board of County Comm'rs of Wyandotte County*, 192 F.R.D. 698 (D. Kan. 2000).

Kendall v. GES Exposition Services, Inc., 174 F.R.D. 684 (D. Nev. 1997) is an oft-quoted case that tries to distinguish between subparts that should be counted as part of the primary interrogatory and those that should be viewed as separate interrogatories:

> [I]n *Ginn* [*v. Gemini, Inc.*, 137 F.R.D. 320 (D. Nev. 1991)], . . . [t]he Court . . . [held] that interrogatory subparts are to be counted as part of but one interrogatory . . . if they are logically or factually subsumed within and necessarily related to the primary question. *Ginn*, 137 F.R.D. at 322.
>
> This Court agrees with that decision and adopts it herein. However, the more difficult question is determining whether the subparts are "logically or factually subsumed within and necessarily related to the primary question." If the questions are relevant to the case, it could be argued that all the interrogatories are "related." If that were the case, then all the interrogatories would only be counted as one and there could never be an excessive number. By the same token, the mere inclusion of "and" or "also" in a question (or double question) does not automatically mean the questions are separate or "discrete" and not subsumed within the initial or primary question.
>
> Probably the best test of whether subsequent questions, within a single interrogatory, are subsumed and related, is to examine whether the first question is primary and subsequent questions are secondary to the primary question. Or, can the subsequent question stand alone? Is it independent of the first question? Genuine subparts should not be counted as separate interrogatories. However, discrete or separate questions should be counted as separate interrogatories, notwithstanding they are joined by a conjunctive word and may be related.

174 F.R.D. at 685; *cited with approval* in Nyfield v. V. I. Tel. Corp., 200 F.R.D. 246, 247 (D.V.I. 2001). (*But see* Safeco of America v. Rawstron, 181 F.R.D. 441, 446 (C.D. Cal. 1998), noting that even "this formula falls short of a bright-line test.").

Two additional points are pertinent to this question. First, determination of whether subparts should be counted as multiple interrogatories can never turn on whether the subparts are separately numbered, else the rule of limitation could always be circumvented. *Prochaska & Assoc. v. Merrill Lynch, Pierce, Fenner & Smith, Inc.*, 155 F.R.D. 189, 191 (D. Neb. 1993). *Cf. Safeco of America*, 181 F.R.D. 441, 444 (C.D. Cal. 1998). Second, while a defendant who objects to interrogatories on the ground of numerosity may be justified in not answering any of them, he could also answer the first 25 and then stop. *In re Indep. Energy Holdings Secs. Litig.*, 2003 WL 42010 (S.D.N.Y. Jan. 6, 2003).

So what should be the disposition of the defendant's motion? Interrogatory No. 1, inclusive of its subparts, should be counted as two interrogatories. The "first" interrogatory seeks information concerning the identity and employment history of each defendant; subsumed within that primary question are subparts asking for dates when prior jobs were held, job titles, and so forth. The "second" interrogatory seeks information about a different primary subject—namely, the history of complaints of brutality against each defendant. Related to that question is information about dates, names of complaining witnesses, nature of complaint, and disposition.

Likewise, Interrogatory No. 2 may be viewed as two interrogatories. The "first" asks for information concerning the "incident" on January 15th involving the plaintiff, including identity of witnesses, their statements, and any written reports. The "second" invokes a separate primary question—the administrative actions taken "subsequent and in relation to the incident." Thus, the plaintiff exceeded the presumptive cap of 25 interrogatories by two without leave of court or stipulation of the parties, and so defendants were within their rights to decline to answer any of them.

Should the court allow the two additional interrogatories? No hard and fast answer is possible, because that is a discretionary judgment. Where a party makes a "particularized showing" that justifies the additional interrogatories, leave to file them should be granted. *Archer Daniels Midland Co. v. Aon Risk Serv., Inc.*, 187 F.R.D. 578, 586 (D. Minn. 1999); *Bell v. Fowler,* 99 F.3d 262, 271 (8th Cir. 1996). *See Whittingham v. Amherst College* 163 F.R.D. 170, 171-72 (D. Mass. 1995). That judicial determination is governed by Rule 26(b)(2). Leave will be denied if (i) the discovery sought is unreasonably cumulative or duplicative, or is obtainable from some other source that is more convenient, less burdensome or less expensive; (ii) the party seeking discovery has had ample opportunity by discovery in the action to obtain the information sought; or (iii) the burden or expense of the proposed discovery outweighs its likely benefit, taking into account the needs of the case, the amount in controversy, the parties' resources, the importance of the issues at stake in the litigation, and the importance of the proposed discovery in resolving the issues. *Duncan v. Paragon Publ'g, Inc.*, 204 F.R.D. 127 (S.D. Ind. 2001). Here, the plaintiff prisoner can argue that the additional interrogatories are the most efficient and least expensive means of getting information that goes to the heart of the case, and that they are not duplicative of other discovery requests.

On the practical side, some courts, including the United States District Court for the District of Maryland, have adopted presumptively proper form interrogatories as an appendix to their local rules. Found as Appendix D to the local rules, they are included as Appendix C to this book. Counsel should check the local rules of each court in which they practice to determine whether there are any such form interrogatories, and if so, to consider using them. This will help limit possible objections by opposing counsel to the number of questions posed.

3. INTERROGATORIES—PROPRIETY OF DEFINITIONS AND INSTRUCTIONS

In accordance with Rule 33, the defendants in a lawsuit propounded interrogatories on the plaintiffs. They were prefaced by a series of definitions and instructions, including the following:

> 4. The term "document" as used in these interrogatories includes any writing of any kind or description, including (but not limited to) the original and all copies and drafts of memoranda, letters, notes, whether in pencil, ink, typewritten, any other medium or on a computer; communications of any kind except oral; drawings of any kind, including (but not limited to) tracing, blueprints, sketches, computer graphics, flow diagrams; photographs; notebooks; computer databases; instructions; invoices, bills and receipts; and any other written, printed, computer-generated, graphic or drawn material.
>
> 5. Where a document is required to be identified, listed or described in response to any one of these interrogatories, the following information shall be given: (a) date; (b) present location; (c) person who prepared document; (d) person or persons to whom it was sent or given or disclosed; (e) name of organization each of the persons named in the answer to (c) and (d) represented or with which each person was connected; (f) substance of the statement or showing contained in the document; and (g) the occasion for and/or circumstances under which it was made.
>
> 6. If a document that you have identified in response to these interrogatories is no longer in your possession, state the name of the custodian and the business or home location and/or address where you believe the document to be located at present, and the basis for such belief.

The defendants filed a motion for a protective order that they not be required to answer any of the interrogatories on the ground that the definitions and instructions made them impermissibly overbroad, onerous, and burdensome to answer.[1] How should the court rule?

---

1. *See* chapter 1, note 1, *supra.*

Comment: Rule 33 does not prohibit the use of definitions or instructions, and the few reported decisions on this issue have held that they may be used, provided that they are reasonable and do not cause the interrogatories to be overbroad or burdensome. *Dang v. Cross*, No. CV-00-13001, 2002 WL 432197 at *3 (C.D. Cal. March 18, 2002); *Temple Univ. v. Salla Bros., Inc.*, 656 F. Supp. 97 (E.D. Pa. 1986); *Harlem River Consumers Co-op., Inc. v. Assoc. Grocers of Harlem, Inc.*, 64 F.R.D. 459 (S.D.N.Y. 1974); *Diversified Prods. Corp. v. Sports Ctr. Co., Inc.*, 42 F.R.D. 3 (D. Md. 1967); *see* 7 James Wm. Moore et al., *Moore's Federal Practice* § 33.31[2] (3d ed. 2001) (collecting cases).

The general rule that can be distilled from these cases is that where definitions and instructions aid in clarity and relate to the subject matter of the inquiry, they are permissible. However, where they create complexity and/or seek tangential information, they may be deemed objectionable on the grounds that they are overbroad, onerous, and burdensome.

In a leading opinion on this issue, *Diversified Products*, the court found that the language in paragraphs (4) and (5) above (modified in the example to include computer data), and especially items (f) and (g), "so expanded the information requested that many of the interrogatories are burdensome." Although the court did not explain its reasoning, it seems obvious that item (f), which calls for a summary of the document, is burdensome because the interrogating party, which presumably has asked for the production of the document, can read it as easily as the responding party. 42 F.R.D. 3. *See* Rule 33(d). Likewise, item (g), which requires explanation of "the occasion for and/or circumstances under which" the document was created, may be something that can be gleaned from the document itself.

In *Harlem River Consumers Co-op., supra,* the court acknowledged the holding in *Diversified Products* but nonetheless authorized comparable definitions and instructions on the ground that they were reasonable in the context in which they were presented. Likewise, in *Temple University, supra,* the court required a response observing an instruction that the respondent explain the whereabouts of any document no longer in its possession (comparable to paragraph (6) above), distinguishing *Diversified Products* on the ground that it sought gratuitous information regarding documents still in the possession of the respondent and subject to production. In that regard, Rule 33(d) expressly requires that a respondent who identifies a document as responsive to an interrogatory should provide "sufficient detail to permit the interrogating party to locate and to identify, as readily as can the party served, the records from which the answer may be ascertained."

Before turning to the specific example under consideration, it is important yet again to remember that the local rules in many jurisdictions provide definitions for certain terms that apply to all interrogatories and may be narrowed but not expanded. *See, e.g.,* Rule 26.5, Local Rules of the District of Massachusetts; Rule 47, Local Rules of the Southern District of New York; Rule 3.02, Local Rules of the Southern District of West Virginia; Rule CV-26, Local Rules of the Western District of Texas; Rule 7-09, Local Rules of the Eastern District of Wisconsin. Such rules may permit an interrogating party to supplement the standard defined terms with additional defined terms if appropriate. Both the interrogating party and the responding party should consult the local rules for definitions in framing interrogatories and in answering or objecting to them.

Applying these principles, the court in the example might rule as follows:

(A) The definition of "document" in paragraph (4), contrary to the court's holding in *Diversified Products*, is helpful because it delineates for the responding party exactly what specific items fall within the meaning of the term—that is, it provides clarity. Moreover, it creates no greater burden on the respondent than would otherwise exist. In that regard, see Rule 34(a), which sets forth a definition of the term "document" that is comparable to the definition above in some respects and broader in others. Paragraph (4) is not objectionable.

(B) Paragraphs 5(a) and (b) likewise are not objectionable, notwithstanding the court's holding to the contrary in *Diversified Products*. As noted above, Rule 33(d), while allowing identification of business records in lieu of an answer, places the burden on the responding party to identify the documents' location. That is all paragraphs 5(a) and (b) do.

(C) Paragraphs 5(c)–(e) are objectionable, for the reasons set forth by the court in *Diversified Products*. The information can be gleaned from the documents themselves.

(D) Paragraph 6 is not objectionable, for the reasons set forth in *Temple University, supra*.

4. THE TIMING OF INTERROGATORIES AND REQUESTS FOR PRODUCTION—HOW SOON CAN YOU ASK, AND WHEN IS IT TOO LATE?

Plaintiff's counsel was poised to file and serve her complaint. Simultaneously, she prepared a set of interrogatories and requests for production for service along with the complaint. She believed that taking discovery at the earliest possible moment would give her a head start and put the other side back on its heels.

Before acting, however, she consulted Rule 33(a) and read that "[w]ithout leave of court or written stipulation, interrogatories may not be served before the time specified in Rule 26(d)." She noted comparable language in Rule 34(b) governing the timing of requests for production. She then turned to Rule 26(d) and saw the following admonition: "Except in categories of proceedings exempted from initial disclosure under Rule 26(a)(1)(E), or when authorized under these rules or by order or agreement of the parties, a party may *not* seek discovery from any source before the parties have conferred as required by Rule 26(f)" (emphasis added). Unable to find any applicable exception, plaintiff's counsel placed the Rule 33 and 34 discovery requests back in the file to await service after the Rule 26(f) conference.

At the 26(f) conference, all counsel agreed that the most efficient way to proceed with discovery would be to conduct depositions first, and so they did. Several months later, and just 30 days before the discovery deadline, counsel realized that she had neglected to serve her Rule 33 and 34 requests. She retrieved them from her file, condensed them to account for the substantial discovery obtained in depositions, and served them on opposing counsel that very day. She reasoned that her discovery requests were still timely as the discovery deadline had not yet elapsed.

When she did not receive responses, she telephoned her adversary. He said, "Your Rule 33 and 34 requests were out of time. You served them on the 30th day before the discovery cutoff. Given that the rules permit 30 days for a response, and that the 30 days are to be counted from the day *after* service, answers would not be due until the day *after* the discovery cutoff. So you are too late." Plaintiff's counsel protested that the Rules were silent on the point, and as she had filed her discovery requests before the expiration of discovery she was entitled to answers. She argued in the alternative that service on the 30th day before the cutoff would require answers to be served on the cutoff date, rather than a day later. Defense counsel refused to budge, however, and so plaintiff's motion to compel followed. How should the court rule?

Comment: Federal Rule 6(a) states in part: "In computing any period of time prescribed or allowed by these rules, by the local rules of any district court, by order of court, or by any applicable statute, the day of the act, event, or default from which the designated period of time begins to run shall not be included."

Thus, plaintiff's counsel was wrong when she argued that discovery requests filed 30 days before termination of discovery would require responses on the cutoff date. The 30 days for responding to Rule 33 and 34 requests would begin running on the 29th day before the discovery cutoff (the day after service), and so the response deadline would be the day *after* the cutoff.

As for plaintiff's counsel's second argument—that mere *service* of interrogatories was proper within the last 30 days before the discovery cutoff date—she was probably wrong on that score as well. The Federal Rules are silent on the point, but the local rules of many district courts do address the question. For example, Rule 104(2) of the Civil Rules of the United States District Court for the District of Maryland says:

> Interrogatories, requests for production, motions for physical and mental examination, and written deposition questions must be made at a sufficiently early time to insure that they are answered before the expiration of the discovery deadline set by the Court. Unless otherwise ordered by the Court, no discovery deadline will be extended because written discovery requests remain unanswered at its expiration.

Rule 26.1(C) of the Rules of the United States District Court for the Eastern District of Oklahoma makes the same point even more succinctly: "All discovery requests shall be served on opposing counsel in sufficient time to allow a response prior to discovery cutoff"; *cf. Zornes v. Specialty Indust.*, 166 F.3d 1212, 1998 WL 886997 (4th Cir. Dec. 21, 1998) (unpublished opinion) (the court discusses the criteria for dismissal with prejudice as a sanction for discovery abuse by plaintiff, including failure to file discovery requests in sufficient time to allow for timely responses prior to discovery cutoff date); *Potomac Elec. Power Co. v. Elec. Motor Supply, Inc.*, 190 F.R.D. 372, 381 (D. Md. 1999) (the court exercises its discretion to waive the deadline requirement for responses to third-party subpoenas where it would be difficult for third parties to timely respond before discovery cutoff date); *Ghandi v. Police Dept. of City of Detroit*, 747 F.2d 338, 354-55 (6th Cir. 1984) (affirming the trial court's decision to nullify a subpoena for documents that were available during discovery and sought on the eve of trial); *McNerney v. Archer Daniels Midland Co.*, 164 F.R.D. 584, 588 (W.D.N.Y. 1995) ("when [a] party . . . is aware of the existence of documents before the discovery cutoff date and issues discovery requests including subpoenas after the discovery deadline has passed, then the subpoenas and discovery requests should be denied").

Even without a local rule or scheduling order explicitly addressing this cutoff question, logic compels the same result. Frequently, for example, local rules or a scheduling order will set forth a date for the filing of dispositive motions, expressed as "no later than 30 days after the conclusion of discovery" or words to that effect. With such a case schedule, the parties need to know a specific end point for discovery in order to prepare their dispositive motions. Interpreting the cutoff as plaintiff's counsel did in the example would have the effect of creating a floating motions deadline up to 30 days beyond the stated deadline. That could interfere with preparation of dispositive motions in two ways—by altering the schedule at the whim (and perhaps to the advantage) of one party, and by affording the possibility of additional discovery that may affect the arguments to be made on dispositive motion. A bright-line rule is necessary to avoid these uncertainties— thus the logic of the requirement that discovery be propounded in time to allow for responses before the discovery cutoff.

Two other considerations beyond scheduling logic suggest that plaintiff's counsel was off-base. They are simple, but every litigator needs to remember them. The first is "be thorough." The second is "better safe than sorry." In the example, the lawyer's prime failing was that she assumed her own point of view was right; she did not take the time to consider counterarguments. And, even if she had some reason to doubt that the discovery cutoff was a cutoff for responses, it would have been better to be cautious and deal with the issue as soon as possible, and not wait until the end of the discovery period.

5. INTERROGATORIES—SUFFICIENCY OF OBJECTIONS

The plaintiff insured brought a declaratory judgment action against her insurance carrier, which had refused to provide coverage for her medical condition. She sought a declaration that the illness was covered by her health insurance policy. In discovery, she propounded the following interrogatories to defendant:

(1) Identify every material and/or principal fact upon which defendant bases its contention that the medical condition at issue in this case is excluded by the terms of plaintiff's health insurance policy.

(2) Identify every conversation and communication between or among defendant's employees concerning the scope of coverage of plaintiff's health insurance policy with the defendant regarding the medical condition at issue in this case, including names, dates, witnesses, the substance of each conversation and communication, and if such communication is contained in a document or electronic message, the date, author, and addressees of the document or electronic message.

Twenty days after service of the interrogatories, defense counsel telephoned plaintiff's counsel and said, "Look, I'm in trial, and I need two more weeks to get you the answers to these interrogatories." Plaintiff's counsel agreed to the request for additional time.

On the agreed-upon extension date, defendant served plaintiff with "Answers and Objections to Plaintiff's Interrogatories." The response to Interrogatory No. 1 was: "The plain language of the policy, as interpreted by the case law, shows that the medical condition at issue in this case is not covered. To the extent plaintiff is asking the defendant to disclose the legal decisions, opinions and analyses that support this answer, defendant objects on the ground that the interrogatory calls for a legal conclusion as well as attorney work-product and attorney-client privileged communications. Further, defendant objects to this interrogatory on the ground of undue burdensomeness."

The defendant's response to Interrogatory No. 2 was: "Defendant objects to this interrogatory on the ground of attorney-client privilege and attorney work-product."

A week later, the defendant filed a document captioned "Supplemental Objections to Plaintiff's Interrogatories," which asserted that interrogatories

1 and 2 were objectionable on the further grounds of overbreadth and vagueness. Plaintiff's counsel filed a motion to compel complete answers to interrogatories 1 and 2, which defendant promptly opposed. The matter is now before the court. How should it rule?

Comment: Before filing the motion to compel, plaintiff's counsel should have consulted the local district rules to determine whether they required the parties to attempt first to resolve their dispute informally. For example, Rule 37.1 of the Local Rules of the United States District Court for the Northern District of Ohio provides:

> Discovery disputes shall be referred to a Judicial Officer only after counsel for the party seeking the disputed discovery has made, and certified to the Court the making of, sincere, good faith efforts to resolve such disputes. The Judicial Officer shall attempt to resolve the dispute by telephone conference. In the event the dispute cannot be resolved by the telephone conference, the parties shall outline their respective positions by letter and the Judicial Officer shall attempt to resolve the dispute without additional legal memoranda. If the Judicial Officer still is unable to resolve the dispute, the parties may simultaneously file their respective memoranda in support of and in opposition to the requested discovery by a date set by the Judicial Officer. . . .

By way of further example, Rule 104.7 of the Local Rules of the United States District Court for the District of Maryland provides:

> Counsel shall confer with one another concerning a discovery dispute and make sincere attempts to resolve the differences between them. The Court will not consider any discovery motion unless the moving party has filed a certificate reciting (a) the date, time and place of the discovery conference, the names of all persons participating therein and any issues remaining to be resolved, or (b) counsel's attempts to hold such a conference without success.

If such a rule exists and is ignored, the court may deny the motion to compel even if it has merit. *See Doe v. Nat'l Hemophilia Found.*, 194 F.R.D. 516, 519 (D. Md. 2000); *Gibbs v. Oklahoma Dep't of Transp.*, No. Civ-90-

1911-C, 1991 WL 405514 at 3 (W.D. Okla., Aug. 21, 1991). Although such denial might ostensibly be "without prejudice," if there is a deadline for filing discovery motions and that deadline was passed, the denial could, in effect, be final. In the District of Maryland, for example, Local Rule 104.8a provides that a party who is dissatisfied with the responses to interrogatories and is unable to negotiate a satisfactory resolution must file its motion to compel "within thirty days of the party's receipt of the response." As such local rules are common, counsel should consult them as soon as they receive unsatisfactory discovery responses.

Apart from the question of pre-motion consultation with opposing counsel, the example presents at least three related problems for the defendant before the merits are considered. First, recall that the parties agreed to an extension of time without consulting the court, much less obtaining its consent. While it is true that Rule 33(b)(3) allows for stipulations by the parties for extensions of time to respond to interrogatories, some districts have a local rule that vitiates the effect of any such agreement, absent court approval. *See, e.g.*, Rule 7.1M of the Local Rules of the United States District Court for the District of Colorado, quoted in *Pham v. Hartford Fire Ins. Co.*, 193 F.R.D. 659, 661 (D. Colo. 2000):

> No agreement of counsel to shorten or extend any time limitation provided by the federal rules of civil . . . procedure . . . will be recognized or enforced, nor will such an agreement be considered just cause for failing to perform within the time limits established by those rules. Only time variances specifically approved by court order upon motion made within the time limits prescribed by those rules will be recognized as having any binding or legal effect.

If a rule like that were applied, the defendant's responses would be untimely; and absent "good cause," all objections to the interrogatories would have been waived, as Rule 33(b)(4) provides that "[a]ny ground [for objection] not stated in a timely objection is waived unless the party's failure to object is excused by the court for good cause." *Hammond v. Lowe's Home Centers, Inc.*, 216 F.R.D. 666, 668 (D. Kan. 2003); *Allen v. Interstate Brands*, 186 F.R.D. 512 (S.D. Ind. 1999), *Jayne H. Lee, Inc. v. Flagstaff Indus. Corp.*, 173 F.R.D. 651, 653 (D. Md. 1997) (failure to object timely to interrogatories waives the basis for objections; incomplete or nonparticularized objections also result in waiver).

The likely untimeliness of defendant's objections in the example is only exacerbated by the staggered filing of responses—in its initial responses, the defendant objected on the grounds of attorney-client privilege, work-product doctrine, and undue burdensomeness. Only in its subsequent filing did the defendant raise overbreadth and vagueness objections. Amended objections that are filed out of time without leave of court or stipulation of the parties do not satisfy Rule 33 and are deemed waived. *Davis v. Fendler*, 650 F.2d 1154, 1160 (9th Cir. 1981); *Safeco Ins. Co. of Am. v. Rawstron*, 183 F.R.D. 668, 671 (C.D. Cal. 1998); *Walker v. Lakewood Condo. Owners Ass'n*, 186 F.R.D. 584 (C.D. Cal. 1999).

The defendant's second problem is that its agreement with plaintiff for an extension of time covered only "answers" to the interrogatories—nothing was said regarding an extension for filing objections. On that ground, the court would be within its discretion under Rule 33(b)(4) to rule that all objections were waived. At a minimum, the court might require that defendant establish that its agreement with plaintiff for an extension of time to file "answers" also embraced objections. *Coregis Ins. Co. v. Baratta & Fenerty, Ltd.*, 187 F.R.D. 528, 530 (E.D. Pa. 1999).

The lack of specificity and precision in its objections is a third problem for the defendant. Rule 33(b)(4) requires that "[a]ll grounds for an objection to an interrogatory shall be stated with specificity." While many lawyers provide merely generalized or boilerplate objections, they should be aware of the volume of case law requiring specificity and holding that the absence of detail could waive the objection. *Alexander v. F.B.I.*, 192 F.R.D. 50, 53 (D.D.C. 2000) (an objection to an interrogatory on the ground of "undue burden" must be coupled with a specific, detailed showing as to how the interrogatory is burdensome); *Etienne v. Wolverine Tube, Inc.*, 185 F.R.D. 653, 656 (D. Kan. 1999) (mere assertion of "overbreadth" does not adequately state objection); *St. Paul Reinsurance Co., Ltd. v. Commercial Fin. Corp.*, 198 F.R.D. 508 (N.D. Iowa 2000); *Marens v. Carrabba's Italian Grill, Inc.*, 196 F.R.D. 35, 38 (D. Md. 2000) ("conclusory assertions of burden or cost are insufficient" to raise valid objections to discovery requests, citing authority; the same is true if a party fails to particularize claims of privilege under Rule 26(b)(5)); *Tucker v. Ohtsu Tire & Rubber Co., Ltd.*, 191 F.R.D. 495, 498 (D. Md. 2000) (generalized, nonspecific assertions of burden, prejudice, and expense are insufficient to present valid objection to discovery requests, citing authority). The mere assertion that an interrogatory is objectionable because it is "overly broad, burdensome, oppressive and irrelevant" does not state a proper objection. *Tucker*, 191 F.R.D. at 511-12; *Burns v. Imagine Films Entm't, Inc.*, 164 F.R.D. 589 (W.D.N.Y. 1996). "[T]o successfully object to an interrogatory, a defendant cannot simply state that the interrogatory is overly broad, burdensome, oppressive and irrelevant, rather, the party opposing discovery must specifically demonstrate how each interrogatory was overly broad, burdensome, oppressive or irrelevant." *Burns*, 164 F.R.D. at 593-94. *See also* chapter 46, *infra*.

As to the claim of privilege, Rule 26(b)(5) provides that

> [w]hen a party withholds information otherwise discoverable . . . by claiming that it is privileged or subject to protection as trial preparation material, the party shall make the claim expressly and shall describe the nature of the documents, communications, or things not produced or disclosed in a manner that, without revealing information itself privileged or protected, will enable other parties to assess the applicability of the privilege or protection.

Thus, the blanket assertion that an interrogatory is objectionable because it seeks to traverse the work-product doctrine or invade the attorney-client privilege will not serve to defeat the inquiry. The objecting party must make a clear showing that the privilege or doctrine applies. *ERA Franchise Sys., Inc. v. Northern Ins. Co. of N.Y.*, 183 F.R.D. 276, 278-79 (D. Kan. 1998); *Ali v. Douglas Cable Communications Ltd. P'ship*, 890 F. Supp. 993, 993-94 (D. Kan. 1995); *Peat, Marwick, Mitchell & Co. v. West*, 748 F.2d 540 (10th Cir. 1984), *cert. denied*, 469 U.S. 1199 (1985); *Nutmeg Ins. Co. v. Atwell, Vogel & Sterling*, 120 F.R.D. 504, at 510 (W.D. La. 1988). Under Rule 26(b)(5), that showing must be made at the time the objection is raised.

When the attorney-client privilege is asserted, the objection should state the attorney involved and the people present, and should provide a description of the communication sufficient to enable the inquiring party to assess the applicability of the claimed privilege. *Pham v. Hartford Fire Ins. Co.*, 193 F.R.D. 659, 662 (D. Colo. 2000). Such a claim fails upon a failure of proof for any element of the privilege. *Jones v. Boeing Co.*, 163 F.R.D. 15, 17 (D. Kan. 1995). Thus, the objecting party must make a showing that (1) it is or sought to become a client; (2) the person to whom the communication was made was a member of the bar of a court or his subordinate and was acting as a lawyer in connection with this communication; (3) the communication related to a fact of which the attorney was informed (a) by the objecting party (b) without the presence of strangers (c) for the purpose of securing primarily either (i) an opinion of law or (ii) legal services or (iii) legal assistance in some legal proceeding, and (d) not for the purpose of committing a crime or tort. *Alexander v. F.B.I.*, 192 F.R.D. 50, 54 (D.D.C. 2000). Failure to object on the ground of attorney-client privilege in a timely and complete manner waives the objection. *Pham*, 193 F.R.D. at 662; *Nguyen v. Excel Corp.*, 197 F.3d 200, 206 (5th Cir. 1999). *But see First Sav. Bank v. First Bank Sys., Inc.*, 902 F. Supp. 1356, 1361-65 (D. Kan. 1995); *Jayne H. Lee, Inc. v Flagstaff Indus. Corp.*, 173 F.R.D. 651, 653 (D. Md. 1997).

In this example, it is likely that the court will find either that the defendant's objections have been waived or, at the least, that the defendant must provide greater substantiation for its objections in order for them to be considered.

If the court were to address the merits, it would likely reach two conclusions. First, Interrogatory No. 1 is wholly appropriate even though a response might involve the application of law to fact. *See* Rule 33(c): "An interrogatory otherwise proper is not necessarily objectionable merely because an answer . . . involves an opinion or contention that relates to a fact or the application of law to fact . . ."; *Steil v. Humana Kansas City, Inc.*, 197 F.R.D. 445, 446 (D. Kan. 2000). Limitation of the inquiry to "material" and "principal" facts, as opposed to "all" facts, makes the interrogatory acceptable in form. *Steil*, 197 F.R.D. at 446. Second, even if some of the information responsive to Interrogatory No. 2 may implicate the attorney-client privilege or work-product doctrine, that does not justify a blanket refusal to provide any answer at all; the respondent must provide as complete an answer as possible, making specific objection—and an adequate showing—as to any information that would violate the privilege or doctrine. *Alexander*, 192 F.R.D. at 54-55.

Practice Tip

Failure to interpose proper objections to interrogatories or document production requests not only waives the objections but also exposes the party to a motion to compel under Rule 37(a) and the possibility of sanctions. *See* chapters 45 and 46, *infra*. Thus, when interrogatories arrive, counsel should immediately docket the deadline for filing a response. If the deadline poses a problem, promptly seek an extension. Memorialize the extension in writing, and if required by the local rules or customs of the court, obtain court approval for the extension, particularly if it would alter a court-imposed deadline. If you obtain an extension, make sure that you meet it and that your filing is in proper form. That means that any objections or claims of privilege must be particularized. Substantive answers must be complete and nonevasive or they may be deemed to be a failure to answer. *See* Rule 37(a)(3).

If, after propounding discovery, you receive a request for a reasonable extension of time to answer interrogatories or document production requests, agree to the extension. Some courts have adopted discovery guidelines, such as Guideline 8, Appendix A, Local Rules, United States District Court for the District of Maryland, that govern how requests for extension must be handled. A failure to agree to a reasonable request for an extension may well produce a motion for additional time to the court, which will not look charitably on a lawyer who is unreasonable on such matters.

Finally, the best way to avoid objections to your interrogatories is to frame them properly in the first place. In this regard, always check to see if the court in which the action is pending has adopted form interrogatories germane to your case; if so, use them. If you receive what you believe are improper objections to interrogatories that you have propounded, try to resolve the dispute with opposing counsel before filing a motion to compel.

6. SUFFICIENCY AND SUPPLEMENTATION OF INTERROGATORY ANSWERS

In a defamation case, interrogatories propounded by the defendant were answered by the plaintiff as follows:

1. If you contend that the defendant made defamatory statements about the plaintiff that were published in newspapers or magazines, please identify every newspaper or magazine article that so defamed the plaintiff by (a) name of the publication; (b) date of publication of the defamatory article; (c) section and page number of the article; and (d) the precise language in the article, attributed to the defendant, that you claim defamed you.

   Answer: Plaintiff has previously produced all newspapers and magazine articles that he believes pertain to this case, including the defamatory articles. The burden of reviewing those articles is no greater on the defendant than it would be on the plaintiff, and so the defendant is referred to those articles.

2. With reference to your allegation at paragraph 13 of the complaint that the defendant defamed the plaintiff by telling and writing to other people that he was "an incompetent boss who should have been fired by the Board of Directors a long time ago," or words to that effect, please identify each person whom you allege heard or read that statement (or that statement in substance) from the defendant by stating: (a) such person's name; (b) his or her last known residence or business address; (c) his or her last known home or business telephone number; (d) the date, if known, when the defamation was communicated to such person; and (e) if it was communicated by letter, memo, or e-mail, the date on which such written communication was generated.

   Answer: John Doe and Mary Roe, as well as members of the Board of Directors, among others. In addition, defendant may have communicated statements to that effect in interoffice memos and e-mails; all office records for the last year are in boxes or on disks in plaintiff's office, and defendant is welcome to inspect these boxes and disks at his convenience. Plaintiff reserves the right to supplement the answer to this interrogatory when further information is obtained during discovery.

3. If you intend to present expert testimony on the issue of damages, please identify every expert whom you will expect to testify, by stating: (a) his or her name; (b) his or her business affiliation, business address and telephone number; (c) his or her professional credentials; and (d) a statement of the opinion to which the expert will testify and the basis therefor.

Answer: Plaintiff will provide this information in accordance with the substance and timing of Rule 26(a)(2) and (b)(4), as directed by the court.

The defendant thought that these answers were inadequate and attempted to negotiate for more complete responses. When that failed, the defendant filed a motion to compel. What will the outcome be?

Comment: Rule 33(d) recites:

Where the answer to an interrogatory may be derived or ascertained from the business records of the party upon whom the interrogatory has been served or from an examination, audit or inspection of such business records, including a compilation, abstract or summary thereof, and the burden of deriving or ascertaining the answer is substantially the same for the party serving the interrogatory as for the party served, it is a sufficient answer to such interrogatory to specify the records from which the answer may be derived or ascertained and to afford to the party serving the interrogatory reasonable opportunity to examine, audit or inspect such records and to make copies, compilation, abstracts or summaries. A specification shall be in sufficient detail to permit the interrogating party to locate and to identify, as readily as can the party served, the records from which the answer may be ascertained.

The Advisory Committee Notes to the 1980 amendments recite that "[t]he final sentence [quoted above] was added to make it clear that a responding party has the duty to specify, by category and location, the records from which answer to interrogatories can be derived."

Measuring the plaintiff's answers to questions 1 and 2 against the Rule and Advisory Committee Notes, it is apparent that the answers are insufficient: The plaintiff has responded to precise interrogatories by simply saying, in effect, "The information you want is in articles that I have already given to you, so you go figure it out, and there may be more information in a stack of other materials in my control, which you are welcome to peruse." In doing this, the plaintiff has impermissibly placed the burden on the defendant to determine what statements the plaintiff contends are defamatory, as well as what newspaper and magazine articles and internal office memos and e-mails plaintiff intends to rely on. Because it is inconceivable that the plaintiff has not already made such determinations, the burden is far lighter on the plaintiff to identify such statements than it would be on the defendant to try to figure it out.

Thus, plaintiff's response has gotten it exactly backwards. It is *his* obligation to identify the information responsive to the interrogatory, and not the defendant's. Of course, the plaintiff might be able to rely on reference to documents, but only when the prerequisites for doing so have been satisfied:

> The producing party must satisfy a number of factors in order to meet its justification burden. First, it must show that a review of the documents will actually reveal answers to the interrogatories. 8A Wright [Miller & Marcus, *Federal Practice and Procedure*, 2d ed. 1994] § 2178, at 330. In other words, the producing party must show that the named documents contain all of the information requested by the interrogatories. *Oleson v. Kmart Corp.*, 175 F.R.D. 560, 564 (D. Kan. 1997); *Thompson v. Glenmede Trust Co.*, 1995 WL 752443, at *3 (E.D. Pa. Dec. 19, 1995). Crucial to this inquiry is that the producing party has adequately and precisely specified for each interrogatory the actual documents where information will be found. 8A Wright, *supra*, § 2178, at 336. Document dumps or vague references to documents do not suffice. *Capacchione v. Charlotte-Mecklenburg Schools*, 182 F.R.D. 486 (W.D.N.C. 1998) (200 boxes); *In re Bilzerian*, 190 B.R. 964 (Bankr. M.D. Fla. 1995) (28 boxes). Depending on the number of documents and the number of interrogatories, indices may be required. *O'Connor v. Boeing North.*, 185 F.R.D. 272, 278 (C.D.Cal. 1999).
>
> . . .
>
> A second burden imposed on the producing party is to justify the actual shifting of the perusal burden from it to the requesting party. . . . Plaintiff has failed to show that it would be no more burdensome for defendants to go through voluminous documents to pull out answers than for plaintiff [citation omitted]. In fact, because plaintiff is now

preparing for the hearing, the Court assumes it has already culled the documents for answers to some or all of the interrogatories. In this situation, it is not equally less burdensome for defendants to obtain the information. *Petroleum Ins. Agency, Inc. v. Hartford Acc. and Indem. Co.*, 111 F.R.D. 318, 322 (D. Mass. 1983). . . .

S.E.C. v. Elfindepan, S.A., 206 F.R.D. 574, 576-77 (M.D.N.C. 2002); *Sabel v. Mead Johnson & Co.*, 110 F.R.D. 553, 556 (D. Mass. 1986) (pharmaceutical company could not respond to interrogatories in products liability suit by telling the interrogator to view the company's new drug application where, given lack of specificity in records and inadequate index, company was better able to cull information from 154,000 pages of documents).

The answer to Interrogatory No. 2 in the defamation case suffers from the further vice that it does not even attempt to identify persons whom the plaintiff believes heard or read the defamatory statement at the office—note the vague phraseology "members of the Board of Directors, among others." The defendant will ask the obvious questions, "Which members of the Board of Directors, and who are the 'others'?" If the plaintiff has possession of that information, he is obliged to give it. If the plaintiff is unsure of which members of the board heard the statement, or who else heard it, he should say so explicitly: "Plaintiff understands from Doe and Roe that members of the Board of Directors heard the statement. Plaintiff does not yet know which board members heard the statement. Further, plaintiff understands from Doe and Roe that there may have been other company officers who heard the statement, but again, plaintiff does not yet know the identity of these persons."

The language in response to Interrogatory No. 2 to the effect that plaintiff reserves the right to supplement his answers when further information becomes known is gratuitous. Rule 26(e), entitled "Supplementation of Disclosures and Responses," *requires* the respondent to supplement discovery responses in certain circumstances. Rule 26(e)(2), in particular, states: "A party is under a duty seasonably to amend a prior response to an interrogatory, request for production, or request for admission if the party learns that the response is in some material respect incomplete or incorrect and if the additional or corrective information has not otherwise been made known to the other parties during the discovery process or in writing."

Failure to so supplement interrogatory answers when required may be sanctionable by entry of an order precluding the offending party from introducing at trial evidence that varies from or supplements its interrogatory answers. *Nicholas v. Pa. State Univ.*, 227 F.3d 133 (3d Cir. 2000); *Rodowicz v. Mass. Mut. Life Ins. Co.*, 279 F.3d 36 (1st Cir. 2002).

The answer to Interrogatory No. 3 is not objectionable. Rule 26(a)(2) and (b)(4) (as well as the other rules governing mandatory disclosures) trump discovery requests seeking the same information and govern the timing of such disclosures. *B.C.F. Oil Ref., Inc. v. Con. Ed. Co. of N.Y., Inc.*, 168 F.R.D. 161, 166 (S.D.N.Y. 1996).

Practice Tip

Rule 37(a)(3) must always be considered in assessing the sufficiency of answers to interrogatories (as well as all other discovery responses and disclosures). This rule states: "For purposes of this subdivision [pertaining to failures to make required discovery and the motions and sanctions that may result therefrom] an evasive or incomplete disclosure, answer or response is treated as a failure to disclose, answer, or respond." The power of Rule 37(a)(3) is apparent. The most common mistake in responding to interrogatories, illustrated in this section, is not outright refusal to respond, but instead providing evasive and incomplete answers. Based on Rule 37(a)(3), a court, confronted with such answers (and the unwillingness of the party to correct them), will probably grant a motion to compel and, if appropriate, impose sanctions.

Accordingly, a lawyer who receives evasive or incomplete answers to a properly framed interrogatory should immediately communicate in writing with the party that provided the deficient answers, identifying the basis for the inadequacy and requesting that responsive answers be provided within a reasonable, but brief, time. If no agreement can be reached or if an agreement is reached but not honored, the position of the party propounding the interrogatories is greatly strengthened on a motion to compel and for sanctions. By the same token, a lawyer who receives such a letter from an adverse party complaining about the insufficiency of the answers should review them carefully and consider the wisdom of reaching agreement for prompt supplementation.

---

7. INTERROGATORIES—USE IN COURT

A. *As Substantive Evidence*

Plaintiff Jones has sued the defendant for damages resulting from an automobile collision, including $250,000 in special damages. Before resting his case, defendant's counsel addresses the court as follows:

> Defense Counsel: Your Honor, before defendant closes its case, we would like to read into evidence defendant's Interrogatory No. 10 and plaintiff's answer under oath.
>
> Plaintiff's Counsel: We object. The plaintiff is available in court, and if defense counsel wants to question or cross-examine plaintiff, he can do so.
>
> The Court: Federal Rule of Civil Procedure 33(c) provides that the answers to interrogatories may be used for any purpose to the extent permitted by the rules of evidence. Unless there is some relevancy objection, I am going to allow defendant's counsel to proceed.
>
> Defense Counsel: Thank you, Your Honor: "Interrogatory 10: 'Please itemize your expenses incurred as a result of the occurrence.'" "Answer, filed on June 7, 2004, under oath and signed by the plaintiff: '(1) property damage, $15,000; (2) medical bills, $15,000.'"

Was the interrogatory answer properly admitted into evidence?

Comment: Yes. Interrogatory answers may be used at trial in the same manner as deposition answers. *See* Rule 33. *See also Exum v. G. E. Co.*, 819 F.2d 1158 (D.C. Cir. 1987); *Carballo-Rodriguez v. Clark Equip. Co.*, 147 F. Supp. 2d 66 (D. Puerto Rico 2001) (holding that answers given by defendant to interrogatories in a separate suit were admissible as admissions of a party-deponent as they contained evidence contrary to the factual position asserted by the defendant in the instant case). *But see Frankel v. Burke's Excavating, Inc.*, 397 F.2d 167 (3d Cir. 1968) (refusal to allow plaintiffs to read into evidence defendants' answer to interrogatory not erroneous because court's instructions to jury resolved the disputed issue in plaintiffs' favor as a matter of law); *In re CFS Related Secs. Fraud Litig.*, 256 F. Supp. 2d 1227 (N.D. Okla. 2003) (holding that the district court has the discretion, in appropriate circumstances, to prohibit the use of interrogatories, depositions, and affidavits with the exception of the limited purposes of impeachment or perjury). *See also* Sandler & Archibald, *Model Witness Examinations*, 2d ed., 235-37 (ABA Litigation Section, 2003).

B. *As Impeachment*

In the same case, plaintiff is on the stand for cross-examination:

> Defense Counsel: Mr. Jones, you testified on direct examination that your expenses, as a result of this occurrence, were approximately $250,000. Is that correct?
>
> Jones: Yes.
>
> Defense Counsel: Do you recall that you were served with interrogatories or a series of written questions in this case?
>
> Jones: Yes.
>
> Defense Counsel: And you and your lawyer prepared the answers to these questions, did you not?
>
> Jones: Indeed.
>
> Defense Counsel: And you reviewed the answers before they were filed in court?
>
> Jones: Of course.
>
> Defense Counsel: That is because you wanted to make sure that the answers were correct and complete before you signed them, swore to them, and filed them, true?
>
> Jones: Absolutely.
>
> Defense Counsel: And so after you reviewed them for accuracy and completeness, you appeared before a Notary Public, did you not, and declared under oath, on penalty of perjury, that the answers were true to the best of your information and belief?
>
> Jones: Yes.
>
> Defense Counsel: Now, Mr. Jones, I want you to read to the jury Interrogatory No. 10 and your answer.
>
> Plaintiff's Counsel: Objection, Your Honor.
>
> The Court: Overruled. You may proceed.

Comment: Interrogatory answers, like deposition answers, may be used to impeach at trial. *See* Rule 33. *See also U. S. Lines Co. v. King*, 363 F.2d 658 (4th Cir. 1966); *Troutman v. S. Ry Co.*, 441 F.2d 586 (5th Cir. 1971), *cert. denied*, 404 U.S. 871 (1971); *Clark Equip. Co. v. Keller*, 570 F.2d 778 (8th Cir. 1978), *cert. denied*, 439 U.S. 825 (1978). *But see DeBenedetto v. Goodyear Tire & Rubber Co.*, 754 F.2d 512 (4th Cir. 1985) (refusal to allow jury to consider interrogatories for purposes of impeaching opposing party not in error, where interrogatories and requests for admissions considered irrelevant in light of the party's admissions at trial); *Williamson v. Yang*, 550 S.E. 2d 456 (Ga. App. 2001) (finding where response to interrogatory did not contradict scientist's subsequent trial testimony, answer to interrogatory was inadmissible for purposes of impeachment). *See also* Sandler & Archibald, *Model Witness Examinations*, 2d ed., 236-37 (ABA Litigation Section, 2003).

8. DOCUMENT REQUESTS—NUMEROSITY, PROPRIETY, TIMING, AND SUFFICIENCY OF OBJECTIONS

A plaintiff brought a personal injury action against the defendant arising out of the collision of their automobiles. Along with her answer, the defendant served a set of 50 requests for production on the plaintiff under Rule 34. Among the requests were the following:

1. Produce for inspection and copying all documents that support the allegations in paragraphs 7, 8, 9, and/or 10 of your complaint.
2. Produce for inspection and copying all documents concerning your damages.
3. Produce for inspection and copying all documents relating to repairs to your automobile related to the incident in question.
4. Produce for inspection and copying all witness statements.
5. Produce for inspection and copying all documents identified in response to the interrogatories.

Plaintiff did not file any responses within 30 days. Defense counsel then telephoned and asked when she might expect the responses. Plaintiff's counsel responded, "In one week." A week later, the plaintiff filed a document captioned "Plaintiff's Objections to Defendant's Requests for Production." In its entirety, the document read: "Plaintiff objects to defendant's requests for production of documents on the ground that they are onerous, burdensome, and vague. Further, request No. 4 invades the work-product doctrine." Defendant thereupon filed a motion to compel, which plaintiff opposed. What will the outcome be?

Comment: As discussed in chapters 5 and 6, *supra*, defendant's counsel, before moving to compel, should have checked the local district court rules to determine whether they required a good faith attempt at informal resolution of any discovery disputes before resorting to a formal motion. *See, e.g.,* Rule 7.1(I) of the Local Rules of the United States District Court for the District of Nebraska, which provides:

> To curtail undue delay in the administration of justice, this court shall refuse to consider any and all motions relating to discovery

unless moving counsel, as part of the motion, shall make a written showing that after personal consultation with counsel for opposing parties and sincere attempts to resolve differences, they are unable to reach an accord. This showing shall recite, additionally, the date, time and place of such conference and the names of all persons participating in them.

If such a rule is ignored, the court may deny the motion to compel even if it has merit. *See Doe v. Nat'l Hemophilia Found.*, 194 F.R.D. 516, 519 (D. Md. 2000); *Gibbs v. Oklahoma Dep't of Transp.*, 1991 WL 405514 at *3 (W.D. Okla., Aug. 21, 1991). Although such denial might ostensibly be "without prejudice," if the deadline imposed under local rules for filing discovery motions has passed, the denial could, in effect, be final. *See supra* at chapter 5.

As also discussed above at chapter 5, the plaintiff himself could have a problem. The parties agreed to an extension of time without consulting the court, much less obtaining its consent. Rule 34(b) allows for stipulations by the parties for extensions of time to respond to requests for production *subject to Rule 29.* Rule 29 allows for such stipulations "[u]nless otherwise directed by the court." Under Rule 29, some districts have a local rule that negates the effect of any agreement between counsel absent court approval. See, for example, Rule 7.1M of the Local Rules of the United States District Court for the District of Colorado, quoted in *Pham v. Hartford Fire Ins. Co.*, 193 F.R.D. 659, 661 (D. Colo. 2000):

> No agreement of counsel to shorten or extend any time limitation provided by the federal rules of civil . . . procedure . . . will be recognized or enforced, nor will such an agreement be considered just cause for failing to perform within the time limits established by those rules. Only time variances specifically approved by court order upon motion made within the time limits prescribed by those rules will be recognized as having any binding or legal effect.

If that rule were applied to the car crash example, plaintiffs' responses might be deemed untimely; in that event, absent "good cause," all objections to the requests for production would have been waived. *Pham*, 193 F.R.D. at 661. It is important to note, however, that Rule 34 does not contain language comparable to that in Rule 33(b)(4), which says: "Any ground [for objection] not stated in a timely objection is waived unless the party's failure to object is excused by the court for good cause." A lawyer with a potential waiver problem may argue that the absence of this language in Rule 34 allows for a broader standard of compliance and does not require a showing of "good cause."

Timing is another threshold issue that should always be considered when issuing Rule 34 requests. Rule 34(b) recites that "[w]ithout leave of court or written stipulation, a request may not be served before the time specified in Rule 26(d)." Here, the facts suggest that the requests for production jumped the gun. Premature requests could give rise to an argument by plaintiff that the motion to compel was not ripe, although defense counsel would argue that plaintiff's failure to make that objection in its responses constituted a "stipulation" in its effect that would trump the otherwise restrictive language of Rule 34(b).

The number of requests could also be an issue, depending on the local rules. While Rule 33 limits the presumptive number of interrogatories to 25, Rule 34 contains no such restriction. Local rules, however, frequently restrict the presumptive number of requests for production. Rule 104(1) of the Rules of the United States District Court for the District of Maryland, for example, provides: "Unless otherwise ordered by the Court, or agreed upon by the parties, no party shall serve upon any other party, at one time or cumulatively, more than 30 requests for production . . . including all parts and subparts." If such rule existed in the district in which the hypothetical case is pending, the plaintiff may be justified in not responding to any of the 50 requests, *In re Indep. Energy Holdings Secs. Litig.*, 2003 WL 42010 (S.D.N.Y. Jan. 6, 2003), although he might answer the first 30 requests and then stop. Of course, the defendant could argue that the plaintiff's failure to make that specific objection constituted a stipulation that 50 requests for production could be filed, or perhaps a waiver of any such objection. *See generally Coregis Ins. Co. v. Baratta & Fenerty, Ltd.*, 187 F.R.D. 528, 529 (E.D. Pa. 1999) (failure to make timely objections to discovery constitutes waiver).

Depending on the applicable local rules, the defendant might also argue that the format of the objections was improper and thus all objections were waived. Rule 104(6) of the Rules of the United States District Court for the District of Maryland, for example, provides that "[r]esponses to interrogatories and requests for production shall set forth each interrogatory or request followed by the answer and/or a brief statement of the grounds for objection, including a citation of the main applicable authorities." *St. Paul Reins.*

Co. v. Commercial Fin. Corp., 198 F.R.D. 508, 511 (N.D. Iowa 2000) (an objection is waived if no explanation or ground for such objection is given).

If the court ever gets to the substance of plaintiff's objections, defendant should be able to defend the breadth of the requests. They are straightforward and relevant. *Steil v. Humana Kansas City, Inc.*, 197 F.R.D. 445, 448 (D. Kan. 2000) (upholding requests for documents pertaining to plaintiff's claim that the treatment at issue was not excluded or was covered by plaintiff's health insurance policy, and request for production of all documents identified in answers to interrogatories).

The request for witness statements, however, invades the attorney work-product doctrine. *Dunn v. State Farm Fire & Cas. Co.*, 927 F.2d 869, 875 (5th Cir. 1991). Thus, discovery of the statements would be subject to the limitations of Rule 26(b)(3), which provides in pertinent part:

> Subject to the provisions of subdivision (b)(4) of this rule, a party may obtain discovery of documents and tangible things otherwise discoverable under subdivision (b)(1) of this rule and prepared in anticipation of litigation or for trial by or for another party or by or for that other party's representative (including the other party's attorney, consultant, surety, indemnitor, insurer, or agent), only upon a showing that the party seeking discovery has substantial need of the materials in the preparation of the party's case and that the party is unable without undue hardship to obtain the substantial equivalent of the materials by other means. . . .

Defendant, unless he can demonstrate that he has no access to the witnesses and that their statements are material, will not meet the requisite standard for their discovery. *See further*, discussion at chapter 10 regarding discovery of witness statements.

Counsel should also bear in mind that altering or failing to preserve evidence in pending or reasonably foreseeable litigation could violate ethical guidelines. See chapter 48, *infra*, for a discussion of the law of spoliation and the risks faced by counsel who engage in nonproduction of documents or sluggish responses to discovery requests, and chapter 9, *infra*, which focuses on the particular problems that stem from discovery of electronically stored information. Rule 3.4 of the Rules of Professional Responsibility, American Bar Association Model Rules of Professional Conduct, "Fairness to Opposing Party and Counsel" (2003), provides that counsel shall not unlawfully obstruct another party's access to evidence or destroy evidence. The ABA's Civil Discovery Standards (August 1999 and August 2004 Amendments), Standard No. 10, entitled "Preservation of Documents," see Appendix D, emphasizes that when counsel learns that litigation is probable, she should inform her client of its duty to preserve potentially relevant documents and consequences resulting if documents are not properly preserved.

9. DISCOVERY OF ELECTRONICALLY STORED INFORMATION

Omnibus Construction Company contracted with Acme Insurance Company to design and build its new corporate headquarters. Omnibus was the lowest bidder of the many companies that submitted bids. Its bid stressed its experience in the design and construction of large commercial projects and its skill in managing construction to finish on time and within budget.

The job ran into trouble almost immediately after the contract was signed. Delays set the project at least six months behind schedule and 15 percent over budget. Acme began to receive complaints from materials suppliers and subcontractors that they were not being paid by Omnibus and were planning to file mechanic's liens. Hearing this, Acme brought suit against Omnibus in federal court alleging breach of contract, fraud, and misrepresentation.

Discovery began following the court's issuance of a pretrial schedule. Acme filed Rule 34 document production requests seeking all records, whether in "hard copy" or electronic form, related to Omnibus's experience in the past five years in designing and building large commercial projects generally, and similar construction projects specifically. The requests sought copies of all relevant e-mails, both existing and deleted, from all persons involved in the bidding and execution of the contract. The request asked for materials on Omnibus's computer hard drives, archived electronic data, and backup tapes. Together with the requests, counsel for Acme sent a letter to counsel for Omnibus demanding that it preserve all electronically stored information relevant to the requests.

Omnibus objected to the requests and filed a Rule 26(c) motion for a protective order. Relying on affidavits from Omnibus executives, it argued that the requested discovery of electronic data was burdensome, that it would be too costly to produce the data, and that such production efforts would interrupt Omnibus's business activities in a substantial manner. Omnibus particularly objected to Acme's request for access to Omnibus's computer hard drives, archival data, and backup data. Omnibus argued further that it already had produced much of the information requested in hard copy and that it should not have to produce duplicate data in an electronic format. Omnibus objected to the demand to preserve data on the ground that this would interfere with the company's document retention policy requiring destruction of records more than one year old. Finally, Omnibus argued that if the court ordered it to comply with the requests, Acme should pay for the expense of production.

In its opposition, Acme asserted that the electronic data was discoverable and that Omnibus, as the producing party, should bear the burden and expense of production. Acme further argued that the fact that it had received "hard copy" information did not prevent discovery of the data in electronic form. Finally, Acme argued that a preservation order should be issued by the court to prevent spoliation of evidence.

How should the court rule?

Comment: The permissible methods and scope of discovery of electronically stored information have been the subject of substantial recent debate and controversy. Courts have wrestled with the questions of how much discovery to allow and how to apportion the burden and expense associated with production. The breadth of the term "electronically stored information" contributes to the problems faced by parties and courts. As one court has observed, the term "electronic records" potentially encompasses voice mail, e-mail messages and files, deleted e-mail, data files, program files, backup files, archival tapes, temporary files, system history files, Web site information in textual, graphical, or audio format, Web site log files, cache files, "cookies," and other electronically stored information. *Kleiner v. Burns*, 2000 WL 1909470 (D. Kan. 2000). Furthermore, because an enormous number of business records are created, edited, revised, and retained in computer format and on workstation systems, laptop computers, personal data devices, and even cell phones, a request for "all relevant" electronic data related to a fact at issue may encompass a huge amount of information and cost. (The 1970 changes to Rule 34(a) made it clear that "records" include electronically prepared and stored information. Commentary to the 1970 changes to the Federal Rules of Civil Procedure, 48 F.R.D. 487, 527. Accordingly, electronically stored data is subject to disclosure under Rule 26(a)(1) and discovery under Rule 34. *Bills v. Kennecott Corp.*, 108 F.R.D. 459, 461 (D. Utah 1985); *Daewoo Elecs. Co. v. United States*, 650 F. Supp 1003 (Court of International Trade, 1986); *Playboy Enterprises Inc. v. Welles*, 60 F. Supp 2d 1050, 1053 (S.D. Cal. 1999); *Rowe Entm't v. The William Morris Agency, Inc.*, 205 F.R.D. 421, 428 (S.D.N.Y. 2002); *In re Bristol-Myers Squibb Sec. Litig.*, 205 F.R.D. 437, 441-42 (D. N.J. 2002) (the only limits on discovery of computerized records are that the "producing party [must] be protected against undue burden and expense and/or invasion of privileged matter" (internal citations omitted)); *Antioch Co. v. Scrapbook Borders*, 210 F.R.D. 645, 652 (D. Minn. 2002) (electronically stored information, including deleted files, are discoverable; Rule 26(a)(1)(B) disclosures require "description and categorization of computerized data including deleted e-mails," and the disclosing party must "take reasonable steps to ensure that it discloses any back-up copies of files or archival tapes that will provide information about any 'deleted electronic data'"); *Thompson v. H.U.D.*, 219 F.R.D. 93 (D. Md. 2003) (electronically stored records are discoverable, subject to Rule 26(b)(2) limitations to avoid burdensomeness) (internal citations omitted); *Zubulake v. UBS Warburg LLC*, 220 F.R.D. 212, 2003 WL 22410619 (S.D.N.Y. Oct. 22, 2003) (holding that the duty to preserve electronically stored materials attaches "when the party has notice that the evidence is relevant to litigation or when a party should have known that the evidence may be relevant to future litigation"); *id.* at *2.

Some courts have gone so far as to order the responding party to develop programs to assist the requesting party in extracting electronically stored information, and to help the requesting party to read and interpret it. On occasion, courts have allowed discovery into the responding party's computer capabilities and capacities. *Bills v. Kennecott Corp.*, 108 F.R.D. 459 (D. Utah 1985).

The difficult issues concern the scope of the production that will be required in a given case and who should bear the burden and expense of the discovery. While saying that electronic data logically is no different from "hard copy" records for purposes of discoverability, courts recognize the sheer magnitude of producing "all relevant" electronic data that could be gleaned from multiple users or sources, especially if discovery of "deleted" files is sought. One court has noted that "[a]ccording to a University of California study, 93% of all information generated during 1999 was generated in digital form, on computers. Only 7% of information originated in other media, such as paper." *In re Bristol-Myers Squibb Sec. Litig.*, 205 F.R.D. at 440, n. 2 (internal citations omitted). Another has observed:

> Computer files, including e-mails, are discoverable. . . . However, the Court is not persuaded by the plaintiff's attempt to equate traditional paper-based discovery with the discovery of e-mail files. Several commentators have noted important differences between the two. . . . Chief among these differences is the sheer volume of electronic information. E-mails have replaced other forms of communication besides just paper-based communication. Many informal messages that were previously relayed by telephone or at the water

cooler are now sent via e-mail. Additionally, computers have the ability to capture several copies (or drafts) of the same e-mail, thus multiplying the volume of documents. All of these e-mails must be scanned for both relevance and privilege. Also, unlike most paper-based discovery, archived e-mails typically lack a coherent filing system. Moreover, dated archival systems commonly store information on magnetic tapes which have become obsolete. Thus, parties incur additional costs in translating the data from the tapes into useable form.

Byers v. Ill. State Police, 2002 WL 1264004 at *10, (N.D. Ill. June 2002).

Courts have looked to the cost-benefit balancing principles in Rule 26(b)(2) to determine the nature and extent of permissible discovery of computerized information in particular cases and have adopted flexible measures for determining which party should pay for such discovery. *McPeek v. Ashcroft*, 202 F.R.D. 31, 34 (D.D.C. 2001) (adopting a "marginal utility" analysis to determine whether a party was required to bear the cost of searching for deleted e-mail from backup tapes. "The more likely it is that the backup tape contains information that is relevant to a claim or defense, the fairer it is that the . . . [defendant] search at its own expense. The less likely it is, the more unjust it would be to make the agency search at its own expense.").

One court has fashioned a much discussed multifactor test to determine who should pay for the production of voluminous electronic records. After noting that "the presumption is that the responding party must bear the expense of complying with discovery requests," the court in *Rowe Entm't v. The William Morris Agency, Inc.*, 205 F.R.D. 421 (S.D.N.Y. 2002), acknowledged that Rule 26(c) permitted a party to request that the court issue a protective order to shift the expense of production entirely or partially to the requesting party. *Id.* at 428.[1] The factors to be considered were: (1) the specificity with which the requesting party identified the electronic data sought; (2) the likelihood of a successful search for the information sought (the greater

---

1. *See also* Oppenheimer Fund, Inc. v. Sanders, 437 U.S. 340, 358 (1978) (responding party ordinarily bears the expense associated with the production of discovery); and Murphy Oil USA, Inc. v. Fluor Daniel, 2002 WL 246439 (E.D. La. 2002) (presumption is that producing party bears the expense of production, but may seek Rule 26(c) relief. When this is done, the Rule 26(b)(2) balancing factors should be applied to determine whether or not to shift the cost to the requesting party).

the likelihood of success, the fairer it is to require the producing party to bear the expense); (3) the availability of the information sought from other sources; (4) the purpose for which the responding party retained the electronic data (if the producing party maintains the data for its own business purposes, it is not unfair to require that it bear the burden of production, but if it maintains data only for purposes of backup in the event of an emergency or simply has neglected to discard such data, it is unfair to require that the producing party bear the expense); (5) the benefit to the parties (if the responding party benefits from the production there is no reason to shift the cost to the requesting party); (6) the total costs of the production (the greater the cost the more likely the court will order total or partial cost shifting to the requesting party); (7) the ability to control the costs of production (if discovery is proceeding on an incremental basis, it is more fair to put the burden on the party that asks for additional discovery following initial discovery to pay for it); and (8) the resources of the parties. *Id.* at 429-32.

Evaluation of these factors necessarily embraces the Rule 26(b)(2) cost-benefit analysis that courts are required to make, either on their own or in connection with a Rule 26(c) motion for protective order, to determine whether potentially burdensome discovery will be permitted. *See* chapter 46, *infra.*

Not all courts agree that the *Rowe* factors are the right ones to apply under Rule 26(b)(2) to determine whether to shift the burden and cost of production of electronic data to the requesting party. In *Zubulake v. UBS Warburg, LLC*, 216 F.R.D. 280 (S.D.N.Y., July 24, 2003) (*Zubulake* III), the court modified the *Rowe* factors because it found that they tended to favor the responding party by too readily shifting the cost of production to the requesting party. *Id.* at 284. Instead, the court adopted the following seven-factor test: (1) the extent to which the request is specifically tailored to discover relevant information; (2) the availability of such information from other sources; (3) the total cost of production, as compared to the amount in controversy; (4) the total cost of production, compared to the resources available to each party; (5) the relative ability of each party to control costs and its incentives to do so; (6) the importance of issues at stake in litigation; and (7) the relative benefits to the parties of obtaining the information. *Id.*

Regardless of what test the court employs, the central issue is the same: Given the potential expense associated with discovery of electronic discovery, courts are concerned about the cost-benefit balance of discovering such information, and they take seriously their obligation under Rule 26(b)(2) to prevent such discovery from becoming unfairly burdensome or expensive. Nor will they allow generalized claims of burden and expense or imbalance in the financial resources of the parties to preclude such discovery where its importance is established.

The discovery of "deleted" data or files has been subject to particular judicial scrutiny.[2] In *Zubulake v. UBS Warburg LLC*, 2003 WL 21087136 (S.D.N.Y. May 13, 2003) (*Zubulake I*), the court noted at *10 that there is substantial confusion about what is meant by a "deleted" electronic file. The court observed that when electronic records are "deleted" they are not "erased" from the computer's storage, but simply designated as "not used," which enables the computer to "write over" them. Until this occurs, however, the "deleted" data can be recovered. Accordingly, the court stated that it is more accurate to refer to deleted electronic data as "residual data," and that such data may also be located in backup or archival files. *Id.*

Since "deleted" electronic data actually exists until it is overwritten, time may be of the essence in pursuing its discovery. To ensure against loss of the ability to discover "deleted" electronic files after they are overwritten, many parties request that the party from which computer-based discovery is sought agree to a preservation order. If the requesting party is unable to obtain a stipulation to that effect, it can move for a protective order. *See, e.g., Antioch Co. v. Scrapbook Borders, Inc.*, 210 F.R.D. 645, 649 (D. Minn. 2002) (court granted plaintiff's unopposed request to order defendant to "preserve all documents relevant to the lawsuit" based on plaintiff's fear that otherwise they would be lost, destroyed, altered, or deleted).

The Civil Litigation Management Manual of the Judicial Conference of the United States, Committee on Court Administration and Case Management, 2001, suggests that courts handling cases involving issues related to discovery of electronic information consider the following procedures to avoid loss or destruction of this data: (1) request that the parties voluntarily

---

2. There is widespread authority that "deleted" electronic data may be the subject of discovery. Antioch Co. v. Scrapbook Borders Inc., 210 F.R.D. 645, 652 (D. Minn. 2002) (deleted computer records including e-mail are discoverable); Simon Prop. Group L.P. v. mySimon, Inc., 194 F.R.D. 639, 640 (S.D.N.Y. 2000) (computer records, including records that have been deleted, are discoverable under Rule 34); Playboy Enterprises v. Welles, 60 F. Supp. 2d 1050, 1053 (S.D. Cal. 1999) (permitting discovery by plaintiff of defendant's computer hard drive because defendant deleted e-mail); and Zubulake v. UBS Warburg, LLC., 2003 U.S. Dist. Lexis 7939 (S.D.N.Y., 2003) (deleted electronic data may be discovered).

agree to take steps to preserve all relevant electronic records; (2) require counsel to agree on measures that will be taken to effect preservation to avoid later accusations of spoliation of evidence; and (3) issue a "freeze order" if the parties cannot agree on the measures that should be taken. Counsel should be aware of the contents of the manual, because trial judges may use it as a reference and adopt its recommendations.

In this regard, courts have given clear guidance on when a duty arises to preserve electronic and other materials that may be the subject of discovery requests. "The duty to preserve material evidence arises not only during litigation but also extends to that period before the litigation when a party reasonably should know that the evidence may be relevant to anticipated litigation." *Silvestri v. G. M.*, 271 F. 3d 583, 591 (4th Cir. 2001); *Kronisch v. United States* 150 F.3d 112, 126 (2d Cir. 1998) (same); *Zubulake v. UBS Warburg LLC*, 220 F.R.D. 212 (S.D.N.Y. 2003) (*Zubulake IV*), at 216; *Thompson v. H.U.D.*, 219 F.R.D. at 99-100. Discussing discovery of e-mail and other electronic materials, the *Zubulake III* court expressed the following additional rules: (1) Once the duty to preserve is triggered, a party need not preserve "every shred" of paper or electronically stored information, but it must not "destroy unique, relevant evidence that might be useful to an adversary," and "is under a duty to preserve what it knows, or reasonably should know, is relevant in the action, is reasonably calculated to lead to the discovery of admissible evidence, is reasonably likely to be requested during discovery and/or is the subject of a pending discovery request," *id.* at 217, 218 (internal citations omitted); (2) the duty to preserve "extends to those employees likely to have relevant information—the 'key players' in the case," *id.*; (3) the party under a duty to preserve need not keep multiple copies of identical documents, or even all existing backup tapes, but:

> Once a party reasonably anticipates litigation, it must suspend its routine document retention/destruction policy and put in place a 'litigation hold' to ensure the preservation of relevant documents. As a general rule, that litigation hold does not apply to inaccessible backup tapes (e.g., those typically maintained solely for the purposes of disaster recovery), which may continue to be recycled on the schedule set forth in the company's policy. On the other hand, if backup tapes are accessible (i.e., actively used for information retrieval), then such tapes *would* likely be subject to the litigation hold. *Id.* at 218 (emphasis in original).

However, "if a company can identify where particular employee documents are stored on backup tapes, then the tapes storing the documents of 'key players' to the existing or threatened litigation should be preserved if the information contained on those tapes is not otherwise available." *Id.*

Lawyers should also be aware that the American Bar Association has adopted civil discovery standards addressing discovery issues not expressly covered by the Federal Rules of Civil Procedure. They appear as Appendix D to this text. Standard No. 29 addresses the duty to preserve, and the discovery of, electronic information. Standard No. 30 addresses the use of technology to facilitate discovery. Taken together, they cover many of the problems discussed by the courts in their effort to balance the costs and burdens of electronic discovery against its benefits. It is a good idea for counsel to familiarize themselves with the details of the ABA standards, as courts may look to them for guidance, and a lawyer who can demonstrate that his or her position on electronic discovery follows the ABA recommendations may have an advantage.

Counsel should likewise bear in mind that altering or failing to preserve evidence in pending or reasonably foreseeable litigation could violate ethical guidelines. Rule 3.4 of the Rules and Professional Responsibility, American Bar Association Model Rules of Professional Conduct, "Fairness to Opposing Party and Counsel" (2003), provides that counsel shall not unlawfully obstruct another party's access to evidence or destroy evidence. The ABA's Civil Discovery Standards (August 1999 and August 2004 Proposed Amendment), Standard no. 10, titled "Preservation of Documents," emphasizes that when counsel learns that litigation is probable, he or she should inform the client of its duty to preserve potentially relevant documents and the consequences resulting if documents are not properly preserved.

While the foregoing suggestions may seem burdensome, counsel would be wise to heed them. Failure to do so could result in the judicial imposition of an adverse inference instruction to the jury as a discovery sanction. That would allow the jury to infer that the lost or destroyed evidence was harmful to the party that lost or destroyed it. *Zubulake IV, supra,* at *5-6. To be entitled to such an instruction, the party seeking discovery must establish that: (1) the party having control over the evidence had an obligation to preserve it at the time it was destroyed; (2) the records were destroyed with a "culpable state of mind" (willful/bad faith, gross negligence, or simple negligence); and (3) the destroyed evidence was 'relevant' to the party's claim or defense such that a reasonable trier of fact could find that it would support that claim or defense. *Zubulake IV, supra* at 220; *Residential Funding Corp. v. DeGeorge Fin. Corp.*, 306 F.3d 99, 108 (2d Cir. 2002); *Thompson v. H.U.D.*, 219 F.R.D. at 101.

The Federal Judicial Center's Complex Litigation Manual, 4th edition, 2004, provides helpful advice regarding discovery of computer-stored data. Judges frequently refer to it for guidance, and thus practitioners should be familiar with its contents as well. The manual observes that computerized data has become commonplace in litigation, and that any discovery plan proposed by counsel to the court should address issues "relating to such information including the search for it and its location, retrieval, form of production, inspection, *preservation*, and use at trial." *Id.* at 78 (emphasis added). The manual further states that "[t]he complexity and rapidly changing character of the technology for the management of computerized materials may make it appropriate for the court to seek the assistance of a special master or neutral expert, or call on the parties to provide the judge with expert assistance in the form of briefings on the relevant technological issues." *Id.* at 82. *See, e.g., Antioch Co. v. Scrapbook Borders Inc.*, 210 F.R.D. 645, 652 (D. Minn. 2002) (discussing the use of an expert to assist the court in resolving discovery issues related to computerized records); and *Simon Prop. Group v. mySimon, Inc.*, 194 F.R.D. 639, 640 (S.D. Ind. 2000) (discussing the use of an expert to assist the court in resolving discovery issues associated with production of electronically stored information).

Lawyers should anticipate that a judge, faced with conflicting positions of adverse experts regarding the feasibility or burdensomeness of discovery of electronic records, may appoint a court expert, as suggested by the Complex Litigation Manual. In that event, the costs to one party or another, or both, may increase substantially; the court may assess the cost of its expert evenly, apportion it between the parties, or assign the entire cost to the party whose position the court rejects. Knowing these possibilities, counsel should gauge at the outset the vulnerability of his expert's opinion to challenge by an objective outsider.

Applying the foregoing authority to the *Omnibus/Acme* example, there is no doubt that the court will order some discovery of Omnibus's electronic records. The outcome of Omnibus's motion for protective order will depend on the factual specificity of its assertions of unfair burden or expense. If Omnibus's counsel demonstrates that (a) there is little likelihood that a search of deleted files will produce relevant information, (b) the discovery sought by Acme is so broad that it entails a review of all electronic files, backup tapes, and archival matter, or (c) the information sought is available from other sources, it likely will persuade the court to restrict that production. Conversely, if Acme shows that (a) Omnibus maintains the requested information for its own business purposes, (b) it will benefit from the production as much as Acme will, (c) the costs of production can be contained, or (d) Omnibus has sufficient resources that the search will not be an unfair burden, the motion is likely to be denied or, at the least, the relief given will be minimal.

Omnibus's chances of success will be greatly enhanced if it proposes a production plan that is fair to Acme and not unduly burdensome to Omnibus. In this regard, Omnibus may argue that it should not have to produce in electronic format records that already have been produced in "hard copy." While some courts have found that a party seeking discovery of electronic records is entitled to such material even if it has already been produced in hard copy, there is authority suggesting that it is not an abuse of discretion for a court to deny such a request. *Bills v. Kennecott Corp.*, 108 F.R.D. 459, 461 (D. Utah 1985); *William v. Owens-Illinois*, 665 F.2d 918, 932-33 (9th Cir. 1982).

Practice Tips

At the outset of the litigation, determine the risks that important electronically stored information will be lost, destroyed, deleted, or overwritten by your adversary. Promptly ask opposing counsel to agree to a preservation order (and agree to one on behalf of your client, if asked). If your proposal is refused without a reasonable explanation, quickly file a motion under Rule 26(c) asking the court to issue a freeze order.

To plan effectively for electronic discovery, you must understand the computer systems used by your client and your adversary, and how electronic data is created, filed, saved, and archived on each party's system. Before propounding a Rule 34 production request for electronically stored data, you should carefully evaluate what materials you want and how they are stored by the other side. The greater the precision of the request, the greater the likelihood that either the adverse party will accede to it, or failing acquiescence, that it will be ordered by the court. Overly broad requests increase the likelihood that a protective order will be issued.

If you do not understand your opponent's computer and electronic records retention systems, consider propounding interrogatories that require a description of those systems. Alternatively, take a Rule 30(b)(6) deposition of someone knowledgeable about the systems. *See generally* chapter 25, *infra*. This information will enable you to craft precise requests that will withstand attack. In formulating your requests, try to anticipate the objections that opposing counsel will make, and consider your response and the court's likely reaction.

Once you have learned as much as you can about the adverse party's computer and electronic data retention systems, prepare a discovery plan for electronic records that outlines the nature and sequence of discovery you want to pursue. Pay careful attention to how you propose to search for deleted data in backup files and archival sources, which party should bear this cost, and the justifications therefor. You may want to use an expert to assist in developing a plan that meets your needs but is not overly burdensome for your opponent. Make sure your plan addresses the handling of confidential commercial information and privileged material. Keep in mind that your client is subject to reciprocal requests; and if you are overly aggressive in your approach, you may receive the same treatment from the opposition.

When you have completed your electronic discovery plan, submit it to opposing counsel and ask for consent or comment. Obviously, it makes sense to negotiate the plan with opposing counsel if possible; the fruits of your agreement should be memorialized in writing. If the parties cannot agree, at least you will have documented your efforts. If your subsequent discovery requests are not answered and you file a Rule 37(a) motion to compel, be prepared to explain why your proposed discovery is not overly burdensome under Rule 26(b)(2), Rule 26(c), and the *Rowe* or *Zubulake* factors.

Anticipate that the court may ask counsel for the names of qualified experts to assist in the technical issues associated with electronic data discovery. Be prepared to offer names.

When opposing a request for discovery of electronic records, be as specific as possible in supporting your arguments of excessive burden or expense. Conclusory assertions will be rejected by the court. You should be prepared to attach affidavits from your client's IT staff or one or more experts documenting the nature of the burden or expense. Accept the fact that the court is unlikely to bar all discovery of electronic data, so be prepared to offer suggestions for a reasonable scope of such discovery. A court is more likely to rule in your favor if you have made a reasonable proposal than if you argue that no such discovery should be allowed.

If you are taking the position that the costs of production of electronic data should be borne by your opponent, use the *Rowe* or *Zubulake* factors to support your argument, providing specific facts to support your position regarding each factor. If approached by opposing counsel with a proposed plan for discovery of electronic data, negotiate in good faith to try to reach agreement. If you act unreasonably, your opponent can be expected to file a motion for protective order. If the court finds that your position is unreasonable, there is a greater likelihood that the discovery allowed will be more intrusive than if you had proposed reasonable alternatives.

Finally, be aware that the American Bar Association Section of Litigation has adopted civil discovery standards that address many of the issues involved in preservation and discovery of electronic information. The current version is included as Appendix D to this book, but note that the guidelines are in the process of being amended. While they are not mandatory, they offer valuable guidance in this challenging area of discovery. Compliance with these standards may help convince your adversary and the court that you have behaved reasonably.

10. DISCOVERY OF WITNESS STATEMENTS

The plaintiff sued defendant in federal court for personal injuries incurred in an automobile accident. Defendant thereafter filed a request for production of documents that included the following: "Please produce all written or recorded statements obtained from any witness or party to the traffic accident."

Plaintiff's counsel reviewed his file and found the following materials responsive to the request: (1) statements of the plaintiff, the defendant, and one eyewitness to the traffic accident recorded on audiotape by the plaintiff's insurance adjuster two days after the accident (and two years before suit was filed), and transcribed by the attorney's secretary after suit was filed; (2) statements of two other eyewitnesses dictated by them to plaintiff's counsel's paralegal and signed by the two witnesses after instigation of suit.

How should plaintiff respond to the request for production?

Comment: The issue is the extent to which the work-product doctrine embodied in Rule 26(b)(3) affords qualified protection from discovery to these materials. *Frontier Refining, Inc. v. Gorman-Rupp Co., Inc.*, 136 F.3d 695, 702 n.10 (10th Cir. 1998). Rule 26(b)(3) covers documents and things "otherwise discoverable under subdivision (b)(1) of this rule." Therefore, if the witness statements sought by defense counsel are within the scope of discovery defined by Rule 26(b)(1)—and surely they are—and are not privileged communications, the work-product question is framed. The resisting party, here the plaintiff, has the burden of establishing that the documents are protected work product and therefore immune from discovery. *Amica Mut. Ins. Co. v. W.C. Bradley Co.*, 217 F.R.D. 79, 82 (D. Mass. 2003); *F.D.I.C. v. Ogden Corp.*, 202 F.3d 454, 460 (1st Cir. 2000).

To enjoy the qualified immunity bestowed by the work-product doctrine, the materials sought must be (1) "documents and tangible things"; (2) "prepared in anticipation of litigation or for trial"; (3) "by or for another party or by or for that other party's representative." Rule 26(b)(3); *Hickman v. Taylor*, 329 U.S. 495, 511-12 (1947); *see also Hertzberg v. Veneman*, 273 F. Supp. 2d 67, 76 n.3 (D.D.C. 2003) quoting Charles Alan Wright, Arthur R. Miller & Richard L. Marcus, *Federal Practice and Procedure* § 2024 at 336 (3d ed. 1994).

How do these criteria apply here? The audiotape recordings of the statements (category 1 above) are certainly "tangible things" potentially covered under the rule. So are the transcriptions of the taped statements (also category 1) and the transcribed statements of the other two witnesses (category 2 above). As a result, the items sought may be protected if the other two tests in the rule are satisfied. Note, however, that "[a]lthough documents and tangibles created by the representative in anticipation of litigation are protected, the underlying facts may be subject to disclosure in ordinary discovery if they are non-privileged." *See Vardon Golf Co., Inc. v. Karsten Mfg. Corp.*, 213 F.R.D. 528, 534 (N.D. Ill. 2003); *Garcia v. City of El-Centro*, 214 F.R.D. 587, 591 (S.D. Cal. 2003) (The work-product rule does not "protect facts concerning the creation of work product or facts contained within the work product. Only when a party seeking discovery attempts to ascertain facts, which inherently reveal the attorney's mental impression does the work product protection extend to the underlying facts" (citations and emphasis omitted).).

Rule 26(b)(3)'s second requirement is that the documents and tangible things be prepared in anticipation of litigation or for trial. Whether the material is created before or after litigation is not determinative. Wright and Miller provide the following "because of" test to determine whether an item in question was prepared in anticipation of litigation: "[T]he test should be whether, in light of the nature of the document and the factual situation in the particular case, the document can fairly be said to have been prepared or obtained because of the prospect of litigation." Charles Alan Wright, Arthur R. Miller & Richard L. Marcus, 8 *Federal Practice and Procedures: Civil* § 2024 (2d ed. 1994); *see In re Grand Jury Subpoena (Mark Torf/Torf Environmental Management)*, 350 F.3d 1010 (9th Cir. 2003); *U.S. v. Adlman*, 134 F.3d 1194, 1203 (2d Cir. 1998) ("A document should be deemed prepared in anticipation of litigation if it was prepared because of existing or expected litigation; it is not necessary that the document be prepared 'primarily' to assist in the litigation." The document at issue was a memorandum prepared by an accountant and lawyer at Arthur Andersen & Co. to evaluate the tax implications of a proposed merger to assist the client in making a decision about the merger, but it was also prepared because of the almost certain prospect that the merger would result in litigation with the Internal Revenue Service. The First Circuit reversed the trial court's rejection of the work-product assertion, and protected the document's confidentiality on that basis.).

Other courts of appeals that have adopted the "because of" test include: *National Union Fire Ins. Co. v. Murray Sheet Metal Co., Inc.*, 967 F.2d 980, 984 (4th Cir. 1992); *Simon v. G.D. Searle & Co.*, 816 F.2d 397, 401 (8th Cir.

1987); *Senate of Puerto Rico v. DOJ*, 823 F.2d 574, 586 n.42 (D.C. Cir. 1987); *Binks Mfg. Co. v. National Presto Indus., Inc.*, 709 F.2d 1109, 1118-19 (7th Cir. 1983*); and *In re Grand Jury Proceedings*, 604 F.2d 798, 803 (3d Cir. 1979).

Materials generated by insurance investigators frequently raise these issues: "Coverage investigations by insurance companies are not *per se* conducted in anticipation of litigation, and a determination as to whether documents generated during such investigations were prepared in anticipation of litigation, as opposed to in the ordinary course of business, should be made on a case-by-case basis." *Amica Mut. Ins. Co.*, 217 F.R.D. at 83; *see also S.D. Warren Co. v. Eastern Elec. Corp.*, 201 F.R.D. 280, 285 (D. Me. 2001) ("[U]nless and until an insurance company can demonstrate that it reasonably considered a claim to be more likely than not headed for litigation, the natural inference is that the documents in its claims file that predate this realization were prepared in the ordinary course of business, i.e., the business of providing insurance coverage to insureds. This approach realistically recognizes that at some point an insurance company shifts its activity from the ordinary course of business to anticipation of litigation, and no hard and fast rule governs when this change occurs" (citation omitted).).

Thus, if plaintiff's counsel in the example can establish that the insurance adjuster interviewed the defendant, the plaintiff, and the first eye-witness, and prepared the tape because of the prospect of litigation, the audiotape and its transcription are work product and will be protected from discovery as long as the third requirement under Rule 26 (b)(3) is met. *See Bartlett v. State Farm Mut. Auto. Ins. Co.*, 206 F.R.D. 623, 629-30 (S.D. Ind. 2002) (Documents in insurer's claims file, including insured's medical and employment chronologies, recap of his medical expenses, and insurer's request to obtain an independent medical examination were protected from discovery by work-product doctrine.); *Carson v. Mar-Tee Inc.*, 165 F.R.D. 48 (E.D. Pa. 1996) (Defendants in personal-injury action arising out of an automobile accident established that the defendant-driver's statement taken by insurance adjuster of owner after the accident was taken in anticipation of litigation.); *Goodyear Tire & Rubber Co. v. Chiles Power Supply, Inc.*, 190 F.R.D. 532 (S.D. Ind. 1999) (Witness statements and summaries of witness interviews prepared by nonparty insurer during investigation of claims were protected because the insured notified its insurer of imminent lawsuits, and the insurer demonstrated that it anticipated litigation when it prepared the documents in question.).

However, if the adjuster taped the party and witness interviews in the ordinary course of an investigation without regard to the prospect of litigation, which the adjuster did not anticipate, those audiotapes would not be protected and would have to be produced to the requesting party. *See* Advisory Committee Note to Rule 26(b)(3) ("Materials assembled in the ordinary course of business, or pursuant to public requirements unrelated to litigation, or for other nonlitigation purposes are not under the qualified immunity provided by this subdivision."). *See also S.D. Warren Co. v. Eastern Elect. Corp.*, 201 F.R.D. at 285 (insurer did not meet its threshold burden of showing that documents in its claims file were created in anticipation of litigation). In *Warren*, the insurer noted that the documents at issue were prepared three months after the accident giving rise to the claim, and that the claim was for a substantial sum, $1.5 million. Nonetheless, the court concluded that other factors indicating the anticipation of litigation must be present to ensure protection of the tape from discovery.

Whether the tape itself is discoverable, plaintiff's counsel should be able to establish that the transcriptions of the taped statements of the parties and the first eyewitness were prepared by the counsel's secretary in anticipation of trial and therefore meet the second requirement for protection. The same holds true for the witness interviews conducted and transcribed by counsel's paralegal.

The last requirement for protection from disclosure is that the material was prepared "by or for another party or by or for that other party's representative." Rule 26(b)(3) provides that the "other party's representatives" includes "[their attorney], consultant, surety, indemnitor, insurer, or agent." However, this list is not exhaustive. The insurance adjuster and the attorney's paralegal and secretary are included among the party's representatives. Therefore, if documents or tangible things were prepared by them in anticipation of litigation, presumptively they would be shielded from discovery by the work-product doctrine.

"Presumptively" is the operative word. Even if plaintiff's counsel meets the three tests under Rule 26(b)(3), as noted above, plaintiff's work-product materials enjoy only *qualified* immunity. "There are two types of work product recognized, ordinary work product and opinion work product, and generally opinion work product, including mental impressions, conclusions, opinions or legal theories, is entitled to nearly absolute protection." *Homgren v. State Farm Mut. Auto. Ins. Co*, 976 F.2d 573, 577 (9th Cir. 1992). "Ordinary work product, by contrast, is subject to disclosure upon a showing by the party seeking discovery of substantial need and its inability to obtain the materials by other means." *Yurick v. Liberty Mut. Ins. Co.*, 201 F.R.D. 465, 472 (D. Ariz. 2001); Rule 26(b)(3).

The courts' application of the "substantial needs" test has not been uniform. Some courts view Rule 26(b)(3) as creating a two-prong test; *see, e.g., Fisher v. Nat'l R.R. Passenger Corp.*, 152 F.R.D. 145, 153 n.10 (S.D. Ind. 1993). Others apply a three-factor test. *See* 8 Charles A. Wright & Richard L. Marcus, *Federal Practice and Procedure* § 2025, at 374 (2d ed. 1994) (describing the test as involving "three foci"). *Fletcher v. Union Pac. R.R. Co.*, 194 F.R.D. 666, 670 (S.D. Cal. 2000) (Plaintiff failed to establish that he had a substantial need for surveillance films taken by railroad to assess his injuries, so as to overcome the work-product protection.); *see also, Hertzberg v. Veneman*, 273 F. Supp. 2d 67 (D.D.C. 2003) (applying the two-prong test). The two-prong approach requires a party seeking discovery of an opponent's trial preparation material, to demonstrate "substantial need" and "undue hardship." *Id.* at 670-71.

"'The substantial need prong examines: 1) whether the information is an essential element in the requesting party's case and 2) whether the party requesting discovery can obtain the facts from an alternate source.'" *Id.* citing 6 James Wm. Moore et al., *Moore's Federal Practice* § 26.70[5][c], at 26-221 to 26-222 (3d ed. 1999). Examples of "essential" materials include test results that cannot be duplicated, photographs taken immediately after an accident when the accident scene has subsequently changed, and contemporaneous statements taken from, or made by, parties or witnesses. By contrast, a party's desire to find corroborating evidence is insufficient to establish substantial need. *Id.*

The second prong examines the burden the requesting party would experience in obtaining the information from an alternate source. *Fletcher*, 194 F.R.D. at 671. Examples of undue hardship include witnesses' inability to recall statements contained in interviews and excessive costs to obtain equivalent information. *Id.*, citing *In re Int'l Sys. Controls Corp. Sec. Litig.*, 693 F.2d 1235, 1240 (5th Cir. 1982) (faulty memory of witness must be substantiated); *Xerox Corp. v. I.B.M. Corp.*, 64 F.R.D. 367, 382 (S.D.N.Y. 1974) (requesting party must depose witnesses to establish that they could not recall the information); and *Castle v. Sangamo Weston, Inc.*, 744 F.2d 1464, 1467 (11th Cir. 1984).

The three-factor approach examines: (1) whether there is "substantial need" for the work product, which requires a showing of something more than relevancy under Rule 26(b)(1); (2) whether substantially equivalent information can be obtained from another source; and (3) whether doing so would create an undue hardship (not merely expense or inconvenience) for the party seeking discovery. *See* 8 *Federal Practice and Procedure* § 2025, at 374 & n. 15.

Even if the plaintiff establishes that the tape is work product, applying the two-prong test to the audiotape statement of the eyewitness taken two days after the accident, defense counsel will be entitled to the tape if he can establish that information contained in the statement is essential in the preparation of the defense and that the substantial equivalent cannot be obtained elsewhere. The first prong might be satisfied if the lawyer demonstrated that neither party had an unobstructed view of the accident scene, but that the first eye witness did and was the only person to see the occurrence from start to finish. The second prong could be met by showing that the first eye witness could no longer recall his statement given contemporaneously with the accident. Note that defense counsel may be required to depose the witness to substantiate the claim of faulty memory.

Finally, recall that plaintiff's counsel has a tape of the defendant's statement, as well as a transcription of that statement. Rule 26(b)(3) carves out an exception to the requesting party's required showing of "substantial need and undue hardship" when the item in issue is "a statement concerning the action or its subject matter previously made by that party." Pursuant to Rule 26(b)(3), plaintiff's counsel must turn the tape of the defendant's statement over to defense counsel.

11. PRIVILEGE LOGS

Defense counsel responded to plaintiff's request for production of documents by producing only a few documents, declining to produce the bulk of the materials sought on the grounds of attorney-client privilege and attorney work-product. Plaintiff's counsel then asked for a list of all withheld documents and the reason why privilege was claimed for each document. Defense counsel refused to create such a list. At trial, plaintiff's counsel subpoenaed the same documents. Defense counsel refused to produce them for the reasons previously given. Plaintiff's counsel then asked the court to compel production on the ground that any privilege was lost due to counsel's failure to provide a privilege log in response to the original document request. How should the court rule?

Comment: Although assertion of a privilege is grounds for refusing to produce requested documents, Rule 26(b)(1), if counsel responding to a document request does not provide an adequate "privilege log," the privilege can be lost at the discretion of the court.

The Rules specify what a party must do in response to a request for production of documents. "The response shall state, with respect to each item or category, that inspection and related activities will be permitted as requested, unless request is objected to, in which event the reasons for the objection shall be stated." Rule 34(b). A written response must be served within 30 days of service of the request. *Id.*

Where the objection to producing the requested documents is based on privilege or attorney work-product, "the party shall make the claim expressly and shall describe the nature of the documents, communications, or things not produced or disclosed in a manner that, without revealing information itself privileged or protected, will enable other parties to assess the applicability of the privilege or protection." Rule 26(b)(5). That is, a privilege log must be prepared.

To properly demonstrate that a privilege exists, the privilege log should contain a brief description or summary of the contents of the document, the date the document was prepared, the person or persons who prepared the document, the person to whom the document was directed, or for whom the document was prepared, the purpose in preparing the document, the privilege or privileges asserted with respect to the document, and how each element of the privilege is met for that document. The summary should be specific enough to permit the court or opposing counsel to determine whether the privilege asserted applies to that document. *Carty v. Government of Virgin Islands,* 203 F.R.D. 229, 230 (D. V.I. 2001), *citing Smith v. Dow Chem. Co.,* 173 F.R.D. 54, 57-58 (W.D.N.Y.1997) [internal citations omitted]. *See also United States v. KPMG, LLP,* 237 F. Supp. 2d 35, 38 (D.D.C. 2002) ("The essential function of a privilege log is to permit the opposing party, and ultimately the court, to evaluate a claim of privilege."). "Other required information, such as the relationship between the individuals listed in the log and the litigation parties, the maintenance of confidentiality and the reasons for any disclosures of the document to individuals not normally within the privilege relationship, is then typically supplied by affidavit or deposition testimony." *Browne v. Ambase Corp.,* 150 F.R.D. 465, 474 (S.D.N.Y. 1993). "Even under this approach, however, if the party invoking the privilege does not provide sufficient detail to demonstrate fulfillment of all the legal requirements for application of the privilege, his claim will be rejected." *Id.,* at 474. *See Fox v. Cal. Sierra Fin. Services,* 120 F.R.D. 520 (N.D. Cal. 1998) (holding that privilege log that failed to properly identify each document claimed to be privileged and/or failed to supply the basis for such privilege is insufficient).

Under Rule 26(b)(5), the party asserting the attorney-client privilege or work-product doctrine has the burden of establishing that the privilege exists. "Mere conclusory or *ipse dixit* assertions of privilege are insufficient to satisfy this burden." *In re Pfohl Bros. Landfill Litig.,* 175 F.R.D. 13, 20 (W.D.N.Y. 1997), *citing United States v. Kovel,* 296 F.2d 918, 923 (2d Cir. 1961).

Finally, "when faced with claims of privilege, courts often undertake *in camera* review in order to supplement the parties' privilege logs and determine the content of the documents. However, *in camera* review of the documents, while potentially helpful to the determination of privilege, is 'not . . . to be routinely undertaken . . . as a substitute for a party's submission of an adequate record for its privilege claims,' especially where, as here, the Court would have to examine a large quantity of documents." *Weber v. Paduano,* 2003 WL 161340 (S.D.N.Y. 2003), *citing Browne v. Ambase Corp.,* 150 F.R.D. 465, 475 (S.D.N.Y. 1993); *see also King v. Conde,* 121 F.R.D. 180, 190 (E.D.N.Y. 1988).

Practice Tip

Here is a model privilege log:

John Smith, et al. v. ABC Company, Inc.
(Civil Nos. 12345 and 34567 Consolidated)
Privilege Log for John Smith and Smith Electronics, LLC

Date	Document Type	# of Pages	Author	Recipient	Subject Matter	Privilege Claimed	Bates Number(s)
Undated	Notes	2	Amy Soll, Esq., of Smith Electronics, LLC	John Smith, President of Smith Electronics, LLC	Advising client regarding legal issues re: executive committee meetings	AC/WP	677-78
12/02/02	Memo	1	Bob Jones, outside counsel for Smith Electronics, LLC	Amy Soll, in-house counsel for Smith Electronics, LLC	Privileged and confidential memorandum re: potential causes of action against ABC, containing Jones' opinions and mental impressions	AC/WP	1008
Undated	Notebook	30	Amy Soll, Esq., of Smith Electronics, LLC	N/A	Trial notebook prepared by Soll containing interview notes, witness lists, prehearing memoranda, opening statements, etc.	AC/WP	910-940

12. INADVERTENT DISCLOSURE OF PRIVILEGED MATERIAL

In response to a request for production of documents, defense counsel reviewed 10 boxes of documents containing thousands of pages of materials. He set aside one box containing attorney-client privileged communications and attorney work-product. Unfortunately, he failed to remove that box from the room prior to inviting plaintiff's counsel to inspect and tab the documents for copying. Plaintiff's counsel inspected the documents, took detailed notes, and tabbed those that she wanted copied, including some documents from the box of privileged material. Prior to copying, defense counsel reviewed the documents and discovered that he had inadvertently disclosed privileged materials. He immediately contacted plaintiff's counsel by telephone and in writing advising that certain documents that were protected by the attorney-client privilege and work-product doctrine had been disclosed by mistake and would not be copied or provided. Defense counsel agreed to provide a privilege log identifying the documents and the grounds on which they were being withheld.

Has defense counsel waived the attorney-client privilege and/or work-product doctrine?

Was plaintiff's counsel under an ethical obligation to refrain from reviewing the privileged documents or under an affirmative duty to notify defense counsel that the documents were inadvertently produced?

Comment: The fear of accidentally turning over the "smoking gun" file sends chills down the spines of all litigators. Judging from the wealth of cases on the subject, this mistake occurs more often than one might guess. The inadvertent production of privileged materials to third parties may implicate the attorney-client privilege, the work-product doctrine, or both. However, whether inadvertent disclosure constitutes a waiver of these privileges does not depend upon which privilege is asserted. "When the disclosure is made to the adverse party, ... the distinction between waiver of attorney client privilege and of work product immunity disappears. . . ." *Hartford Fire Ins. v. Garvey*, 109 F.R.D. 323, 328 (N.D. Cal. 1985).

Unfortunately, there is no consensus as to the effect of inadvertent disclosures of confidential communications. *Alldread v. City of Grenada*, 988 F.2d 1425, 1434 (5th Cir. 1993). Three distinct tests have evolved—each with different criteria and considerations. These are generally referred to as (i) the "strict test" or "per se waiver rule," (ii) the "lenient" or "no waiver" test, and (iii) the "intermediate" or "middle" test. *McCafferty's Inc. v. The Bank of Glen Burnie*, 179 F.R.D. 163, 167 (D. Md. 1998).

Courts applying the "strict" test or per se waiver rule hold that the privilege is lost even if the disclosure of privileged materials is inadvertent. *See In re Sealed Case*, 877 F.2d 976, 980-81 (D.C. Cir. 1989); *In re Grand Jury Proceedings*, 727 F.2d 1352, 1356 (4th Cir. 1984); *Int'l Digital Systems Corp. v. Digital Equip. Corp.*, 120 F.R.D. 445 (D. Mass. 1988). "[T]he holder of the privilege bears the burden of maintaining the confidentiality of privileged information, . . . absent extraordinary circumstances, disclosure waives the privilege with respect to the privileged documents, regardless of whether the disclosure is voluntary or inadvertent." *In re United Mine Workers of America Employee Benefit Plans Litig.*, 156 F.R.D. 507, 512 (D.D.C. 1994), citing *In re Sealed Case*, 877 F.2d at 980 ("Short of court-compelled disclosure, *cf. Transamerica Computer Co. v. IBM Corp.*, 573 F.2d 646, 651 (9th Cir. 1978), or other equally extraordinary circumstances, we will not distinguish between various degrees of 'voluntariness' in waivers of the attorney-client privilege."), *United Mine Workers of America, Int'l Union v. Arch Mineral Corp.*, 145 F.R.D. 3, 6 (D.D.C. 1992) (privilege waived where documents had been misappropriated and leaked to opposing counsel); *Wichita Land & Cattle Co. v. Am. Fed. Bank*, 148 F.R.D. 456, 458-59 (D.D.C. 1992) (law firm's inadvertent disclosure of two privileged documents that were among 40 boxes of documents produced to defense counsel waived the attorney-client privilege).

Courts applying the per se waiver rule will deem a document disclosed where an opposing party has learned the "gist" of the document's contents. *Wichita Land & Cattle*, 148 F.R.D. at 459, quoting *Chubb Integrated Systems Ltd. v. Nat'l Bank of Wash.*, 103 F.R.D. 52, 63 (D.D.C. 1984). Once the court concludes that a waiver has occurred, it must determine the scope of the waiver. "[A] waiver of the privilege in an attorney-client communication extends 'to all other communications relating to the same subject.'" *In re Sealed Case*, 877 F.2d at 980-81, quoting *In re Sealed Case*, 676 F.2d 793, 809 (D.C. Cir. 1982).

Applying the per se waiver rule to the example, defense attorney's inadvertent disclosure of the privileged documents waived the privilege. Plaintiff's counsel took detailed notes of the documents, learning at least the "gist," if not the entirety, of their contents. Since there were no extraordinary circumstances excusing the production, defense counsel will be required to produce the documents to plaintiff's counsel regardless of the measures taken by defense attorney to correct his mistake.

Courts applying the "no waiver" test examine the conduct of the client—the holder of the privilege—to determine if a waiver has occurred. *See Georgetown Manor, Inc. v. Ethan Allen, Inc.*, 753 F. Supp. 936 (S.D. Fla. 1991) (inadvertent production of a transcript of an attorney-client privileged conversation did not waive privilege); *Mendenhall v. Barber-Greene Co.*, 531 F. Supp. 951 (N.D. Ill. 1982) (no waiver occurred when plaintiff's attorney unintentionally provided privileged documents to defendant's attorney, but later refused to turn over copies of the documents); *State Comp. Ins. Fund v. WPS, Inc.*, 82 Cal. Rptr. 2d 799, 805-06 (Ct. App. 2d Dist. 4th Div. 1999). Under this test, the mere inadvertent disclosure of privileged documents by an attorney, by itself, does not waive the client's privilege. "We are taught from first year law school that waiver imports the 'intentional relinquishment or abandonment of a known right.' Inadvertent production is the antithesis of that concept." *Mendenhall*, 531 F. Supp. at 955 (internal quotation omitted). To find a waiver under this test, a court must examine "the subjective intent of the holder of the privilege and the relevant surrounding circumstances for any manifestation of the holder's consent to disclose the information." *State Comp. Insur. Fund*, 82 Cal. Rptr. 2d at 652-53.

Applying this test to the example, the defense attorney's client may not be disadvantaged. The client did not intend to waive the privilege, and his lawyer's immediate actions to rectify his mistake showed that the client wanted to maintain the privilege. Unless plaintiff's counsel can prove defendant's consent to the waiver, the court will find the privilege intact.

Most courts follow neither the per se waiver rule nor the no-waiver test. Instead, they hold that inadvertent disclosure may or may not result in waiver of the privilege, depending on the facts surrounding a particular disclosure. "This analysis serves the purpose of the attorney client privilege, the protection of communications which the client fully intended would remain confidential, yet at the same time will not relieve those claiming the privilege of the consequences of their carelessness if the circumstances surrounding the disclosure do not clearly demonstrate that continued protection is warranted." *Alldread*, 988 F.2d at 1434; *see also Gray v. Bicknell*, 86 F.3d 1472, 1483-84 (8th Cir. 1996) ("The middle test is best suited to achieving a fair result. It accounts for the errors that inevitably occur in modern, document-intensive litigation, but treats carelessness with privileged material as an indication of waiver."); *Hydraflow, Inc. v. Enidine Inc.*, 145 F.R.D. 626, 637 (W.D.N.Y. 1993).

Courts applying the intermediate test for waiver of privilege often employ the five-part test set forth in *Hartford Fire Ins. Co.*, 109 F.R.D. at 332:

(1) the reasonableness of the precautions taken to prevent inadvertent disclosure in view of the extent of the document production;

(2) the number of inadvertent disclosures;

(3) the extent of the disclosure;

(4) any delay and measures taken to rectify the disclosure; and

(5) whether the overriding interests of justice would or would not be served by relieving a party of its error. *Sampson Fire Sales v. Oaks*, 201 F.R.D. 351, 360 (M.D. Pa. 2001).

As the intermediate test is fact-driven, there is no judicial trend that favors one outcome or the other. In the following cases, the intermediate test was applied and the courts concluded that no waiver resulted from inadvertent production: *United States v. TRW, Inc.*, 204 F.R.D. 170 (C.D. Cal. 2001); *Sampson Fire Sales, Inc. v. Oaks*, 201 F.R.D. 351 (M.D. Pa. 2001); *In re Copper Market Antitrust Litig.*, 200 F.R.D. 213 (S.D.N.Y. 2001); *Starway v. Independent School Dist. No. 625*, 187 F.R.D. 595 (D. Minn. 1999); *Sanner v. The Bd. of Trade of the City of Chicago*, 181 F.R.D. 374 (N.D. Ill. 1998); *Fidelity and Deposit Co. of Md. v. McCulloch, Jr.*, 168 F.R.D. 516 (E.D. Pa. 1996); *Milford Power Ltd. P'ship v. New England Power Co.*, 896 F. Supp. 53 (D. Mass. 1995); *Berg Electronics, Inc. v. Molex, Inc.*, 875 F. Supp. 261 (D. Del. 1995); *Hydraflow, Inc. v. Enidine Inc.*, 145 F.R.D. 626 (W.D.N.Y. 1993); *Monarch Cement Co. v. Lone Star Industries, Inc.*, 132 F.R.D. 558 (D. Kan. 1990).

Other courts applying the same test did find a waiver. *See Amgen Inc. v. Hoechst Marion Roussel, Inc.*, 190 F.R.D. 287 (D. Mass. 2000); *Local 851 of the Int'l Brhd. of Teamsters v. Kuehne & Nagel Air Freight, Inc.*, 36 F. Supp. 2d 127 (E.D.N.Y. 1999); *United States v. Gangi*, 1 F. Supp. 2d 256 (S.D.N.Y. 1998); *Ciba-Geigy Corp. v. Sandoz Ltd.*, 916 F. Supp. 404 (D. N.J. 1995); *Fox v. Massey-Ferguson, Inc.*, 172 F.R.D. 653 (E.D. Mich. 1995); *Edwards v. Whitaker*, 868 F. Supp. 226 (M.D. Tenn. 1994) (waived attorney-client privilege; did not waive attorney work-product privilege); *Parkway Gallery Furniture, Inc. v. Kittinger/Pa. House Group*, 116 F.R.D. 46 (M.D.N.C. 1987).

In one case applying the intermediate approach, *McCafferty's v. Bank of Glen Burnie*, 179 F.R.D. 163 (D. Md. 1998), the court identified circumstances that may constitute an inadvertent disclosure of privileged information that waives the privilege. They are where (1) conversations between attorneys and clients in a public place are overheard by others; (2) there is indiscriminate mingling of attorney-client privileged documents with documents that will be subject to routine disclosure to third persons without having taken precautions to protect the privileged documents from disclosure; (3) privileged documents are stolen or taken because they were not adequately protected; (4) privileged documents are kept in file cabinets routinely used by others; and (5) privileged papers are left in places accessible to the public (internal citations omitted). *Id.* at 168.

Examples of precautions that show a continued intent to maintain confidentiality, and thus militate against a finding of inadvertent disclosure, include: (1) labeling privileged documents as such at their origination; (2) segregating such documents in their own separate files; (3) establishing policies to limit access to privileged materials; (4) shredding, not simply discarding, privileged documents that are no longer needed; and (5) if unauthorized individuals do gain access to privileged materials, taking "immediate remedial steps" to obtain their return. *Id.* (internal citations omitted).

Applying the intermediate test to the example, a court might rule either way. Thousands of pages of documents were produced, which favors non-waiver. However, the defense attorney had segregated the privileged materials, making it incumbent upon him to guard those documents. That carelessness may count against him. In addition, he produced an entire box of privileged material, which also favors a finding of waiver. On the other hand, he quickly realized his mistake, notified plaintiff's counsel, and refused to produce the material. Both parties had ample time to obtain judicial intervention absent agreement. This favors non-waiver.

What about the ethical obligations of a lawyer who receives the privileged materials? An attorney who receives what is plainly a "smoking gun" may be under competing ethical obligations. While a lawyer is duty-bound to advocate zealously for his or her client, Rule 4.4 of the ABA Model Rules of Professional Conduct "operates as a 'brake' on the zeal with which a lawyer may represent a client." ABA-AMRPC Rule 4.4, Respect for Rights of Third Persons, Scope of Rule 4.4.

Model Rule 4.4 was amended in 2002 by adding paragraph (b) and comments [2] and [3] to specifically address inadvertent disclosures: "(b) A lawyer who receives a document relating to the representation of the lawyer's client and knows or reasonably should know that the document was inadvertently sent shall promptly notify the sender."

Comments [2] and [3] provide:

[2] Paragraph (b) recognizes that lawyers sometimes receive documents that were mistakenly sent or produced by opposing parties or their lawyers. If a lawyer knows or reasonably should know that such a document was sent inadvertently, then this Rule requires the lawyer to promptly notify the sender in order to permit that person to take protective measures. Whether the lawyer is required to take additional steps, such as returning the original document, is a matter of law beyond the scope of these Rules, as is the question of whether the privileged status of a document has been waived. Similarly, this Rule does not address the legal duties of a lawyer who received a document that the lawyer knows or reasonably should know may have been wrongfully obtained by the sending person. For purposes of this Rule, 'document' includes e-mail or other electronic modes of transmission subject to being read or put into readable form.

[3] Some lawyers may choose to return a document unread, for example, when the lawyer learns before receiving the document that it was inadvertently sent to the wrong address. Where a lawyer is not required by applicable law to do so, the decision to voluntarily return such a document is a matter of professional judgment ordinarily reserved to the lawyer. See Rules 1.2 and 1.4. ABA-AMRPC Rule 4.4 (b), Comments [2] and [3] (August 2003).

An ABA ethics opinion predating the 2002 amendment required much more than notification. The opinion concluded that a lawyer who receives documents that were clearly sent by mistake and that looked as though they were intended to be confidential must notify the sender, resist the temptation to examine the materials, and wait for the sender's instructions about what to do with them. ABA Formal Ethics Op. 92-368 (1992). The Annotation to the Model Rules of Professional Conduct summarized cases and ethics opinions decided after Ethics Op. 92-368, but prior to the 2002 amendment, as follows:

Although new Model Rule 4.4(b) does not go that far, many jurisdictions have lined up behind this approach. See, e.g., Transp. Equip.

Sales Corp. v. BMY Wheeled Vehicles, 930 F. Supp. 1187 (N.D. Ohio 1996); Am. Express v. Accu-Weather, Inc., Nos. 91 CIV 6485 (RWS) & 92 CIV 705 (RWS), 1996 WL 346388 (S.D.N.Y. 1996) (sanctioning lawyer who opened package containing inadvertently released confidential materials after being requested not to so by sender); State Comp. Ins. Fund v. W.P.S. Inc., 82 Cal. Rptr. 2d 799 (Ct. App. 1999); Ill. Ethics Op. 98-4 (1999); Ky. Ethics Op. E-374 (1995); N.Y. County Ethics Op. 730 (2002); N.C. Ethics Op. 252 (1997) (lawyer who received opposing party's claim file from his liability carrier should have stopped reading when he realized it had been sent in error, and should have notified opposing counsel); Va. Ethics Op. 1702 (1997); see also D.C. Ethics Op. 256 (1995) (if receiving lawyer unaware of inadvertence of disclosure until after reading documents, no ethical violation); Fla. Ethics Op. 93-3 (1994) (lawyer who receives confidential documents sent inadvertently by opposing counsel must promptly notify sender; it is up to sender to take further action); Or. Ethics Op. 1998-150 (1998) (lawyer who receives privileged document unintentionally included in discovery response must return it; may seek ruling on admissibility of information at trial).

Other jurisdictions, however, do not take the obligation quite so far. See, e.g., In re Meador, 968 S.W.2d 346 (Tex. 1998) (lawyer who receives privileged materials inadvertently sent by opponent in discovery ordinarily has no duty to notify opponent or return the materials); Me. Ethics Op. 146 (1994) (lawyer may use privileged document inadvertently sent by opposing counsel as permitted by rules of procedure and evidence, but should notify opposing counsel and, if asked, send opposing counsel a copy); Mich. Ethics Op. RI-179 (1993) (lawyer who asks opponent for unprivileged documents not required to return them when opponent later claims they were actually privileged); cf. Ohio Sup. Ct. Ethics Op. 93-11 (1993) (lawyer who innocently obtains apparently privileged document while conducting public-records search may read it and share information with client; lawyer must notify source of document and return copy if requested). ABA-AMRPC Rule 4.4, Annotation, "A Lawyer's Duties upon Fortuitous Receipt of Documents That Look Confidential" (August 2003).

Under the ABA Model Rule, plaintiff's attorney should have notified defense counsel of the inadvertent production. However, as just explained, several states' ethics standards require more. To determine the actual obligation, an attorney should examine the ethics opinions and case law in the states where the case is pending and where he is a member of the bar.

13. MOTIONS FOR MENTAL OR PHYSICAL EXAMINATION

A worker sued his employer for race-based discrimination under Title VII and included a state claim for intentional infliction of severe emotional distress. The plaintiff sought damages for emotional injuries and past and future medical expenses associated with treatment for them.

During discovery, defense counsel wrote plaintiff's counsel asking that a mental examination of the plaintiff be scheduled with the defendant's psychiatrist. Plaintiff's counsel agreed and a date was set. One week before the scheduled exam, defense counsel wrote to plaintiff's counsel to advise that the designated psychiatrist was not available and that the examination would be conducted by a clinical psychologist, Dr. Jones. Plaintiff's counsel immediately objected on the grounds that Dr. Jones was a psychologist, not a psychiatrist, and that he had a reputation for always testifying on behalf of defendants. Objection was made on the further ground that defendant had not identified the tests or other evaluative procedures that Dr. Jones planned to administer. Plaintiff's counsel demanded that she be present at any examination to videotape the proceedings and prevent anything untoward from occurring.

Defense counsel responded that he was not required to identify the tests that Dr. Jones would administer as long as they were within the range of what psychologists normally do. Further, he refused to permit plaintiff's counsel to attend and videotape the examination. Plaintiff's counsel refused to produce the plaintiff for examination, and defense counsel thereupon filed a motion to compel. How should the court rule?

Comment: This dispute is governed by Rule 35. When the mental or physical condition, including the blood group, of a party or a person in the custody or under the legal control of a party is in controversy, a court may order the party to submit to a mental or physical examination by "a suitably licensed or certified examiner," or produce the person in the party's custody or legal control for such an examination. Recognizing the intrusive nature of such discovery, the rule further provides that the order may be made only after a showing of good cause and notice to the person to be examined and all parties that "shall specify the time, place, manner, conditions, and scope of the examination and the person or persons by whom it is to be made." Rule 35(a).

Rule 35(b) states that the party or person examined under Rule 35(a) is entitled to receive a copy of the report of the examination that sets out in detail its findings, including the results of all tests made, diagnoses or conclusions, and all like reports from all earlier examinations of the same condition. If the examining professional refuses to provide the report, the court may order it, and if the report still is not produced, may exclude the testimony of the examiner at trial. Rule 35(b)(1). The court may also impose any other sanction allowed by Rule 37(b)(2)(A)-(C). *See* Rule 37(b)(2)(E). However, if the court orders a mental or physical examination and the party or person to be examined refuses to submit to it, sanctions may not include contempt. Rule 37(b)(2)(D).

Rule 35 is the only discovery method that expressly requires a motion and court order. In practice, however, most mental and physical examinations of a party are scheduled by stipulation of counsel. *Hardy v. Riser*, 309 F. Supp. 1234, 1237 n.3 (N.D. Miss. 1970) (Even though Rule 35 requires a motion, it is customary for counsel to arrange an examination by stipulation, "with the rule standing as a compulsory sanction which helps produce such stipulations." Internal citation omitted); *Liechty v. Terrill Trucking Co.*, 53 F.R.D. 590 (E.D. Tenn. 1971) (same); Wright, Miller & Marcus, *Federal Practice and Procedure* (2d ed. 1994) § 2234, n.3, Commentary to the 1970 Changes to the Rules of Civil Procedure, 48 F.R.D. 529 ("Examinations [under Rule 35] are very frequently made by agreement. . . .").

The requirements for a Rule 35 motion are specific and stringent. As the Supreme Court said in *Schlagenhauf v. Holder*, 379 U.S. 104 (1964), the "in controversy" and "good cause" requirements of Rule 35 are limitations on the use of the rule which ". . . are not met by mere conclusory allegations of the pleadings—nor by mere relevance to the case—but require an affirmative showing by the movant that each condition as to which the examination is sought is really and genuinely in controversy and that good cause exists for ordering each particular examination." *Id.* at 118. According to the Court, these requirements may be established by the pleadings alone in certain cases, such as when the plaintiff asserts a mental or physical injury, or, if the pleadings alone are insufficient, by the filing of affidavits, or if the need for the examination is contested, by an evidentiary hearing. *Id.* at 119.

Rule 35 does not say who may select the examining health care professional. Courts have found that while the party seeking the examination "does not have an absolute right to choose the doctor who will perform the examination," absent a "valid objection" to the physician chosen, the choice of the party that seeks the examination should be respected. *Looney v. Nat'l R.R. Passenger Corp.*, 142 F.R.D. 264 (D. Mass. 1992); *Great W. Life Assur. Co. v. Levithan*, 153 F.R.D. 74, 76 (E.D. Pa. 1994).

Under Rule 35, are there limits to the kinds of examinations that are permissible, especially if they could be invasive or painful? Courts try to balance the trial preparation needs of the moving party for information about an opponent's mental or physical condition against the privacy interests of the person to be examined. In *Pena v. Troup*, 163 F.R.D. 352, 353 (D. Colo. 1995) the court noted that "in determining what kinds of [Rule 35] examinations to authorize, [it] must balance the desire to insure the safety and freedom from pain of the party to be examined against the need for the facts in the interest of truth and justice." That court adopted a "burden-shifting approach" requiring the party opposing a Rule 35 mental or physical examination "to show that the proposed test is prima facie potentially dangerous." *Id.* Once this showing is made, "the burden shifts to the party seeking the examinations to demonstrate the need for the examination and its safety." *Id.*; *Stinchcomb v. United States*, 132 F.R.D. 29, 30 (E.D. Pa. 1990) ("The court may require a showing of medical acceptance and safety [before ordering a Rule 35 examination], and may weigh the need for a procedure against the pain and safety risks associated with it.").

A related issue is whether a party may be ordered to undergo several examinations—by professionals from multiple medical specialties. This will depend on the facts and the nature of the claim. In *McKitis v. Defazio*, 187 F.R.D. 225 (D. Md. 1999), the court ordered the plaintiff to be examined by a psychiatrist and neurologist despite her earlier examination by an orthopedic surgeon. The court noted that the plaintiff herself proposed to call "an orthopedist, a neurologist, an internist, a neurosurgeon, a plastic surgeon and two psychologists" as witnesses at trial, and that where a plaintiff claims damages for multiple injuries the treatment of which falls within multiple medical specialties, the defendant may be entitled to a physical examination of the plaintiff by more than one medical specialist. *Id.* at 227; *See Vopelak v. Williams*, 42 F.R.D. 387, 389 (N.D. Ohio 1967) ("It seems fair to say that under certain circumstances, a second examination is authorized by the rule . . .").

A party may agree that a Rule 35 examination is warranted but object to the particular health care provider designated by the moving party to conduct the examination. Some courts have refused to allow the examination to be done by the person proposed if that choice appears to be unfair or improper. *McKitis, supra* at 227, collecting cases.

For example, one court rejected as an examining physician a doctor who was a client of the attorney seeking the examination. *Main v. Tony L. Sheston—Luxor Cab Co.*, 249 Iowa 973, 89 N.W.2d 865 (1958). Another court held that a refusal by the attorney seeking a medical examination of a litigant to answer questions about the existence of a business relationship with the doctor designated to conduct the examination disqualified the doctor. *Adkins v. Eitel*, 2 Ohio App. 2d 46, 206 N.E. 2d 573 (1965).

However, objections regarding possible bias by the examiner, or the existence of a relationship between the examiner and the attorney for the movant, may not lead to change in the examiner, because a court may say that such concerns go to the weight of the examiner's opinion and may be raised during cross-examination. *McKitis, supra* at 227; *Powell v. United States*, 149 F.R.D. 122, 124 (E.D. Pa. 1993) (rejecting an objection to the examiner because he allegedly had a preconceived notion that two-thirds of plaintiffs he examined on behalf of insurance companies are untruthful regarding their claimed injuries).

Sometimes the lawyer representing the person to be examined seeks to attend the examination to observe the proceedings. The party seeking the examination almost always objects. While some courts have allowed counsel to attend Rule 35 examinations, *Vreeland v. Ethan Allen*, 151 F.R.D. 551 (S.D.N.Y. 1993), and *Gensbauer v. May Dept. Stores Co.*, 184 F.R.D. 552 (E.D. Pa. 1999), most courts have not, expressing concern that to do so would run the risk of transforming a medical examination into an adversarial proceeding. *McKitis v. Defazio*, 187 F.R.D. 225, 228 (D. Md. 1999) ("It is difficult to imagine a more disruptive result than to convert what is intended to be a medical examination into an adversary proceeding attended by counsel."); *Romano v. II Morrow, Inc.*, 173 F.R.D. 271 (D. Or. 1997); *Tomlin v. Holecek*, 150 F.R.D. 628 (D. Minn. 1993); *Warrick v. Brode*, 46 F.R.D. 427 (D. Del. 1969); and *Dziwanoski v. Ocean Carriers Corp.*, 26 F.R.D. 595 (D. Md. 1960).

In the example, it is clear that the pleadings alone are sufficient to demonstrate that the plaintiff's mental condition is "in controversy" for purposes of Rule 35, because the plaintiff alleges intentional infliction of severe emotional distress. There is plainly good cause to order the examination. Although the defendant attempted informally to arrange the examination rather than file a motion as contemplated by the rule, this is accepted practice. As for substituting a clinical psychologist for a psychiatrist, Rule 35 authorizes the examination to be conducted by a "suitably licensed or certified examiner." The fact that the proposed examiner is not a psychiatrist is no basis for denying the examination so long as he has the credentials to perform the examination. Moreover, given the presumption that the moving party's choice of examiner is permitted, the plaintiff is unlikely to convince the court that Dr. Jones should not conduct the examination. His professional identification with defendants likely would go to the weight of his findings, and not to whether he can conduct the examination.

As for plaintiff's argument that the defendant has not identified with necessary detail the nature of the tests to be performed, the court may well agree, given Rule 35's requirement that a motion for a mental or physical examination "shall specify the time, place, manner, conditions, and scope of the examination." The court likely will require a fuller description of the tests to be performed before allowing the examination. Finally, it is probable that the court will not permit plaintiff's counsel to attend and videotape the examination.

Practice Tips

1. In requesting a Rule 35 mental or physical examination, be certain you can demonstrate that the condition to be examined is in controversy, and identify the facts you will rely on to support this position if challenged. If the pleadings alone are insufficient, be prepared to use affidavits and other discovery responses, if available, to demonstrate that the "in controversy" requirement has been met. If you are opposing a Rule 35 request or motion on the basis that the condition to be examined is not in controversy or that good cause does not exist to warrant the examination, be prepared to demonstrate with particularity why this is so. Conclusory assertions likely will not be accepted by the court.

2. If you wish to schedule a Rule 35 examination, consider whether to do so informally by contacting counsel for the party to be examined, or formally by filing a motion under Rule 35. Most courts dislike unnecessary motions, so the most practical approach is to attempt to schedule the examination informally. If that does not succeed, your motion should describe your unsuccessful efforts to schedule the exam without court intervention. Be sure to

include in your motion facts relating to each of the items listed in Rule 35(a)—time, place, manner, conditions, scope of exam, and the person who will conduct it.

3. If the examination is to be conducted by agreement, document it, as well as the particular information required by Rule 35(a) regarding the nature of the examination/tests, qualifications of the person to perform them, and the date, time, and place of the examination.

4. Remember that courts usually deny requests by counsel to attend and observe or videotape Rule 35 examinations. Do not ask for that unless you have an exceptionally strong justification. Be prepared to provide specific information to the court to persuade it that your request should be granted.

5. If you seek multiple examinations by specialists in different fields, be sure you can demonstrate that the condition to be examined by each specialist can be demonstrated to be "in controversy" and that there is "good cause" to justify the request. If you seek tests that may be painful or dangerous, or if you want the person to be examined to travel to an inconvenient location for testing, you will need to make a more compelling showing of good cause. If objecting to a request for multiple examinations, be sure that you can demonstrate why the test or examination objected to is not in controversy, or why there is not good cause to order the examination. Refer to the Rule 26(b)(2) balancing factors in your analysis.

6. If objecting to the particular examining specialist, demonstrate with specificity why it would be unfair or improper for the designated person to conduct the examination. A mere allegation of bias is unlikely to impress the court unless you can show that the bias will produce an unfair result. A more concrete objection, for example, demonstrating that the doctor designated to conduct the examination is related to an adverse party or his attorney, or has a business relationship with him, will have a much greater chance of success.

14. REQUESTS FOR ADMISSION

Fifteen days before the discovery cutoff, plaintiff's counsel in an accident case filed 75 requests for admission. One of the requests asked the defendant to admit that "at the time of the accident, the driver of the vehicle was under the control of the defendant." Another request sought an admission that "at the time of the accident the driver was operating the motor vehicle under the influence of Oxycontin." Still another request stated, "the driver of the defendant's motor vehicle had a record of two prior motor vehicle collisions for which the driver was convicted of driving while intoxicated."

The defense attorney has objected to the requests for admissions on two grounds. First, the requests would require responses after the discovery deadline and thus are too late. Second, the requests are too numerous and overly burdensome. To play it safe, however, defendant has also filed a pro forma denial of each request.

Plaintiff has moved to compel a response. How should the court rule?

Comment: It is likely that the plaintiff filed the requests too late (as the answers would be due after the discovery cutoff), and thus defendant presumptively was under no obligation to respond. *See* Robert L. Haig, ed., *Business and Commercial Litigation in Federal Courts,* § 22.2 (West Group and ABA 1998); and cases cited therein, including *O'Neill v. Medad,* 166 F.R.D. 19, 21 (E.D. Mich. 1996). So long as the requests are filed before the discovery deadline, however, counsel should check the local rules and the text of the court's scheduling order to reconfirm that it has no duty to respond. *See generally* chapter 4, *supra.* As a precaution, however, instead of simply ignoring the requests and risking their admission (*see* Rule 36(a)), counsel should file a motion for a protective order.

The strength of defendant's assertion that the requests were too numerous and overly burdensome would depend on the facts of the case and the nature of the requests. Bear in mind, however, that the federal rules do not set a limit on the number of requests for admission (in contrast to interrogatories, which are presumptively limited to 25, including subparts). Of course, counsel should always check the local rules to determine whether they set a limit on requests for admission.

Requests for admission may ask the adverse party to admit a question relating to the application of law to facts. (Thus, in the example, the request relating to the control of the driver by the defendant—the driver's employer—is proper.) Advisory Committee Notes to the 1970 Amendments, 48 F.R.D. 487, 530-34 (1970); *McSparran v. Hanigan*, 225 F. Supp. 628 (E.D. Pa. 1963), *aff'd*, 356 F.2d 983 (3d Cir. 1966). Requests for admission should be clear and concise. A poorly drafted request may yield a qualified response that is unhelpful.

In responding to a request for admission, a party may admit the request in whole or part, deny the request, or state that it lacks sufficient knowledge to admit or deny even upon reasonable inquiry. A denial must fairly meet the substance of the request. If part of the request is true and part is false, the responding party should so specify in its response. *See* Haig at 22.4.

An improper response may cause the request to be deemed admitted or the imposition of other sanctions. Certainly, if there is no response at all within the time allotted, the matter will be deemed admitted. Rule 36(a) provides:

> Each matter of which an admission is requested shall be separately set forth. The matter is admitted unless, within 30 days after service of the request, or within such shorter or longer time as the court may allow or as the parties may agree to in writing, subject to Rule 29, the party to whom the request is directed serves upon the party requesting the admission a written answer or objection address to the matter, signed by the party or by the party's attorney.

Rule 36(b) provides that the admission may be used "for purposes of the pending action only" and is not deemed an admission for other purposes or proceedings.

A requesting party who receives a response stating that the responding party is unable to admit or deny may file a motion to challenge the sufficiency of the answer if, for example, the moving party believes that the responding party did not fulfill its obligation to make a reasonable inquiry. In the example, although the defendant may not know the driving record of the particular driver, he is obligated to make reasonable inquiry.

Haig, *supra,* section 22.1-22.11, contains a thorough discussion of requests for admission, noting several pitfalls to be avoided in responding. For example, "a party responding to a request for an admission may have already made a binding admission in another place, and thus should be mindful of that possibility to avoid the risk of being inconsistent—or sanctioned."

Id. § 22.2 at 451. The authors recommend that a responding party promptly seek to amend any inconsistent pleadings (whether in the case in which the requests for admissions were served or in another case) because "[a] court may view a failure to act quickly in this situation as a form of sanctionable gamesmanship." *Id.* at 452.

Counsel or his client risks sanctions if either fails to provide a straight-forward response to a straightforward request. *Herrera v. Scully*, 143 F.R.D. 545, 548 (S.D.N.Y. 1992) ("A party who fails to respond to a request for admission in violation of Rule 36 is liable . . . for reasonable expenses. . . ."); *Holmgren v. State Farm Mut. Auto. Ins. Co.*, 976 F. 2d 573 (9th Cir. 1992) (insurer sanctioned for responding with blanket denials to requests that it admit that the insured's collision with plaintiff was caused by insured's driving through stop sign; that insured was operating her vehicle under the influence of alcohol; and that at the time of the accident the insured's blood alcohol content was 2 ½ times greater than the presumptive level of intoxication under Montana law. The court rejected the insurer's strained justifications for the blanket denials, *e.g.*, the possibility that there were other causes of the accident besides its insured's poor driving.).

Courts have also sanctioned evasive responses. *See Swarthmore Radiation Oncology, Inc. v. Lapes*, 1993 WL 475507 (E.D. Pa. 1993) (court deemed request admitted where responding party admitted part of the requests and then inserted extraneous material in the response. The court said that the responding party should have instead either specified the untrue portions of the request or clarified any potentially misleading features of the response). *See also* Rule 37(a)(3) (evasive or incomplete discovery responses or disclosures are deemed to be a failure to respond; if that rule is applied to evasive answers to a Rule 36 request for admission, the failure to respond would result in an admission of the facts in the request). Finally, in *Boyle v. Leviton Mfg. Co.*, 94 F.R.D. 33 (S.D. Ind. 1981), the court held the responding party responsible for "the preparation and filing of elaborate briefs" concerning the application of law to facts in support of a motion for summary judgment, "when that briefing would not have been necessary if proper admissions had been made." Haig, *supra* § 22.9 at 471.

Section 2

Depositions

Depositions 2

85

OVERVIEW

Most civil cases settle or are otherwise resolved prior to trial. It is therefore no surprise that depositions are a key element in advancing the prosecution or defense of a case. Depositions enable counsel to discover facts about the case, meet the adverse witnesses and assess their character and credibility, freeze the witnesses' testimony, establish a foundation for subsequent impeachment, neutralize potentially harmful witnesses, and perpetuate testimony.

Here we address some of the major practical and procedural problems encountered in taking and defending depositions. These include: the basics of taking a deposition; assertion of objections and privileges during deposition; misconduct by counsel during a deposition; ethical considerations in representing a corporate client's employee during deposition; who may attend a deposition; and the uses of a deposition at trial.

15. NOTICE OF DEPOSITION—TIMING

Plaintiff's counsel filed his complaint and then noticed the defendant's deposition before receiving the answer. Attached to the notice, which scheduled the deposition for 10 days later, was a request for production of documents. Defense counsel objected. He said that he would seek a protective order unless the plaintiff's lawyer agreed to reschedule the deposition to a date after the exchange of Rule 33 and Rule 34 discovery. How should plaintiff's counsel respond?

Comment: Rule 30(a) provides that a party may take the deposition of any person without leave of court except as otherwise provided in the Rule. (If the deposition is of a nonparty, attendance may be compelled by subpoena.) Absent leave of court, however, depositions are not permitted before a Rule 26(f) discovery conference. Thus, "[a]lthough in the typical case an Answer is filed before depositions are noticed, there is no per se rule requiring this sequence. In fact, a party can take the deposition of any person without leave of the court unless the deposition is noticed for a time prior to the parties' Rule 26(f) conference." *Connell v. City of New York,* 230 F. Supp. 2d 432, 436 (S.D.N.Y. 2002).

A party who wishes to take a deposition must "give reasonable notice in writing to every other party to the action." Rule 30(b). The "reasonableness" of the notice is a function of the other factors in the case. "The rules do not require any particular number of days, so that reasonableness may depend on the particular circumstances." *Hart v. U.S.,* 772 F.2d 285, 286 (6th Cir. 1985);

Vardon Golf Co., Inc. v. Supreme Golf Sales, Inc., No. 89-C-2654, 1989 WL 153335, at *1 (N.D. Ill. Nov. 2, 1989). "When determining whether the period of time between which the notice of deposition was received and the time at which the deposition is to take place is an unreasonably short time, the Court shall take into consideration any special need for haste that the noticing party may have." *Forstater v. State Farm Mut. Auto. Ins. Co.*, 1992 WL 70402 (E.D. Pa. 1992). *See also F.A.A. v. Landy,* 705 F.2d 624 (2d Cir. 1983), *cert. denied,* 464 U.S. 895 (1983) (court permitted four days' notice for an out-of-town deposition); *Ranger Transp. Inc. v. Wal-Mart Stores,* 903 F.2d 1185 (8th Cir. 1990) (court approved depositions where formal notice was received only two days prior to scheduled depositions but informal notice was given eight days earlier); and *Radio Corp. of Am. v. Rauland Corp.,* 21 F.R.D. 113 (N.D. Ill. 1957) (court approved a one-day written notice for a deposition to take place in Norway where both parties' counsel were present in Norway). *But see Lloyd v. Cessna Aircraft Co.,* 430 F. Supp. 25 (E.D. Tenn. 1976) (court held that notice of depositions scheduled to take place in Washington, D.C., and Los Angeles, California, given to parties in Tennessee only two working days prior to the depositions was unreasonable); and *Mims v. Cent. Mfrs. Mut. Ins. Co.,* 178 F.2d 56 (5th Cir. 1950) (court held defendant's notice to take more than 15 depositions on one day in locations across the country unreasonable).

A notice of deposition generally must be in writing. Rule 30(b)(1). "Written notice may be dispensed with only in the most unusual circumstances." *Lauson v. Stop-N-Go Foods, Inc.*, 133 F.R.D. 92 (W.D.N.Y. 1990) citing *C & F Packing Co., Inc. v. Doskocil Companies, Inc.,* 126 F.R.D. 662, 678 (N.D. Ill. 1989). *See also Story v. Quarterback Sports Fed'n, Inc.,* 46 F.R.D. 432 (D. Minn., 1969) (court held that the plaintiff retained discovery priority because only it had noted depositions in writing, even though the parties, according to defense counsel, had orally agreed that defendant would proceed first with plaintiff's deposition).

In the example, the court would probably grant the protective order, although not for the reason argued by defense counsel. The problem was not that written discovery should be filed first. Rather, the notice was too early: It impermissibly preceded the Rule 26(d) discovery conference. *But see Rodriguez v. Biltoria Realty LLC*, 203 F. Supp. 2d 290 (E.D.N.Y. 2002) (court refused to grant co-defendant a protective order delaying the deposition of co-plaintiff, although it was scheduled prior to the conference, where she was a foreign citizen of little means who was scheduled to return to her country in several weeks upon expiration of her visa, and her claim was limited in scope).

Plaintiff's counsel should also have considered that the threat by defense counsel to file a motion for protective order, if effectuated, might prevent plaintiff from using the deposition at trial. Rule 32(a)(3) states: " . . . [N]or shall a deposition be used against a party who, having received less than 11 days notice of a deposition, has promptly upon receiving such notice filed a motion for a protective order under Rule 26 (c)(2) requesting that the deposition not be held or held at a different time or place and such motion is pending at the time the deposition is held." *Spangler v. Southeastern Greyhound Lines,* 10 F.R.D. 591 (E.D. Tenn. 1950) (notices filed within 10 days of trial were unreasonable considering the short time between the notices and the trial). *See also Cahn v. Cahn,* 626 A.2d 296 (Conn. 1993) (applying *Spangler*). *But see Bohmfalk v. Linwood,* 742 S.W.2d 518 (Tex. App. Dallas, 1987) (holding that counsel's failure to file motion for protective order in response to four-day advance notice of a deposition constituted a waiver of any objections he may have had regarding admissibility of the deposition based on insufficiency of notice).

Some courts have adopted local rules defining the "reasonable notice" requirement of Rule 30(b)(1). For example, in the United States District Court for the District of Maryland, Guideline 8(b), Appendix A to the Local Rules of Court states that "[u]nless otherwise ordered by the Court or agreed upon by the parties, eleven days notice shall be deemed to be 'reasonable notice' within the meaning of Fed. R. Civ. P. 30(b)(1), for noting depositions." In contrast, the United States District Court for the District of Kansas Local Rule 30.1 provides that "reasonable notice for the taking of depositions shall be five days." Counsel should always check the local rules to determine whether they designate a reasonable period of time for noting depositions.

Plaintiff's counsel made yet another timing error. By requesting production of documents at the deposition, he effectively conceded the propriety of at least 30 days' notice (the period provided for a response under Rule 34) and waived entitlement to such production if the deposition were to occur as noticed. "It is well settled that Fed. R. Civ. P. 30(b)(5) provides that any deposition notice which is served on a 'party deponent' and which requests documents to be produced at the deposition must comply with the thirty-day notice requirement set forth in Fed. R. Civ. P. 34." *Epling v. UCB Films, Inc.,* 2000 WL 1466216 at *8 (D. Kan. 2000). "A party may not unilaterally shorten that response period by noticing a deposition and requesting document production at that deposition." *Id. at *8, citing Premier Resort, Krabi, Ltd. v. Mohawk, Inc.,* 1997 WL 18154, at *1.

16. TAKING A DEPOSITION—THE BASICS

Erin Jackson, a young lawyer representing the plaintiff in a toxic tort case, is preparing to take her first deposition. Jackson hopes that the witness, who lives near a sewage plant, will testify that he has seen sewage being pumped from the plant into the bay. What considerations should Jackson bear in mind as she prepares for the deposition?

Comment: Rule 30 (a)(2) limits to 10 the number of depositions that one party may take without leave of court. Thus, at the outset, Jackson should determine whether this witness is within her allotted 10; if not, she should seek leave of court to take this deposition. She should also bear in mind that the 2000 amendments to paragraph 2 of Rule 30 impose a durational limitation of one seven-hour day (not counting breaks) on each deposition. Often, of course, counsel stipulate to a large number of depositions, as well as larger durational limits—but Jackson should take care to consult the local rules to confirm the procedure for entering into any such stipulations.

Jackson should also consider the reasons for taking a deposition. They include learning the deponent's knowledge of the facts (both direct knowledge and hearsay—the rule against hearsay does not apply in depositions); ascertaining the substance of a potential trial witness's testimony; assessing the witness's demeanor, character, and credibility; and freezing the witness's testimony. If Jackson locks in the witness's testimony at deposition, and the testimony changes at trial, his recollection can be refreshed by the transcript of the deposition—or he can be effectively impeached.

Another reason to take a deposition is to perpetuate testimony so that if the witness fails to appear for trial for one reason or another (for example, the witness is beyond the reach of the court's jurisdiction, or the witness dies), the transcript may be read to the judge or jury—and in the case of a video deposition, the video may be shown. Still another reason to take a deposition is to "neutralize" a potentially harmful witness by showing that the witness has a personal stake in the outcome of the case or a bias for one reason or another. The interrogating lawyer may be able to establish at deposition that the witness has no recollection of specific events—or that his view of events was blocked in some manner.

During the deposition, Jackson should not ask a witness more than one question at a time, and she should refrain from asking questions intended merely to harass or annoy the witness. She should review the rules regarding objections and instructions not to answer. *See generally* chapters 17 (Depositions—Making Procedural and Evidentiary Objections), 18 (Asserting Privileges During Deposition), and 19 (Instructing a Witness Not to Answer a Question), *infra.*

She should also consider the various techniques in asking questions and the applicability of each to the topic at hand. Open-ended questions, for example, are useful in obtaining a narrative answer: "Tell us what you observed that day." Closed-ended or leading questions pin a witness down: "You agree that the traffic light was red at the time of the collision?" As the primary purpose of the deposition of a fact witness is usually to gain as much information as possible, open-ended questions are the norm, but a closed-ended question may be necessary to lock in a witness's testimony. If the intent of a particular question is to lock in a witness, a leading question may trigger an objection that could be sustained at trial, depending on the circumstances—so the interrogator should frame the question in a nonleading, but nonetheless closed-end, fashion. "Was the traffic light red, yes or no?"

Novice lawyers sometimes make two mistakes—neglecting to arrange for the attendance of a court reporter, and forgetting to have the witness sworn. An experienced court reporter, however, will automatically swear in the witness at the start of the deposition.

The format of a deposition may vary from case to case. Usually, counsel introduces herself, explains the purpose of the deposition to the witness, and clarifies that if the witness needs to take a break or does not understand the question, he should stop the questioner and say so. Often counsel will begin the questioning with the witness's background, education, employment, and present occupation to put the witness at ease and obtain information that may prove useful during courtroom interrogation. Other preliminary topics include the witness's litigation experience as a party and as a witness, as well as the relationship of the witness to the parties in the litigation at hand. Once the preliminaries are done, counsel will then turn to the specific topics to be covered in that deposition. Some lawyers, however, prefer to start a deposition by "cutting to the chase," that is, honing in on one or several critical areas immediately to catch the witness off-guard, and then returning to background questioning and other areas of secondary interest.

Jackson may wish to consult other secondary sources that discuss in greater detail the purposes, techniques, and procedures for depositions. *See*, for example, Henry L. Hecht, *Effective Depositions* (ABA Litigation Section 1997). *See also* section 2, *passim.*

17. DEPOSITIONS—MAKING PROCEDURAL AND EVIDENTIARY OBJECTIONS

Plaintiff has sued the defendant corporation for gender discrimination under Title VII. The following exchange takes place during the deposition of defendant's human resources officer:

> Q: Plaintiff's Attorney: How many successful gender discrimination complaints have been brought against your company in the last 10 years?"
>
> A: Well, let me think . . .
>
> Defendant's Attorney: Wait a minute, don't say any more. I object to this question. It is vague, assumes facts not in evidence, is argumentative, and irrelevant. Also, it calls for the disclosure of privileged information, and the answer given, if affirmative, will be inadmissible in evidence under FRE 404(a) as impermissible character evidence. You also are asking the witness to testify to a legal conclusion as to what constitutes a "successful" gender discrimination claim. In addition, to ask this witness to give the details about such a long period of time is burdensome, oppressive, and subjects my client to unreasonable expense. I instruct the witness that if, and only if, he is certain that he knows the answer, and he can do so without disclosing any information that might be privileged, he may give it. But don't speculate or guess. Finally, counsel, if you persist in asking irrelevant and objectionable questions, I am going to terminate this deposition and we will leave.
>
> Plaintiff's Attorney: Counsel, please identify the privilege that you are asserting, and give me some basic information so I can tell whether I agree that it is applicable.
>
> Defendant's Attorney: No. I am not obligated to do so. The witness may proceed as I directed.

Comment: This example concerns objections that properly may be made during a deposition. There are two categories of such objections: (a) procedural objections, addressing the notice, method, conduct, and transcription of the deposition, and (b) evidentiary objections, addressing the substance of the questions. As will be seen, the objecting attorney here, who gave a speech sadly common in many depositions, made many errors.

First, procedural objections—Rule 30(c) requires that the following objections, if made during a deposition with the intent to preserve them, must be noted on the record: objections to (1) the qualifications of the officer taking the deposition; (2) the manner of the taking of the deposition; (3) the evidence presented during the deposition; (4) the conduct of a party during the deposition; and (5) any other aspect of the deposition. The deposition should proceed subject to the objection once made. This allows the objecting party to make a record that will permit a later challenge to the use of the deposition in court without obstructing the deposition itself. Likewise, it gives the deposing lawyer the chance to cure the problem. Rule 32(b) states that objections may be made to the use of a deposition at a trial or hearing for any reason that would require exclusion of evidence if the deponent were testifying at trial, subject to Rule 32(d)(3), discussed below.

Timing of objections is critical. Rule 32(d)(1) states that an error or irregularity in the notice of a deposition is waived if not made by written objection promptly served after the deposition has been noted. Similarly, Rule 32(d)(2) provides that an error or irregularity regarding the qualification of the officer taking the deposition is waived unless made before the deposition begins or as soon thereafter as reasonably could be discovered.

As a practical matter, the timing requirements of Rule 32(d)(3) are the most significant. The rule provides that an error or irregularity during the examination of a deponent in the manner of taking the deposition; in the form of any question asked or answer given; in the conduct of the parties; or errors of any kind that might be obviated, removed, or cured if promptly made, are waived unless timely made during the deposition. This means that objections to the form of the questions asked must be made during the deposition or they are waived; the questioning lawyer, once alerted to the objection, might cure it by rephrasing the question. This rule is designed to prevent a lawyer from intentionally withholding objections to the form of questions during the deposition and then raising objection for the first time at trial or a hearing when the deponent may not be present to testify and it is too late for the questioning party to cure the error.

Evidentiary objections are the second category addressed in this problem: Rule 26(b)(1) states that the scope of discovery includes nonprivileged information relevant to the claims and defenses in the pleadings. Information that is not admissible into evidence may still be discovered if it appears reasonably calculated to lead to the discovery of admissible evidence. Thus, the fact that a deponent testifies to hearsay does not mean that the inquiry is improper so long as it is relevant and reasonably calculated to lead to the identity of facts that are admissible.

Rule 32(d)(3) provides that objections as to the competency of a witness or the relevance or materiality of testimony are not waived by failure to object during the deposition unless the ground for the objection is one that might have been obviated or removed if made during the deposition. Thus, as a rule of thumb, to avoid the possibility of waiver of an objection, a lawyer should make all objections during a deposition where the ground for the objection might be removed if opposing counsel were alerted at that time. This covers most objections, including, for example, an objection for failure to lay a proper foundation for a hearsay exception, or an objection based on insufficient authentication of evidence. It is difficult, however, to imagine many situations where making an objection based solely on relevance or hearsay would permit the interrogating attorney to cure the objection, as the evidence either will or will not be determined to be relevant or, in the case of hearsay, admissible based on some exception.[1]

Rule 30(d)(1) governs the manner of making objections during a deposition. It is important and runs contrary to the deposition styles of many lawyers in past years. An objection shall be stated concisely and in a nonargumentative, nonsuggestive manner. Counsel may not instruct his witness not to answer unless necessary to preserve a privilege, enforce a limit on evidence imposed by the court, or enable the lawyer to make a motion under Rule 30(d)(4).[2]

The rule, however, does allow an attorney unilaterally to suspend the deposition if it is being taken in bad faith or a manner that is unreasonably annoying, embarrassing, or oppressive to the deponent. If that happens, the rule requires the attorney suspending the deposition promptly to make a motion to the court to terminate the deposition or to order a stop to the offensive conduct. Be careful, however; suspending a deposition under Rule 30(d)(4) is an extreme, infrequent measure, and a call to a judge on the phone about deposition misconduct may not receive a congenial reception. In short, do not suspend a deposition unless the record contains a strong

---

1. In point of fact, for the reasons discussed in this section, if the proper foundation is laid for a question that asks for an answer containing hearsay, the defending lawyer need not object to the ultimate question in order to preserve his hearsay objection at trial.

2. See chapters 18 (Asserting Privileges During Deposition) and 19 (Instructing a Witness Not to Answer a Question), *infra*.

factual basis to demonstrate that the interrogating counsel is acting in bad faith and is more interested in harassing or abusing the witness than in discovering facts.

Objections to the Form of the Question: While the combined effect of Rule 30(c) and FRE 611(c) is that a party may not ask leading questions during a deposition unless he or she would be able to do so at trial, neither the rules of procedure nor evidence define the other types of questions that are objectionable as to form. However, case law and treatises have identified the following types of questions that are objectionable as to form; objection to any such question must be made during a deposition or else it is waived:

- Questions that are overly broad;
- Questions calling for an overly long narrative answer;
- Compound questions;
- Questions already asked and responsively and completely answered;[3]
- Questions calling for speculation, conjecture, or an opinion regarding the veracity of another person;
- Questions that are ambiguous, imprecise, unintelligible, or that call for a vague answer;
- Questions that are argumentative;
- Questions that contain improper characterization of evidence or misquote prior testimony of the deponent or another;
- Questions that assume the truth of disputed facts or facts not in evidence;
- Leading questions that do not comply with FRE 611(c); and
- Questions calling for an opinion that would not be allowed by FRE 701 or 702.

Boyd v. Univ. of Md. Med. Syst., 1998 WL 256627 (D. Md. 1998); *In re Stratosphere Corp. Sec. Litig.*, 182 F.R.D. 614, 618 (D. Nev. 1998*); Sequoia Prop. and Equip. Ltd. P'ship v. United States*, 2002 WL 507537 (E.D. Cal. 2002) at *2; Graham, *Handbook of Federal Evidence* § 611.14 (4th ed. 1996). Note, however, that in many courts, by local rule, practice, or case-specific

---

3. Rule 37(a)(3) states that an answer or discovery disclosure that is incomplete or evasive is deemed to be a failure to answer. Thus, during a deposition a lawyer is entitled to pursue a question until a complete and responsive answer is given.

order, a lawyer's initial objection on any of those grounds is limited to "Objection—Form." The questioning lawyer can ask for an explanation if he wants to try to cure any problem.

In the example, while it was proper for the defense attorney to make an objection to the form of the question, the manner in which the objection was made clearly violated Rule 30(d)(1): It was argumentative, suggestive, and not concise. Such objections, called "speaking objections," are improper because they are calculated to coach the witness. *In re Stratosphere Corp. Sec. Litig.*, 182 F.R.D. at 617; *Quantachrome Corp. v. Micrometrics Instrument Corp.*, 189 F.R.D. 697, 700 (S.D. Fla. 1999); *McDonough v. Keniston*, 188 F.R.D. 22, 23 (D. N.H. 1998) ("Speaking objections and coaching objections are simply not permitted in depositions in federal cases.").

Some courts have adopted discovery guidelines to implement Rule 30(d)(1). For example, Discovery Guideline 5.b., adopted by the United States District Court for the District of Maryland, provides:

> During the taking of a deposition, it is presumptively improper for an attorney to make objections which are not consistent with Fed. R. Civ. P. 30(d)(1). Objections should be stated as simply, concisely and non-argumentatively as possible to avoid coaching or making suggestions to the deponent, and to minimize interruptions in the questioning of the deponent (for example: "objection, leading"; "objection, asked and answered"; "objection, compound question"; "objection, form"). If an attorney desires to make an objection for the record during the taking of a deposition that reasonably could have the effect of coaching or suggesting to the deponent how to answer, then the deponent, at the request of any of the attorneys present, or, at the request of a party if underrepresented by an attorney, shall be excused from the deposition during the making of the objection.
>
> Appendix A, Local Rules of the United States District Court for the District of Maryland.

See also McDonough v. Keniston, 188 F.R.D. at 24, citing L.R. 39.16, United States District Court, District of New Hampshire ("[in] stating an objection counsel shall state only the basis of the objection (e.g., 'leading' or 'nonresponsive', or 'hearsay')"). *Calzaturficio S.C.A.R.P.A. s.p.a. v. Fabiano Shoe*, 201 F.R.D. 33, 40 (D. Mass. 2001) ("A deposition is meant to be a question-and-answer conversation between the deposing lawyer and the witness. There is no proper need for the witness's own lawyer to act as an intermediary, interpreting questions, deciding which questions the witness should answer, and the witness to formulate answers.") (citing *Hall v. Clifton Precision*, 150 F.R.D. 525, 528 (E.D. Pa. 1993)); *Van Pilsum v. Iowa State University of Science and Technology*, 152 F.R.D. 179, 181 (S.D. Iowa 1993) ("Merely because depositions do not take place in the presence of a judge does not mean lawyers can forget their responsibilities as officers of the court. They should conduct themselves accordingly.").

Defense counsel's objection on the ground of relevance was unnecessary because it was preserved under Rule 32(d)(3). *In re Stratosphere Sec. Litig.*, 182 F.R.D. at 618; *Quantachrome Corp. v. Micrometrics Instrument Corp.*, 189 F.R.D. 697, 699 ("It is arguable whether objections based on relevancy should even be made during the deposition"); *Sequoia Prop. and Equip. Ltd. P'ship v. United States* (2002 WL 507537 (E.D. Cal.) at *2 ("Generally it is unnecessary to make an objection [during a deposition] based on irrelevancy."). Defense counsel's threat to suspend the deposition and walk out was improper because under Rule 30(d)(4) such action is proper only if the deposition is being conducted in bad faith or the questioning is oppressive, neither of which occurred in the example.

Defense counsel's instruction to the deponent not to disclose privileged information was appropriate. Rule 26(b)(1) exempts privileged information from discovery, and Rule 30(d)(1) allows an attorney to instruct a deponent not to answer a question that calls for the disclosure of privileged information. In fact, a failure to instruct not to answer in such circumstances likely would waive the privilege. However, defense counsel in the example failed to explain the basis for the assertion of privilege. Rule 26(b)(5) requires that:

> [w]hen a party withholds information otherwise discoverable under these rules by claiming that it is privileged or subject to protection as trial preparation material, the party shall make the claim expressly and shall describe the nature of the documents, communications, or things not produced or disclosed in a manner that, without revealing information itself privileged or protected, will enable other parties to assess the applicability of the privilege or protection.

Finally, in context, it appears that the instruction not to answer was given for reasons mostly unrelated to privilege, and that is not proper.

Practice Tips

In considering possible objections at deposition one should review Rules 26, 30, and 32 as well as any local rules of court, discovery guidelines, or case law in the circuit and district in which the deposition will be taken that regulate the taking of depositions. Particular care should be taken to review Rule 30(d)(1-4), which governs objections, instructions not to answer, and unilateral suspension of a deposition for improper or abusive conduct to allow the filing of a motion with the court. Further, counsel should make only those procedural or evidentiary objections that must be made in order to avoid waiver. Objections should be stated as concisely and nonargumentatively as possible. If for some reason an objection must be made that reasonably could have the effect of coaching the deponent, the deponent should be excused and the objection put on the record in the witness's absence. When instructing the witness not to answer a question on the basis of privilege, make sure to state all of the information required by Rule 26(b)(5). Finally, suspend the taking of a deposition only if the record justifies it under the very limited circumstances allowed by Rule 30(d)(4). Then file a motion with the court immediately.

18. ASSERTING PRIVILEGES DURING DEPOSITION

Plaintiff has brought a Section 1983 action against police officers, asserting violations of the Fourth and Fourteenth amendments. The following exchange occurs during plaintiff's deposition of one of the officers:

> Plaintiff's Counsel: Officer, please tell me each conversation you have had with any person since the incident that led to this lawsuit in which you have given any statements or otherwise discussed the incident.
> Defense Counsel: Objection, the question calls for attorney-client and work-product information, and to the extent that it does, I instruct my client not to answer.
> Plaintiff's Counsel: Well, I think that it is improper for you to instruct your client not to give me an answer, based on whatever privilege you are asserting. In any event, I certainly want to know about statements that he gave to people other than his counsel, which clearly are not privileged. And just because he talked to you, that does not automatically mean that the substance of such communication is not discoverable. There may have been third parties present, or he may have waived the privilege, or what you and he said may not have been covered by the privilege. As for your work-product claim, that depends on a lot of factors as well. You need to identify for me each communication that you contend is covered by a privilege, and give me some information about the nature of the communication, who was present, and the like, so I can decide whether or not I agree that the privilege properly was asserted, or if it was waived.
> Defense Counsel: I disagree. I don't have to spend time giving all that information. I'm permitted to instruct my client not to answer a question that calls for disclosure of privileged information or work product.

Who is correct?

Comment: Rule 26(b)(1) excludes privileged information from discovery. Discovery of work product, which technically is not "privileged," is limited by the work-product doctrine, codified at Rule 26(b)(3) and discussed *supra* at chapter 8 (Document Requests—Numerosity, Propriety, and the Timing and Sufficiency of Objections), chapter 10 (Discovery of Witness Statements), chapter 11 (Privilege Logs), and below.[1] Rule 30(d)(1) permits an attorney to instruct a deponent not to answer a question if it calls for the disclosure of privileged information. Therefore, assuming the attorney-client privilege and work-product doctrines were applicable, defense counsel was warranted in instructing the deponent not to answer the question posed.

That is not the end of the inquiry, however. The primary problem posed by the example is not whether an instruction not to answer is available, but how much information defense counsel should have provided. As things stand, there are so few details that plaintiff's counsel has no meaningful way to determine whether the assertions of privilege are proper. Likewise, if a motion to compel is filed, the transcript of the deposition would give the court insufficient information to make a ruling. Addressing these issues, Rule 26(b)(5) requires that :

> [w]hen a party withholds information otherwise discoverable under these rules by claiming that it is privileged or subject to protection as trial preparation material, the party shall make the claim expressly and shall describe the nature of the documents, communications, or things not produced or disclosed in a manner that, without revealing information itself privileged or protected, will enable the parties to assess the applicability of the privilege or protection.[2]

As with most privileges, the attorney-client privilege and work-product doctrine have many elements. Even if initially applicable, they may subsequently be waived. The elements of the attorney-client privilege, for example, are: (1) it must be asserted by one who is or sought to become a client; (2) the person to whom the communication was made (a) is a member of the bar, or is his or her subordinate and (b) the communication was made in connection with that person acting in the capacity of a lawyer; (3) the communication

---

1. "Technically, the work product doctrine is not a privilege, but confers upon materials within its scope an immunity from discovery. However, the doctrine has so frequently been referred to as a privilege, that any distinction which once existed is now regarded as largely academic." Nutramax Labs. v. Twin Labs, Inc. 183 F.R.D. 458, 463 n.8 (D. Md. 1998); Musselman v. Phillips, 176 F.R.D. 194, 195 n.1 (D. Md. 1997).

2. Although the attorney-client privilege and work-product doctrine are the most frequently asserted privileges, Rule 26(b)(5) applies to all statutory and common law privileges, 8 WRIGHT, MILLER, & MARCUS, FEDERAL PRACTICE AND PROCEDURE: CIVIL 2d ed., § 2016. Whatever the privilege, a party asserting it must provide sufficient information to enable the inquiring party to assess the validity of the claim.

related to a fact of which the attorney was informed (a) by the client (b) without the presence of third parties (c) for the purpose of securing primarily either an opinion on law, or legal services, or assistance in some legal proceeding, and not (d) for the purpose of committing a crime or tort; and (4) the privilege has been (a) claimed by the client but (b) not waived. Edna S. Epstein, *The Attorney-Client Privilege and the Work-Product Doctrine* (4th ed., 2001), citing *United States v. United Shoe Mach. Corp.*, 89 F. Supp. 357 (D. Mass. 1950). Unless counsel asserting the privilege can establish that each of these elements is satisfied, the privilege cannot be invoked.

Similarly, Rule 26(b)(3) identifies the elements of the work-product doctrine as follows: (1) documents and tangible things; (2) prepared in anticipation of litigation or for trial; (3) by or for a party's representative (including an attorney, consultant, surety, indemnitor, insurer, or agent). In addition, unlike the attorney-client privilege, which, if applicable and not waived, is absolute, the work-product doctrine provides only a qualified immunity from discovery. Rule 26(b)(3) permits discovery of work product upon a showing of (1) substantial need, and (2) inability without undue hardship to obtain the substantial equivalent of the materials by other means. Again, unless counsel can demonstrate that the elements of the doctrine have been satisfied, discovery will be allowed.[3]

Rule 26(b)(5) provides that a claim of privilege must be accompanied by a description of "The nature of the documents, communications, or things not produced or disclosed in a manner that . . . will enable other parties to access the applicability of the privilege. . . ."

It is often difficult to determine how to comply with the Rule 26(b)(5) disclosure requirements without revealing the privileged information itself. To assist in this exercise, some courts have adopted discovery guidelines that state what must be disclosed during a deposition when a privilege is asserted. For example, Discovery Guideline 6 of the United States District Court for the District of Maryland states:

> (a) When a claim of privilege is asserted during a deposition, and information is not provided on the basis of such assertion: (i) In ac-

---

3. If it is determined that counsel resisting discovery has not made the proper showing, however, the court still must "protect against disclosure of the mental impressions, conclusions, opinions, or legal theories of an attorney or other representative of a party concerning the litigation." Rule 26(b)(3). *See also* chapter 37, *infra* (Discovery of Oral Communications and Privileged Documents Shared with Expert).

cordance with Fed. R. Civ. P. 26(b)(5), the person asserting the privilege shall identify during the deposition the nature of he privilege (including work product) that is being claimed. (ii) After a claim of privilege has been asserted, the person seeking disclosure shall have reasonable latitude during the deposition to question the witness to establish other relevant information concerning the assertion of privilege, including: (i) the applicability of the particular privilege being asserted; (ii) any circumstances which may constitute an exception to the assertion of the privilege; (iii) any circumstances which may result in the privilege having been waived; (iv) any circumstances that may overcome a claim of qualified privilege. In accordance with Fed. R. 26(b)(5), the party asserting the privilege, in providing the foregoing information, shall not be required to reveal the information which is itself privileged or protected from disclosure.

See also Moloney v. United States, 204 F.R.D. 16, 20-21 (D. Mass. 2001) (The requirement of Fed. R. Civ. P. 26(b)(5) to provide details regarding the assertion of a privilege applies to depositions as well as written discovery. The correct procedure is to allow the examining counsel to make a record that would permit meaningful judicial evaluation of the privilege claimed, to include the nature of the privilege claimed, and the basic rationale for asserting the privilege (citing 7 *Moore's Federal Practice*, § 30.43[2], Mathew Bender 3d ed.)); *Caplan v. Fellheimer Eichen Braverman & Kasskey*, 162 F.R.D. 490, 491-92 (E.D. Pa. 1995) (To properly assert a privilege during a deposition, Rule 26(b)(5) requires a party to define the privilege to permit the opposing party to determine whether to challenge the assertion and, if a challenge is filed, to permit the court to rule.); 8 Wright, Miller & Marcus, *Federal Practice and Procedure: Civil*, 2d ed., § 22016.1 ("An existing privilege exemption from discovery must be raised in a proper fashion to be effective in justifying a refusal to provide discovery. . . . In the deposition context, as at trial, the objection should ordinarily be asserted when a question seeking privileged material is asked, and the questioner may explore the propriety of the objection with questions going to the availability of the privilege."). The commentary to Rule 26(b)(5) cautions, however, that the duty to disclose particularized information regarding an assertion of privilege should not be unduly burdensome:

[Rule 26(b)(5)] does not attempt to define for each case what information must be provided when a party asserts a claim of privilege or work product protection. Details regarding time, persons present, general subject matter, etc., may be appropriate if only a few items are withheld, but may be unduly burdensome when voluminous documents are claimed to be privileged or protected, particularly if the items can be described by categories. A party can seek relief through a protective order . . . if compliance with the requirement for providing [details regarding the privilege asserted] . . . would be an unreasonable burden.

Commentary on the 1993 Amendments to the Federal Rules of Civil Procedure, 146 F.R.D. 401, 639 (1993). Compliance with Rule 26(b)(5) is not simply a procedural nicety. Failure to do so may constitute a waiver of the privilege attempted to be asserted. 8 Wright, Miller & Marcus, *Federal Practice and Procedure: Civil*, 2d ed., § 2016.1 and 2016.0 (collecting cases).

Practice Tip

Under Rule 30(d)(1), a lawyer who intends to assert a privilege as the basis for an instruction not to answer a question should follow the instruction with a concise statement of the information discussed above. For example, counsel could say, "I object on the ground of attorney-client privilege and instruct my client not to answer. My client and I had a confidential conversation—no one else was present—in which we discussed the incident in question, he asked me certain questions, and I gave him certain advice. He has never shared that communication with anyone else."

The inquiring lawyer should make sure that the information complies with Rule 26(b)(5) and the guidance of the above cited cases, and should be prepared to conduct additional examination of the witness to learn sufficient facts about the nature of the privilege asserted, the general type of information at issue, and whether there are any facts that would support an argument that the privilege does not apply or has been waived. The deponent, in turn, is not required to disclose so much information that the privileged facts themselves are revealed. In the illustration immediately above, it seems that the defending lawyer has fairly demonstrated the existence of the privilege. If he had merely said, however, "Objection—instruct not to answer on the ground of privilege," the interrogating lawyer should have followed up with questions establishing that the communication was between the lawyer and client only, with no one else present, that it involved legal advice as opposed to a nonprivileged topic, and that such communication was never divulged to another.

19. INSTRUCTING A WITNESS NOT TO ANSWER A QUESTION

A former wife sued her ex-spouse for failure to pay alimony as required by their marital property settlement agreement. The ex-husband defended on the ground that the parties had agreed prior to entering the contract that the alimony payments were in reality for child support, and that once the children reached majority it was agreed that he would stop paying.

At the ex-wife's deposition the defense attorney asked her the following questions:

> Q. "On the evening before you and your former husband signed the marital property settlement agreement, did the two of you discuss child support?"
> A. "I do not remember."
> Q. "Didn't the two of you agree prior to signing the agreement to treat the alimony payments as child support payments?"

Plaintiff's counsel instructed her client not to answer the question and then turned to defense counsel and remarked, "The question is improper in the context of this case. You are way off-base here. Whatever the parties discussed prior to signing the written agreement is irrelevant and is barred by the parol evidence rule. The contract is clear, and the discussions and intentions of the parties prior to the signing of the agreement are inadmissible." Defense counsel then asked the witness, "Are you going to follow your lawyer's instructions?" When she said, "Yes," he turned to the stenographer and said, "Certify the question." The deposition continued and ultimately defendant filed a motion to compel.

How should the court rule?

Comment: The court will probably order the witness to answer the question at deposition, but the answer will be deemed inadmissible at trial if the contract is found to be wholly integrated.

Apart from three exceptions discussed below, it is improper to instruct a witness not to answer questions during depositions. *See Ralston Purina Co. v. McFarland,* 550 F.2d 967, 973 (4th Cir. 1977); *Boyd v. Univ. of Md. Med. Systems,* 173 F.R.D. 143, 144, 149 (D. Md. 1997); *Gagne v. O'Donoghue,* No. CIV.A.94-1158., 1998 WL 408962, at *5 (Mass. Super. July 14, 1998).

Rule 26(b)(1) recognizes that litigants are permitted to obtain discovery about any matter not privileged that is relevant to the subject matter involved in the case. While a party may object to an irrelevant line of questioning even though such objection is not necessary, instructing the witness not to answer because the question calls for inadmissible facts may be sanctionable. *See* chapter 19, *supra*; *Boyd*, 173 F.R.D. 143 (D. Md. 1997); *In re Stratosphere Corp. Sec. Litig.*, 182 F.R.D. 614 (D. Nev. 1998); *Calzaturficio S.C.A.R.P.A. s.p.a. v. Fabiano Shoe Co., Inc.*, 201 F.R.D. 33 (D. Mass. 2001).

Rule 30(d) (1) establishes three circumstances when an instruction not to answer may be given: (1) protection of a privilege; (2) enforcement of a limitation on evidence directed by the court; or (3) in anticipation of a motion under Rule 30(d)(4) for a protective order against questions presented in bad faith or to annoy, embarrass, or oppress the deponent.

The propriety of instructing a witness not to answer a question to protect a privilege is well recognized. Indeed, failure to instruct a witness to refuse to answer could result in the loss of the privilege. And if a lawyer, in an effort to cooperate, seeks agreement from the questioner that answering a question that seeks privileged material will not be deemed a waiver, he has fallen into a trap. Despite any agreement, once the information is divulged the privilege could be lost. *See Nguyen v. Excel Corp.*, 197 F.3d 200, 206 (5th Cir. 1999) ("A client waives the attorney-client privilege . . . by failing to assert it when confidential information is sought in legal proceedings."); *Gebbie v. Cadle Co.*, 714 A.2d 678 (Conn. App. 1998) (mortgagor's attorney's answers in pretrial deposition regarding mortgagor's understanding of the loan agreement waived attorney-client privilege); *Madanes v. Madanes*, 199 F.R.D. 135 (S.D.N.Y. 2001) (where defendant selectively disclosed portions of communications with former attorney during deposition, defendant waived claims of attorney-client privilege to all communications with former attorney with regard to same subject matter). In instances where counsel are concerned about confidential, as distinguished from privileged, information, the parties should try to agree on a protective order limiting accessibility to such information. *See* chapter 46 (Motion for Protective Order), *infra*.

It is also improper to ask questions during a deposition that are beyond the scope of discovery, asked in bad faith, or asked in such a manner as to unreasonably annoy, embarrass, or oppress the deponent or party. Rule 30(d) (4). Of course, there is no universally accepted test for when questions are harassing. One or two isolated questions that are off-track usually will not justify an instruction not to answer. On the other hand, repeatedly asking the same question or "bearing down" on the deponent in an irrelevant area (e.g., focusing on the opponent's personal life in a commercial case) might well justify an instruction not to answer. Deciding whether a question or series of questions is sufficiently far out of bounds is not easy, and an instruction not to answer is given at counsel's peril. *Miller v. Waseca Med. Ctr.,* 205 F.R.D. 537 (D. Minn. 2002). If the court concludes that counsel was wrong to instruct a witness not to answer, sanctions may be imposed. *See* Rule 30(d)(3) and section 4, "Sanctions and Protective Orders," *infra.* Moreover, the local rules of many United States district courts and local discovery guidelines presumptively prohibit instructions not to answer during depositions. *See, e.g.,* Local Discovery Guideline 5(d) (D. Md. 1995). *See also Fondren v. Republic Am. Life Ins. Co.,* 190 F.R.D. 597 (M.D. Okla. 1999), which held that an attorney who instructed a witness not to answer, but did not intend to present a motion for protective order and failed to meet the necessary showing of an unreasonable annoyance, embarrassment, or oppression, or that the deposition was otherwise conducted in bad faith, was subject to an award of reasonable expenses incurred in making the motion to compel, including counsel fees.

Even if there is an instruction not to answer a given question, the deposition should continue if practical. In instances where the question or series of questions is critical at the moment, however, a call to the court may be necessary.

When the deposition does continue without an immediate call to the court, the witness's lawyer should consider seeking a protective order to sustain the instruction not to answer. Alternatively, counsel can defend his instruction in response to a motion to compel and for sanctions.

When an instruction not to answer is given during a deposition, it is not necessary for opposing counsel to preserve the record by making any statement at all, much less the arcane—but very common—formulation, "Certify the question." Counsel may say that, however, in order to highlight the issue in the transcript so that the relevant testimony and instruction can be found quickly when preparing a motion to compel. Counsel's question to the witness, "Are you going to follow your lawyer's instruction?" is gratuitous on one level—can there be any doubt as to the answer?—but it is one means of dramatically underscoring the record. *See* Stuart W. Gold & Henry L. Hecht, chapter 14, "Defending at a Deposition," in *Effective Depositions* (American Bar Association 2001).

20. MISCONDUCT BY COUNSEL AT A DEPOSITION

Plaintiff's counsel was having difficulty scheduling by agreement the deposition of the defendant, who lived in a distant state and frequently traveled internationally on business. Finally, counsel simply noticed the deposition on a date convenient for himself. When defendant and his lawyer failed to appear, plaintiff's counsel moved under Rule 37(d)(1) to compel the defendant's attendance. The motion was granted, with the costs of the frustrated deposition and motion charged to the defendant.

The rescheduled deposition began at 9:00 a.m. in the office of defense counsel. Soon thereafter, the defendant started leaning over and consulting his lawyer before answering each question. After a few minutes, plaintiff's lawyer interjected, "Counsel, if your client needs to consult with you occasionally, even though it's objectionable I'll be reasonable and allow it. But I will not permit coaching before he answers every question." Defense counsel retorted, "I think your client is a liar who has fabricated his claim, and I don't think much more of you. I don't give a damn whether you object to my consultations with my client. I'll do as I please."

Shocked by this, plaintiff's counsel was tempted to respond in kind, but recognized that an argument on the record would simply waste time. He thought for a moment and then said: "Pursuant to Rule 30(d)(4), I'm going to call chambers and take this up with the judge." "Not on my telephone, you're not," defense counsel shot back. Plaintiff's counsel did not have his cell phone and so had only two choices—terminate or resume the examination. As to the first option, he was concerned that Rule 30(c) might prevent him from reconvening the deposition on a later date ("All objections made at the time of the examination . . . to the conduct of any party . . . shall be noted by the officer upon the record of the deposition; but the examination shall proceed, with the testimony being taken subject to the objections."). So he decided to resume and simply make a record of his objections to defense counsel's conduct. Not surprisingly, defense counsel made a speech summarizing her own record of what had happened. By that time well over an hour had elapsed since the questioning had been interrupted.

Plaintiff's counsel then resumed his questioning. Once again, defense counsel repeatedly interrupted, used insulting language, gave commentary after many of the questions were asked, and instructed her client not to answer questions because they were "stupid," "improperly phrased," "clearly irrelevant," "harassing," or had been "asked and answered." Frequently she told her client, "I know you don't know the answer to that question, but if you do, go ahead and give it." Invariably he would respond that he did not know the answer. At the stroke of 5:00 p.m., defense counsel announced that under the Rule 30(d)(2) "seven hour rule" (*see* chapter 16, *supra*) the deposition was over, grabbed her client by the shoulder, and pulled him out the door. When he returned to his office, plaintiff's counsel filed a motion to compel and for unspecified sanctions under Rule 37. The motion has come on for hearing.

Comment: Although plaintiff's counsel limited the grounds for his motion to Rule 37, in fact there are multiple sources of authority for the court to discipline counsel and impose sanctions for misconduct in depositions (and for that matter, discovery generally). Rule 30(d)(3) provides that "[i]f the court finds that any impediment, delay, or other conduct has frustrated the fair examination of the deponent, it may impose upon the persons responsible an appropriate sanction, including the reasonable costs and attorney's fees incurred by any parties as a result thereof."

Rule 37 provides a host of remedies for contumacious conduct by counsel or his client. *See* Rule 37(a)(2)(B), (a)(3), (a)(4), (b) and (d). A court may also sanction counsel pursuant to 28 U.S.C. § 1927, which states in pertinent part that "[a]ny attorney . . . who so multiplies the proceedings in any case unreasonably and vexatiously may be required by the court to satisfy personally the excess costs, expenses, and attorneys' fees reasonably incurred because of such conduct." *See Higginbotham v. KCS International, Inc.,* 202 F.R.D. 444, 459 (D. Md. 2001), citing *Resolution Trust Corp. v. Dabney,* 73 F.3d 262, 267 (10th Cir. 1995); *Kotsilieris v. Chalmers,* 966 F.2d 1181, 1183 (7th Cir. 1992). Further, a local rule of court may provide for sanctions. In addition, the court has the inherent authority to redress discovery misconduct upon a finding that counsel has acted in bad faith. *Poole ex rel. Elliott v. Textron, Inc.,* 192 F.R.D. 494, 497 (D. Md. 2000); *Paramount Communications, Inc. v. QVC Network Inc.,* 637 A.2d 34 (S.C. Del. 1994). (Some circuits have required that misconduct punished under the court's inherent powers must be shown by clear and convincing evidence, and that such powers should be used sparingly. *See generally Chambers v. NASCO, Inc.,* 501 U.S. 32, 46 (1991); *Higginbotham, supra.*; *Burda v. M. Ecker Co.,* 2 F.3d 769, 777 (7th Cir. 1993)). Finally, all courts are authorized to refer a matter to the appropriate bar's disciplinary authority to determine whether discipline of counsel is warranted.

While there are many bases for sanctioning deposition misconduct, an aggrieved lawyer must remember that there may be a federal or local rule requiring good faith efforts to resolve discovery dispute before a motion for sanctions may be filed. Rule 37(a)(2)(B), for example, requires, as a predicate for a motion to compel a witness to answer a deposition question, ". . . a certification that the movant has in good faith conferred or attempted to confer with the person or party failing to make the discovery in an effort to secure the information or material without court action." *See also* Rule 37(a)(4)(A).

In this example, plaintiff's counsel might certify that he tried in good faith to deal with the problem at the deposition, but to no avail. He could also argue that the transcript of defense counsel's comments and behavior demonstrated the futility of any such efforts, and therefore they should not be imposed as a precondition to the motion—especially where defense counsel refused to cooperate in contacting the court for an immediate ruling as permitted by Rule 30(d)(4).

Finally, plaintiff's counsel might assert that certification of efforts to solve the problem should not be required because the misconduct constituted a contempt of court sanctionable under Rule 37(b)(1). That portion of the rule has no certification requirement and provides that "[i]f a deponent fails to . . . answer a question after being directed to do so by the court . . . the failure may be considered a contempt of that court."

Here, plaintiff's lawyer would argue that the deposition was being taken pursuant to court order (based on the defendant's failure to appear for the deposition when originally noticed) and thus defendant was bound to answer all proper questions. The strength of that argument could turn on the specificity of the language in the order compelling the defendant's appearance. In this case (and in retrospect), plaintiff's counsel would have been well advised to propose language for the order providing that failure to answer proper questions would be deemed contemptible under Rule 37(b)(1). Whether such language would be inferred from an order simply compelling defendant's attendance at a deposition on a particular date and at a specified time and place is uncertain.

Turning to the substance of defense counsel's behavior, plaintiff's counsel was quite right that "off the record" communications between an attorney and a witness generally are improper. The only exception is where the consultation is for the purpose of determining whether a privilege should be invoked as the basis for an instruction not to answer. *Calzaturficio S.C.A.R.P.A.*

s.p.a. v. Fabiano Shoe Co., Inc., 201 F.R.D. 33, 39 (D. Mass. 2001); *Morales v. Zondo, Inc.*, 204 F.R.D. 50, 53 (S.D.N.Y. 2001), citing 7 James Wm. Moore et al., *Moore's Federal Practice* ¶ 30.42[2] (3d ed. 1997). Thus defense counsel's refusal to obey the rules when cautioned to do so by counsel—especially when her remaining obstructive behavior is taken into account—is sanctionable. *Id.* Conspicuous in that regard are her running commentaries, speaking objections, frivolous objections, ill-disguised instructions to her client, and instructions not to answer, all of which run afoul of Rule 30(d)(1): "Any objection during a deposition must be stated concisely and in a non-argumentative and non-suggestive manner. A person may instruct a deponent not to answer only when necessary to preserve a privilege, to enforce a limitation directed by the court, or to present a motion under Rule 30(d)(4)." *Cf. Calzaturficio, supra* (attorney's sanctionable conduct included conferences with witnesses during questioning, instructions not to finish answers, suggestions as to how to answer questions, rephrasing of questions, instructions not to answer on grounds other than privilege, assertion of "asked and answered" 81 times, and ad hominem attacks on opposing counsel.).

It is also important that defense counsel's conduct seems to have been in purposeful disregard of the rules rather than in mere ignorance of them. Her misbehavior escalated dramatically once she knew that plaintiff's counsel would be unable to reach the court for a ruling—and she readily cited to Rule 30(d)(2) when she terminated the session. Purposeful disregard of the rules is far more likely to result in the imposition of sanctions than a violation caused by a misunderstanding of their constraints. *Higginbotham, supra*, at 458.

Counsel's sustained incivility may provide yet another basis for sanctions. *See, e.g., Freeman v. Schointuck*, 192 F.R.D. 187 (D. Md. 2000). "[I]solated acts of discourtesy or loss of temper can be expected, even from the best of counsel, and excused by the court, [but] systematic and deliberate abuses . . . cannot go unsanctioned as they are destructive of the very fabric which holds together the process of pretrial discovery—cooperative exchange of information without the need for constant court intervention." *Freeman, supra* at 190. *See also In re First City Bancorp. of Texas, Inc.*, 282 F.3d 864, 866 (5th Cir. 2002), *supra* at 866; *Mruz v. Caring, Inc.*, 166 F. Supp. 2d 61 (D.N.J. 2001); *but see Saldana v. Kmart Corp.*, 260 F.3d 228, 235 (3d Cir. 2001).

What specific sanctions might be sought or imposed here, beyond an order compelling testimony and restricting the lawyer's conduct? Rule

37(a)(4)(a) provides that if a motion to compel answers to deposition questions is granted, "the court shall, after affording an opportunity to be heard, require the party or deponent whose conduct necessitated the motion . . . or both of them to pay to the moving party the reasonable expenses incurred in making the motion, including attorney's fees, unless the court finds that . . . the opposing party's nondisclosure, response, or objection was substantially justified, or that other circumstances make an award of expenses unjust." Thus, reimbursement of fees and expenses is mandatory absent substantial justification or other supervening circumstances. Beyond that, the trial court has the discretion to impose additional sanctions as it deems fit, with the guiding principle one of proportionality between the offense and the sanction. *Bonds v. D.C.*, 93 F.3d 801, 808 (D.C. Cir. 1996). The Supreme Court has expressly held that "[s]anctions must be chosen to employ 'the least possible power to the end proposed.'" *In re First City Bancorporation of Texas, Inc., supra* at 867, quoting *Spallone v. U.S.*, 493 U.S. 265, 280 (1990), quoting in turn *Anderson v. Dunn*, 6 Wheat. 204, 231, 5 L. Ed. 242 (1821).

Accordingly, it would be within the court's discretion here to award plaintiff's counsel the costs of his aborted deposition, including attorney's fees, as well as the right to reconvene the deposition for as much time as needed to conduct a fair examination of the defendant. *See* Rule 30(d)(2). The court may want to caution the defense counsel that a repeat performance could result in further sanctions under Rule 37(b)(2)(A), (B), (C), or (D). Given the nature of the misconduct at issue, the court could even go so far as to charge counsel—and not her client—with all or a portion of the costs and fees that plaintiff was caused to expend on the first deposition. *Cobell v. Norton*, 2003 WL 255968 (D.D.C., Feb. 5, 2003). Nonmonetary sanctions, including a letter of apology from defense counsel to plaintiff and his lawyer, as well as a mandated course in professionalism for lawyers, have been imposed by courts in cases like this. *Freeman v. Schointuck, supra* at 190. *But see Saldana, supra* at 236-38, discussed in *Mruz v. Caring, Inc., supra* at 70 (these cases may be distinguishable because the sanctions were imposed under the inherent powers of the court rather than pursuant to statute or rule of procedure).

As a final point, the cases make clear that two wrongs will not make a right. That is, confronted with an obnoxious, harassing opponent bent on undermining the discovery process, a lawyer should never rise to the bait and respond in kind. Rather, counsel should simply mind the rules. Presented with the proper record, the courts will not hesitate to enforce them.

Practice Tips

It is important for every lawyer to understand the full range of remedies available when confronted by an obstreperous, obnoxious opponent who will not allow his or her client's deposition to be taken in an orderly manner. The goal of the interrogating lawyer, however, is to get information, not sanctions, and so the question remains, *what do you do* when faced with misbehavior to get the discovery that you want? One technique, assuming that the court is unreachable by telephone during the deposition, is simply to slog through your questions, one at a time, and let the opposing lawyer bury himself in multiple offensive comments, objections, and interjections. Then take the transcript to the presiding judge or magistrate judge, and on that basis, apart from any other sanctions sought, ask the court to reconvene the deposition in front of the magistrate judge or a specially appointed master with the power to rule on objections, instruct counsel to behave on pain of sanctions, and likewise order the witness to answer the questions or similarly face sanctions. The costs of that procedure, of course, should be borne by the party whose misconduct made it necessary.

21. VIDEO DEPOSITIONS

Plaintiff's counsel noted the video deposition of one of his own expert witnesses, advising defense counsel that the expert would be unavailable at trial and that plaintiff intended to use the video in lieu of the expert's live testimony. Defense counsel responded that (a) he wanted to depose the expert without any video recording before plaintiff's counsel took the expert's video deposition, and (b) he would object to plaintiff's use of the video at trial on the ground that a trial witness was required to appear in person. How should each issue be resolved?

Comment: Defense counsel may depose the witness first, for discovery purposes, prior to the videotaped deposition even if the videotaped deposition is noticed first and notwithstanding objections of opposing counsel. Although there is no case law on point, common practice and a reading of the discovery rules support this proposition. Prior to either deposition, unless otherwise ordered by the court, the parties must "as soon as practicable . . . confer . . . to develop a proposed discovery plan. . . ." Rule 26(f). Following that meeting, however, "[u]nless the court upon motion, for the convenience of the parties and witnesses and in the interests of justice, orders otherwise, methods of discovery may be used in any sequence, and the fact that a party is conducting discovery, whether by deposition or otherwise, does not operate to delay any other party's discovery." Rule 26(d). The commentary to the rule observes: "The principal effects of this new provision are first, to eliminate any fixed priority in the sequence of discovery, and second, to make clear and explicit the court's power to establish priority by an order issued in a particular case." *See* Advisory Committee Notes to the 1970 Amendments, 48 F.R.D. 487, 492-508 (1970).

Therefore, the fact that plaintiff's counsel noticed the video deposition first does not necessarily give him the right to go first. In fact, because plaintiff's counsel intends to take a *de bene esse* deposition to be used at trial in the witness's absence, the most reasonable approach would be to allow defense counsel to take a discovery deposition first so as to prepare for the trial deposition.

If plaintiff's counsel refuses to agree to this sequence, defense counsel may file a motion for a protective order if he "has in good faith conferred or attempted to confer with other affected parties in an effort to resolve the dispute without court action." Rule 26(c). *See also Keller v. Edwards,* 206 F.R.D.

412, 416 (D. Md., 2002) (holding that "[i]f objections to the service of the deposition notice, or sequence and timing of the deposition in dispute cannot be resolved with opposing counsel through the good faith discussions contemplated by Discovery Guideline 1.d., then a motion for protective order must be filed pursuant to Rule 26(c) requesting that the court order that the deposition not take place or delay it until after other discovery has been presented."). The court may then determine if the proposed discovery sequence should be altered by applying the Rule 26(b)(2) balancing factors, which include whether: "(i) the discovery sought is unreasonably cumulative or duplicative, or is obtainable from some other source that is more convenient, less burdensome, or less expensive; (ii) the party seeking discovery has had ample opportunity by discovery in the action to obtain the information sought; or (iii) the burden or expense of the proposed discovery outweighs its likely benefit, taking into account the needs of the case, the amount in controversy, the parties' resources, the importance of the issues at stake in the litigation, and the importance of the proposed discovery in resolving the issues." Rule 26(b)(2).

The propriety of a video deposition is well accepted. Rule 30(b)(2) states that: "[t]he party taking the deposition shall state in the notice the method by which the testimony shall be recorded. Unless the court orders otherwise, it may be recorded by sound, sound-and-visual, or stenographic means, and the party taking the deposition shall bear the cost of the recording." In fact, some courts have considered the costs of the video recording a recoverable expense. *See Morrison v. Reichhold Chemicals, Inc.*, 97 F.3d 460 (11th Cir. 1996) (where party taking deposition properly notices that deposition is to be videotaped and opposing party fails to object to the manner of recordation, video depositions are taxable as costs); *Gilluly v. Miller,* 891 P.2d 1147 (Mont. 1995) (videotaped depositions filed with the court and used at trial are not solely for the convenience of the litigant and therefore may properly constitute recoverable costs). *But see DiCecco v. Dillard House,* 149 F.R.D. 239 (N.D. Ga. 1993) (prevailing party is not entitled to recover expenses associated with videotaping of depositions where parties made prior agreement to share the costs of the depositions); and *Migis v. Pearle Vision, Inc.,* 135 F.3d 1041 (5th Cir. 1998) (denying cost of videotaped deposition to successful Title VII plaintiff for failure to demonstrate that taped deposition was necessary to case).

What about the plaintiff's proposed reliance on the video deposition at trial? Rule 32, FRE 804(b)(1) and the case law permit the use of the videotaped deposition under these circumstances. *See Miller v. Solaglas California, Inc.,* 870 P.2d 559, 570 (Colo. App., 1993) ("We conclude that timely notice, in a trial data certificate [constituting formal notice by counsel that the case is ready for trial], of the intent to call a witness by way of video deposition constitutes appropriate 'application and notice' under the rule," citing C.R.C.P. 32(a)(3)(E)); and *Robert v. Colson,* 729 So. 2d 1243, 1249 (Miss. 1999) ("We also take this opportunity to direct trial courts to allow the use of video depositions at the discretion of the party taking the deposition without any requirement of stipulation by the other party or prior court approval. Trial courts shall allow non-stenographic depositions unless a deposition taken by stenographic means is necessary to assure the accuracy of the recording.") Should plaintiff's counsel choose to proceed in this manner, he should understand, however, that ". . . a transcript will be required by Rule 26(a)(3)(B) and Rule 32(c) if the deposition is later to be offered as evidence at trial or on a dispositive motion under Rule 56." Rule 30(b) Advisory Committee Notes 1993 Amendments.

Useful tips for video depositions can be found on the Internet. See, for example, http://www.videoresources.com/litigationsupport/videodepositions tips.html. Tips include the following: Choose an appropriate setting for the deposition. "There is little worse than having your deponent giggled at because he appears to be wearing a potted plant on his head. Choose a neutral setting, avoid distracting art, wallpaper, or other objects behind the deponent." *Id.* Make sure that the room will be quiet during the deposition. *Id.* Consider using a visual aid during the testimony. For example, a surgeon can describe an operative technique using a model that can be videotaped. A mechanic can display a damaged piece of machinery. An accountant or economist can perform calculations on a blackboard or white poster board. Fred Misko, Jr., *VideoTape Depositions* at 1-2 (http://www.misko.com/library/video.pdf).

Audio quality should be assured by fitting each of the participants with a lapel microphone and using a table microphone for backup. Be careful not to inadvertently record your whispered conversations with your client or co-counsel, because they could be picked up by the microphone. *Id.*

The preferred seating arrangement is "to seat the witness at one end of the table with a camera opposite. Other participants should sit at least one or two chairs away from the deponent. This will avoid annoying severe profile views of the witness who must repeatedly turn to face off-camera participants." *Id.*

Finally, it is critical that you prepare and test in advance your arrangements for playing back the videotape deposition in the courtroom. Misko recommends having "one good quality television monitor of 19 inches or larger, simply placed at the jury rail" because this is the approximate distance that jurors are accustomed to in watching television. Misko, *supra*, at 7.

22. WHO MAY ATTEND A DEPOSITION?

Three inmates in a federal prison brought a civil rights action against four prison guards, alleging deprivation of the inmates' First Amendment right to practice their religion. The suit alleged that: (i) the defendants had prevented the plaintiffs from praying communally; (ii) the plaintiffs' special dietary needs were ignored; (iii) the guards had prevented the plaintiffs from proselytizing to fellow inmates; and (iv) the guards had deprived the plaintiffs of their religious texts.

The plaintiffs noticed the video deposition of one of the guards under Rule 30. Three motions were filed in advance of the deposition: (i) a television station moved to intervene to have a reporter attend the deposition, or obtain a copy of the videotape immediately upon conclusion of the deposition; (ii) the plaintiffs moved for a protective order that the remaining defendant guards be excluded from the deposition; and (iii) the guard whose deposition was noticed moved that none of the plaintiffs be permitted to attend. The motions came on for hearing. How should the court rule?

Comment: "Although the public traditionally has a right to attend judicial proceedings, 'pretrial depositions and interrogatories are not public components of a civil trial,' and as a result, pretrial discovery proceedings are generally 'conducted in private as a matter of modern practice.'" *New York v. Microsoft Corp.*, 206 F.R.D. 19, 22 (D.D.C. 2002), quoting *Seattle Times Co. v. Rhinehart*, 467 U.S. 20, 33 [remainder of citation omitted]; *Felling v. Knight*, 211 F.R.D. 552, 553 (S.D. Ind. 2003). (There is an exception for certain antitrust actions where Congress has legislated that "[u]nder 15 U.S.C. § 30 (1973), depositions conducted in cases brought by the United States under the Sherman Act are 'open to the public as freely as are trials.'" *Amato v. City of Richmond*, 157 F.R.D. 26, 27 (E.D. Va. 1994).) This does not mean that the public does not have the right to inspect the fruits of deposition discovery—the transcript or videotape—at an appropriate time and in an appropriate manner, but simply that the public has no right to observe the deposition process "in real time" as it is unfolding. *Id.*, at 554-55; *see also Northern States Power Co. v. Westinghouse Elec. Corp.*, 156 F.R.D. 168, 172 (D. Minn. 1994) (nonparty intervenors had no right to attend depositions, but might be entitled, at some point, to access to discovery that had already taken place).

Further, a court may sometimes restrict the right of a *party* to observe or participate in a deposition in its own case. Rule 26 (c) (5) authorizes the court to enter an order "that discovery be conducted with no one present except persons designated by the court" where "good cause" has been shown for the entry of an order "which justice requires to protect a party or persons from annoyance, embarrassment, oppression, or undue burden or expense." A court may even exclude a party from a deposition that it has noticed of the opposing party, although such authority should be used only in unusual circumstances. *Galella v. Onassis*, 487 F.2d 986, 997 (2d Cir. 1973); *Visor v. Sprint/United Management Co.*, 1997 WL 567923, at *2 (D. Colo. Aug. 18, 1997) (holding that although parties have a presumptive right to participate in depositions, that right may be curtailed upon a showing of compelling or extraordinary circumstances). The specific protection to be afforded the parties—including the right to exclude another party—is within the discretion of the district court and may be reversed only on a clear showing of abuse of discretion. *Id.* at 997.

The court's power to limit attendance during depositions is buttressed by a doctrine of constitutional dimension: No one has an absolute due process right to attend his own civil trial (including pretrial depositions), *Hines v. Wilkinson*, 163 F.R.D. 262, 265 (S.D. Ohio 1995), although the involuntary exclusion of a party from civil trial is justified only under specific circumstances that comport with due process, as when the party is obstreperous and disruptive in court. *Id.*; *Helminski v. Ayerst Labs.*, 766 F.2d 208, 216 (6th Cir. 1985).

In deciding whether a plaintiff inmate, over the defendant's opposition, may attend the deposition of a defendant guard, courts have generally tried to determine whether the inmate poses a threat to the security and integrity of the prison. Generalized allegations to that effect are usually insufficient (e.g., a claim that allowing the prisoner to attend questioning of his jailer will upset the "balance of power" that is necessary to maintain order). Rather, the defendant must show facts, such as: the inmate has a history of violent behavior; he has habitually ignored direct orders of the correctional staff; he has instigated disturbances by other inmates; and/or he has been verbally abusive and threatening to the staff. *In re Collins*, 73 F.3d 614 (6th Cir. 1995); *Hines v. Wilkinson, supra*. At least one court has broadened these criteria to include "where the deposition will take place, the security issues involved in transporting a prisoner, the importance of the deponent, [as well as] the prisoner's individual security history." *James v. Roberts*, 163 F.R.D. 260, 266 (S.D. Ohio 1995).

Similar concerns about deposition attendance sometimes arise in cases other than prisoners' actions. Consider, for example, the well-known case of *Galella v. Onassis, supra*, in which Jacqueline Kennedy Onassis was sued on a variety of tort theories by Ron Galella, a photographer who shadowed her and made his living by selling his photographs of her and her children. There, the trial court excluded Galella from Onassis's pretrial deposition. On appeal, the Court of Appeals affirmed, though it noted that it might have reached a different decision had it been the trial court. Before the lawsuit, Galella had intentionally touched Onassis and her daughter in his efforts to obtain photographs, causing them fear of further unwanted contact; he had followed Onassis too closely in an automobile; he endangered the safety of her children while they were swimming, water skiing, and horseback riding; and he violated several restraining orders requiring him to keep a reasonable distance from Onassis and her children at all times. In these circumstances, the appellate court found that the trial court acted within its discretion under Rule 30(c) to bar Galella from Onassis's deposition.

In commercial cases, especially those involving claims among competitors, concerns about guarding trade secrets and other confidential information may justify restriction of a deposition to outside litigation counsel, with a "seal" order barring transcript review by the parties or their in-house personnel. *Compaq Computer Corp. v. Packard Bell Elect., Inc.*, 163 F.R.D. 329 (N.D. Cal. 1995*); see also* Rule 45(c)(3)(B)(i): "If a subpoena requires disclosure of a trade secret or other confidential research, development, or commercial information . . . if the party in whose behalf the subpoena is issued shows a substantial need for the testimony or material that cannot be otherwise met without undue hardship . . . , the court may order appearance or production only upon specified conditions."

The prisoners' rights example also raises the question of whether the party who has noticed the deposition of a witness or adverse party can obtain an order barring adverse parties from attending. Such a request seeks to achieve, in a deposition, a kind of witness sequestration common in trials.

Such relief is in fact available upon a "strong" and "compelling" showing that the adverse parties' testimony may be influenced, even unintentionally, if they are allowed to attend the remaining depositions. Such "strong" and "compelling" showing is not made, however, merely by making the obvious point that the testimony of one witness, if heard by a party, may influence its testimony. Rather, the movant must demonstrate that the facts of the case, and the relationships among the adverse parties, are not of a "garden variety" or "boilerplate" type but instead are extraordinary, and must strongly argue for independent testimony that bears no palpable risk of taint. *In re Levine*, 101 B.R. 260 (D. Colo. 1989); *see also Jones v. Circle K Stores, Inc.*, 185 F.R.D. 223 (M.D.N.C. 1999) (failure to show good cause for sequestration of other witnesses); *Alexander v. FBI*, 186 F.R.D. 21, 53 (D.D.C. 1998) (no compelling or extraordinary reason shown for excluding possible witnesses from depositions); *Lee v. Denver Sheriff's Dept.*, 181 F.R.D. 651 (D. Colo. 1998) (plaintiff prisoner failed to show "extraordinary and exceptional circumstances" that would warrant excluding defendants from each other's deposition).

Some courts have adopted local rules or discovery guidelines that address who may attend a deposition. For example, Guideline 5(h), Appendix A, Local Rules for the United States District Court for the District of Maryland states: "Unless otherwise ordered by the Court, the following persons may, without advance notice, attend a deposition: individual parties; a representative of non-individual parties; and expert witnesses of parties. Except for the persons identified above, counsel shall notify other parties not later than five . . . business days before the taking of a deposition if counsel desires to have a non-party present during a deposition. If the parties are unable to agree to the attendance of this person, then the person shall not be entitled to attend the deposition unless the party desiring to have the person attend obtains a Court order permitting him/her to do so." Again, make sure that you check the local rules.

Remember also that FRE 615, which provides for sequestration of non-party witnesses at trial upon request by a party, does not apply to pretrial depositions. Rule 30(c). Thus, other deponents are not automatically excluded from a deposition on request of a party, but may be excluded only for good cause pursuant to a protective order under Rule 26(c)(5).

Even if the public or the media cannot attend a deposition, is there a right to later access to the record of such deposition? The general rule is that civil discovery, once it has been taken, is subject to public disclosure absent a protective order maintaining confidentiality for good cause shown. Once good cause for secrecy no longer exists, any protective order should be lifted and access to such discovery should be granted to the public. *Felling v. Knight*, *supra*, at 554; *Kimberlin v. Quinlan*, 145 F.R.D. 1 (D.D.C. 1992) (holding that CNN does not have a right to attend and report on depositions, but that once a deposition is completed and filed, "the rights of CNN and the general public to inspect these materials are governed by different standards.").

Applying these rules to the prisoners' rights case, the media have no right to attend the plaintiffs' deposition, and if either party objects, the TV station's motion to attend should be denied. Once the deposition is completed, however, barring some reason to maintain its confidentiality (for example, a concern that premature disclosure of one defendant's testimony might educate the other defendants on how to testify, *In re Levine, supra*, or the risk that the media might manipulate the testimony by using selective "sound bites" from the tape and thus prejudice further proceedings, *Felling v. Knight, supra*), the transcript and the video should be made available.

On the question of attendance by other guards, the plaintiffs must make a particularized showing that there is some reason to fear that the testimony of one of the guards will influence the testimony of another. That is not self-evident here, and certainly something other than mere concern by the plaintiffs is necessary (for example, evidence that these guards are particularly close to each other and have colluded on matters before).

The same holds true in reverse. If the guard wants to exclude the plaintiffs on the ground of risk of collusive testimony, he must show that the exposure of any of the plaintiffs to the guard's testimony somehow will cause all of the plaintiffs to square their stories with one another; that, however, seems a farfetched allegation in this case, because the plaintiffs presumably have ample opportunity to get their stories straight, as do the guards, which would argue against granting either party's motion to exclude. If the guard wants to exclude the plaintiffs on security grounds, then a showing must be made that the plaintiffs actually pose a security or harassment risk. Again, a mere allegation to that effect will not suffice.

23. SUBMISSION OF DEPOSITION TRANSCRIPT TO WITNESS FOR REVIEW AND SIGNATURE

There were three witnesses to the auto accident—the plaintiff whose car was struck, the defendant whose car hit the plaintiff's car, and a pedestrian who happened to be walking by. In a diversity action brought in federal court, the plaintiff testified on deposition that the light was green as he entered the intersection and was broadsided by the defendant. The defendant, on the other hand, testified that his light had just turned green as he entered the intersection, when the plaintiff materialized in front of him out of nowhere. Both parties noticed the deposition of the pedestrian, who appeared without an attorney. She testified that from her vantage point it appeared as if the plaintiff had entered the intersection at an excessive rate of speed as his light was turning from yellow to red.

At the end of the pedestrian's testimony but before the record was closed, defense counsel advised her that under Rule 30(e) she had the right to review the transcript of her deposition within 30 days of its preparation and make typographical changes—or alternatively, she could waive that right. Plaintiff's counsel responded, "Counselor, I disagree with your limited characterization of what changes she can make—she is not limited to typos; she can change anything she wants. Also, whether or not she desires to exercise her right to review the transcript or waive it, I want her to review the transcript, and I direct her to do so."

The witness indicated that she was unsure as to how to proceed and the deposition ended on that note. Later, when she learned that the transcript was available for review, she decided to consult an attorney. She told the attorney what had happened, and then added: "You know, whether or not I can be compelled to review my transcript, the fact is that I realized after it was over that I had made a serious mistake that should be corrected. I confused the defendant with the plaintiff. In hindsight, it was the plaintiff who had the green light, not the defendant." Her lawyer then advised her to complete an errata sheet explaining the changes and the reason she made them. She did so. Upon reading her changes, defense counsel moved to strike the errata sheet, arguing that she was bound by her original answer because her alteration was not merely typographical, but rather, constituted an impermissible substantive change. The motion has come on for hearing.

Comment: The threshold issue is whether a party other than the deponent has the right to require review and signature of a deposition transcript. The short answer is that such party can request the review, but not compel it, absent order of court. The first sentence of Rule 30(e) recites that "[i]f requested by the deponent *or a party* before completion of the deposition, the deponent shall have 30 days after being notified by the officer that the transcript or recording is available in which to review the transcript or recording and, if there are changes in form or substance, to sign a statement reciting such changes and the reasons given by the deponent for making them" (emphasis added). Plaintiff's counsel was therefore within his rights to ask, if not insist, that the witness review her transcript, whether or not the deponent independently wanted to do so. Absent an order of court, of course, the lawyer cannot compel such review if the witness simply refuses. Still, such refusal in the face of a party request can set up powerful impeachment in the event that the witness, for the first time at trial, deviates from her testimony on deposition.

The more fundamental question is whether there are any limits on the types of changes that a deponent may make to the transcript. As noted above, Rule 30(e) allows for "changes in form or substance." Cases that postdate the 1993 amendments to Rule 30(e) and interpret this power fall into three categories.

The first group of cases allows a deponent to make *any* changes, including changes that create inconsistencies with the prior recorded testimony, provided that they are made in strict conformity with the requirements of the rule: (a) the request for review must be made by a party or the deponent before completion of the deposition; (b) the changes must be made within 30 days of notification that the transcript is available for review; (c) the deponent must sign a statement reciting the changes and the reasons for making them; and (d) the changes must be appended to the transcript during the period allowed. *Foutz v. Town of Vinton, Virginia*, 211 F.R.D. 293 (W.D. Va. 2002); *Holland v. Cedar Creek Mining, Inc.*, 198 F.R.D. 651 (S.D.W. Va. 2001); *Rios v. AT&T Corp.*, 36 F. Supp. 2d 1064 (N.D. Ill. 1999); *Hlinko v. Virgin Atl. Airways*, 1997 WL 68563 (S.D.N.Y. Feb. 19, 1997); *Podell v. Citicorp Diners Club, Inc.*, 914 F. Supp. 1025 (S.D.N.Y. 1996), *aff'd*, 112 F.3d 98 (2d Cir. 1997).

The second category of decisions permits changes that may appear to create substantive inconsistencies with prior testimony provided that an adequate reason is given for the change which, in effect, reconciles, explains, or clarifies the inconsistency. *Herring v. Teradyne, Inc.*, 2002 WL 32068318 (S.D. Cal., Nov. 4, 2002) (change for purpose of clarification is an adequate reason); *Lamarche v. Metro. Life Ins. Co.*, 236 F. Supp. 2d 34 (D. Me. 2002) (party offered sufficient justification for changing deposition answer from "no" to "yes" by filing, along with certification of accuracy of remainder of deposition transcript, statement that he had misunderstood question and had been fatigued due to diabetic condition and lack of food at time of original answer); *DeLoach v. Philip Morris Companies, Inc.*, 206 F.R.D. 568 (M.D.N.C. 2002) (change to deposition transcript which simply explained deponent's answer in more detail, and which was not contradictory to his testimony, was permissible under rule governing deposition changes); *Elwell v. Conair, Inc.*, 145 F. Supp. 2d 79 (D. Me. 2001); *Duff v. Lobdell-Emery Mfg. Co.*, 926 F. Supp. 799 (N.D. Ind. 1996).

The third category disallows any substantive changes, applying the same logic that rejects a party's attempt to defeat summary judgment by submitting an affidavit that contravenes the affiant's prior sworn answer at deposition. *Garcia v. Pueblo Country Club*, 299 F.3d 1233, 1242 (10th Cir. 2002); *S.E.C. v. Parkersburg Wireless, L.L.C.*, 156 F.R.D. 529, 535 (D.D.C. 1994); *Rios v. Welch*, 856 F. Supp. 1499 (D. Kan. 1994). Under these cases, changes can be made only for items such as misspellings, transcription errors, and the like.

In all cases where changes are allowed, the prior deposition testimony is available for impeachment. *Foutz v. Town of Vinton, Virginia, supra.* Likewise, a substantive change in deposition testimony, even if explained and allowed, may entitle the interrogating party to reopen the deposition to explore further the reasons for the change. *Foutz v. Town of Vinton, Virginia, supra*; *Holland v. Cedar Creek Mining, Inc., supra.* Of the three categories, the majority of courts appear to apply the most liberal standard (i.e., any changes are acceptable), while a distinct minority apply the most conservative standard (i.e., no substantive changes). In all cases where a contradicting change is made, however, a deponent should offer a reasonable explanation for it in order to (a) increase the likelihood that the change will be allowed; and (b) lessen its impeachment effect on cross-examination.

Applying that reasoning to this example, the deponent may attempt to explain her change in testimony by saying that she was confused by the nomenclature of litigation—she simply reversed the terms "plaintiff" and "defendant." If, on the other hand, her explanation is that she thought long and hard after the deposition and realized that she had been mistaken, the court, even if it allows the correction, might well permit further questioning on deposition, setting the groundwork for effective impeachment at trial based on her earlier contradictory sworn testimony.

24. COMPENSATION FOR TREATING PHYSICIAN'S DEPOSITION PREPARATION AND TESTIMONY

Plaintiff in a personal injury action named his treating physician as a possible fact witness at trial. Defense counsel then subpoenaed the doctor for his deposition, attaching a notice of deposition and check for $50 for the witness fee and costs of transportation in accordance with 28 U.S.C. § 1821(b) and (c)(2).

When he learned of the subpoena, plaintiff's counsel telephoned defense counsel and told him that the doctor wanted to be paid for his time spent preparing for the deposition as well as the time spent in deposition at the rate he charged for an office medical consultation—$350 an hour. This was reasonable, the plaintiff's lawyer said, because the doctor's time spent on this case would prevent him from seeing patients and earning his standard fees for such work. The doctor, plaintiff's counsel added, was not demanding any premium beyond the income that he would otherwise earn.

Defense counsel disagreed. He pointed out that the plaintiff had not identified his doctor as an expert witness: The doctor was simply a fact witness whose direct testimony would be limited to the facts of his examination, diagnosis, and treatment of the plaintiff. Accordingly, said defense counsel, the doctor was entitled only to the payment provided by the statutory schedule of payment for a fact witness. The parties were unable to resolve the dispute. Plaintiff's counsel therefore filed a motion for a protective order that her client's treating physician be paid his standard hourly rates for deposition preparation and testimony as a condition of going forward.

Comment: The cases are split on this issue, even though the better-reasoned rule, since the 1993 amendments to Rule 26 (discussed below), is that reasonable hourly fees should be allowed. Absent controlling authority in the district court where the case is pending (or a local rule setting the fee for a treating physician called for deposition), a lawyer can argue either position, depending on his client's interest in the issue.[1]

---

1. Rule 104.11.b of the United States District Court for the District of Maryland, for example, titled "Limitation on the amount of fees of treating physician," provides that "[u]nless otherwise ordered by the Court, a treating physician shall not charge a fee higher than the hourly fee that he or she customarily charges for in-office patient consultation or $200 per hour, whichever is lower, for any work that he or she performs in connection with any discovery matter or for the taking of a *de bene esse* deposition."

In *Demar v. United States*, 199 F.R.D. 617 (N.D. Ill. 2001), the magistrate judge held that a treating physician was not entitled to be paid as an expert, but rather, was limited to the statutory $40 per diem plus travel expenses under 28 U.S.C. § 1821. In so ruling, the court reviewed conflicting authorities on this question, including *Fisher v. Ford Motor Co.*, 178 F.R.D. 195, 197-98 (N.D. Ohio 1998); *Mangla v. Univ. of Rochester*, 168 F.R.D. 137, 139-40 (W.D.N.Y. 1996); and *Baker v. Taco Bell Corp.*, 163 F.R.D. 348, 350 (D. Colo. 1995) (all of which limit payment to the statutory rate), as well as *Harvey v. Shultz*, 2000 WL 33170885 (D. Kan. Nov. 16, 2000); *Haslett v. Tex. Industries, Inc.* 1999 WL 354227 (N.D. Tex. May 20, 1999); *Coleman v. Dydula*, 190 F.R.D. 320 (W.D.N.Y. 1999); and *Scheinholtz v. Bridgestone/ Firestone, Inc.*, 187 F.R.D. 221, 222 (E.D. Pa. 1999) (which allow payment of reasonable hourly fees).

The court's ruling that hourly fees were inappropriate was grounded on the "undisputed" finding that the treating physician in that case "[was] a fact witness and not an expert witness." 199 F.R.D. at 618. From that premise, the court reasoned that Rule 26(b)(4)(C), which provides for payment of reasonable fees to an expert for participation in discovery, was inapplicable. As a result, said the *Demar* court, a treating physician was limited to recovery of the statutory fee mandated by 28 U.S.C. § 1821. The court disagreed with *Haslett, supra*, which had held that treating physicians should be compensated for discovery at their normal rate because they (1) provide "invaluable" services to the public; (2) should be remunerated for their time when they cannot deliver medical care; (3) often have substantial overhead costs that they incur whether they are treating a patient or testifying about one; and (4) are entitled to payment "commensurate with their professional standing and special expertise." *Id.* at 619. In rejecting this analysis, the *Demar* court reasoned that the medical profession was entitled to no greater deference than any other specialized occupation, including engineering, law, accountancy, or consultancy. If other professions were to be granted the same entitlement as medicine, who would decide which professions qualified and which did not? Satisfied that a bright-line test between expert and fact witnesses made more sense, the court limited the treating physician to the statutory fee.

A subsequent unreported decision in the same division of the same district, however, *Hoover v. United States*, 2002 WL 1949734 (N.D. Ill. Aug. 22, 2002), held precisely the reverse, allowing a treating physician reasonable fees under Rule 26(b)(4)(C). Like the *Demar* court, the *Hoover* court reviewed the conflicting authorities, including *Grant v. Otis Elevator Co.*, 199 F.R.D. 673 (N.D. Okla. 2001), and *Bovey v. Mitsubishi Motor Mfg. of Am.*, 88 Fair Empl. Prac. Cas. (BNA) 866 (C.D. Ill. 2002), which allowed reasonable expert fees.[2]

Analyzing the 1993 amendments to Rule 26, the *Hoover* court concluded that the drafters contemplated that testimonial expert witnesses entitled to reasonable compensation by the adverse party fell into two categories: (1) retained experts disclosed as witnesses, from whom a written report was required; and (2) nonretained experts disclosed as witnesses, who may offer testimony at trial under FRE 702,[3] but were not obliged to submit a report.[4] A treating physician fell into the latter category, as invariably he or she would be (1) qualified "as an expert by knowledge, skill, experience, training, or education," and (2) providing "scientific, technical or other specialized knowl-

---

2. Other cases allowing reasonable fees include Sublette v. Glidden Co., 1998 WL 398156 (E.D. Pa. June 25, 1998); Magee v. Paul Revere Life Ins. Co., 172 F.R.D. 627, 645-46 (E.D.N.Y. 1997); Slywka v. CMI-Equip. & Eng'g, Inc., 1997 WL 129378 at *1 (M.D. Pa. March 14, 1997); Mathis v. NYNEX, 165 F.R.D. 23, 26 (E.D.N.Y. 1997); U.S. Energy Corp. v. NUKEM, Inc., 163 F.R.D. 344, 346-47 (D. Colo. 1995); Hose v. Chicago and N. W. Transp. Co., 154 F.R.D. 222, 225-27 (S.D. Iowa 1994); Dominguez v. Syntex Lab., Inc. 149 F.R.D. 166, 170 (S.D. Ind. 1993); Jochims v. Isuzu Motors, Ltd., 141 F.R.D. 493, 497 (S.D. Iowa 1992); and Goldwater v. Postmaster Gen. of the United States, 136 F.R.D. 337 (D. Conn. 1991).

Further cases limiting payment to the statutory fee include N. Shore Concrete & Assoc. v. City of New York, 1996 WL 391597 (E.D.N.Y. July 10, 1996) (analogous nonmedical expert); Richardson v. Consol. Rail Corp., 17 F.3d 213 (7th Cir. 1994); O'Connor v. Commonwealth Edison Co., 13 F.3d 1090 (7th Cir. 1994); Patel v. Gayes, 984 F.2d 214, 217 (7th Cir. 1993) (interpreting Rule 26 prior to the 1993 amendments, *see infra*); and Sipes v. United States, 111 F.R.D. 56 (S.D. Cal. 1986).

3. FRE 702 provides in part that "[i]f scientific, technical, or other specialized knowledge will assist the trier of fact to understand the evidence or to determine a fact in issue, a witness qualified as an expert by knowledge, skill, experience, training, or education, may testify thereto in the form of an opinion. . . ."

4. *See also* Coleman v. Dydula, *supra* at 323; Salas v. United States, 165 F.R.D. 31 (W.D.N.Y. 1995); Wreath v. United States, 161 F.R.D. 448, 450 (D. Kan. 1995). The *Hoover* court observed in this regard that the 1970 version of Rule 26 (which the 1993 amendments superseded) recognized only the former category of testimonial expert, and not the latter.

edge [that would] assist the trier of fact to understand the evidence or to determine a fact in issue." *Id.*[5]

The court distinguished, on two grounds, cases reaching a different conclusion. First, *Baker v. Taco Bell Corp., supra; Mangala v. Univ. of Rochester, supra;* and cases following their reasoning had held that treating physicians, unlike retained experts, testify to opinions based upon personal knowledge, rather than information acquired from outside sources, and that the former renders the treating doctor a fact witness, not an expert witness. The *Hoover* court rejected this analysis both as a matter of interpretation of Rule 26 and as a matter of logic:

> [A] treating physician who testifies about the examination, diagnosis, and treatment of a patient necessarily draws upon his or her skill, training and experience as a doctor. And the physician can only do so as an expert under Rule 702—which makes the treater an expert under Rule 26(a)(2)(A), who is subject to deposition under Rule 26(b)(4)(A) and who, under the terms of Rule 26(b)(4)(C)(i), is entitled to payment of a reasonable fee for the deposition.

Hoover v. United States, supra at *6.

Second, the *Demar* decision and cases following its line of reasoning found as a matter of policy that doctors should not be treated in a manner different from other specialized professionals. The *Hoover* court observed, however, that *Demar* failed to analyze Rule 26(b)(4)(C), which requires "payment of a reasonable fee to all experts who are disclosed under Rule 26(a)(2)(A) and deposed under Rule 26(b)(4)—irrespective of whether they are retained experts, and irrespective of whether they are required to submit a report under Rule 26(a)(2)(B)." *Hoover v. United States,* supra at *7. This law trumped the *Demar* policy argument.

In the example, defense counsel could argue that even assuming that the plaintiff's treating physician might otherwise be entitled to reasonable fees, in this case plaintiff did not name his doctor as a witness who would provide

---

5. The court in *Grant v. Otis Elevator Co., supra,* similarly postulated that "almost all of a treating physician's testimony concerning diagnosis, treatment and prognosis, is expert testimony under Fed. R. Evid. 702. A treating physician would be a 'fact' witness only in rare situations, such as where the physician also witnessed the accident or incident in question." 199 F.R.D. at 676.

expert testimony, and thus such fees should not be allowed. Indeed, Rule 26(a)(2)(A) requires that "[i]n addition to the disclosures required by paragraph (1) [of Rule 26(a)], a party shall disclose to other parties the identity of any person who may be used at trial to present evidence under Rules 702, 703, or 705 of the Federal Rules of Evidence."

Thus, plaintiff should identify the doctor in discovery as someone who may be called as a witness to present evidence under Rules 702, 703, or 705 of the Federal Rules of Evidence notwithstanding that his testimony will be limited to the "facts" of the examination, treatment, and diagnosis of the plaintiff. Doing that will increase the likelihood of recovering reasonable fees and minimize the chance that the doctor will be required to file a report as provided by Rule 26(a)(2)(B).

An alternative argument supports the treating doctor's entitlement to a reasonable fee for the income lost by not being able to see patients. Under Rule 26(b)(2), the court on its own initiative or upon motion of a party can exercise control over discovery to prevent abusive, burdensomeness or unfair consequences. In the example, the doctor's position is that it would be unfair to dock his earnings for the day, and limit him to what he could otherwise earn in under ten minutes. That argument would be no less reasonable if made by an architect, accountant, lawyer or engineer who would lose income if subpoenaed to give deposition testimony as a fact witness or as a hybrid fact-expert witness under Rule 26(a)(2)(A).[6] If the court is convinced that disallowance of a reasonable fee would be unfair, it has ample authority under Rule 26(b)(2) to order the party taking the deposition to pay a reasonable fee regardless of the language of Rule 26(b)(4).

---

6. In fact, a laborer earning $15 an hour, supporting a family of four, would be placed at even a greater disadvantage if limited to the statutory fee for a day's testimony—but that is all that he would get if he were a fact witness.

25. DEPOSITIONS OF CORPORATIONS AND OTHER ENTITIES UNDER RULE 30(b)(6)

The plaintiffs brought suit under 42 U.S.C. § 1983 for civil rights violations after their daughter was shot and killed by Sgt. Smith of the City police force while she was riding as a passenger in a car. Plaintiffs noted the deposition of defendant City under Rule 30(b)(6), asking that the City "designate one or more officers, directors, or managing agents, or other persons who consent to testify on its behalf," on the following matters: (i) Sgt. Smith's training history; (ii) Sgt. Smith's disciplinary history; and (iii) the City Police Department's policies, practices, guidelines, and procedures over the last 10 years concerning the use of deadly force.

Three officers, Lts. A, B, and C, were designated by the City in response to the notice. At the deposition, however, Lt. A, who was designated to testify concerning Sgt. Smith's training history, said that he was unfamiliar with the details of Sgt. Smith's training specifically related to the use of firearms directed at moving vehicles.

Lt. B testified that he was unprepared to provide any background on the prior discipline against Sgt. Smith, such as when specific incidents occurred, the circumstances surrounding them, or whether Sgt. Smith had served either of two suspensions ordered against him. Likewise, he was unable to say whether Sgt. Smith received any counseling or action under the Police Department's Early Warning System program that identified officers who received frequent complaints of unnecessary or excessive force.

Lt. C was instructed by counsel not to answer questions as to whether certain behavior by a police officer would violate departmental policies and procedures on the ground that these hypothetical questions were outside the scope of the designation of the matters on which examination was requested in the Rule 30(d)(6) deposition notice. Plaintiff's counsel suspended the depositions and moved the court to compel defendants to designate witnesses who were prepared to testify concerning Sgt. Smith's training and disciplinary history and to require Lt. C to testify concerning the matters that defense counsel argued were outside the scope of the designations. How should the court rule?

Comment: A deposition notice pursuant to Rule 30(b)(6) can be an excellent discovery tool when a lawyer knows that a corporation, government agency, or other entity has useful information, but cannot identify the persons within the entity who possess that knowledge.

However, if treated carelessly by the party deponent, ". . . the Rule 30(b)(6) deposition will engender needless discovery disputes that only increase the cost of litigation and may come back to haunt the corporation at trial." U.S. Magistrate Judge Sydney N. Schenkier, "Deposing Corporations and Other Fictive Persons: Some Thoughts on Rule 30(b)(6)," *Litigation* (the journal of the ABA Section of Litigation) 29:2 (Winter 2003): 62. A Rule 36(b)(6) deposition can breed disputes if treated carelessly by the noticing party as well. The example, taken from *Detoy v. City and County of San Francisco,* 196 F.R.D. 362 (N.D. Cal. 2000), illustrates some of the disputes that can occur in a Rule 30(b)(6) deposition.

The starting point for the resolution of any Rule 30(b)(6) problem is its text, which provides:

> A party may in the party's notice and in a subpoena name as the deponent a public or private corporation or partnership or association or governmental agency and describe with reasonable particularity the matters on which examination is requested. In that event, the organization so named shall designate one or more officers, directors, or managing agents, or other persons who consent to testify on its behalf, and may set forth, for each person designated, the matters on which the person will testify. A subpoena shall advise a non-party organization of its duty to make such a designation. The persons so designated shall testify as to matters known or reasonably available to the organization.

In *Detoy,* Magistrate Judge Larson granted plaintiffs' motion to compel the defendants to designate witnesses prepared to testify regarding "Sgt. Smith's" training and disciplinary history. Those subjects, and the police department's policy and procedures, were at the heart of the case; to prevail against the City, the plaintiff had to show that the police department and the City engaged in a pattern and practice of permitting or ratifying unconstitutional force by police officers.

The court further required defendants to ensure that such witnesses were adequately prepared to testify—that is, that each witness had reviewed all pertinent documents and was familiar with them. The court ordered that plaintiff's counsel allow the witnesses to review files and documents during their depositions if necessary to refresh their recollections. If witnesses other than those initially designated were available to testify regarding discrete aspects of the defendant officer's training history, they had to be made available for deposition as Rule 30(b)(6) witnesses whose testimony would be binding on the police department and City.

The case law is unsettled as to whether witness testimony at a Rule 30(b)(6) deposition is limited to the subject matter of the designation in the notice. A deposing party is thus left to choose between not asking questions outside the designation or re-opening the deposition at a different time under Rule 30(b)(1). This process is complicated by the Rule 30(a)(2)(A) limitation of ten depositions per party, unless a local rule or court order provides otherwise. The court in *Paparelli v. Prudential Ins. Co. of Am.*, 108 F.R.D. 727, 730 (D. Mass. 1985), strictly construed the scope of a 30(b)(6) deposition: "Accordingly, I rule that if a party opts to employ the procedures of Rule 30(b)(6), F. R. Civ. P., to depose a representative of a corporation, that party must confine the examination to the matters stated 'with reasonable particularity' which are contained in the Notice of Deposition."

At the same time, the *Paparelli* court held that the defending party may not instruct the witness not to answer questions outside the scope of the designations, but rather should adjourn the deposition to seek a protective order. *Id.* at 731.

The *Detoy* police officer opinion criticized *Paparelli* for appearing to ignore the liberal discovery requirements of Rule 26(b)(1), which states that "[p]arties may obtain discovery regarding any matter not privileged that is relevant to the subject matter involved in the pending action . . ." *Paparelli* forecloses the opposing party from two of the most significant benefits of the deposition as a tool in the discovery process: (i) the ability to explore previously undisclosed areas of a case that are revealed by a deponent during deposition questioning; and (ii) the ability to observe a deponent's response to an unexpected question. *Detoy*, 196 F.R.D., *366. According to the *Detoy* court, limiting the scope of a Rule 30(b)(6) deposition to what is noticed in the deposition subpoena frustrates the objectives of Rule 30(b)(6) whenever a deposing party seeks information relevant to the subject matter of the pending litigation that was not specified.

The court in *King v. Pratt & Whitney, a Div. of United Technologies Corp.*, 161 F.R.D. 475 (S.D. Fla. 1995), interpreted the "reasonable particularity" requirement of Rule 30(b)(6) as designed to ensure that the party produces a witness prepared to testify about the designated matters. According to *King*, this means that the description of the scope of the deposition in the notice is the minimum about which the witness must be prepared to testify, not the maximum. The *King* court also disagreed with the decision in *Paparelli*, reasoning as follows: (i) Rule 30(b)(6) obligates the responding entity to provide a witness who can answer questions regarding the subject matter listed in the notice; (ii) if the designated deponent cannot answer those questions, then the entity has failed to comply with its Rule 30(b)(6) obligations and may be subject to sanctions. The entity has an affirmative duty to produce a representative who can answer questions that are both within the scope of the matters described within the notice and are "known or reasonably available to the corporation"; (iii) if the examining party asks questions outside the scope of the matters described in the matters, the general deposition rules govern (i.e., Rule 26(b)(1)), so that relevant questions can be asked and no special protection is conferred on a deponent by virtue of the fact that the deposition was noticed under Rule 30(b)(6); however, (iv) if the deponent does not know the answer to questions outside the scope of the matters described in the matters, then that is the examining party's problem.

The *King* court thus concluded that Rule 30(b)(6) cannot be used to limit what is asked of a designated witness at deposition. Once the witness satisfies the minimum standard, the scope of the deposition is determined solely by the standard of relevance under Rule 26—that is, whether the evidence sought may lead to the discovery of admissible evidence. *Overseas Private Inv. Corp. v. Mandelbaum*, 185 F.R.D. 67 (D.D.C. 1999) (once a corporate defendant produces a witness capable of responding to questions in Rule 30(b)(6), the scope of inquiry is limited only by Rule 26(b)(1). *Id.* at 68). While the *Detoy* court agreed with *King* that Rule 30(b)(6) cannot be used to limit the scope of examination, the court recognized that the witness's counsel may fear that the designating entity could be bound by the witness's answers to questions that could not have been anticipated, or that the answers could act as admissions by the designating entity. 196 F.R.D. 362, *367. 7 *Moore's Federal Practice* at 30-56.5 (3d ed. 2003) states that "[t]he better view" is reflected in the *King* holding that a Rule 30(b)(6) deponent may be questioned as broadly as any other deponent. *See also Cabot Corp. v. Yamulla Enterprises. Inc.*, 194 F.R.D. 499 (M.D. Pa. 2000) (specifically rejecting *Paparelli*, the court ruled that the scope of a Rule 30(b)(6) deposition is not limited to matters described in the notice).

In addressing this concern, *Detoy* first concluded that it was artificial and a waste of time and resources to adjourn a Rule 30(b)(6) deposition and require that it be re-noticed for the witness to appear on his or her own behalf. *Id.* The court reasoned that if a witness was able to testify on behalf of an entity, he was certainly able to testify at the same deposition for himself. Likewise, treating the witness's testimony as two depositions for purposes of the local rules' limit on the number of depositions would simply encourage defending counsel to take a hard line and force an opponent to expend its deposition allotment. The *Detoy* court thus held that if defense counsel objected to questions as falling outside the scope of the Rule 30(b)(6) designation, he should state the objection, and the witness should then answer to the best of his ability, subject to the objection. The witness's counsel should not instruct him not to answer except as authorized by Rule 30(d)(1) to preserve a privilege, enforce a limitation on evidence directed by the court, or present a Rule 30(d)(4) motion that the deposition is being conducted in bad faith or in such a way to unreasonably annoy, embarrass, or oppress an opponent or a party.

Counsel for the witness may note on the record, according to the *Detoy* court, that answers to questions beyond the Rule 30(b)(6) designation are not intended as the answers as the designating party and do not bind it. At trial, counsel may request a jury instruction that such answers were merely the answers or opinions of individual fact witnesses, not admissions of the party. Such an instruction may not be granted, however. "It is surprising how many counsel do not realize that a deposition of a corporate employee concerning matters falling within the scope of employment produces admissions. . . . It makes no difference whether the employee is designated . . . pursuant to [Rule] 30(b)(6). Any statement made during employment and within the scope of employment is a [Fed. Evid.] Rule 801(d)(2)(D) statement [i.e., an admission]." Stern, Saltzburg & Capra, 2 *Trying Cases to Win* 5 (2003 Supp.).

If the rule suggested by *King, Detoy,* and *Moore's Federal Practice* were to become widely accepted—if every Rule 30(b)(6) deponent were fair game for a general discovery deposition—then one result could be that 30(b)(6) designees would become entirely "synthetic" witnesses. That is, companies would select witnesses without personal knowledge of the dispute or even the company, and then train them to respond to the information sought by the notice. That, of course, would be inefficient and foolish, as it would ensure that those witnesses most knowledgeable on the 30(b)(6) questions would not testify.

The summer 2003 issue of the ABA's Section of Litigation newsletter, *PreTrial Practice & Discovery,* contains a useful article by Jonathan Handler on key 30(b)(6) concepts. Handler notes that attorney-client privilege and work-product issues frequently will arise when a corporation's attorney prepares a Rule 30(b)(6) designee witness. Despite the lawyer's role in such circumstances, "a deponent has the obligation to recite all facts about which he or she is questioned even though those facts may have been provided by the deponent's lawyer. If the deponent's attorney believes those facts are protected by the work product doctrine or the attorney-client privilege, he or she should seek a protective order." *Id.* at 4.

Handler also points out that there is a split of authority concerning the extent to which the 30(b)(6) testimony binds the corporation. Compare *Worthington Pump Corp. v. Hoffert Marine, Inc.,* 1982 U.S. Dist. LEXIS 17968, at *8 (N.D.N.J. Feb. 19, 1982) ((30)(b)(6) testimony represents the corporation's final statement on a particular issue, which it can neither amend nor modify) with *W.R. Grace & Co. v. Viskase Corp.,* 1991 U.S. Dist. LEXIS 14651, at *5 (N.D. Ill. Oct. 11, 1991) ((30)(b)(6) witness cannot conclusively bind a corporation; such testimony is not a judicial admission but, rather, only an evidentiary admission that the corporation may further explain or contradict). *See* Handler at 4.

Handler's article concludes by alerting counsel to consider challenging the scope of an overly broad 30(b)(6) deposition notice:

> Under the prevailing interpretation of Rule 30(b)(6), a corporation may now essentially be required to create one or more omniscient witnesses who can provide a binding synthesis of every fact and defense in the case. As a result, a party who receives such a broad deposition notice should carefully consider challenging its scope rather than merely submitting to the deposition as noticed. Even if the courts are willing to try to pare back the scope of overly broad notices, Rule 30(b)(6) will continue to pose significant risks to corporations on the receiving end while offering a potential bonanza of useful information to artful counsel on the deposing side who understand the intricacies of this powerful tool. Handler, *supra,* at 6.

Lawyers must also be aware that courts take seriously the obligation imposed by Rule 30(b)(6) to produce a witness who is prepared to testify meaningfully about the subject matters identified in the deposition notice. Courts have not hesitated to impose sanctions against the party designating the witness and/or its attorney in the absence of such preparation, reasoning that a failure to produce a sufficiently knowledgeable witness is tantamount to a failure to attend the deposition. *See, e.g., Black Horse Lane Assoc. v. Dow Chem. Corp.*, 228 F.3d 275 (3d Cir. 2000) (failure to produce a witness at a 30(b)(6) deposition capable of testifying meaningfully to each of the topics is tantamount to a failure to attend the deposition, warranting sanctions) and *Resolution Trust Corp. v. Southern Union Co. Inc.*, 985 F.2d 196 (5th Cir. 1993) (same). *See also* chapter 47 (Rule 37(d) Sanctions for Failure of a Party to Attend Its Own Deposition or Respond to Interrogatories or Document Production Requests), *infra*.

Practice Tip

When noting a Rule 30(b)(6) deposition, take care to identify with precision the topics about which the witness is being asked to testify. Do not designate an excessive number of topics, because to do so simply invites an objection and motion for protective order. If you receive a Rule 30(b)(6) deposition notice, promptly and carefully review it to determine whether the topics listed are improper or burdensome. If they are, immediately notify opposing counsel and make a good faith effort to reach a compromise, documenting these efforts. If unsuccessful, promptly file a motion for a protective order. When preparing a Rule 30(b)(6) designee to testify, ensure that he or she is adequately prepared, remembering that the witness is not bound by his or her own actual knowledge, but must be prepared to testify about information known and reasonably available to the organization.

Anticipate that a dispute may arise if the deposing party does not think that the witness was prepared adequately, and make sure you are able to document to the court that reasonable preparation efforts were made. Stress to the witness that he or she must be very careful in answering each question, because the court may rule that any testimony he gives is an admission by the organization under FRE 801(d)(2)(C) or (D). Counsel should be prepared to make proper objections to questions during the deposition; a casual answer to a poorly framed question as to which there is no timely objection may be a cause for considerable regret at trial.

When you receive the transcript of a Rule 30(b)(6) deposition, make sure the designee carefully reviews it, and if substantive corrections are needed, ensure that they are made. While this may result in a motion for additional deposition time to explore the substantive corrections, it is more important to ensure correctness than to avoid the possibility of a continued deposition. *See* chapter 23 (Submission of Deposition Transcript to Witness for Review and Signature), *infra*. Finally, if a dispute arises during a 30(b)(6) deposition as to whether a question is within the scope of the notice, try to resolve the argument without suspending the deposition. One way to do this is to object but permit the witness to answer, clearly indicating on the record that from the perspective of the party being deposed the answer is not that of the organization but is limited to the personal knowledge of the witness.

26. DISCOVERY OF ORAL COMMUNICATIONS AND PRIVILEGED DOCUMENTS PROVIDED TO A WITNESS

Plaintiff's counsel is poised to depose an eyewitness to a motor vehicle collision. The witness is cooperative and agrees to meet with the lawyer before the deposition to prepare. During the meeting, plaintiff's counsel provides his chronology of events and presents an abbreviated opening statement to orient the witness.

During the deposition, defense counsel learns of this meeting and the information provided to the witness. She wants to see the chronology and asks the witness to repeat the opening statement. Plaintiff's counsel objects on the grounds of attorney-client privilege and work-product doctrine. How should the issue be resolved?

Comment: The party asserting the attorney-client privilege has the burden of proving that the privilege applies to a given set of documents or communications. *In re Grand Jury Subpoenas (Hirsch)*, 803 F.2d 493, 496 (9th Cir. 1986); *Nishika, Ltd. v. Fuji Photo Film Co., Ltd.*, 181 F.R.D. 465, 466 (D. Nev. 1998). Here, plaintiff's counsel cannot meet that burden. The privilege applies only if (1) the asserted holder of the privilege is or sought to become a client; (2) the person to whom the communication was made (a) is a member of the bar of a court or his subordinate, and (b) in connection with the communication is acting as a lawyer; (3) the communication relates to a fact of which the attorney was informed (a) by his client (b) without the presence of strangers (c) for the purpose of securing primarily either (i) an opinion on law or (ii) legal services or (iii) assistance in some legal proceeding, and not (d) for the purpose of committing a crime or tort; and (4) the privilege has been (a) claimed and (b) not waived by the client. The attorney-client privilege is triggered only by a client's request for legal, as contrasted with business, advice and is limited to communications made to attorneys (or subordinates) solely for the purpose of the client seeking legal advice and the counsel providing it. *Energy Capital Corp. v. U.S.,* 45 Fed. Cl. 481, 485 (Fed. Cl. 2000) *citing United States v. United Shoe Machinery Corp.,* 89 F. Supp. 357, 358-59 (D. Mass. 1950).

In the example, the communication took place between an attorney and a nonparty witness, not a client. Any attorney-client privilege that may have protected the chronology before it was shared with the nonparty witness was waived upon the disclosure. *See In re Columbia/HCA Healthcare Corp. Bill-*

ing Practices Litigation, 293 F.3d 289, 294 (6th Cir. 2002) ("As a general rule, the attorney-client privilege is waived by voluntary disclosure of private communications by an individual or corporation to third parties.").

What about work-product protection for the chronology or opening statement? Of course, "[t]o constitute work product under Fed. R. Civ. P. 26(b)(3), the material must be documents and tangible things, prepared in anticipation of litigation or for trial, and prepared by or for another party or for that other party's representative." *Audiotext Communications Network, Inc. v. U.S. Telecom, Inc.*, 164 F.R.D. 250, 252 (D. Kan., 1996) quoting *Sunbird Air Servs., Inc. v. Beech Aircraft Corp.*, No 89-2181-V, unpublished op. at 5 (D. Kan. Sept. 4, 1992). Thus the written chronology qualifies as work product, but the oral opening statement does not. The workproduct doctrine may not protect disclosure of the written chronology, however, because such protection may be lost by using materials for a "testimonial purpose" such as preparing a witness to testify. *Nutramax Laboratories, Inc. v. Twin Laboratories, Inc.*, 183 F.R.D. 458 (D. Md. 1998).

Courts have ruled that FRE 612, the "refreshed recollection" rule, applies to depositions through Rule 30(c), *Nutramax, supra*, at 461-62. FRE 612 provides that writings used by a witness to refresh his memory either while testifying or before testifying are fair game for the adverse party, who is entitled "to have the writing produced at the hearing, to inspect it, to cross-examine the witness thereon, and to introduce in evidence those portions which relate to the testimony of the witness." FRE 612.

The Advisory Committee Notes say, however, that "nothing in the Rule [should] be considered as barring the assertion of a privilege with respect to writings used by a witness to refresh his memory." *Suss v. MSX Intern. Eng'g Services, Inc.*, 212 F.R.D. 159, 163 (S.D.N.Y. 2002), *citing* Advisory Comm. Notes, Fed. R. Evid. 612 (1974). "In applying Rule 612, courts must balance the tension between the disclosure needed for effective cross-examination and the protection against disclosure afforded by any relevant privilege." *Id.* "As a threshold matter, Rule 612 applies, by its terms, only to writings used to refresh a witness' memory; otherwise, the Rule bestows no rights on adverse parties." *Arkwright Mutual Ins. Co. v. Nat'l Union Fire Ins. Co. of Pittsburgh, Pa.*, 1994 WL 510043 at *16, *citing* 28 Charles A. Wright & Victor J. Gold, *Federal Practice and Procedure* § 6185 (1993).

Thus, defense counsel must demonstrate in her motion to compel discovery that the chronology shared with the witness was used for that purpose. "The purposes of disclosure under Rule 612 are to test the credibility of a witness's claim that memory has been revived and to expose any discrepancies between the writing and the testimony." *S & A Painting Co., Inc. v. O.W.B. Corporation,* 103 F.R.D. 407, 410 (W.D. Pa. 1984), *citing* McCormick, *Evidence* § 9 at 17 (1972). "A party must meet three conditions before obtaining 'documents used by a witness prior to testifying: (1) the witness must use the writing to refresh his or her memory; (2) the witness must use the writing for the purpose of testifying; and (3) the court must determine that production is necessary in the interest of justice.'" *Audiotext Communications Network, Inc. v. U.S. Telecom, Inc.,* 164 F.R.D. 250, 254 (D. Kan. 1996), quoting *Butler Mfg. Co. v. Americold Corp.,* 148 F.R.D. 275, 277-78 (D. Kan. 1993).

Even "where the party seeking production has not established that the witness used the writing to refresh his memory, a court may nonetheless order production where the writing had 'sufficient impact' on the witness' testimony to warrant the application of Rule 612." *Arkwright Mutual Ins. Co.,* 1994 WL 510043 at *16 (citing *Berkey Photo, Inc. v. Eastman Kodak Co.,* 74 F.R.D. 613, 615-17 (S.D.N.Y. 1977)), *Nutramax Laboratories Inc.,* 183 F.R.D. 458 (D. Md. 1998) (identifying multifactor test for determining when work-product doctrine does not shield discovery of documents used to prepare a witness to testify at a deposition, under Fed. R. Evid. 612). *But see Leucadia, Inc. v. Reliance Ins. Co.,* 101 F.R.D. 674, 679 (S.D.N.Y. 1983) (holding that the privilege was preserved where the witness, during her testimony, did not rely on the document reviewed).

27. DISCOVERY OF JURY CONSULTANT AND FOCUS GROUP MATERIALS AND RELATED COMMUNICATIONS

A&F, an accounting firm, and its client, Big, Inc., are co-defendants in a federal securities class action involving Big, Inc.'s alleged accounting fraud. A&F and Big have cross-claimed against each other, with Big maintaining that A&F negligently performed its audit of Big, and A&F contending that Big misled A&F's auditors. A&F has hired Dr. McGee, a jury/trial consultant, to advise on trial strategy and prepare witnesses. A&F has also conducted an abbreviated mock trial before a jury of randomly selected residents in the venue where the action is pending.

At the deposition of A&F's senior auditor, Big, Inc.'s counsel asks the witness whether he ever met with Dr. McGee and if so, to describe the substance of their communications. The lawyer also asks the witness if he had testified before a mock jury or focus group, and if so, to describe the reactions of the jury.

A&F's lawyer objects and instructs the witness not to answer on the grounds of attorney-client privilege and work- product doctrine. Big, Inc. subsequently files a request for documents seeking all reports or other documents generated by Dr. McGee in connection with his consultation for A&F, as well as all documents identifying the mock jurors. A&F objects and moves for a protective order. How should the court rule?

Comment: Litigation consultant and focus group materials and communications may be protected by the attorney work-product doctrine codified at Rule 26(b)(3). The doctrine applies to "documents and tangible things . . . prepared in anticipation of litigation or for trial by or for another party or by or for that other party's representative (including the other party's attorney, consultant, surety, indemnitor, insurer, or agent) . . . ." *Id. See generally* chapters 5 (Interrogatories—Sufficiency of Objections), 6 (Sufficiency and Supplementation of Interrogatory Answers), 8 (Document Requests—Numerosity, Propriety, Timing, and Sufficiency of Objections), 10 (Discovery of Witness Statements), and 11 (Privilege Logs). This protection is not absolute, however; a party may obtain discovery of work product upon "a showing that the party seeking discovery has substantial need of the materials in the preparation of the party's case and that the party is unable without undue hardship to obtain the substantial equivalent by other means." Even if that showing is made, however, the court, in ordering the disclosure, "shall protect against disclosure of the mental impressions, conclusions, opinions, or legal theories of an attorney or other representative of a party concerning the litigation."

On its face, the protection of Rule 26(b)(3) extends only to "documents and tangible things." However, in *Hickman v. Taylor*, 329 U.S. 495, 510-11 (1947), the Supreme Court made it clear that intangible work product is also protected:

> Proper preparation of a client's case demands that he assemble information, sift what he considers to be the relevant from the irrelevant facts, prepare his legal theories and plan his strategy without undue and needless interference. That is the historical and the necessary way in which lawyers act within the framework of our system of jurisprudence to promote justice and to protect their clients' interests. This work is reflected, of course, in interviews, statements, memoranda, correspondence, briefs, mental impressions, personal belief, and countless other tangible and intangible ways . . . roughly termed the "work product of the lawyer." Were such materials open to opposing counsel on mere demand, much of what is now put down in writing would remain unwritten. An attorney's thoughts, heretofore inviolate, would not be his own. Inefficiency, unfairness and sharp practices would inevitably develop in the giving of legal advice and in the preparation of cases for trial.

In *In re Cendant Corp. Sec. Litig.*, 343 F. 3d 658 (3d Cir. 2003), the Third Circuit ruled that Cendant was not entitled to discover the substance of conversations among appellant Ernst & Young's auditor witness, its counsel, and jury consultant. The court reasoned that these discussions were understood and intended to be confidential by all participants. In addition, counsel provided the consultant with documents that reflected counsel's mental impressions, opinions, conclusions, and legal theories. The court observed that the trial consultant's notes of the discussions might also reflect the mental impressions, opinions, conclusions, and legal theories of counsel. As a result, the court concluded that discovery of such information went "to the core of the work product doctrine and, therefore, [was] discoverable only upon a showing of extraordinary circumstances." 2003 WL 22133429, at *8. The *Cendant* court did, however, permit Cendant to ask whether the auditor witness's testimony was practiced or rehearsed with the trial consultant, but cautioned that such questioning should be circumscribed. *Id.*

Notably, *Cendant* rejected the argument that Rule 26(b)(3)'s work-product protection is superseded by Rule 26(b)(4)(B), which governs discovery of "facts known and opinions held by an expert who has been employed by another party in anticipation of litigation or preparation for trial and who is not expected to be called as a witness at trial." Although the first sentence of Rule 26(b)(3) (the protection against disclosure of the mental impressions, conclusions, opinions, or legal theories of an attorney or representative of a party) is subject to the provisions of subdivision (b)(4) of the Rule, according to the court, subdivision (b)(4) does not limit the second sentence of 23(b)(3) restricting the disclosure of work product containing mental impressions or legal theories. 2003 WL 22133429, at *6. Thus, 26(b)(3) provides work-product protection independently of Rule 26(b)(4).

It is not clear whether communications among client, attorney, and litigation consultant are protected by the attorney-client privilege. *Blumenthal v. Drudge*, 186 F.R.D. 236 (D.D.C. 1999), held that the attorney-client privilege does not protect such communications. The court reasoned that "[n]ormally, the attorney-client privilege is destroyed once information is shared with any person other than the attorney and the client because the presence of a third party is inconsistent with the client's intent that the communication remain confidential." 186 F.R.D. at 243. Although the *Blumenthal* court recognized that in some cases the privilege is extended to nonlawyers who are "employed to assist the lawyer in the rendition of professional legal services," it held that such extension must be "strictly confined within the narrowest possible limits consistent with the logic of its principle and should only occur when the communication was made in confidence for the purposes of obtaining legal advice from the lawyer." *Id.* In the end, *Blumenthal* declined to apply the attorney-client privilege because it appeared that the litigation consultant was retained "for the value of his own advice, not to assist the defendant's attorneys in providing their legal advice." *Id.*

In *United States v. Stewart*, 287 F. Supp. 2d 461 (S.D.N.Y. 2003), the defendant, Martha Stewart, had sent her daughter a copy of an e-mail that Stewart had earlier sent her attorney, giving details regarding a stock sale that was central to the government's charge of fraud against Stewart. The government argued that any attorney-client privilege was thereby waived, and that the e-mail could be used in the prosecution. The court concurred that the privilege had been waived by Stewart's sharing of the e-mail with her daughter, but held the e-mail protected from disclosure or usage by the government nonetheless on the ground of work product. The court reasoned that Stewart would not have generated the e-mail but for the prosecution, and that her daughter, though she was not her mother's lawyer, was assisting in Stewart's defense as a confidential consultant.

If communications between a party and its litigation consultant are aimed at developing a trial strategy, they might arguably be protected under *Blumenthal* because such communications are made "in confidence for the purposes of obtaining legal advice from the lawyer." In fact, in a concurring opinion in *Cendant, supra,* Judge Garth argued for the application of the attorney-client privilege to communications among Ernst & Young, its counsel, and the litigation consultant because the consultant's function was to assist counsel in the formulation of legal advice. 2003 WL 22133429, at *9 (Garth, J., concurring). Following the same logic, some commentators have observed that the function of a litigation consultant is not to provide his own advice, as found by the *Blumenthal* court, but rather to assist the client's attorneys in providing the attorneys' legal advice. *See* Davis & Beisecker, "Discovering Trial Consultant Work Product: A New Way to Borrow an Adversary's Wits?," 17 *American Journal of Trial Advocacy* 581, 626-27 (1994):

> As every trial lawyer knows, the client's communication of the facts of the case is an ongoing process, certainly continuing through the trial preparation stage. Intertwined with the client's responses to mock questions, and the consultant's reactions thereto, will inevitably be client communications of facts, concerns, fears, recollections, and even questions about alternatives, such as settlement, which are clearly for the purpose of obtaining professional services and intended by the client to be a confidential part of the relationship with counsel. Extirpating the comments of the consultant from this context may well be impossible without bringing along these communications and thus frustrating the purpose of the attorney-client privilege.

Discovery of the substance of communications of mock jurors or focus groups and their identities should also be protected, although no cases have directly addressed this issue. Commentators have observed that classifying the deliberations of mock juries or focus groups as factual or opinion work product, thereby protecting them under Rule 26(b)(3) from disclosure, could be problematic because such deliberations are "no more than impressions of outsiders, not attorney theories." Davis & Beisecker, *supra*, 17 *American Journal of Trial Advocacy* at 624. Commentators who oppose this view argue that "imbedded within the deliberations are the presentations and the arguments they contain; certainly an adversary [able to discover the substance of the deliberations] would have little difficulty inferring the contentions offered on both sides of the controversy." *Id*. Thus, the work-product protection afforded by Rule 26(b)(3) might well apply.

Apart from work-product issues, there is another reason not to permit discovery of deliberations and comments of mock jurors. They simply are not relevant and are not within the scope of permitted discovery under Rule 26(b)(1). What mock jurors and focus groups do and say could not be part of proof. Perhaps the strongest argument for any type of mock jury or focus group disclosure is that the identities of the participants must be disclosed so that opposing counsel can ensure that no mock jurors or focus group participants sit on the jury at the actual trial. The argument, of course, would be that such individuals would be biased or come to court with preconceived notions of the case. However, only to the extent that the mock jurors resided in the same venue in which the case is pending should such disclosure be considered. Further, a simple *in camera* review of the names by the court, as opposed to disclosure of the names to counsel, could ensure that no mock juror became a real juror.

28. ETHICAL CONSIDERATIONS IN REPRESENTING YOUR CORPORATE CLIENT'S EMPLOYEES IN DEPOSITION

John Smith represents Phil Burton, Inc., which manufactures curtain rods. In civil litigation initiated by stockholders, Smith is called upon to represent the company's chief operating officer (COO) in a Rule 30(b)(1) deposition noted by the plaintiffs. During the questioning, it becomes apparent to Smith that the COO engaged in conduct that could expose the company, if not the witness himself, to civil and criminal liability. Smith remains silent as the COO testifies about committing these improprieties. The deposition is suspended at the day's end and is set to resume in three weeks. Should Smith continue to represent the COO?

Comment: As Lawrence J. Fox observes in "Your Client's Employee is Being Deposed: Are You Ethically Prepared?" 29 *Litigation* No. 4 (Summer 2003) at 17, when a lawyer represents a corporation, he does not represent its employees unless such an engagement is specifically undertaken. A corporation's lawyer is duty-bound and well advised to make that absolutely clear. Even then, a join representation requires an absence of conflict between the employee and the corporation.

In the example, Smith had an ethical obligation to determine, based on his assessment of the employee's potential testimony, whether joint representation would be allowable or advisable. *See, e.g.,* Model Rule 1.7, *Conflicts of Interest.*[1] If the employee's testimony could create criminal or civil

---

1. ABA Model Rule of Professional Conduct 1.7:

    (a) Except as provided in paragraph (b), a lawyer shall not represent a client if the representation involves a concurrent conflict of interest. A concurrent conflict of interest exists if:

        (1)   the representation of one client will be directly adverse to another client; or

        (2)   there is a significant risk that the representation of one or more clients will be materially limited by the lawyer's responsibilities to another client, a former client or a third person or by a personal interest of the lawyer.

    (b) Notwithstanding the existence of a concurrent conflict of interest under paragraph (a), a lawyer may represent a client if:

        (1)   the lawyer reasonably believes that the lawyer will be able to provide competent and diligent representation to each affected client;

liability on either his part or that of the corporation, an irreconcilable conflict of interest might exist between the two. And, if that were the case, obviously Smith could not represent both. See Model Rule 1.7(b)(3). Joint representation would create a material limitation on the advice counsel could give either client.

Whether Smith could have foreseen the problem with the COO's testimony before the deposition depends partly on the witness's candor with Smith during preparation for his testimony. But, at the deposition, once Smith reasonably believed that a conflict might exist, should he have stopped the deposition then and there? Certainly, if he thought that the witness might be incriminating himself, he should have advised him of his Fifth Amendment rights (which in turn would have brought the conflict problem into bold relief). However those issues might have been resolved, by the end of the first day of deposition it was clear that the COO needed independent counsel.

There are at least two ways to avoid such difficult problems. First, right from the start, retain separate counsel for the employee for purposes of the deposition. Second, seek that lawyer's consent for corporate counsel to represent the employee in the deposition under whatever guidelines the separate counsel deems appropriate. The latter approach minimizes suspicions that might otherwise be triggered in the mind of adverse lawyer by the appearance of separate counsel on behalf of the corporate officer. It is still potentially hazardous, however, because the COO will probably remain loyal to his employer during the deposition. Corporate counsel thus may be well advised to protect the witness's interests by bringing in separate counsel who has no prospect of divided loyalties. Such a lawyer would not be subject to any criticism that his advice or instructions to the witness are tainted by the lawyer's loyalty to the company, and thus may favor the company's interests at the expense of the witness.

---

(2)   the representation is not prohibited by law;

(3)   the representation does not involve the assertion of a claim by one client against another client represented by the lawyer in the same litigation or other proceeding before a tribunal; and

(4)   each affected client gives informed consent, confirmed in writing.

29. DISCOVERY OF FOREIGN CITIZENS AND RESIDENTS

The plaintiff is a U.S. citizen, residing in New York, who occasionally makes business loans. The defendant is a citizen of Great Britain domiciled in London. Defendant approached plaintiff for a $200,000 business loan; she agreed to make the loan; and the parties entered into a loan agreement in New York. Defendant defaulted on loan repayment, and plaintiff brought suit against him in the United States District Court for the Southern District of New York. Defendant was personally served with process in New York, where he was attending a convention. He promptly retained New York counsel and then returned to England.

Defense counsel filed an answer denying liability. The court then issued its standard scheduling order which said, in part, that "this action is exempted from the disclosure requirements of Fed. R. Civ. P. 26(a)(1), 26(d) and 26(f)." Three days later defense counsel was served with Rule 33 interrogatories and Rule 34 requests for production directed to the defendant, as well as a Rule 30 notice of deposition for the defendant to appear and give testimony six weeks later at the office of plaintiff's counsel in New York. Defense counsel also received a copy of a Rule 45 subpoena duces tecum and Rule 30 notice of deposition addressed to the defendant's brother, an American citizen domiciled in London, who was not a party, but who plaintiff believed had discoverable information and documents. The subpoena had been signed by the clerk of the Southern District, was mailed by certified mail to the witness, and was returnable two months later at the American Embassy in London.

Defense counsel had no experience representing foreign-based clients in litigation, but thought the fact that his client was a British citizen living in London, and that his client's brother, though an American citizen, was also domiciled in London, might give rise to objections to American-style discovery. He decided to research the issue and raise whatever colorable objections he might find. What arguments are available to him?

Comment: The Federal Rules of Civil Procedure govern discovery against a foreign party that has been properly served, is subject to personal jurisdiction in the forum, and is located in the United States. 28 U.S.C. §§ 1331, 1332; Rules 26-37, F.R.C.P. Likewise, the Rules govern discovery in suits brought in the United States by foreign citizens. *Jack v. Trans World Airlines, Inc.* 1994 WL 90107 (N.D. Cal. 1994). The Rules also control discovery of nonparty foreign citizens who are located in the United States. *See, e.g.,* Rule 45, F.R.C.P.

The extent to which the Rules govern discovery in a suit brought against a foreign national who lives outside the United States, however, are more complex, and involve the interplay between the Rules and any discovery conventions or treaties to which the United States and the country of citizenship of the foreign national are signatories. *See, e.g.*, Rule 28(b) ("Depositions may be taken in a foreign country (1) pursuant to any applicable treaty or convention . . .").[1]

There are two principal conventions of which the United States is a member: the Hague Convention on the Taking of Evidence Abroad in Civil or Commercial Matters and the Inter-American Convention on Letters Rogatory.[2] *See generally* Robert L. Haig ed., *Business and Commercial Litigation in Federal Courts*, vol. 2, § 17.12 (West Group & ABA 1998), which contains a definitive analysis of the scope and manner of, and problems associated with, foreign depositions, and was a primary source for portions of the discussion below.

The text of the Hague Convention, 23 U.S.T. 2555, T.I.A.S. No 7444 (1970), and a list of all signatories (which includes the United Kingdom) may be found following 28 U.S.C.A. § 1781 (West). The Hague Convention facilitates the issuance of letters of request seeking production of testimony and documentary or other physical evidence. It requires each signatory to designate an authority to receive such letters from the judicial authorities of other signatories and transmit them to the domestic authorities competent to enforce their execution and compel responses. There is a big exception, however: the Hague Convention allows signatories to declare that they will not execute letters of request issued "for the purpose of obtaining pretrial discovery of documents as known in Common Law countries," *id.* at Art. 23— which would of course defeat the purpose for which they would often be issued in the first place. A number of signatories, including the United King-

---

1. A related act of questions is presented when parties seek domestic discovery under the federal rules in aid of foreign judicial proceedings. 28 U.S.C. § 1782(a). That topic is beyond the scope of this chapter. As this book was going to press, however, the Supreme Court, in *Intel Corp. v. Advanced Micro Devices, Inc.*, 124 S.Ct. 2466, 159 L. Ed. 2d 355 (2004) substantially liberalized the discretion vested in district courts to allow such discovery. That case, and cases interpreting *Intel*, should be considered when this issue arises.

2. In the absence of treaty or convention between the United States and the country at issue, letters rogatory are nonetheless available. As discussed below, however, their utility is severely limited.

dom, have made such declaration, but, of that group, some (including the United Kingdom) have allowed narrowly defined requests, proscribing only broad, indefinite inquiries.[3] *See* Haig, *supra.*

The Inter-American Convention on Letters Rogatory, 14 I.L.M. 339 (1975) (reproduced following 28 U.S.C.A. § 1781 (West)), to which there are 19 signatory countries including the United States, provides another means of international discovery. It follows the same model as the Hague Convention with certain technical differences.

Finally, in the absence of treaty or convention, letters rogatory are available. Rule 28(b)(2). These are formal requests from a court in one country to the appropriate judicial authority in another country requesting testimonial or documentary evidence. *See* United States Department of State, *Preparation of Letters Rogatory, www.travel.state.gov/letters_rogatory.* Foreign courts are under no obligation to execute letters rogatory, however, and those that do may place restrictions on them that limit their usefulness. Usually, the procedures of the foreign courts are used, which may exclude participation of U.S. counsel, and such procedures may not provide for administration of an oath or preparation of a verbatim transcript, which may limit the evidentiary value of the information obtained.

The Federal Rules of Civil Procedure provide far greater latitude in methods and range of discovery than either convention or letters rogatory. Thus the plaintiff's goal in the example should be to use the Rules to the fullest extent possible. The question is whether the Rules or the Conventions control in a case where the parties are citizens of signatory countries.

There is a wealth of case law on this subject, beginning with *Société Nationale Industrielle Aérospatiale v. United States District Court for the Southern District of Iowa*, 482 U.S. 522 (1987). In that case, the Supreme Court rejected the argument that the methods of discovery set forth in the Hague Convention were exclusive or mandatory for discovery targets who live abroad, holding that the trial court should determine the propriety of specific discovery requests "based on its knowledge of the case and of the claims and interests of the parties and the governments whose statutes and policies they invoke." *Id.* at 546. Following *Aérospatiale*, the lower courts

---

3. The Hague Convention also provides for the taking of testimony before diplomatic officers, consular agents, and specially appointed commissioners of a signatory, subject to a number of restrictions, not the least of which is that such testimony cannot be compelled. *Id.* at Arts. 15-17.

have found that a determination of which rules should apply requires analysis of the nature of the discovery sought, the sovereign interests at issue, and the likelihood that the Convention's procedures will be effective. *First Am. Corp. v. Price Waterhouse LLP*, 154 F.3d 16 (2d Cir. 1998); *Bodner v. Paribas*, 202 F.R.D. 370 (E.D.N.Y. 2000); *In re Vitamins Antitrust Litig.*, 120 F. Supp. 2d 45 (D.D.C. 2000); *In re Aircrash Disaster Near Roselawn, Indiana Oct. 31, 1994*, 172 F.R.D. 295 (N.D. Ill. 1997); *In re Benton Graphics v. Uddeholm Corp.*, 118 F.R.D. 386 (D.N.J. 1987). *Cf.* Haig, *supra.*

Generally, courts will employ the Federal Rules of Civil Procedure where the discovery requests are germane, nonintrusive and not unduly burdensome. *Bodner v. Paribas, supra at* 370; *Valois of America, Inc. v. Risdon Corp.*, 183 F.R.D. 344, 346 (D. Conn. 1997); *In re Aircrash Disaster, supra at* 308. A foreign defendant seeking to invoke the Hague Convention must identify with specificity its objections to the discovery requests served under the Rules, and bears the burden of persuading the court that the Convention, rather than the Rules, should control. *Id.*

In resisting application of the Federal Rules of Civil Procedure, a foreign defendant will sometimes invoke a "blocking statute" adopted by his country. This is a statute prohibiting or restricting imposition of civil discovery by U.S. courts abroad and imposing criminal sanctions for violation thereof. In *Société Internationale pour Participations Industrielles et Commerciales S.A. v. Rogers*, 357 U.S. 197 (1958), the Supreme Court held that a trial court erred when it dismissed a case as a sanction against the plaintiff, which had failed to comply with an order compelling discovery on the ground that to do so would have exposed plaintiff to criminal sanctions under its country's law. Following that decision, courts have considered two issues in cases presenting this conflict: (i) whether discovery should be ordered notwithstanding a conflict with foreign law, and if so, (ii) whether sanctions should be imposed for failure to comply with the discovery order. *Cochran Consulting, Inc. v. Uwatec USA, Inc.*, 102 F.3d 1224 (Fed. Cir. 1996); *Minpeco, S.A. v. Conticommodity Services, Inc.*, 116 F.R.D. 517 (S.D.N.Y. 1987).

Turning to the example, defense counsel should carefully evaluate the scope of Rule 33 and 34 discovery requests in the context of plaintiff's claim, and compare his findings with pertinent British and U.S. judicial opinions on the permissible scope of such discovery and the interplay between the Hague Convention and the Federal Rules of Civil Procedure on that point.

Assuming that the requests do not go far afield, it is likely that the Rules will be deemed to govern. *In re Aircrash, supra* at 309.

Defense counsel thus may be unable to prevent his client's deposition. If it does take place, there are two related issues. First, what is the permissible scope of the deposition? Second, where should it take place?

As to the first question, the same factors that determine the reasonableness of the Rule 33 and Rule 34 requests will determine the proper scope of the deposition.

As to the second question, the defendant may argue that it would pose a hardship for him to be deposed in the United States, and thus his deposition should be scheduled for the American Embassy in London. On this point, the defendant can note that plaintiff's counsel has, in essence, acknowledged, by issuing to the defendant's brother a nonparty subpoena returnable at the American Embassy in London, that it would be no impediment for him to travel there to take discovery. The courts have considerable discretion in deciding whether a defendant should be compelled to travel to the jurisdiction where suit was filed in order to be deposed. *In re Edelman*, 295 F.3d 171 (2d. Cir. 2002); *Custom Form Mfg., Inc. v. Omron Corp.*, 196 F.R.D. 333 (N.D. Ind. 2000).

Of course, if the defendant argues that he should be questioned in England, the plaintiff should determine whether: (a) taking the defendant's deposition in England is permissible under British law; and (b) how the courts of the two countries have resolved the question of which rules govern the conduct of the deposition—looking to decisional law applying the Hague Convention and the Federal Rules. (In that regard, *see* Rule 28(b).) The answers to these questions would affect plaintiff's response to any objection by defendant to taking the deposition in New York.

The next set of problems concerns the subpoena and notice of deposition served on the defendant's brother. Defense counsel may be able to prevent questioning based on those documents if the deposition is noticed in a foreign jurisdiction that does not permit the taking of evidence from a foreign national. *In re Bridgestone/Firestone, Inc. Tires Prod. Liab. Litig.*, 190 F. Supp. 2d 1125 (S.D. Ind. 2002); *In re Tygg-Hansa Ins. Co., Ltd.*, 896 F. Supp. 624 (E.D. La. 1995). Otherwise, there will be little to prevent the brother's testimony. Great Britain has no such restriction, and so the deposition should go forward (although counsel may be able to delay it on procedural grounds discussed below).

Title 28 U.S.C. § 1783, titled "Subpoena of person in foreign country," provides:

(a) A court of the United States may order the issuance of a subpoena requiring the appearance as a witness before it, or before a person or body designated by it, of a national or resident of the United States who is in a foreign country, or requiring the production of a specified document or other thing by him, if the court finds that particular testimony or the production of the document or other thing by him is necessary in the interest of justice, and, in other than a criminal action or proceeding, if the court finds, in addition, that it is not possible to obtain his testimony in admissible form without his personal appearance or to obtain the production of the document or other thing in any other manner.

(b) The subpoena shall designate the time and place for the appearance or for the production of the document or other thing. Service of the subpoena . . . shall be effected in accordance with the provisions of the Federal Rules of Civil Procedure relating to service of process on a person in a foreign country. The person serving the subpoena shall tender to the person to whom the subpoena is addressed his estimated necessary travel and attendance expenses, the amount of which shall be determined by the court and stated in the order directing the issuance of the subpoena.

Thus the brother, an American citizen living in England, is subject to process requiring his appearance for deposition, but the subpoena requires special findings by a court and may not simply be issued by a clerk of court under Rule 45(a)(3). Further, service of the subpoena is governed by Rule 4(f), titled "Service Upon Individuals in a Foreign Country":

Unless otherwise provided by federal law, service upon an individual from whom a waiver has not been obtained and filed, other than an infant or an incompetent person, may be effected in a place not within any judicial district of the United States:

(1) by any internationally agreed means reasonably calculated to give notice, such as those means authorized by the Hague Convention on the Service Abroad of Judicial and Extrajudicial Documents; or

(2) if there is no internationally agreed means of service or the applicable international agreement allows other means of service, provided that service is reasonably calculated to give notice:

    (A) in the manner prescribed by the law of the foreign country for service in that country in an action in any of its courts of general jurisdiction; or

    (B) as directed by the foreign authority in response to a letter rogatory or letter of request; or

    (C) unless prohibited by the law of the foreign country, by

        (i) delivery to the individual personally of a copy of the summons and the complaint; or

        (ii) any form of mail requiring a signed receipt, to be addressed and dispatched by the clerk of the court to the party to be served; or

(3) by other means not prohibited by international agreement as may be directed by the court.

Accordingly, service by certified mail—possibly the swiftest means of service under the circumstances—may or may not be acceptable. If it is not, then, as noted above, the witness may be able to delay his deposition—but ultimately, if service is properly effected, will be unable to prevent it.

Practice Tip

The subject of foreign discovery is obviously exceedingly complex and broad-ranging—the procedural and substantive issues that might arise are as varied as the number of countries in which discovery is sought. This discussion is only a starting point for research and analysis. The authorities cited here are useful tools, but when in doubt, a lawyer should not hesitate to contact the legal officer at the embassy or consulate of the country in question and ask appropriate questions.

30. USE OF ADVERSE PARTY'S DEPOSITION AT TRIAL

During his deposition, the defendant truck driver testified that his co-defendant employer was aware of his poor driving record before entrusting him with the truck; the truck driver described a conversation to that effect with his employer, a man named Weeks. The plaintiff does not want to call the driver as a trial witness because he may try to alter his testimony or explain it away. However, the plaintiff does want to get the driver's clear admission into evidence. Accordingly, at trial plaintiff's counsel does the following:

> The Court: Mr. Darrow, call your next witness, please.
>
> Mr. Darrow: Your Honor, we ask permission to read into evidence a portion of the deposition of co-defendant Hannibal Smith.
>
> Defense Counsel: I object. Mr. Smith is present in court and available to testify. Also, he is adverse to his employer—my client—on the issue of negligent entrustment and his deposition testimony on that issue cannot be admitted against my client.
>
> The Court: Plaintiff's counsel has the right to use the deposition of an opposing party for any purpose. He can read into evidence portions or all of the deposition of the driver, and this evidence can be considered as part of the plaintiff's case against both defendants. You have the right to introduce any other part of the deposition that ought, in fairness, to be considered with those portions introduced by plaintiff's counsel.
>
> Mr. Darrow: If the Court please, I read to the jury from page 38 of the defendant driver's deposition, commencing at line 3: "Mr. Weeks, president of the tire company, told me that I had too many car accidents, and if I had another accident, I would have to find another job, because he couldn't take the chance of being sued on my account."

See Sandler & Archibald, *Model Witness Examinations*, 2d ed., p 231 (ABA 2003).

Is the court's ruling correct?

Comment: Yes. In this example, plaintiff's counsel properly used the co-defendant driver's deposition testimony as substantive evidence and not just as impeachment. Thus, he has placed the burden on the defense attorney to rebut the driver's admission. He could also have used the deposition in court in other ways, such as in cross-examination of Weeks, the president of the company, to impeach him by prior inconsistent statement if he had denied, in direct examination, that he had made such a statement to his employee. *See* Rule 32; FRE 613; *Fey v. Walston & Co., Inc.*, 493 F.2d 1036 (7th Cir. 1974). In addition, the deposition testimony could also have been used as substantive evidence pursuant to FRE 801(d)(1)(A) if Smith made the statement within the scope of his employment, was available for trial, and then offered inconsistent trial testimony. Additionally, FRE 801(d)(2)(D) (admissions of party opponent) provides for the admissibility of statements, against a party, by the party's agent or employee. "Rule 801(d)(2)(A) merely renders a statement nonhearsay if it was made by the party against whom it is offered . . . the statements need neither be incriminating, inculpatory, against interest, nor otherwise inherently damaging to the declarant's case." *United States v. Reed*, 227 F.3d 763, 770 (7th Cir. 2000) *citing United States v. McGee,* 189 F.3d 626, 631-32 (7th Cir. 1999). "Rule 801(d)(2)(A) simply admits those statements made by one party, but offered as evidence by the opposing party." *United States v. Reed,* 227 F.3d 763, 770 (7th Cir. 2000).

However, the court must find that the declarant in fact was an agent of the adverse party when the statement was made before ruling the testimony admissible on that ground. *Bourjaily v. United States*, 483 U.S. 171 (1987). The statement itself may be used to determine whether it was made within the scope of employment. FRE 801(d)(2)(A). *See also, e.g., Sea-Land Serv. v. Lozen Int'l*, 285 F.3d 808 (9th Cir. 2002); *Weston-Smith v. Cooley Dickinson Hosp., Inc.,* 282 F.3d 60, 66 (1st Cir. 2002); *Albright v. Virtue*, 273 F.3d 564, 569 (3d Cir. 2001); *Yates v. Rexton, Inc.,* 267 F.3d 793, 802 (8th Cir. 2001).[1] Moreover, "[w]hile the hiring/firing/promoting/demoting decision making authority of the declarant may be critical in employment cases in which the admission deals with hiring/firing/promoting/demoting-type decisions, no similar requirement exists in other contexts. The only requirement is that the

---

1. *But note*, "The contents of the statement [of a nonparty offered as an admission against a party] shall be considered *but are not alone sufficient* to establish the declarant's authority under . . . [Rule 801(d)(2)(C) [pertaining to admissions by a party's agent], [or] the agency or employment relationship and scope thereof under subdivision (D)" (emphasis added). FRE 801(d)(2)(A). Additional evidence that might make the point includes an admission from another party representative as to the authority of the nonparty to make the statement on behalf of the party, or a document that supports either the admission or the authority of the person to make it, or comparable evidence. *See* FRE 104(a).

subject matter of the admission match the subject matter of the employee's job description." *Aliotta v. Nat'l R.R. Passenger Corp.*, 315 F.3d 756, 762 (7th Cir 2003). "It clarifies matters to consider how 'scope of employment' is defined in other tort claims. For a statement to qualify as an admission, the employee who made it need only be performing the duties of his employment when he comes in contact with the particular facts at issue." *Id.*; *Wilkinson v. Carnival Cruise Lines, Inc.*, 920 F.2d 1560, 1566-67 & n.12 (11th Cir. 1991); *see, e.g., Grayson v. Williams*, 256 F.2d 61, 66 (10th Cir. 1958). Compare *Nat'l Ass'n. for Advancement of Colored People, et al. v. State of Florida, Dept. of Corr., et al*, 122 F. Supp. 2d 1335, 1341 (M.D. Fla., 2000) (holding that "[a]ny information, communications or other evidence obtained by Plaintiff's counsel in the course of interviewing former employees of the Department may not be later used by the Plaintiff's against the Department as a binding admission for the purposes of Rule 801(d)(2)(d).").

In so holding, the court, citing to *Orlowski v. Dominick's Finer Foods, Inc.*, 937 F. Supp. 723, 730 (N.D. Ill. 1996), stated that it "does not intend the prohibition to be interpreted as a blanket prohibition of the use of such information as evidence. Simply, the Plaintiffs may not consider former employees as 'non-parties' for the purposes of ethical rules, but later assert that the former employees are 'parties' for the purpose of making a binding admission against the interests of the Department."

The easiest way to keep these rules straight is to remember the interplay between Rule 32(a) (2), which allows admissions made in deposition into evidence against the party that made the admission, and FRE 801(d)(2), which enumerates five types of admissions, each of which, if memorialized in a deposition, can be introduced as substantive evidence under Rule 32(a)(2). These are: (1) the party's own statement in an individual or representative capacity (FRE 801(d)(2)(A)); (2) the statement made by a third party but adopted by the party as his own (FRE 801(d)(2)(B)); (3) the statement of a person authorized by the party to make statements on the party's behalf (FRE 801(d)(2)(C)); (4) the statement of an agent, servant, or employee of a party made while employed and within the scope of the employee's job responsibilities (FRE 801(d)(2)(D)); and (5) the statement of a co-conspirator made during the conspiracy and in furtherance thereof (FRE 801(d)(2)(E)). In sum, under FRE 801(d)(2), there are four distinct circumstances in which the statements of a nonparty are deemed to be the admission of a party, and if any of these "vicarious admissions" are memorialized in a deposition, they may be used as substantive evidence against the party at trial without the need to demonstrate the unavailability of the declarant.

Counsel should also bear in mind FRE 801(d)(1)(A), which provides that if a person testifies in a deposition and later is called as a witness at trial and testifies inconsistently with the deposition testimony, it is admissible as substantive evidence. Thus, in the example, if plaintiff's counsel had elected to call the employee as a witness at trial to testify as to the statement of Weeks, the company president, and the employee denied that Weeks had made it, the deposition testimony would have been admissible as substantive evidence to prove Weeks' admission under FRE 801(d)(1)(A). The distinction between FRE 801(d)(1)(A) and 801(d)(2) is that under the former, the person deposed must also testify at trial, inconsistently with her prior deposition testimony. Under the latter, if the deposition testimony of a nonparty qualifies as a vicarious admission of a party, it is admissible into evidence against the party regardless of whether the deponent is called to testify at trial. *See* Sandler & Archibald, *Model Witness Examinations*, 2d ed., pp. 231-32 (ABA 2003).

31. USE AT TRIAL OF DEPOSITION OF UNAVAILABLE WITNESS

Defense Counsel: Your Honor, at this point defendants would like to read in evidence the deposition of James McCullough. Mr. McCullough, whose deposition was taken last April, is now in Lewiston, Maine, a distance greater than 100 miles from this court-house. We are prepared to present evidence to this effect, if that is necessary.

The Court: Is there any dispute as to the location of the witness?

Plaintiff's Counsel: No, Your Honor, but I object to counsel's effort to use the deposition in lieu of live testimony. When he took Mr. McCullough's deposition, there was no indication that he would not be available for trial. Had I known that would be the case, I would have conducted my deposition cross-examination in a far different fashion.

The Court: Objection overruled. Counsel, you may proceed.

Defense Counsel: Thank you, Your Honor. I ask that my co-counsel, Mr. Ames, take the witness stand. I will read the questions asked of Mr. McCullough during his deposition and Mr. Ames will read Mr. McCullough's answers. Your Honor, will you explain to the jury the nature and effect of a deposition?

The Court: Very well. (Court explains nature and effect of a deposition; how it is taken; the fact that it is evidence just as if McCullough were personally on the witness stand.)

Counsel then reads the questions and co-counsel reads the answers.

Was the court correct in overruling plaintiff's objection to the testimony? *See* Sandler & Archibald, *Model Witness Examinations*, 2d ed., p. 231 (ABA 2003).

Comment: Yes. Rule 32(a)(3)(B) provides that the deposition of a witness may be used by any party for any purpose if the court finds "that the witness is at a greater distance than 100 miles from the place of trial or hearing, or is out of the United States, unless it appears that the absence of the witness was procured by the party offering the deposition." *See Tatman v. Collins*, 938 F.2d 509 (4th Cir. 1991); *Jauch v. Corley*, 830 F.2d 47 (5th Cir. 1987); *cf. Rosebud Sioux Tribe v. A & P Steel, Inc.*, 733 F.2d 509 (8th Cir.) (reading of deposition into evidence constituted an unfair manipulation of the rules of evidence when unavailability of witness was due to invocation of Fifth Amendment), *cert. denied*, 469 U.S. 1072 (1984).

Rule 32(a)(3) provides other exceptions that allow for use of a deposition at trial as affirmative evidence: (a) the death of the witness; (b) age, illness, infirmity, or imprisonment; (c) the witness's avoidance of subpoena; or (d) some other exceptional circumstance exists as to make it desirable, in the interest of justice, to allow the deposition to be used. Rule 32(a)(3). The burden is on the proponent of the deposition testimony to establish the exception. *Allgeier v. United States,* 909 F. 2d 869, 876 (6th Cir., 1990). *See also Frazier v. Forgione,* 881 F. Supp. 879, 880 (W.D.N.Y. 1995). Therefore, "in considering the use of depositions at a trial or hearing, . . . the problem has two aspects. First, the conditions set forth in Rule 32(a) must exist before the deposition can be used at all. *See* Appendix 1. Second . . . it must be determined whether the matters contained in it are admissible under the rules of evidence." *Kolb v. Suffolk County,* 109 F.R.D. 125, 127 (E.D.N.Y. 1985) citing Wright, Miller & Marcus, *Federal Practice and Procedure* § 2142 at 159 (2d ed. 1994).

Moreover, to successfully invoke the exception (assuming that the evidence is otherwise admissible), the proponent must show the court that efforts have been made to secure the witness's attendance: "[T]o establish the unavailability as predicate for the admission of depositions, Federal Rule of Evidence 804(a)(5) requires an attempt to secure the presence of a witness by 'process or other reasonable means.'" *United States v. Aguilar-Tamayo,* 300 F.3d 562, 565 (5th Cir. 2002). *Accord, In re Warmus,* 276 B.R. 688 (S.D. Fla. 2002) (holding that trustee must exercise "appropriate diligence" to ensure witness's presence at trial and that service of subpoena, alone, was insufficient to prove this); *Clay v. Buzas,* 208 F.R.D. 636 (holding that where employer had sufficient motive and opportunity in a prior case to develop deponent's testimony, plaintiff could use prior depositions of other employees alleging sexual harassment by the employer, but that she would have to establish the deponents' unavailability for trial).

In dealing with the evidentiary aspect of the use of depositions, the key rules to consult are FRE 804(a), which identifies five circumstances in which a deponent may be "unavailable" at trial and FRE 804(b)(1), the "prior testimony" exception to the hearsay rule. FRE 804(b)(1) permits introduction into evidence of a prior deposition of a witness unavailable at trial if two conditions are met: (a) the party against whom the deposition testimony is offered must be the same party as (or a successor in interest to) the party in the action in which the deposition was taken, and (b) that party must have had the same motive and opportunity at the time the deposition was taken to develop the testimony of the witness that it has to develop this same witness's' testimony at trial.

At one time, a distinction was drawn between trial depositions and discovery depositions. That is no longer the case. Most courts hold that discovery depositions, like trial depositions, may be used at trial against an unavailable witness. *See Battle v. Mem'l Hosp.*, 228 F.3d 544, 551 (5th Cir. 2000) (nothing prevents the use of a discovery [as opposed to a trial] deposition at trial, particularly against the party who conducted it); *Savoie v. Lafourche Boat Rentals, Inc.*, 627 F. 2d 722, 724 (5th Cir. 1980); and *Spangler v. Sears, Roebuck and Co.*, 138 F.R.D. 122, 123 (S.D. Ind. 1991) ("Thus, while a party may not propound interrogatories, submit requests for admissions, seek production of documents or things or seek to amend its pleadings based on newly discovered materials after the discovery cut-off, a party may still prepare for trial by taking the depositions of witnesses whose unavailability for trial is anticipated.").

Two final points should be noted. First, lawyers should be attuned to the formalities of in-court procedure. When a deposition of an unavailable witness is introduced into evidence and read to the jury, it is customary for counsel to request, and for the court to give, an explanatory comment to the jury to the effect that the deposition testimony is equivalent to "live" testimony from a witness at trial. For that reason, the deposition transcript should not be marked as an exhibit, nor should it be given to the jury—because a transcript of in-court testimony would not be handled that way.

Second, subject to the court's discretion, counsel has several choices in how to use the deposition at trial in addition to simply reading it to the jury. It can be presented by video or, alternatively, the lawyer can have an associate sit in the witness box and play the role of the deponent answering the lawyer's questions. Either of these techniques may be preferable to the lawyer or clerk reading the transcript, which can become an exercise that risks losing the jury's attention. *See* Sandler & Archibald, *Model Witness Examinations*, 2d ed., p. 233 (ABA 2003).

32. USE OF DEPOSITION FOR IMPEACHMENT AT TRIAL

Ms. Smith, a party in a lawsuit, gave testimony at trial that was inconsistent with her prior deposition testimony. Opposing counsel wanted to use her deposition transcript to impeach her. In developing his impeachment and dramatizing the difference between her present and former testimony, the lawyer asked a series of preliminary questions. Smith's lawyer objected to each of these preliminary questions on the grounds that it was not relevant to the impeachment and unfairly distracted the jury. The objections were overruled by the bench. The colloquy (with the court's rulings omitted) was as follows:

Q: Miss Smith, do you recall that you were summoned to appear in my office over one year ago?

A: I do.

Q: You remember coming to the office with your lawyer?

Smith's Attorney: Objection.

A: Of course.

Q: And we sat down at a table in my library, and a court reporter was there who took down questions that I asked you and your answers to those questions?

Smith's Attorney: Objection.

A: I remember that.

Q: The testimony was recorded by the court reporter then just as it is being recorded today, except there was no judge or jury present, is that correct?

Smith's Attorney: Objection.

A: Correct.

Q: And you were under oath then just as you are now?

Smith's Attorney: Objection.

A: Yes, I was.

Q: The lawyer who accompanied you to my office is the same lawyer who represents you today, is that right?

Smith's Attorney: Objection.

A:. That's true.

Q: And when you finished your deposition, your testimony was typed up by the court reporter word for word as you gave it, and it was submitted to you to read and to correct any mistakes, isn't that true?

Smith's Attorney: Objection.

A: It was.

Q: Did you in fact read your deposition?

Smith's Attorney: Objection.

A. I did.

Q: You found some mistakes in the transcript, didn't you?

Smith's Attorney: Objection.

A: Right.

Q: And you made notes of the corrections you felt had to be made, didn't you?

Smith's Attorney: Objection.

A: I made notes.

Q: And then you signed your deposition as corrected by you before a Notary Public, isn't that true?

Smith's Attorney: Objection.

A: True enough.

Q: Miss Smith, I am now going to read to you beginning at line 7 on page 81 of the transcript of your deposition testimony as typed by the court reporter and corrected by you: "Q: What color was the traffic light at the time of the collision?" "A: Green."

Now, Miss Smith, what I have just read was your testimony under oath on April 14, 2000, wasn't it?

A: I can't remember what I said at that time, but I suppose that what you read is what I said then, if that's what it says.

Q: Well, you are not suggesting that what I read was anything but your previous testimony, are you?

A:. No, I am not.

Q: Now, is your testimony today correct under oath, or was your testimony correct as you gave it in April 2000?

A: I'm testifying now to the best of my recollection.

Should Smith's counsel's objections have been sustained?

Comment: No. On cross-examination counsel has the right to pose detailed questions to illustrate the significance of the deposition and to emphasize the subsequent inconsistent testimony at trial. *See generally* Rule 32(a); *Aetna Cas. & Sur. Co. v. Guynes,* 713 F.2d 1187 (5th Cir. 1983) (previous deposition testimony used to impeach trial witness testimony); *Shearing v.*

Iolab Corp., 975 F.2d 1541 (Fed. Cir. 1992) (at trial, attempted impeachment of witnesses occurred when they had recollections that had not been mentioned in previous depositions); *Coletti v. Cudd Pressure Control*, 165 F.3d 767, 774 (10th Cir. 1999). *But see New Mexico Sav. & Loan Ass'n v. United States Fid. & Guar. Co.*, 454 F.2d 328, 336 (10th Cir. 1972) (party may not introduce deposition testimony as substantive evidence or to impeach when witness merely cannot remember facts to which the witness previously testified).

To be sure, counsel endeavoring to impeach the witness could have employed a less detailed approach by using the transcript simply to remind the witness that she had testified in deposition contrary to her trial testimony. That might go as follows:

Q: Miss Smith you just testified that you saw the infant touch the screen door and fall?

A: That's right.

Q: But you testified over a year ago in your deposition that you were, and I quote, "at the time of the incident in another room looking after my little boy?"

Q: I might have said that.

Interrogating Counsel: No further questions.

See Herbert J. Stern, *Trying Cases to Win, Cross-Examination* (John Wiley & Sons 1993); Sandler & Archibald, *Model Witness Examinations*, 2d ed., pp. 228-30 (ABA 2003).

The virtue of the longer, more detailed approach, in contrast to the second, shorter technique, is jury appeal. The jury may not readily understand the shorthand reference to the prior deposition. A lawyer usually will want to ask the more detailed litany of questions to let the jury know the significance of the deposition, the conditions under which it was taken and recorded, and to emphasize the subsequent inconsistent trial testimony.

An ultimate impeaching question is optional: "Now, is your testimony today correct under oath, or was your testimony correct as you gave it in April 2000?" Some lawyers ask this to dramatize the inconsistency between the two versions and the witness's likely unreliability. Others prefer to end by simply identifying the inconsistency, saving for closing argument an explanation of the significance of the inconsistency. The advantage of the first approach is that it is more dramatic and may have a greater impact on the jury. Its potential weakness is that the witness, when confronted with a question that amounts to "Are you lying now, or were you lying then?" may persuasively explain the inconsistency, or even appear sympathetic. *See* FRE 613.

Practice Tip

An attorney attempting to impeach the witness through use of a prior inconsistent oral or written statement should bear in mind that such impeachment requires that: (a) the prior statement be inconsistent; (b) the inconsistency relate to a relevant subject; and (c) there be compliance with the rule requiring disclosure of the prior statement to opposing counsel upon request, as well as the opportunity for explanation or denial. *Firemen's Fund Ins. Co. v. Thien,* 8 F.3d 1307 (8th Cir. 1993); *United States v. Rogers,* 549 F.2d 490 (8th Cir. 1976), *cert. denied,* 431 U.S. 918 (1977); *United States v. Strother,* 49 F.3d 869, 874 (2d Cir. 1995). Also, be aware that the prior statement generally is offered only for its impeachment value, that is, simply to diminish the credibility of the trial testimony of the witness. Under FRE 801(d)(1)(A), however, the witness's inconsistent deposition testimony is admissible substantively as well. Thus, in the example, if the lawyer examining Ms. Smith must prove that the light was green at the time of the collision (as she testified in her deposition—but denied on direct examination), her deposition testimony may be introduced both to impeach her trial testimony by prior inconsistent statement and as substantive evidence that the light was green.

Section 3

Experts

Experts **3**

OVERVIEW

Planning for expert discovery requires a sound understanding of the evidentiary basis for such testimony. FRE 702 governs the admissibility of expert testimony in federal litigation. Expert testimony is admissible if the witness is qualified by his or her expertise to render an opinion on the matter at issue in the case, and such opinion testimony will assist the judge or jury in understanding the evidence or in determining a fact in issue. The requirements for such testimony are that: (1) the expert's opinion must be based on sufficient facts or data; (2) it must be based on methods or principles that are reliable; and (3) the application of the methods or principles to the facts of the case must be reliable. In planning discovery relating to experts, counsel must be fully familiar not only with FRE 702, but with FRE 703, 704, and 705 as well. In addition, counsel should know and understand the import of *Daubert v. Merrell Dow Pharm., Inc.,* 509 U.S. 579 (1993); *Kumho Tire v. Carmichael,* 526 U.S. 137 (1996); and the principal cases that follow them in the jurisdiction where the litigation is pending.

Disclosure requirements relating to the use of experts are also critical. Rule 26(a)(2)(B) requires, except as otherwise stipulated by the parties or directed by the court, that a party shall make comprehensive disclosures regarding "a witness who was retained or specially employed to provide expert testimony in the case, or whose duties as an employee of the party regularly involved giving expert testimony." Rule 26(a)(2)(B) also mandates the issuance of a written report signed by the expert that contains: (1) a complete statement of all opinions to be expressed, and the basis or reasons therefor; (2) the data or other information considered by the witness in forming opinions; (3) any exhibits to be used as a summary of or support for the opinions to be expressed; (4) the qualifications of the witness, including a list of publications authored within the last 10 years; (5) the compensation received for the study and testimony performed; and (6) a list of any other cases in which the witness has provided expert testimony, either in trial or in deposition, for the preceding four years.

One tactical consideration that always arises is whether it is even advisable to conduct the deposition of the opposing experts. Although Rule 26(b)(4) authorizes such discovery, a deposition may enable the expert to expand the scope of his testimony beyond his original opinion. *See* Rule 26(a)(2)(B), and discussion *infra* at chapter 36 (Taking the Expert's Deposition—The Basics); *see also* chapter 34 (Timing and Supplementation of Expert Disclosures), *infra*.

The chapters in this section address some of the difficult issues that frequently arise with the discovery of experts: whether draft reports are discoverable; the timing of expert depositions; the reasonableness of fees charged by the adverse expert; the supplementation of expert disclosures; the discovery of privileged documents and oral communications with experts; issues relating to "hybrid" fact/expert witnesses; and expert discovery and its relationship to *Daubert* and succeeding cases.

33. THE TIMING OF AN EXPERT DEPOSITION

The plaintiffs sued the architect who designed their new house, alleging professional negligence in the specifications for the foundation and basement. They claimed that the frame of the house had to be torn down during construction and the foundation and basement redesigned due to his poor performance. The complaint did not identify, however, the specific design flaws or the precise breach of professional standards that caused the damages. With the complaint, the plaintiffs served a notice of deposition of the defendant architect, scheduling it for 10 days after the response to the complaint was due.

Defense counsel telephoned plaintiff's counsel and told her that he would not produce the architect for deposition until the plaintiffs and their expert witness had been deposed. "Your complaint doesn't say exactly what my client did wrong, and until I know your theory of the case and have deposed your client and your client's expert, I am not going to expose my client to interrogation." Plaintiff's counsel filed a motion to compel defendant's deposition under Rule 37(a)(2)(B). How should the court rule?

Comment: The starting point for the resolution of this problem is Rule 26(d), which provides that "[e]xcept in categories of proceedings exempted from initial disclosure under Rule 26(a)(1)(E), or when authorized under these rules or by order or agreement of the parties, a party may not seek discovery from any source before the parties have conferred as required by Rule 26(f)." Rule 26(f), in turn, provides that "[e]xcept in categories of proceedings exempted from initial disclosure under Rule 26(a)(1)(E) or when otherwise ordered, the parties must, as soon as practicable and in any event at least 21 days before a scheduling conference is held or a scheduling order is due under Rule 16(b), confer to consider the nature and basis of their claims and defenses and the possibilities for a prompt settlement or resolution of the case, to make or arrange for the disclosures required by Rule 26(a)(1), and to develop a proposed discovery plan. . . ."

Thus, unless it is subject to an exception under Rule 26(d), the defendant architect's deposition would be premature before the mandated conference. One exception is Rule 26(a)(1)(E), which exempts certain categories of actions from the proscriptive portions of Rule 26(d), but a professional negligence claim is not among them. A more significant exception is the portion of the rule that allows changes in the order of discovery "when authorized under these rules or by order," meaning either an order of the judge handling the case or a local court rule that supplements the requirements of Rule 26.

In the District of Maryland, for example, Local Rule 104.4(b) provides that "[i]n actions in which Fed. R. Civ. P. 26(a)(1) does not apply, discovery shall not commence until a scheduling order has been entered unless otherwise ordered by the Court or agreed to by the parties." (Local Rule 104.4(a) provides that in action in which Rule 26(a)(1) applies, discovery shall not commence until after the mandated disclosures, which typically follow entry of the scheduling order.) The practical effect of this rule is to stay all discovery until after entry of the scheduling order. This means that the basis for the plaintiff's claim will have to be disclosed before discovery, eliminating the concern expressed by the defendant in the example that he might be subject to interrogation without notice of the elements of the claim against him and without the opportunity to depose his adversary's expert first.

In addition to consulting the local rules, it is also instructive to review the discovery guidelines that explain and interpret the local rules. Using the District of Maryland again as an example, Appendix A to the Local Rules, titled "Discovery Guidelines of the United States District Court for the District of Maryland," provides that "[c]ompliance with these Guidelines will be considered by the Court in resolving discovery disputes, including whether sanctions should be awarded pursuant to Fed. R. Civ. P. 37." Such guidelines come very close to having the force of law. Of relevance here is Guideline 4, titled "Scheduling Depositions," which provides that "[a]ttorneys are expected to make a good faith effort to coordinate deposition dates with opposing counsel, parties, and non-party deponents, prior to noting a deposition." The Discovery Guidelines of the United

States District Court for the Northern District of Ohio state that "parties are encouraged to cooperate with each other in arranging and conducting discovery . . ." and that "[c]ounsel are expected to make a timely and good faith effort to confer and agree to schedules for the taking of depositions." The Discovery Guidelines of the United States District Court for the Northern District of Georgia provide that "[a]ny party who desires to use the testimony of an expert witness shall designate the expert sufficiently early in the discovery period to permit the opposing party the opportunity to depose the expert and, if desired, to name its own expert witness sufficiently in advance of the close of discovery so that a similar discovery deposition of the second expert might also be conducted prior to the close of discovery."

Applying these rules to the example, it is obvious that the architect's deposition was noticed improperly and too early by plaintiff's counsel. No Rule 26(f) conference had been held; no scheduling order had been issued; and plaintiff's counsel had not conferred in good faith with defense counsel in trying to reach a mutually agreeable date for the architect's interrogation. While all of this is clear, was defense counsel also entitled under the rules to (a) refuse to produce his client when commanded by the notice of deposition, and (b) insist that he be able to take the depositions of the plaintiff and the plaintiff's expert before producing his client?

In *Keller v. Edwards,* 206 F.R.D. 412 (D. Md. 2002), the case on which the example is based, the court confronted just this situation. It noted that a party served with "a valid notice of deposition" may not simply refuse to produce his client until certain conditions are fulfilled. Instead, he must bring his concerns to the court in a motion for protective order under Rule 26(c) (having first sought to resolve his differences with opposing counsel as mandated by the Discovery Guidelines). In this case, however, given the defect in the notice and timing of the deposition, the architect could not have been compelled to attend even if he had decided to forego the expense of seeking a protective order under Rule 26(c) and simply not appeared. Nonetheless, a cautious defense counsel would both (a) attempt to negotiate an agreeable date for his client's deposition, and (b) move for a protective order notwithstanding the additional expense.

The court then proceeded, under Rules 26(b)(2) and 26(c)(1-3), which empower the court to resolve issues regarding the sequence and timing of depositions, to consider when, and under what circumstances, the deposition of a defendant sued for professional malpractice should take place.

[T]he answer to the question of whether a medical malpractice defendant should be deposed before the plaintiff and her expert witness, or vice versa, depends on the circumstances of each case. Factors that influence the decision include: (a) the specificity of the allegations of negligence in the pleadings . . . (b) the complexity of the claim; (c) the number of defendants sued, and how clearly it may be determined what each allegedly did that was negligent; (d) whether formal or informal discovery already has taken place that informs the defendant of the factual basis for the claims; (e) the presence or absence of articulable prejudice to either the plaintiff or the defendant by delaying the deposition of the defendant until after the plaintiff and her standard of care expert have been deposed; and (f) the plaintiff's need to obtain sufficient information from the defendant to enable plaintiff's expert witness to prepare complete Rule 26(a)(2)(B) disclosures. It is the obligation of counsel when filing either a motion to compel the defendant's deposition, or a motion for a protective order to prevent it, to bring to the court's attention relevant facts to address these factors. 206 F.R.D. at 416-17.

In the end, the court held that the sparse information in the complaint entitled the defendant physician to defer his deposition until there was a full response to the following interrogatory: "If you contend that the Defendant, Dr. Edwards, violated the applicable standard of care in connection with his treatment of Mr. Keller, then state with particularity the facts on which you intend to rely to support this claim." Dr. Edwards's deposition did not have to await the deposition of the plaintiff and the plaintiff's expert, however; there was no apparent prejudice from having defendant's deposition proceed first, assuming a satisfactory response to the interrogatory just described.

In general, the current rules of discovery procedure largely eliminate the horse race that once took place among counsel to be the first to issue discovery. The present rules place a premium on communication and cooperation to resolve, without judicial intervention, the sequence and timing of discovery. If there is an irreconcilable dispute between the parties, the court can step in. Finally, the party who notices an adverse expert's deposition before that party's own expert has been noticed for deposition will ordinarily be entitled to a priority assuming there is no prejudice to the other side.

34. TIMING AND SUPPLEMENTATION OF EXPERT DISCLOSURES

The plaintiff, a resident of one state, brought suit in federal court against her internist, who lived in a neighboring state, for medical malpractice. The plaintiff alleged that the defendant had failed to diagnose her colon cancer early enough to enable her to have surgery that could have successfully removed the cancerous growth. She further claimed that surgery was no longer possible, so that she was left with less effective treatments and a diminished life expectancy. The defendant answered, denying liability. The court issued a scheduling order on February 1, requiring the plaintiff to make her Rule 26(a)(2)(B) expert witness disclosure within 30 days. The defendant, in turn, was required to make his expert disclosure within 30 days thereafter. June 25 was set as the discovery cutoff date.

Plaintiff filed her Rule 26(a)(2)(B) expert disclosure on March 1. Her expert's opinion was that the defendant had breached the standard of care by failing to administer certain tests that would have detected the cancer long before the plaintiff became symptomatic. The disclosure further stated that there was a substantial probability that plaintiff could have undergone surgery that would have removed all of the cancerous growth had the diagnosis been timely made.

Defendant timely filed his Rule 26(a)(2)(B) expert disclosure. The defense expert expressed the opinion that there was no negligence because the tests that the plaintiff's expert said should have been done were appropriate only if there had been a positive response to certain preliminary tests. Those preliminary tests were negative, however, and so no further tests were indicated.

Plaintiff's expert was deposed on June 15. He repeated the opinion that was disclosed in plaintiff's Rule 26(a)(2)(B) report. On June 20, defendant's expert was deposed. During his testimony, he provided information supporting his opinions that undermined the credibility of plaintiff's expert.

On June 30, five days after the discovery cutoff, plaintiff's expert wrote to plaintiff's counsel. He advised that he had read the transcript of the defense expert witness and had looked again at the medical records. Based on that review, he had concluded that the defendant had violated the standard of care in a second way. Specifically, once the cancer had been detected, plaintiff's internist had failed to recommend an aggressive course of radiation and chemotherapy, resulting in a further delay and making successful intervention impossible. In the opinion of plaintiff's expert, this second breach of the standard of care was independent of the failure to perform tests. He said that it caused a reduction in plaintiff's life expectancy from 10 years to just a few months.

Plaintiff's counsel was preoccupied with another trial when he received the letter, and did not get around to sending a copy to defense counsel until July 30. In his cover letter, plaintiff's counsel advised that at the pretrial conference, scheduled for the following week, he would move to amend the pretrial order to add the new opinion listed in the June 30 letter. He also planned to ask the judge to allow plaintiff's expert to express his additional opinions at the trial, scheduled to start two weeks later. Defense counsel wrote back immediately, objecting to the intended course of action and protesting the eleventh-hour surprise. How should the judge rule?

Comment: Unless the trial judge finds that the late disclosure of an additional opinion from plaintiff's expert was substantially justified (or that its timing did not harm the defendant), the court should not allow the new opinion to be introduced. This result comes from the interplay of the disclosure requirements of Rule 26(a)(2), the supplementation requirements of Rule 26(e), and the sanctions provisions in Rule 37.

Rule 26(a)(2)(C) requires that pretrial disclosures, including expert disclosures, must be made at times and in a sequence directed by the court, usually in a scheduling order. Absent court direction or a stipulation by the parties, Rule 26(a)(2)(C) provides that expert disclosures must be made not later than 90 days before trial or the date the case is to be ready for trial. However, if the expert evidence is intended solely to contradict or rebut evidence from an adverse party on the same subject, the rebuttal disclosure must be made within 30 days after receipt of the disclosure that is to be rebutted.

Rule 26(e) governs the supplementation of previously disclosed information, including expert disclosures. It states that a party that previously made a discovery disclosure is under a duty to supplement or correct that disclosure to include after-acquired evidence: (a) if ordered to do so by the court; or (b) at "appropriate intervals" upon learning that the earlier disclosure was in some material way incomplete or incorrect, unless the required corrective information has not otherwise been made known to the adverse parties during discovery or in writing.

As for the expert disclosures required by Rule 26(a)(2)(B), in addition to supplementing the written report as required by Rule 26(e), the party sponsoring the expert must supplement information provided in the expert's deposition. Finally, Rule 26(e)(1) states that any supplementation to expert disclosures or deposition testimony must be made not later than the deadline for Rule 26(a)(3) pretrial disclosures of trial witnesses and exhibits, which is 30 days before trial unless otherwise ordered by the court.

Rule 37(c) excludes from use at trial, hearings, or in support of any motions, any information that a party failed to disclose or supplement under Rule 26(a) or 26(e) if the failure is "without substantial justification." Wright, Miller & Marcus, *Federal Practice and Procedure: Civil*, 2d ed., § 2289.1 (1994). Even if the failure to disclose was substantially justified, the proffered evidence nonetheless must be excluded unless it is harmless to the adverse party.

The Advisory Committee notes to Rule 37 reflect that the exclusionary sanction imposed by Rule 37(c) "provides a strong inducement for disclosure of material that the disclosing party would expect to use as evidence, whether at trial, at a hearing, or on a motion. . . ." 146 F.R.D. 691. The commentary further clarifies that the sanction in Rule 37(c) is "a self-executing sanction for failure to make a disclosure required by Rule 26(a), without the need for a motion [to compel production] under [Rule] . . . [37](a)(2)(A)." *Id.* The commentary adds, however, that "[l]imiting the automatic sanction to violations 'without substantial justification,' coupled with the exception for violations that are 'harmless,' is needed to avoid unduly harsh penalties." *Id.*

Courts have struggled to define "substantial justification" and "harmless error." Various formulas have been suggested to determine when to exclude expert testimony that has not been disclosed in accordance with the Rules. For example, in *Rambus v. Infineon Technologies AG*, 145 F. Supp. 2d 721 (E.D. Va. 2001) the district court adopted a five-factor test, first stated in an unpublished Fourth Circuit opinion, for applying the automatic exclusion in Rule 37(c).[1] The factors are: (1) the surprise to the party against whom the witness was to have testified; (2) the ability of the party against whom the expert will testify to cure the surprise; (3) the extent to which allowing the

---

1. Burlington Ins. Co. v. Shipp, 215 F.3d 1317 (table), 2000 WL 62037 (4th Cir. May 15, 2000).

testimony would disrupt the trial; (4) the explanation for the party's failure to name the expert, or disclose the opinion, before trial; and (5) the importance of the testimony to the sponsoring party. *Id.* at 726. The *Rambus* factors recently were adopted by the Fourth Circuit in *Southern States Rack and Fixture, Inc. v. Sherwin Williams, Inc.*, 318 F.3d 592 (4th Cir. 2003).

Other courts have used similar, but slightly different, factors: *Woodworker's Supply, Inc. v. Principal Mut. Life Ins. Co.*, 170 F.3d 985, 993 (10th Cir. 1999) (adopting the following test under Rule 37(c): (1) the prejudice/surprise to the party against whom the expert will testify; (2) the ability to cure the prejudice/surprise; (3) the disruption to the trial in introducing the testimony; and (4) the moving party's bad faith or willfulness); and *United States v. $9,041,598.68*, 163 F.3d 238 (5th Cir. 1998) (adopting the following test under Rule 37(c): (1) the importance of the witness's testimony; (2) the prejudice to the opposing party of allowing the witness to testify; (3) the possibility of curing the prejudice with a continuance of the trial; and (4) the explanation, if any, for the failure to identify the witness [or disclose the information]).

Regardless of the precise formula used, the inquiry essentially is the same. Courts will focus on the importance of the expert's testimony; the surprise or prejudice to the party against whom the expert will testify; whether this can be cured before trial (either in the time remaining before trial, or by continuing the trial); the disruption, if any, to the trial by allowing the testimony; the reason why the required disclosure was not made; and any aggravating factors underlying the failure to disclose, such as bad faith or willfulness.

Applying these factors to the example, it is clear that the additional opinion of plaintiff's expert is both important to the plaintiff's case and prejudicial to that of the defendant. Moreover, coming long after the discovery cutoff, with only two weeks remaining before trial, disclosure of the new opinion would impose a considerable burden on the defendant both to depose plaintiff's expert about the new opinions and attempt to develop rebuttal evidence. And, while courts sometimes order last minute discovery as a way to cure such problems, it exacts a high penalty from counsel, who are otherwise busy preparing for trial; and it may entail additional, substantial expense. Whether the court would grant a continuance of the trial to allow the defendant additional discovery might depend on whether the case has been postponed before, the extent of the disruption and cost of doing so, and the persuasiveness of the explanation given by plaintiff's counsel for the belated disclosure. If the court determines that plaintiff's counsel was negligent or purposeful in trying to surprise the defendant, it is likely that a continuance would not be granted and that the expert's supplemental opinion would be deemed inadmissible.

Practice Tip

This example illustrates the importance of complying with the deadlines for making expert disclosures under Rule 26(a)(2) and promptly supplementing them in accordance with Rule 26(e). The price tag for failing to do so, absent substantial justification and prejudice to the opposing party, is the harsh sanction of exclusion of the expert's testimony. That could be fatal to the case of the party that ignored the disclosure/supplementation requirements of the rules.

---

35. EXPERT DISCLOSURES—TREATING PHYSICIAN OR OTHER HYBRID FACT/EXPERT WITNESS

Mike Adams, a citizen of Maryland, was injured by a truck owned by the Coastal Commercial Trucking Company, a Delaware company based in Virginia. He retained a lawyer who brought suit on his behalf in federal court. The complaint alleged that Adams suffered permanent injury and loss of past and future income, as well as physical and emotional pain and suffering.

In response to the defendant's interrogatories asking for the identity of persons with knowledge of facts relevant to the damages claimed by Adams, his attorney identified Robert Burke, M.D., the orthopedic surgeon who treated Adams after the accident. Shortly after the deadline for filing the plaintiff's Rule 26(a)(2)(B) expert disclosures had passed, defense counsel called plaintiff's counsel and advised that he would be filing a motion to preclude any trial testimony by Dr. Burke because the plaintiff had not provided the information required by Rule 26(a)(2)(B) for Dr. Burke. *See* chapter 34, *supra*. Plaintiff's counsel countered that no disclosure was required because Burke was a treating physician—that is, a fact witness—and that he should be allowed to testify at trial. How should the court resolve this dispute?

Comment: Plaintiff's counsel is correct. If the factual basis for the trial testimony that Dr. Burke would give comes from his treatment of the plaintiff and is not information Burke learned outside of his role as a treating physician, the plaintiff is required to provide only the doctor's name under Rule 26(a)(2)(A).

Rule 26(a)(2) controls this dispute. Rule 26(a)(2)(A) provides that a party must disclose the "identity of any person who may be used at trial to present evidence under [Evidence] Rules 702, 703 or 705" [all dealing with expert testimony]. Rule 26(a)(2)(B) requires that, except as stipulated by the parties or directed by the Court, a party shall make comprehensive disclosures regarding "a witness who is retained or specially employed to provide expert testimony in the case or whose duties as an employee of the party regularly involve giving expert testimony." As for these witnesses, colloquially referred to as "retained experts," Rule 26(a)(2)(B) also requires a written report signed by the expert that contains: (1) a complete statement of all opinions to be expressed, and the basis and reasons for them; (2) the data or other information considered by the witness in forming the opinions; (3) any exhibits to be used as a summary of or support for the opinions to be expressed; (4) the qualifications of the witness, including a list of publications authored within the last 10 years; (5) the compensation received for the study and testimony performed; and (6) a list of any other cases in which the witness has provided expert testimony, either in trial or in deposition, for the preceding four years. A failure to provide the appropriate Rule 26(a)(2) disclosures may lead the court to exclude the expert's testimony at trial absent a determination that there was substantial justification for the failure, and there is no prejudice to the adverse party. *See* chapter 43 *infra* (Rule 26(a) Disclosures and Rule 37(c) Motion for Failure to Disclose, Misleading Disclosures, or Refusal to Admit).

What distinguishes the minimal disclosure required by Rule 26(a)(2)(A) from the comprehensive disclosures required by Rule 26(a)(2)(B)? Rule 26(a)(2)(B) applies when the expert is retained to provide testimony or is an employee of a party whose duties regularly involve giving expert testimony. Rule 26(a)(2)(A) covers persons like treating physicians who occupy a hybrid role: They are "fact witnesses" in the sense that they have firsthand knowledge of relevant facts, but they also have the training, skill, education, and experience that would qualify them to give opinion testimony under FRE 702. A helpful case that discusses the intricacies involving Rule 26(a)(2) disclosures and the difference between "hybrid fact/experts" and "retained experts" is *Sullivan v. Glock*, 175 F.R.D. 497 (D. Md. 1997). *Sullivan* confirms that a witness who is a "hybrid fact/expert" is subject only to the minimal disclosure requirement of Rule 26(a)(2)(A). However, the decision notes that an adverse party may nonetheless discover the opinion of the hybrid expert by skillful use of other discovery such as interrogatories. *Id.* at 502, n.7.

Many courts have permitted testimony on a wide range of topics such as causation, diagnosis, prognosis, and extent of injury when the hybrid expert is a treating physician. See, for example, *Shapardon v. W. Beach Estates*, 172 F.R.D. 415, 416-17 (D. Haw. 1997), and *Hall v. Sykes*, 164 F.R.D. 46, 48 (E.D. Va. 1995). As the comprehensive Rule 26(a)(2)(B) disclosures do not apply to hybrid witnesses, however, courts have been careful to scrutinize the sources of information that forms the basis for the treating physician's opinion. The *Sullivan* court, cautioning that "[a] witness can be a hybrid witness as to certain opinions, but a retained expert as to others," adopted the following rule: "To the extent that the source of the facts which form the basis for a treating physician's opinions derive from information learned during the actual treatment of the patient—as opposed to being subsequently supplied by the attorney involved in litigating the case involving the [patient's] condition or injury, then no Rule 26(a)(2)(B) statement should be required." *Id.* at 500-01. *See Piper v. Harnischfeger Corp.*, 170 F.R.D. 173 (D. Nev. 1997); *Garza v. Abbott Lab.*, No. 95 C 3560, 1996 WL 494266 (N.D. Ill. Aug. 27, 1996); *Thomas v. Consol. Rail Corp.*, 169 F.R.D. 1, 2 (D. Mass. 1996). Conversely, if the opinions to be offered by a treating physician are based on information from a source other than the treatment of the patient, counsel would be wise to provide a Rule 26(a)(2)(B) disclosure as to those opinions.

While the treating physician is the quintessential example of a Rule 26(a)(2)(A) hybrid fact/expert witness, there is no limit to the types of cases where such witnesses may be found. For example, in a products liability case for negligent design, the engineers and design professionals employed by the defendant probably would qualify as hybrid fact/expert witnesses. Similarly, the defendant in a professional malpractice case likely would qualify as a hybrid fact/expert witness. Since Rule 26(a)(2)(A) requires disclosure of only the names of these witnesses, it would be wise to include as a standard interrogatory the one that the court proposed in *Sullivan*, *supra*, 175 F.R.D. at 502 n.7: "For each witness identified by you in connection with the disclosures required by Fed. R. Civ. P. 26(a)(2)(A), provide a complete statement of the opinions to be expressed and basis and reasons therefor." Depending upon the substance of the witness's opinions, counsel should consider following up with a deposition. On the other hand, if the adverse party does not identify the Rule 26(a)(2)(A) witnesses and their expected opinions in response to a *Sullivan*-type interrogatory, a motion to exclude any opinion testimony at trial under Rule 37 would be appropriate.

Practice Tip

Counsel must have a clear understanding of the difference between a "hybrid" fact/expert witness and a "retained expert," as well as the different disclosures required for each under Rule 26(a)(2). Failure to appreciate this difference may cause the lawyer who is pursuing discovery to overlook potential discovery from a persuasive expert witness. Likewise, the lawyer sponsoring the witness may be penalized by an order of court excluding the testimony at trial. Counsel should always remember that Rule 26(a)(2) pertains to the required pretrial disclosure of expert information only, and does not preclude discovery of expert opinions by other discovery methods such as interrogatories, document requests, or depositions. Finally, if the proponent of a hybrid fact/expert witness is uncertain about disclosures, she should make them rather than risk preclusion.

36. TAKING AN EXPERT'S DEPOSITION—THE BASICS

Steve Johnson, a young lawyer, decided to take the deposition of the adverse party's expert witness in a complex toxic tort case. He had never before taken an expert's deposition, and so he decided to review the matter with a senior partner. In preparation for his meeting with the partner, Johnson decided to sketch out some ideas relating to the deposition and the topics that he might cover. What issues might he consider?

Comment: Rule 26(b)(4) authorizes the deposition of an adverse testifying expert. As Rule 26(a)(2)(B) mandates the creation and production of an expert report, however, Johnson may conclude that he does not need to take the expert's deposition. *See* Greg Joseph, "Expert Approaches," *Litigation,* vol. 26, no. 4 (2002), at 20. Rule 26(b)(4) requires the disclosure of the following information from the expert: a complete statement of all opinions and basis and reasons; the information considered by the expert in forming the opinion; any exhibits to be used in support of the opinions; the qualifications of the expert including a list of all publications the expert authored within the last 10 years; the fees to be paid to the expert; and a list of cases in which the expert testified in trial or deposition over the preceding 10 years.

In fact, there can be some risk in taking the adverse expert's deposition. Doing so may expose Johnson to trial testimony from the expert that could not otherwise come in. For example, if the expert's mandatory disclosure does not reveal an opinion that he attempts to raise at trial, Johnson can have it excluded. *See* Rule 37(c)(1). However, if Johnson deposes the expert and asks, "Do you have any other opinions you intend to give during trial?" and the expert offers a view not previously disclosed, that answer could serve as an admissible supplement to the mandatory disclosures under Rule 26(a)(2)(B), and the information frozen in place by the mandatory disclosure would be thawed.

Instead of the expert's deposition and in supplement to the mandatory disclosures, Johnson might issue a subpoena duces tecum to the expert for production of all documents, correspondence, texts, computer data, e-mails, and the like that he consulted or that formed part of the basis for his analysis and conclusions. *See* Rules 34 and 45.

Despite these possibilities, most experts are deposed. If Johnson follows that course, he would do well to consult pertinent articles and texts that discuss taking expert depositions. *See, e.g.*, Raoul Kennedy, "Expert Witness Depositions," in *Effective Depositions* at p. 389 (Henry L. Hecht ed., American Bar Association 1991); Morgan Chu, "Discovery of Experts," in *Expert Witnesses* at p. 171 (Faust Rossi ed., American Bar Association 1991).[1]

Basic topics Johnson should cover in the deposition include the following (many of these topics overlap, and the order in which the questions are posed is a matter of judgment):

1. Present occupation.
2. Education and employment background.
3. Prior experience as an expert (including special areas of expertise; the area of specialty involved in the case; prior instances of serving as an expert, including for which side (plaintiff or defendant) the expert testified and the result of each case; any problems in the expert's career, such as law suits, verdicts against the expert or his firm for malpractice).
4. Specific assignment in the case (what the expert was engaged to do; what opinions she or he will express at trial; review correspondence related to the assignment).
5. Review of documents (including all documents the expert produced under Rule 26. The Rule requires the expert to produce at least: a complete statement of opinions, data, or other information considered in forming the opinion; exhibits that support the opinion; the expert's qualifications and publications; the rate of compensation of the expert, and the list of other cases in which the expert has participated for at least the preceding four years. The notice for deposition should have included a subpoena duces tecum for the expert to bring to the deposition his or her pertinent files, including correspondence, draft reports (*see* chapter 40, Discovery of Draft Report by Testifying Expert, *infra*), time sheets and billing records, all written mate-

---

1. Although these articles were written before *Daubert*, discussed at chapter 40, *infra*, they still provide sound advice on the elements of an expert deposition. For additional considerations after *Daubert*, *see* LAWRENCE J. ZWEIFACH, PRACTISING LAW INSTITUTE, TAKING AND DEFENDING DEPOSITIONS IN COMMERCIAL CASE 2000; DEPOSING THE EXPERT WITNESS (2000); and MASSACHUSETTS CONTINUING LEGAL EDUCATION, INC., MASSACHUSETTS DISCOVERY PRACTICE, vol. II ch. 22 (John A. Houlihan ed., 2000).

rial that the expert reviewed, considered, or relied upon to form his opinions or conclusions).

6. Use of assistants and other help (e.g., determine if the assistants did more of the work than the expert).

7. Amount of time devoted to the case and basis of compensation (is the expert paid up to date; compare the hourly rate for the party who retained the expert to the fee the expert is charging for his deposition).

8. Time spent talking to counsel, witnesses, or other experts (*see* chapter 37, Discovery of Oral Communications and Privileged Documents Shared With Expert), *infra.*

9. Opinions and conclusions reached and about which the expert will testify.

10. The basis of each opinion (including all documents reviewed, learned treatises, textbooks, or other material relied upon and individuals with whom the expert's assistant spoke to fulfill his or her assignment).

11. The report (review the report and draft reports (*see* chapters 37 and 40, *infra*) and all facts serving as the basis of the report, and determine if the expert plans to file additional reports).

12. Future work the expert might undertake in the case, including the formation of other opinions. (Here counsel can restrict the expert's testimony to current opinions and reports by confirming that there is no further work to be accomplished by the expert or additional opinions to be offered at trial. If further opinions are anticipated, arrangements can be made to continue the deposition at a later time.)

13. Disagreements the expert has with the opinions and conclusions of the other side's expert and the reasons for disagreement.

37. DISCOVERY OF ORAL COMMUNICATIONS AND PRIVILEGED DOCUMENTS SHARED WITH EXPERT

Last week, defense counsel and the president of the defendant corporation met with the defense expert to prepare him for his deposition on the following day. Counsel started the session by summarizing the facts supporting his theory of the case. Counsel then gave the opening statement that he intended to use at trial. During the session counsel showed the expert a chronology of significant facts. Then counsel gave the expert a memorandum written by the lawyer's law clerk reflecting their mental impressions of the case, and asked the expert for his thoughts. Counsel also showed the expert a letter that the lawyer had written to the defendant's insurance carrier summarizing his opinion of the case.

After reading the letter, the expert told the lawyer, "Your thoughts are not necessarily correct here, and I do not find them particularly helpful." Defense counsel concluded the meeting by reviewing the prior correspondence that he had sent the expert, including the retainer letter, in which counsel had written, "I know that you will spare nothing to help us in this case."

During the expert's deposition this morning, the following exchange occurred:

Plaintiff's counsel:
Q: "Did you meet with counsel to prepare for your deposition?"
A: "Yes, I did."
Q: "When?"
A: "Yesterday."
Q: "Where did you meet?"
A: "In counsel's office."
Q: "Who was present during the meeting?"
A: "Defense counsel and the CEO of the company."
Q: "Describe what was said during the meeting."
Defense counsel: "Objection. You know that the meeting with my expert is confidential, because it is subject to the attorney-client privilege and the work-product doctrine.
Plaintiff's counsel: "Not so. I am entitled to know what happened at the meeting."
Defense counsel: "Well, I will allow him to testify about what we did without disclosing any substantive discussions or communications, including what was contained in any documents we reviewed."

Plaintiff's counsel: "I do not agree to that, but let's at least have him describe, generally, what was said, and identify what he reviewed and what he considered."

Defense counsel: "Fine, let's proceed."

The expert testified that he heard the defense theory of the case as well as a mock opening statement; he examined a chronology prepared by defense counsel; he reviewed a law clerk's memorandum which contained the lawyers' mental impressions of the case; he read a letter from defense counsel to the insurance company expressing his view of the case; and he reviewed previous correspondence sent to him by defense counsel.

Plaintiff's counsel then pressed for the specific content of each communication and asked whether the expert considered the lawyer's comments and any of the documents in reaching his opinions. Defense counsel instructed the witness not to answer on the grounds of attorney-client privilege and work-product doctrine. (See chapter 19, *supra*, for issues relating to instructions to deponent not to answer a question.)

The deposition was terminated in the late morning. Plaintiff's counsel soon filed a motion to compel. (See chapter 5, *supra*, for issues relating to the duty of counsel to confer in good faith regarding discovery disputes.) Defense counsel opposed the motion, arguing that the communications in question reflected his mental impressions and analysis of the case and were insulated from disclosure by Rule 26(b)(3), which protects an attorney's mental impressions from discovery. Counsel further argued that the discussions with the expert were in the presence of the client and thus insulated from discovery by the attorney-client privilege.

Plaintiff's counsel responded that Rule 26(a)(2) requires disclosure of underlying data considered by the expert, and that FRE 612(b) buttresses this right of disclosure by providing that a party is entitled to all material used to refresh a witness's recollection or upon which he has relied in his testimony. Plaintiff's counsel further argued that FRE 705 provides additional support for disclosure by requiring an expert to disclose underlying facts and data on cross-examination.

How should the court rule?

Comment: Rule 26(b)(3) codifies the work-product doctrine, shielding an attorney's mental impressions concerning litigation from disclosure. Despite that general rule, however, most federal courts have interpreted Rule

26(a)(2)(B) (requiring disclosure of data or other information considered by an expert to form his or her opinions) and FRE 612 (requiring disclosure of material shown to a witness in preparation for testimony) to require disclosure of counsel's mental impressions that were conveyed to an expert in preparation for his or her testimony. *See Berkey Photo Inc. v. Eastman Kodak Co.*, 74 F.R.D. 613 (S.D.N.Y. 1977); *Intermedics, Inc. v. Ventritex, Inc.*, 139 F.R.D. 384 (N. D. Cal. 1991), which held that all information provided to experts by counsel should be produced to opposing counsel; *Prucha v. M&N Modern Hydraulic Press Co.*, 76 F.R.D. 207 (W.D. Wis. 1977); *Wheeling-Pittsburgh Steel Corp. v. Underwriters Laboratories*, 81 F.R.D. 8 (N.D. Ill. 1980).[1]

A minority of courts have distinguished between "core" opinion work product and fact work product supplied to an expert, holding that Rule 26(a)(2)(B) requires disclosure of the latter but not the former. In *Bogosian v. Gulf Oil Corp.*, 738 F.2d 587 (3d Cir. 1984), the court considered the applicability of the attorney work-product doctrine to more than 100 documents provided to an expert. The documents were alleged to contain both "fact" and "opinion" work product. In reversing the trial court's finding that all work-product materials shared with the testifying expert should be disclosed, the Court of Appeals held that "[e]xamination and cross-examination of the expert can be comprehensive and effective on the rel-

---

1. Note that some courts take a different approach for nonexpert witnesses. *See* Bogosian v. Gulf Oil Corp., 738 F.2d 587 (3d Cir. 1984); Sporck v. Peil, 759 F. 2d 312 (3d Cir. 1985), *cert. denied,* 106 S. Ct. 238 (1985) (holding that FRE 612 did not apply to the case because counsel seeking discovery had not established that the nonexpert witness used the writing to refresh memory or for purposes of testifying, and that production was necessary and in the interests of justice); *see also* Nutramax Laboratories Inc. v. Twin Laboratories, Inc., 183 F.R.D. 458 (D. Md. 1988), which held that documents provided by counsel to nonexpert witnesses were not discoverable without proof that they used the documents to refresh their memory for the purpose of testifying. As to experts, however, counsel should assume that disclosure of his mental impression will be compelled. But even then, many courts will review the requested documents in camera to balance the competing issues of preserving the privilege invoked and permitting the disclosure requested. *See generally* EDNA SELAN EPSTEIN, THE ATTORNEY-CLIENT PRIVILEGE AND THE WORK-PRODUCT DOCTRINE 4th ed. 634-37 (ABA 2002). Finally, the client's presence when the disclosures were made is irrelevant—no attorney-client privilege exists when a third party, in this case the expert, is present. *See supra*, chapters 17 (Depositions—Making Procedural and Evidentiary Objections), 18 (Asserting Privileges During Deposition), and 26 (Discovery of Oral Communications and Privileged Documents Provided to a Witness).

evant issue of the basis for an expert's opinion without an inquiry into the lawyer's role in assisting with the formulation of the theory." *Bogosian,* 738 F.2d at 595. Applying that rule to the example, defense counsel's mental impressions might not be discoverable. *See Magee v. Paul Revere Life Ins. Co.,* 172 F.R.D. 627 (E.D.N.Y. 1997); *Krisa v. Equitable Life Assur. Soc.,* 196 F.R.D. 627, 642 (E.D.N.Y. 1997) (Disclosure of core work product, including mental impressions, by attorney to a testifying expert does not abrogate protection accorded such information and as such is not discoverable.). *Bogosian,* however, predates Rule 26(a)(2)(B), which was not adopted until 1993, by nine years, and thus may no longer be persuasive authority.

In fact, most courts hold that core opinion, as well as fact/work product provided to the expert, must be disclosed. *Intermedics, Inc. v. Ventritex, Inc.,* 139 F.R.D. 384 (N. D. Cal. 1991); s*ee, e.g., Aniero Concrete Co., et al. v. N.Y. City Sch. Constr. Auth.,* 2002 WL 257685 (S.D.N.Y. Feb. 22, 2002), and *Musselman v. Phillips,* 176 F.R.D. (D. Md. 1977). *See also James Julian, Inc. v. Raytheon Co.,* 93 F.R.D. 138 (D. Del. 1982). Counsel must be familiar with the case law of the jurisdiction in which the suit is pending to determine whether any disclosures to an expert will remain shielded from discovery.

Applying these standards to the example, it is likely that all of the communications by counsel to the expert would be found discoverable by the court. Defense counsel may be able to persuade the court that the expert did not consider certain documents or oral communications when formulating his opinions, such as the correspondence with the insurance company or even the mock opening statement, and thus such information should remain confidential. Even if those communications were reviewed to some degree by the expert, counsel might nonetheless argue that no reliance was placed on them by the expert in formulating his opinion.

The point is obvious and important: The trend in the courts is to require production of *all* materials given to an expert, absent extraordinary circumstances. As the Court of Appeals for the Federal Circuit has put it, "The 1993 amendments to Rule 26 of the Federal Rules of Civil Procedure make clear that documents and information disclosed to a testifying expert in connection with his testimony are discoverable by opposing party, *whether or not the expert relies on the documents and information in preparing his report.*" *In re Pioneer Hi Bred Intern., Inc.,* 238 F.3d 1370, 1375 (Fed. Cir. 2001) (emphasis added).

Practice Tip

Unless there is contrary authority in the jurisdiction where the litigation is pending, a lawyer must assume that virtually all communications with a testimonial expert will be discoverable. Therefore, do not show an expert work product that has not been previously disclosed, or that you do not want to have disclosed prior to trial. Rather, limit disclosure to documents on the public record, documents that have already been produced and previously undisclosed documents that you are comfortable producing to the adverse party. Do not share with an expert an impeaching document not previously disclosed. Do not make or disclose to the expert any written and oral communications that include facts or opinions that you do not want to share with opposing counsel before trial.

If you want to compel production of documents shown to an adverse expert, establish in deposition or by affidavit that the expert reviewed the documents and considered them. In that regard, some courts will not compel disclosure of privileged documents or communications to the expert unless he has "considered" the material. (For discovery arising out of focus group sessions, see chapter 27, *supra*; for discovery issues arising out of disclosure of documents to fact witnesses during their preparation for deposition, see chapter 26, *supra*.)

38. DISCOVERY OF FACTS KNOWN OR OPINIONS HELD BY EXPERT NOT EXPECTED TO TESTIFY AT TRIAL

Plaintiff's counsel in a products liability case retained two mechanical engineers as experts. The first, Edward Bixby, was retained to testify at trial. The second, William Tell, was retained as a nontestifying consultant to help the lawyers understand the complex technology involved in the machinery at issue in the case.

The two experts had several telephone conversations about the case. They also met to discuss it. During the meeting, Tell (the nontestifying expert) disclosed calculations he had made regarding the machinery, as well as an unpublished paper he had written that criticized the defendant's manufacturing process for the machinery. During defense counsel's deposition of Bixby, he described his dealings with Tell. Bixby insisted, however, that he did not rely on any of Tell's information in formulating his opinions. On instructions from counsel, Bixby declined to disclose the contents of the oral or written communications from Tell. Defense counsel has decided that, rather than try to compel Bixby to disclose the information provided by Tell, he will take Tell's deposition to get that information. Plaintiff's counsel refuses, citing Rule 26(b)(4)(B).

How should the court rule?

Comment: Under Rule 26(b)(4)(B) as interpreted by the courts, the defendant should prevail if he can show that (a) the comments and unpublished paper could not be obtained elsewhere, and (b) the information is critical to his case. Plaintiff's counsel would argue that Bixby's statement that he did not rely on Tell's information prevents defense counsel from making either showing. Defense counsel would then respond that (a) Bixby's self-serving statements about what he relied on can only be tested by disclosure of Tell's materials, and that (b) in any event, Tell's unique expert insights, which can only be obtained from him, may be critical to his case, regardless of what Bixby relied on.

The rules distinguish between experts engaged to testify—Rules 26(a)(2)(B) and 26(b)(4)(A)—and experts engaged to consult but not testify—Rule 26(b)(4)(B). Courts are divided, however, in their interpretation of the rules governing discovery of nontestifying experts. Generally, unless discovery is being sought under Rule 35 from an examining physician (who is, in effect, a nontestifying expert) or a similar person, Rule 26 (b)(4)(B) prohibits a party from discovering facts known or opinions held by a nontestifying expert unless the party can demonstrate that exceptional circumstances exist "under which it is impracticable for the party seeking discovery to obtain facts or opinions on the same subject by other means." *See Marsh v. Jackson*, 141 F.R.D. 431 (W.D. Va. 1992). The litigant seeking such discovery "carries a heavy burden in demonstrating the existence of exceptional circumstances." *Disidore v. Mail Contractors of Am., Inc.*, 196 F.R.D. 410, 415 (D. Kan. 2000), *quoting Ager v. Jane C. Stormont Hosp. & Training Sch. for Nurses*, 622 F.2d 496, 503 (10th Cir. 1980). *See* Douglas Emerick, "Discovery of the Non-Testifying Expert Witnesses' Identity Under the Federal Rules of Civil Procedure: You Can't Tell the Players Without a Program," 37 *Hastings Law Journal* 201 (1985).

Significantly, the protection afforded the nontestifying expert extends to situations where he or she has been identified as a testifying expert, but the designation is later withdrawn. "The court cannot find, then, that the shift in designation affects the witness's current status as a non-testifying expert witness and deny him the protection afforded such a witness." *Ross v. Burlington Northern R. Co.*, 136 F.R.D. 638, 639 (N.D. Ill. 1991).

The district court recognized four interests weighing against allowing an opposing party to depose or call at trial a consultative, nontestifying expert witness: (1) an "important interest in allowing counsel to obtain the expert advice they need in order properly to evaluate and present their clients' position without fear that every consultation with an expert may yield grist for the adversary's mill," which the court found underlies Fed. R. Civ. P. 26(b)(4)(B)'s limitation on discovery of consultative, as opposed to testifying experts; (2) unfairness of allowing an opposing party to benefit from a party's effort and expense incurred in preparing its case; (3) fear of restraint on the willingness of experts to serve as consultants if their testimony could be compelled; and (4) the substantial risk of "explosive" prejudice stemming from the fact of the prior retention of an expert by the opposing party. *House v. Combined Ins. Co. of Am.*, 168 F.R.D. 236, 241 (N.D. Iowa 1996), citing *Rubel v. Eli Lilly & Co.*, 160 F.R.D.458, 460 (S.D.N.Y. 1995). *See also Reeves v. Boyd & Sons, Inc.*, 654 N.E.2d 864 (Ind. App. 1995) (plaintiff in a personal injury case was not permitted to depose defendant's medical expert witness when defendant decided not to call the expert as a witness and plaintiff failed to show exceptional circumstances), and *In re Shell Oil Refinery*, 132 F.R.D. 437 (E.D. La. 1990).

The key question in determining whether to allow the deposition of a nontestifying expert is the meaning of the term "exceptional circumstances."

This turns on whether (a) the party seeking discovery can obtain equivalent information by alternate means and (b) the information is important to the case. *See Hartford Fire Ins. v. Pure Air on the Lake Ltd.*, 154 F.R.D. 202 (N.D. Ind. 1993). Exceptional circumstances have been recognized "where the object or condition observed by the non-testifying expert is no longer observable by an expert of the party seeking discovery" and it is not possible to replicate the expert discovery on a contested issue at a reasonable cost. *Long-Term Capital Holdings, LP v. United States*, No. 01-CV-1290, 2003 WL 21269586, at *2 (D. Conn. May 6, 2003), citing *Bank Brussels Lambert v. Chase Manhattan Bank, N.A.*, 175 F.R.D. 34, 44 (S.D.N.Y. 1997).

Notwithstanding this apparent bright-line test, however, decisions vary. In *Pearl Brewing Co. v. Joseph Schlitz Brewing Co.*, 415 F. Supp. 1122 (S.D. Tex. 1976), for example, the court permitted the deposition of a nontestifying expert who had prepared certain computer programs in support of the case. These programs had been reviewed by the testifying expert. *Accord, Heitmann v. Concrete Pipe Machinery*, 98 F.R.D. 740 (E.D. Mo. 1983); *Spearman Indust., Inc. v. St. Paul Fire and Marine Ins. Co.*, 128 F. Supp. 2d 1148 (N.D. Ill. 2001). *But see Eliasen v. Hamilton*, 111 F.R.D. 396 (N.D. Ill. 1986), in which the court denied a request for the deposition of a nontestifying expert even though the testifying expert relied upon a report prepared by the nontestifying expert. The same result was reached in *Crockett v. Virginia Folding Box Co.*, 61 F.R.D. 312 (E.D. Va. 1974) (request to depose non-testifying expert denied for lack of showing that the requested information was important to the case); *Winchester v. Hertrich*, 658 A.2d 1016 (Del. Super. 1995); *FMC Corp. v. Vendo Co.*, 196 F. Supp. 2d 1023 (E.D. Cal. 2002).

Trial counsel might confer informally with an expert in anticipation of litigation but not retain or specially employ him. Generally speaking, such an expert is immune from discovery. The Advisory Committee comments to Rule 26(b)(4)(b) state that the rule addresses only those experts retained or specially engaged. *See Kuster v. Harner*, 109 F.R.D 372 (D. Minn. 1986). On the other hand, if counsel consults informally with an expert who performs the same analysis as the retained nontestifying expert in the example, the request for discovery of the informally consulted expert should be evaluated by the same criteria as those used to adjudicate the request for discovery of the nontestifying expert who was formally engaged.

Can counsel, at the least, discover the *identity* of a nontestifying witness—perhaps by propounding interrogatories like these? "(1) Have you retained or specially employed any experts in anticipation of litigation whom you do not expect to call at trial? (2) If so, please describe the types of experts retained (in other words, their fields of expertise) and the nature of the services that they performed in anticipation of litigation or trial." *See* Henry L. Hecht, *Effective Depositions* 398 (Section of Litigation, American Bar Association, 1997).

The Advisory Committee notes to the Rules provide that "as an ancillary procedure, a party may on a proper showing require the other party to name experts retained or engaged, but not those informally consulted. The question immediately arises as to what constitutes "a proper showing"—is that synonymous with "extraordinary circumstances"? Cases such as *Ager v. Jane C. Stormont Hosp. & Training Sch.*, 622 F.2d 496 (10th Cir. 1980); *Kuster v. Harner,* 109 F.R.D. 372 (D. Minn. 1986); and *In re Pizza Time Theatre Sec. Litig.,* 113 F.R.D. 94 (N.D. Cal. 1986) hold that the identity of an expert engaged in anticipation of litigation but not expected to testify is not discoverable except upon a showing of exceptional circumstances. *Baki v. B. F. Diamond Construction Co.,* 71 F.R.D. 179, 182 (D. Md. 1976), reaches a different result ("the names and addresses, and other identifying information, of experts, who have been retained or specially employed in anticipation of litigation or preparation for trial and who are not expected to be called as witnesses at trial, may be obtained through properly framed interrogatories without any special showing of exceptional circumstances in the absence of some indication that such information by reason of facts peculiar to the case at issue, is irrelevant, privileged, or form some other reason should not be disclosed"); *Arco Pipeline Co. v. S/S Trade Star*, 81 F.R.D. 416 (E.D. Pa. 1978). Consider: "Experts' Identities under the Federal Rules of Civil Procedure," 80 *Michigan Law Review* 513 (1982), as well as *Hecht, supra,* at 397-98.

Practice Tip

Care should always be taken to insulate the nontestifying expert from the testifying expert. Do not let them communicate directly with each other. Counsel can sometimes serve as a bridge for such communications. However, this bridge can lead to disaster if counsel shares privileged information or work product with the testifying expert. *See* chapter 37, *supra*.

39. DEPOSING OPPOSING PARTY'S FORMER EXPERT IN THE SAME CASE

The plaintiff filed suit against his employer for breach of employment contract. The employer consulted an economist to testify as its expert witness on damages. But the economist developed an opinion adverse to the employer, so defense counsel dismissed the expert and told plaintiff's counsel that the defense would not call the economist at trial. The plaintiff then noticed the economist's deposition. Defense counsel objected and filed a motion for protective order. How should the court rule?

Comment: The case law is clear. A party cannot call as a deposition or trial witness an expert who was designated by the adverse party but whose designation was withdrawn. The courts treat a discharged expert witness in the same manner as a nontestifying expert (*see* chapter 38, *supra*). *See Ferguson v. Michael Foods, Inc.,* 189 F.R.D. 408 (D. Minn. 1999) (Court denied plaintiff's motion to call defendant's former medical expert as an adverse witness during her case in chief, reasoning that such a step could unfairly prejudice the case if the jury learned that the expert was originally hired by the opposing party.); *Durflinger v. Artiles,* 727 F. 2d 888 (10th Cir. 1984) (In a medical malpractice case, plaintiffs notified defendants of their withdrawal of one of their expert witnesses. None of the expert's information had been shared with defense counsel prior to this withdrawal. Defense counsel then contacted the expert, requested a copy of his completed report, and indicated they would call him to testify at trial. The court excluded the proffered evidence, finding that defense counsel violated the principles of fairness outlined in Rule 26(b)(4)(B).).

Communication with or retention of opposing counsel's former expert is prohibited, and it could result in the disqualification of the expert or the attorney making the contact. *See Cordy v. Sherwin-Williams Co.,* 156 F.R.D. 575 (D.N.J. 1994) (In a personal injury suit, plaintiff filed a motion seeking disqualification of the defense expert and counsel. The court held that both should be disqualified as the expert had previously been designated by the plaintiff and counsel knowingly had hired him as defense expert in spite of this.); *Campbell Indust. v. M/V Gemini,* 619 F.2d 24 (9th Cir. 1980) (As a result of defense counsel's ex parte communication with plaintiff's expert, expert's testimony was precluded on behalf of the defense.).

40. DISCOVERY OF DRAFT REPORT BY TESTIFYING EXPERT

Two years ago, John Smith invested $1 million with a stockbroker. Smith instructed the broker that he was looking for long-term growth. The broker advised Smith that his money would be invested in blue chip stocks that should yield, on average, a 15 percent annual return. A year later, Smith's principal had dwindled to $500,000, even though the S&P index was up approximately 10 percent from the previous year. Smith hired a lawyer to represent his interests. The lawyer's investigation suggested that (a) the broker had invested Smith's money in speculative stocks that were unsuitable given Smith's investment objectives; and (b) the broker was churning the account. There was no arbitration requirement in Smith's customer agreement, so his lawyer sued the broker in federal court and simultaneously retained a securities expert to render an opinion and testify on behalf of Smith.

A month later Smith's lawyer received a document from the expert labeled "Draft," stating that the trades "appear to have been" unsuitable; that the frequency of trading suggested churning; and that damages amounted to $600,000. After reading the draft, counsel picked up the telephone, called the expert and left the following message: "I think your draft could be tightened up in two ways. First, can't you strengthen your conclusion to say that the trading *was* unsuitable? Also, there has to be a way to increase the damages calculation—after all, the broker promised a 15 percent return, and some blue chip stocks that would have been suitable for Smith, but that weren't purchased, went up 25 percent last year."

Several days later, the expert sent to Smith's lawyer a document captioned "Final Report," which concluded that "the trades were clearly unsuitable" and set damages at $700,000. Smith's lawyer forwarded a copy of the final report to defense counsel.

At the expert's deposition, defense counsel asked the expert whether he had written any draft reports. The expert acknowledged that he had indeed given Smith's lawyer a draft. Defense counsel thereupon asked for a copy. Smith's lawyer refused, and both counsel called the magistrate judge for a ruling.

Smith's lawyer argued that the draft was properly withheld for two reasons. First, the production of *drafts* by a testimonial expert is not mandated by Rule 26(a)(2)(B), which requires production of a testimonial expert's "official" report ("Except as otherwise stipulated or directed by the court, this disclosure shall . . . be accompanied by a written report prepared and signed by the witness . . .”). Second, Rule 26(b)(3) expressly protects this work product from disclosure:

> Subject to the provisions of subdivision (b)(4) . . ., a party may obtain discovery of documents . . . prepared in anticipation of litigation or for trial by or for another party or by or for that other party's representative (including the other party's . . . consultant . . .) only upon a showing that the party seeking discovery has substantial need of the materials . . . and that the party is unable without undue hardship to obtain the substantial equivalent of the materials by other means. In ordering discovery of such materials when the required showing has been made, the court shall protect against disclosure of the mental impressions, conclusions, opinions or legal theories of an attorney or other representative of a party concerning the litigation.

Defense counsel responded that, while Rule 26(a)(2)(B) requires production of final reports, it does not bar discovery of draft reports. To the contrary, the rule expressly requires that the report "contain . . . the data or other information considered by the witness in forming the opinions"—and that, said defense counsel, necessarily embraces data used in drafts, whether included in the final report or not. Defense counsel further argued that he was entitled to the draft because the limitations on discovery in Rule 26(b)(3) are subject to Rule 26(b)(4), which authorizes discovery of testifying expert witnesses without any restrictions, and he had propounded Rule 34 document requests that included drafts of expert opinions.

Comment: Federal courts disagree about the discoverability of draft expert reports. Compare *Krisa v. The Equitable Life Assur. Soc.*, 196 F.R.D. 254, 256-57 (M.D. Pa. 2000) (directing production of draft reports) and *County of Suffolk v. Long Island Lighting Co.*, 122 F.R.D. 120, 122 (E.D.N.Y. 1997) ("courts have defined the scope of . . . [Fed. R. Civ. P. 26(b)(4)] to allow 'disclosure of drafts of reports or memoranda experts have generated as they develop the opinions they will present at trial'") with *The Nexxus Products Co. v. CVS N.Y., Inc.*, 188 F.R.D. at 10-11 (draft expert reports not discoverable because they are a type of opinion work product) and *Moore v. R.J. Reynolds Tobacco Co.*, 194 F.R.D. 659, 662 (S.D. Iowa 2000) (same).

The majority of decisions, however, do permit discovery of testimonial experts' draft reports. Rule 26(b)(4)(A) authorizes the deposition of "any person who has been identified as an expert whose opinions may be presented at trial." There is no limit on the right of deposing counsel to inquire into the preliminary opinions of such an expert witness, in marked contrast to the limits placed on discoverability of a nontestimonial consulting expert witness, set forth at Rule 26(b)(4)(B). The Advisory Committee notes to the 1970 Amendments that added subdivision (b)(4) authorizing discovery of expert witnesses support this conclusion: "These new provisions of subdivision (b)(4) . . . reject as ill-considered the decisions which have sought to bring expert information within the work-product doctrine." 48 F.R.D. at 504-05 (1970) (internal citations omitted).

The relationship between attorney work product and discoverability of a testimonial expert's draft reports is discussed at 10 Fed. Proc., L. Ed. §§ 26:157 and 26:162 (2002). "Items which are not work product gain no special protected status merely because they are sent to an expert, but conversely, attorney work product does not lose its special status merely because it is transmitted to an expert, unless it is used to prepare the expert's testimony for a deposition or at trial." § 26:162. Here, Smith's lawyer might argue that the contrast in the language between the draft report and the final report would disclose his mental impressions, which are quintessential attorney work-product and should be exempt from disclosure. In fact, however, the draft report contains no attorney work-product and would not be exempt from disclosure on that basis. Nondisclosure of the draft report merely conceals the extent of Smith's lawyer's input and influence in the final report, including strengthening the language on nonsuitability and a significant upward adjustment in damages, which are clearly fit topics for cross-examination.

On the other hand, if the draft report does contain the lawyer's mental impressions and other work product that the expert discarded in fashioning his final opinion and report, then counsel might succeed in maintaining confidentiality of at least those portions of the draft. Counsel would argue that his input formed no portion of the basis for the expert's final analysis, conclusion, or testimony and should be redacted from the draft report if produced. *See Krisa v. Equitable Life Assur. Soc., supra,* at 257. However, given the fact that Rule 26(a)(2)(B) expressly provides for disclosure of "the data or other information *considered*" by the expert (emphasis added), which is considerably broader than just the information relied on in forming the expert's opinion, a strong argument for disclosure can be made. As the commentary to Rule 26(a)(2)(B) states:

> The report is to disclose the data and other information considered by the expert. . . . Given this obligation of disclosure, litigants should no longer be able to argue that materials furnished to their experts to be used in forming their opinions—whether or not ultimately relied on by the expert—are privileged or otherwise protected from disclosure when such persons are testifying or being deposed.
>
> Commentary to the 1993 Changes to the Federal Rules of Civil Procedure, 146 F.R.D. 401, 634.

One course favored by many attorneys is to advise their testimonial experts at the outset that their preliminary impressions should be reviewed with counsel before a written report is prepared. That reduces the likelihood of discovery of preliminary findings to the extent adverse counsel limits his interrogation to "draft reports." It begs the question, however, if adverse counsel then inquires into discussions between the lawyer and the expert in anticipation of the report's preparation. *See* chapters 36 and 37, *supra*. On balance, counsel would be well advised to assume that all drafts of the expert's report are discoverable, and that all input from lawyer to expert, whether written or oral, may be discoverable. In that regard, at least one court has held that an attorney who counseled his expert witness to destroy the drafts of his expert report prior to his deposition would be subject to sanctions for spoliation if the adverse party could show that it was prejudiced. *W.R. Grace & Co.-Conn. v. Zotos International, Inc.*, No. 98-CV-838S(F) 2000 WL 1843258 (W.D.N.Y. Nov. 2, 2000). Finally, it is always good practice to consult the local rules of the district court in which the issue is pending, as they may mandate the scope of required disclosure.

41. DISCOVERY AND *DAUBERT*

The McKenzie Manufacturing Co. makes and sells a portable compressor used to power construction tools. Jones, a construction worker who was seriously injured by a fall from a two-story scaffold, has sued McKenzie, alleging that his injuries were caused by a malfunction of a McKenzie compressor that caused his power tool to jam, which in turn threw him off-balance. Jones alleges negligent design and manufacture of the compressor. The case is pending in federal court.

Pursuant to the court's scheduling order, counsel for Jones and McKenzie timely exchanged Rule 26(a)(2)(B) expert disclosures. The plaintiff's expert engineer, Dr. Adams, concluded that the McKenzie product was negligently designed and manufactured because the metal pins holding the compressor to its frame were too weak to secure it under foreseeable work conditions. The opinion was largely based on destructive testing done by Adams in her laboratory at the local university, where she is a professor in the engineering department.

After reviewing Dr. Adams's report with its own expert witness, McKenzie's lawyer noted Adams's deposition. During the deposition, defense counsel sought to ask Adams about the facts and data upon which she relied to reach her opinions, the tests used, their origin, their use within the engineering community, the error rates associated with the testing, and any peer-review literature discussing the reliability and validity of such tests. Before each question on these topics, plaintiff's counsel objected on the ground of relevance. Defense counsel responded, "I am entitled to this information under *Daubert*."[1] Plaintiff's counsel responded, "You're wrong. All you're entitled to in discovery is the information described in Rule 26(a)(2), which says nothing at all about tests and principles used, error rates, acceptance within a scientific or technical community, or whether they have been peer reviewed. Your questions are beyond the scope of discovery allowed by Rule 26(b)(1), and I instruct the witness not to answer them."

Defense counsel filed a motion asking the court to order a resumption of the deposition to allow him to discover the information that plaintiff's counsel instructed the witness not to provide. How should the court rule?

Comment: The court should grant the motion: the questions were proper and the information sought is discoverable. Under Rule 26(b)(1), discov-

---

1. *Daubert v. Merrell Dow Pharm., Inc.*, 509 U.S. 579 (1993).

ery includes nonprivileged facts relevant to the claims and defenses raised by the parties' pleadings. Clearly, information underlying the expert's opinion is relevant to the claims and defenses raised in the pleadings, and Rule 26(a)(2) provides for substantial preliminary disclosure of expert opinions and supporting bases. In addition, Rule 26(b)(4)(A) permits a party to "depose any person who has been identified as an expert whose opinions may be presented at trial" and delays the deposition of an expert until after the Rule 26(a)(2)(B) disclosures have been made. It is equally clear that the word "expert" in Rules 26(a)(2) and 26(b)(4)(A) means a witness called to testify under FRE 702 as to an opinion or otherwise involving scientific, technical, or specialized matters. Commentary to the 1993 Changes to the Federal Rules of Civil Procedure, 146 F.R.D. 401, 635.

In *Daubert*, the Court clarified the standards that trial courts should use under FRE 104(a) (which requires that the court make a preliminary determination as to the admissibility of evidence and the qualification of witnesses) and FRE 702 (which addresses expert opinion testimony). In doing so, it departed from the "general acceptance test" for admissibility of scientific evidence announced in *Frye v. United States*, 293 F. 1013 (D.C. Cir. 1923) and almost universally followed thereafter. Now, to determine admissibility of expert testimony, trial courts, following *Daubert*, are to assess whether: (a) the proffered expert evidence is relevant to the issues to be decided; (b) it will help the jury understand the evidence or determine disputed facts; and (c) the science used by the expert fits the issues to be resolved in the litigation. *Id.* at 591. The Court identified four nonexclusive factors that a trial court should use to evaluate whether expert evidence meets the requirements of FRE 702: whether (1) the expert's opinions are based on methodology that can be tested; (2) the methodology has been subject to peer review; (3) there is a known, and if so, acceptable error rate associated with the methodology used; and (4) the methodology has been generally accepted within the relevant scientific or technical community. *Id.* at 593-95. Thus, *Daubert* focuses on the methodology used by the expert rather than the specific conclusions reached. *Id.* at 592-93.

In 1999, the Supreme Court decided *Kumho Tire*, which made the *Daubert* factors relevant to all expert testimony, not just novel scientific evidence.[2] As a result, the four *Daubert/Kumho Tire* factors are relevant discovery for all expert witnesses. This is further underscored by the December 1, 2000, changes to FRE 702, which added three requirements to the foundation necessary to support admissibility of expert evidence: (1) the expert's opinion must be based on sufficient facts or data; (2) it must be based on methods or principles that are reliable; and (3) the application of the methods or principles to the facts of the case must be reliable.

As the Committee notes explain, the three new factors complement the *Daubert/Kumho Tire* factors, but have potentially broader applicability, as they include other factors that may be relevant but are not within the holdings of *Daubert and Kumho Tire. See* Commentary to the December 2000 changes to FRE 72, 192 F.R.D. 399, 418-24 (2000). Examples include whether: (1) the expert proposes to testify about matters that directly result from research conducted independent of the litigation; (2) the expert unjustifiably extrapolated from an accepted premise to an unwarranted conclusion; (3) the expert adequately accounted for obvious alternative explanations; (4) the expert is being as careful in his "forensic" work as in his regular nonlitigation-related consulting; and (5) the field of expertise claimed by the expert is known to reach reliable results for the type of opinion the expert would give. *Id.* at 419.

This means that a litigator must be familiar with the elements of the Rule 26(a)(2)(B) expert disclosures, the *Daubert/Kumho Tire* factors, and the foundational requirements of newly revised FRE 702. The lawyer must also know where each of these considerations fits into the pretrial/trial continuum, in order to (a) comply fully with the obligations to provide discovery to the other side and (b) obtain sufficient discovery about the opposing expert opinions. The price tag for failure to satisfy both obligations could be steep. Failure to provide the required expert disclosures and discovery likely will result in exclusion of the expert's testimony in whole or in part under Rule 37(c). Failure to discover enough information about the opinion that will be offered by an adverse party may result in surprise at trial and the admission into evidence of very damaging testimony.

Counsel should approach the discovery of adverse expert testimony with the following considerations in mind in order to avoid these pitfalls. First, Rule 26(a)(2) establishes a mandatory minimum amount of

---

2. Kumho Tire Co. v. Carmichael, 526 U.S. 137 (1999).

expert information that must be disclosed to an adverse party, and Rule 37(c) provides the "hammer" to ensure that it is provided.[3] Second, the *Daubert/Kumho Tire*/FRE 702 requirements identify the foundational prerequisites for acceptance of expert testimony at trial. Thus, to be fully prepared, it is critical to discover both the opinions and factual basis for an adverse expert's testimony as well as the facts that will be relevant to the admissibility of that evidence at trial.

This point is illustrated by *Samuel v. Ford*, 96 F. Supp. 2d 491 (D. Md. 2000), in which the court fashioned a *Daubert/Kumho Tire* "checklist," attached to the opinion as an appendix, that counsel were asked to follow when seeking to challenge the admissibility of an expert's testimony at trial. The checklist requires the following information: (1) the name of the expert whose opinion(s) is challenged; (2) a brief summary of the opinion(s) challenged, including a reference to the source of the opinion (such as the Rule 26(a)(2)(B) disclosure, deposition transcript, etc.); (3) a brief description of the methodology/reasoning used by the expert to reach the challenged opinion(s), including a reference to the source materials; (4) a brief explanation of the basis for the challenge to the reasoning/methodology used by the expert, including a reference to the source material for the challenge; (5) a discussion of the known or potential error rate associated with the methodology employed by the expert, if known; (6); a summary of the relevant peer review material, if available, with citation to the source; and (7) a discussion of whether the methods/principles used have been generally accepted within the relevant scientific or technical community, with citation to references. *Samuel*, 96 F. Supp. 2d at 504. A court may not insist on such a detailed checklist in connection with challenges to expert testimony, but it is a useful reference tool. *In re Westminster Associates, Ltd.*, 265 B.R. 329, 332 (Bankr. M.D. Fla. 2001) ("Although *Daubert* set forth several factors a court should consider when deciding whether to admit scientific testimony, the Rule 702 inquiry is a flexible one and the *Daubert* factors do not constitute a definitive checklist.").

Although counsel may discover the facts relevant to the *Daubert/*

---

3. Rule 37(c) allows the court to sanction a party that fails fully to make the FRCP 26(a)(2) disclosures by excluding its expert's testimony, in whole or part. *See* chapter 43 (Rule 26(a) Disclosures and Rule 37(c) Motion for Failure to Disclose, Misleading Disclosures, or Refusal to Admit).

Kumho Tire factors through any combination of the five main discovery methods, the best way to develop this information is to depose the expert after obtaining the Rule 26(a)(2)(b) disclosure and (pursuant to Rule 34) all documents relating to the expert's analysis and opinions. Counsel should be mindful that the pretrial scheduling order may impose a deadline for filing motions in limine challenging an expert's opinions. It is therefore important to be sure that the discovery is concluded sufficiently in advance of the deadline to permit proper preparation of the motion and supporting materials. The materials obtained in discovery will be invaluable in making a thorough *Daubert/Kumho Tire/* FRE 702 challenge. And, as FRE 104(a) and 1101(d)(1) allow the court to suspend applicability of the rules of evidence (except for privilege) in deciding such a challenge, detailed discovery may eliminate the need for a hearing where live testimony is presented.

Practice Tip

If the scheduling order does not have a deadline for filing motions challenging expert testimony, an attorney who proposes to make such a challenge should contact the court before the discovery cutoff, inform chambers (and opposing counsel) of the likelihood of a *Daubert/Kumho Tire/*FRE 702 challenge, and request imposition of a deadline. It is important to do this sufficiently far in advance of trial to allow the court to schedule an FRE 104(a) hearing. In cases involving multiple experts, highly technical subjects, or strong challenges to the methods and principles used by an expert, an FRE 104(a) hearing can last for days; the court must consider and address all of the *Daubert/Kumho Tire/*FRE 702 factors in order to make a proper ruling. Obviously, such a rigorous hearing cannot easily take place on the eve of (much less during) trial. An eleventh-hour filing of an expert exclusion motion is not likely to be welcomed by the court; allowing inadequate time for consideration may diminish the moving party's chances of success.

Further, asking the court to impose a deadline highlights the possibility that an FRE 104(a) hearing may have to be held before trial. Finally, the existence of a deadline allows each lawyer the comfort of knowing that if the deadline passes without a challenge to his expert, he need not worry that one will be filed on the eve of trial.

---

42. REASONABLENESS OF FEES AND EXPENSES CHARGED TO DEPOSING PARTY BY ADVERSE EXPERT

A patient sued his doctor for medical malpractice. The medical issues in the case were arcane and complex, and it was only with difficulty that defense counsel was able to locate and retain a qualified medical expert. As her initial task, the expert prepared an affidavit in support of defendant's motion for summary judgment. She later wrote a report. Upon receipt of the expert's affidavit and report, plaintiff's counsel noticed the expert's deposition for his office. The expert, who lived on the opposite coast, flew into town for the deposition, which proceeded without incident. Nothing was said by either counsel before or during the deposition about the amount or payment of the expert's fees and expenses. Two weeks later, the defense expert sent a bill to plaintiff's counsel as follows:

4/1—4/8	prep for deposition (home)	15.0 hours
4/8	travel to deposition	7.5 hours
4/9	prep for deposition (counsel's office)	10.0 hours
4/10	deposition	7.0 hours
4/11	return home from deposition	7.5 hours
		47.0 hours

47.0 hours @ $500 an hour $23,500.00

Expenses: Airfare, taxi, meals, drinks, hotel (including
                       mini-bar and movie) $2,332.00

Total Amount Due $25,832.00

Payment Due Within Ten (10) Days

The bill was not paid. The expert called defense counsel, who in turn telephoned plaintiff's counsel. Plaintiff's counsel got right to the point: "I will not pay this ridiculous bill. We didn't agree that I would pay anything, much less $500 an hour. As to the deposition itself, it took seven hours, instead of two or three, only because there were numerous inconsistencies between your expert's affidavit and her written report, which were further complicated by additional inconsistencies in her testimony. Why should I pay for that? And even if I were obligated to pay for her time actually testifying, I see no reason why I should pay for her time spent rehearsing with you—that's for your client's benefit, not mine! Further, it is not my fault that your expert lives on the opposite side of the country—why should I pay for her plane fare, when you could have hired somebody who lives close by? And do you really expect me to subsidize her bar tab and entertainment? Forget it." Defense counsel responded, "Look, I disagree with everything you've said, but rather than fight about it, why don't we settle this matter for 75 cents on the dollar?" Plaintiff's counsel refused to negotiate for any compromise, and the conversation ended.

Defense counsel thereafter filed a motion under Rule 26(b)(4)(C) seeking an order compelling payment of the fees and expenses charged by the expert witness. Defense counsel also sought an award of attorney's fees and costs incurred in bringing the motion pursuant to Rules 11 and 37. Plaintiff's counsel opposed the motion. How should the court rule?

Comment: Rule 26(b)(4)(A) provides in part that "[a] party may depose any person who has been identified as an expert whose opinions may be presented at trial. . . ." Rule 26(b)(4)(C) says that "[u]nless manifest injustice would result, (i) the court shall require that the party seeking discovery pay the expert a reasonable fee for time spent in responding to discovery under this subdivision. . . ." The operative words are "shall" and "reasonable." Ordinarily, the expert witness is entitled to *some* compensation from the deposing party, regardless of who ultimately prevails in the action. *United States v. City of Twin Falls*, 806 F.2d 862, 879 (9th Cir. 1986). Thus, plaintiff's counsel's claim that he is not obliged to pay anything because there was no agreement to do so is wrong. His best line of defense is that the amount claimed is unreasonable.

In *Goldwater v. Postmaster Gen'l of the United States*, 136 F.R.D. 337 (D. Conn. 1991), the court identified six criteria to determine the "reasonableness" of an expert's fees: (1) the witness's area of expertise; (2) the education and training required to provide the expert insight that is sought; (3) the prevailing rates of other comparably respected available experts; (4) the nature, quality, and complexity of the discovery responses provided; (5) the cost of living in the particular geographic area; and (6) any other factor likely to be of assistance to the court in balancing the interests implicated by Rule 26.

The court in *Jochims v. Isuzu Motors, Ltd.*, 141 F.R.D. 493 (S.D. Iowa 1992), accepted the *Goldwater* approach but differed with some of the criteria outlined there, reasoning that "the cost of living in a particular geographic area is [not] directly relevant to a reasonable fee and, in any event, this factor is frequently . . . calibrated into prevailing market rates." 141 F.R.D. at 496. The *Jochims* court proposed two other factors: (1) the fee actually being charged to the party who retained the expert; and (2) fees traditionally charged by the expert on related matters. Numerous courts have adopted this test. *See, e.g., Hose v. Chicago & N.W. Transp. Co.*, 154 F.R.D. 222 (S.D. Iowa 1994); *Dominguez v. Syntex Laboratories, Inc.*, 149 F.R.D. 158 (S.D. Ind.), *upon reconsideration*, 149 F.R.D. 166 (S.D. Ind. 1993). Ultimately, however, a court may use any test or set of criteria it wishes to determine the reasonableness of claimed fees and expenses; as may be expected, the reported decisions often seem to conflict. *See generally* Wright, Miller & Marcus, 8 *Federal Practice and Procedure: Civil* 2d ed., § 2034.

Some courts use the fee charged by the opposing expert as a useful benchmark for setting the fee of the expert deposed. *See, e.g., Bowen v. Monahan,* 163 F.R.D. 571 (D. Neb. 1995). Other courts mandate that a medical expert charge no greater hourly rate for a deposition (or in-court testimony, for that matter) than he or she charges for the provision of medical services. Even if the expert in the example can justify a rate of $500 an hour by reference to such benchmarks, however, the court may reduce the amount allowable on the ground that the total claimed is simply "unconscionable" given all the circumstances. *Cabana* v. *Forcier*, 200 F.R.D. 9 (D. Mass. 2001).

Cases vary widely on payment for deposition preparation. In the example, the expert seeks payment for 15 hours of preparation time at her own office, and an additional 10 hours of time spent in the office of the defense attorney preparing her. The assertion of plaintiff's counsel that he is not obligated to pay for *any* preparation time, on the theory that it is really in aid of defendant's case, finds support in a minority of cases. *See, e.g., McBrian v. Liebert Corp.* 173 F.R.D. 491 (N.D. Ill. 1997); *Baker v. Taco Bell,* 163 F.R.D. 348 (D. Colo. 1995). The majority of cases, however, hold that time spent in actual preparation for the deposition, as opposed to time spent generally preparing for the case or time spent in educating the expert's lawyer, is compensable. *New York v. Solvent Chem. Co., Inc.*, 2002 WL 31190938 (W.D.N.Y. 2002); *Magee v. Paul Revere Life Ins. Co.*, 172 F.R.D. 627, 647 (E.D.N.Y. 1997); *Hose v. Chicago & N. W. Transp. Co., supra* at 224. Even then, however, compensation must be reasonable in light of the totality of circumstances. *New York v. Solvent Chem. Co., Inc., supra.*; *Fleming v. United States*, 205 F.R.D. 188 (W.D.

Va. 2000); *Collins v. Village of Woodridge*, 197 F.R.D. 354 (N.D. Ill. 1999). Applying the majority rule to the example, the court might allow part of the time spent in preparation by the expert in her office and disallow the time spent in consultation with defense counsel.

Plaintiff's counsel objected to paying for the expert's travel time from one coast to the other, as well as the associated expenses. Most courts, however, allow reasonable compensation for such expenses. *Frederick v. Columbia University*, 212 F.R.D. 176 (S.D.N.Y. 2003); *New York v. Solvent Chem. Co., Inc., supra.*; *Silberman v. Innovation Luggage, Inc.*, 2002 WL 1870383 (S.D.N.Y. 2002); *Fleming v. United States, supra.* Cases holding *contra* include *McBrian, Inc. v. Liebert Corp., supra,* and *Rosenblum v. Warner & Sons, Inc.*, 148 F.R.D. 237 (N.D. Ind. 1993). Some courts permit such payment at a reduced rate. *Grdinich v. Bradlees*, 187 F.R.D. 77 (S.D.N.Y. 1999). Applying that rule here, plaintiff's counsel knew that if he wanted to take the defense expert's deposition, either he would have to travel to the expert or she would have to travel to him. (The argument that defendant could have retained an expert nearby, thus saving on travel expense, is a fact-intensive question that plaintiff's counsel could have raised with the court before noticing the deposition at the site of his choice.) In these circumstances, the court might well order the plaintiff to pay the expert for a round-trip tourist ticket and reasonable hotel expenses, but disallow compensation for the mini-bar bills and in-room movie charges, which bear no relation to the costs of travel or to the case.

Some federal districts have local rules that address one or more of the expert compensation issues raised in this case. It is thus essential to consult such rules. On the issues of travel time and time spent in preparation for deposition, *see, e.g.,* Local Rule 104(11)(a) of the Civil Rules of the United States District Court for the District of Maryland: "Unless otherwise ordered by the Court, any reasonable fee charged by an expert for the time spent in a discovery deposition and in traveling to and from the deposition shall be paid by the party taking the deposition. The fee charged by the expert for time spent preparing for the deposition shall be paid by the party designating the expert. The expert may not charge an opposing party for a discovery deposition a fee at any hourly rate higher than the rate that he or she charges for the preparation of his or her report."

In the example, plaintiff's counsel argues that he should not have to pay for seven hours of deposition when the job could have been completed in two or three but for numerous conflicting statements made by the expert in her affidavit and report. Here again, his view is unlikely to prevail: Courts usually decline to parse the substance of a deposition to determine the reasonableness of the time spent. *New York v. Solvent Chem. Co., Inc., supra* (alleged "lack of knowledge" of the expert on the critical issues is irrelevant to compensation obligation); *EEOC v. Johnson & Higgins, Inc.*, 1999 WL 32909 (S.D.N.Y. 1999) (deposing party was obligated to pay expert witness fees even though certain experts allegedly were redundant or were testifying on irrelevant issues). At least one court, however, has reduced the number of deposition hours for which an expert must be compensated by the adverse party as a means of lowering the expert's effective hourly rate. *Cabana v. Forcier, supra.*

The final issue is the propriety of an award of attorneys' fees and costs incurred by defense counsel in filing the motion to compel payment. Rule 11 is an improper basis on which to ground such motion, as it provides, at subsection (d), that "Subdivisions (a) through (c) of this rule [which provisions permit sanctions to be imposed by the court] do not apply to disclosures and discovery requests, responses, objections, and motions that are subject to the provisions of Rule 26 through 37." Rule 37(a)(4) does provide a basis for such award, however. In this case an award might well be justified—even assuming the expert is not entitled to all of the fees and expenses claimed—because plaintiff's counsel refused to pay *any* fees or expenses despite the mandatory language of the rule, and subsequently declined defense counsel's invitation to negotiate for a compromise resolution. *New York v. Solvent Chem. Co., Inc., supra.* A modest compromise offer, even if not accepted by defense counsel, might have saved the plaintiff some money.

Practice Tip

Several themes emerge from the somewhat disparate decisions on these issues: (1) counsel should consult the local rules before retaining an expert; (2) counsel should be aware of the prevailing rates charged by comparable experts (as well as the rate charged by the opposing expert) and try to negotiate with the expert for rates that are consistent with that—alternatively, counsel should be prepared to show why the specialized knowledge of the expert commands a premium over rates typically charged; (3) time spent in preparation for which compensation is sought should be limited to preparation for the deposition, and the details of such preparation should be carefully documented in order to justify the claim; (4) if the distance that the expert must travel is an issue, counsel should be able to show that a comparable expert more conveniently located was not available; (5) costs should be kept to the necessary minimum; (6) counsel objecting to the fees and expenses sought by an expert should honestly negotiate for a compromise in order to better defend against a motion for sanctions; and (7) unless you already know what rates, charges, and expenses the expert you are deposing will charge, find out before the deposition and try to resolve the problem before it arises.

Section 4:

Sanctions and Protective Orders

Sanctions and Protective Orders $\Large 4$

OVERVIEW

Ask a civil litigator for the first words that come to mind when you say "discovery" and the likely responses will be "dispute," "motion," and "sanctions." Discovery, more than any other aspect of pretrial procedure, generates disputes that lead to the filing of motions and often the imposition of sanctions.

The Federal Rules of Civil Procedure contain a complex and often confusing series of rules that govern discovery motions and the sanctions that may be imposed for violations of the discovery rules. Rule 11, perhaps the best known sanction rule, does not apply to discovery requests, responses, or objections, although it is applicable to discovery motions. However, Rule 26(g) imposes on counsel and parties similar obligations of good faith and fair dealing in the conduct of discovery. And, as does Rule 11, Rule 26(g) states that the signature of an attorney or party on a discovery request, disclosure, response or objection constitutes a certification that to the best of the signer's knowledge, information, and belief, formed after a reasonable inquiry, the disclosure, response, or objection is complete and correct, and consistent with existing law or a good faith argument to modify or reverse existing law. The signature further certifies that the discovery request, response, or objection is not filed for an improper purpose, that is it not unreasonable, and that it is not excessively burdensome.

Rule 26(g) also requires the court to impose appropriate sanctions against a party that violates the rule. In this regard, discovery sanctions under Rule 26(g) and Rule 37, the other discovery sanction rule, differ from Rule 11 sanctions. Following the 1993 changes to the Rules of Civil Procedure, courts no longer are required to impose sanctions for Rule 11 violations, but retain broad discretion whether to do so. Rule 11(c). In contrast, discovery sanctions under Rules 26(g) and 37 "shall" be imposed unless the court finds that the party whose conduct was in violation of the rules was substantially justified in its conduct; the misconduct was harmless; or that the imposition of a sanction would be unfair. While the court continues to have discretion whether to impose sanctions under Rules 26(g) and 37, that discretion is circumscribed.

The sanctions that may be imposed for discovery violations include both *compensatory* sanctions, such as an award of costs and reasonable attorney's fees to the prevailing party in the dispute, and *coercive* sanctions, designed to punish the wrongdoer and deter others from similar misconduct. Examples of coercive sanctions include ordering that certain evidence may not be introduced at trial; that certain claims or defenses may not be proved at trial; that claims, defenses, or pleadings be stricken; that an action be dismissed; that a default judgment be entered; or that a party or attorney be held in contempt. Rule 37(b)(2).

The discovery rules guarantee due process to the party facing a sanctions motion by requiring that it be given an opportunity to be heard before sanctions are imposed. This requirement, however, may be satisfied by allowing the parties to file written submissions; in-court hearings are not required. See Rule 37. Given the nature of discovery practice and the need for speedy resolution of discovery disputes, it is likely that an in-court hearing will not be held before discovery sanctions motions are ruled on by the court.

The discovery rules also reflect an expectation that the parties will try to resolve their discovery disputes without involving the court. Only when a lawyer has tried and failed to solve a discovery problem may he file a motion seeking court assistance, and the motion must certify that the good faith compromise efforts have occurred. Rules 26 (c) and (g); Rule 37(a) and (d).

There are two broad categories of discovery motions: motions for protective orders under Rule 26(c), and motions seeking orders to compel discovery or sanction the failure to provide discovery under Rule 37. The former allows a party that receives an objectionable or oppressive discovery request to ask the court to issue an order that relieves it from complying with the objectionable request. The latter permits a party that has received incomplete or evasive discovery responses to seek a court order directing that the discovery be made or sanctioning the offending party for failing to do so. Rules 26(c) and 37 must also be read in conjunction with Rules 26(b)(1), which defines the scope of permissible discovery, and Rule 26(b)(2), which requires the court, on its own or in response to a motion for a protective order, to issue appropriate orders limiting or blocking objectionable, overly burdensome, or expensive discovery. Rule 26(b)(2) contains a series of cost-benefit factors the court is to consider to ensure that only discovery that is fair and reasonable, given the nature of the case, is permitted.

Finally, when considering the types of discovery motions that may be filed, a lawyer must refer to Rule 26(a), which identifies three types of required disclosures. They are similar to discovery in that they communicate factual information, but differ from discovery because they are obligations imposed on parties by the rules of procedure and the court's scheduling order, and do not depend on the filing of a request by a party. The disclosures are: Rule 26(a)(1) initial disclosures; Rule 26(a)(2) expert witness disclosures; and Rule 26(a)(3) pretrial disclosures.

Rule 37 identifies five discrete types of discovery motions that may be filed, each with its own set of standards. Rule 37(a) permits the filing of a motion to compel a discovery disclosure or discovery response. Rule 37(b) permits a party that has already obtained an order compelling a disclosure or discovery to seek sanctions against the party that failed to obey the prior discovery order. Rule 37(b)(2)(B) identifies five nonexclusive types of sanctions that the court may impose against a party that has disobeyed a prior discovery order. They include such very severe sanctions as ordering that the disobedient party may not introduce evidence at trial, ordering that certain facts will be taken as having been established at trial, ordering that the party is precluded from pursuing various claims or defenses at trial, ordering the entry of a default judgment against the party, dismissing the case, or holding a party or lawyer in contempt of court.

Rule 37(c) deals with motions seeking sanctions for failure to make discovery disclosures, making misleading discovery disclosures, and failures to admit the genuineness of facts or authenticity of documents. If a court grants a Rule 37(c) motion, it may also impose certain of the severe Rule 37(b)(2)(B) sanctions, including preclusion of evidence at trial, striking pleadings, foreclosing defenses or claims, or entering a default judgment or dismissal.

Rule 37(d) permits a court to sanction a party that refuses to attend its own deposition, does not properly name a Rule 30(b)(6) designee to testify as its representative in a deposition, or completely fails to file answers to interrogatories or document production requests. As with Rule 37(c), permissible sanctions include the very serious sanctions listed in Rule 37(b)(2)(B).

Finally, Rule 37(g) permits a court to sanction a party or attorney who fails to participate in good faith in the development of a discovery plan as required by Rule 26(f).

Given the number and differences among the possible discovery motions and sanctions, a lawyer must know when each motion is appropriate and what sanctions are available. This is crucial not only to securing the right relief for an opponent's discovery abuses, but also to knowing how to respond to discovery so as to avoid the risk of sanctions.

In addition, discovery-related sanctions may be imposed by courts (1) based on their inherent authority to govern actions, upon a finding of bad faith or willful violation of discovery rules, *Chambers v. NASCO*, 501 U.S. 32 (1991); *United States v. Horn*, 29 F.3d 754, 760 (1st Cir. 1994); *United States v. Shaffer Equipment Co.*, 11 F.3d 450 (4th Cir. 1993); and (2) under 28 U.S.C. § 1927, to penalize an attorney who "so multiplies the proceedings in any case unreasonably and vexatiously" that other parties incur costs and expenses. Finally, Rule of Professional Conduct 3.2, which prohibits as unprofessional conduct the delay or making of litigation unreasonably expensive, may be violated by abuse of the discovery process, causing the court to refer the offending lawyer to the appropriate disciplinary authorities.

These various rules are discussed in the chapters below and summarized in a chart at chapter 50, *infra*.

43. RULE 26(A) DISCLOSURES AND RULE 37(C) MOTION FOR FAILURE TO DISCLOSE, MISLEADING DISCLOSURES, OR REFUSAL TO ADMIT

Trial is scheduled to begin in two weeks. Plaintiff's counsel has advised the defendant's lawyer that plaintiff intends to ask the court to allow him to supplement his list of trial exhibits. He wants to include records from the plaintiff's treating physicians that support the claim that the defendant's negligence prevented successful intervention in the treatment of plaintiff's cancer. Plaintiff's counsel advises that he will make this request of the court informally at the pretrial conference next week.

Defense counsel objects on the ground that these new documents were not listed in plaintiff's Rule 26(a)(1) initial disclosures, nor were they identified in plaintiff's Rule 26(a)(3) pretrial disclosures (which were filed four weeks earlier in conformity with the scheduling order). Defense counsel also notes that the documents were not identified or produced in response to his document production requests, nor were they disclosed in a timely Rule 26(e) supplemental disclosure. Moreover, the deadline for supplementing the Rule 26(a) disclosures has passed and trial is now only two weeks away. Defense counsel maintains that his case is severely prejudiced by plaintiff's attempted last-minute maneuver. He asks the court for a preclusive order and for sanctions.

How should the court rule?

Comment: The resolution of these questions is governed by Rules 26(a)(1)-(3), Rule 26(e)(1), and Rule 37(c). Rule 26(a) requires three types of disclosures, whether or not there is any discovery request from an adverse party: Rule 26(a)(1) *initial disclosures*; Rule 26(a)(2) *expert disclosures*; and Rule 26(a)(3) *pretrial disclosures*. Rule 26(e)(1) requires the timely supplementation of the Rule 26(a) disclosures, and Rule 37(c) allows for imposition of sanctions for failures to make Rule 26 disclosures or supplement other discovery requests.

Rule 26(a)(1) Initial Disclosures: The 1993 amendments added Rule 26(a)(1), which requires each party to disclose: (1) the name and other identifying information for individuals likely to have discoverable information relevant to disputed facts alleged with particularity in the pleadings; (2) a copy or description of documents/data compilations/ and tangible things relevant to disputed facts alleged with particularity in the pleadings; (3) a computation of any category of damages claimed; and (4) any insurance agreement that is a potential source for indemnifying that party or reimbursing his or her expenses associated with the litigation. The hope was that these four disclosures would provide basic information, thereby facilitating case evaluation and discovery planning. Commentary to the 1993 Rule Changes, 146 F.R.D. at 627-28.

To accomplish its goal of keeping expenses to a minimum and expediting prompt exchange of crucial information, the new rule also provided that, absent agreement of the parties, local rule of court, or order of the court, formal discovery would not take place until after the Rule 26(a)(1) disclosures had been made. Rule 26(d).

Unfortunately, Rule 26(a)(1) did not produce the desired effect. First, because a party was required to disclose the identity of witnesses and documents "relevant to disputed facts alleged with particularity in the pleadings," the new rule could be read to force that party to volunteer information that was harmful to its case, and that it did not intend to use at trial. This turned the adversary process upside down and created a serious conflict of interest for the disclosing party. It also was seen as likely to increase the costs of pretrial proceedings by inviting disputes about the meaning of the words "relevant to disputed facts alleged with particularity." *See* Dissenting Statement of Justices Scalia, Thomas and Souter to the 1993 Changes to the Rules of Civil Procedure, 146 F.R.D. at 510-13.

Second, as originally enacted, Rule 26(a)(1) contained "opt-out" language that allowed courts to adopt local rules and standing orders and permitted the parties to stipulate to exempt cases from the Rule 26(a)(1) disclosures. *Id.* at 629. The unpopularity of the Rule 26(a)(1) disclosures and the availability of "opt-out" provisions caused many federal courts to adopt local rules or standing orders to eliminate such disclosures. However, there was no uniformity in these "opt-out" provisions, making it difficult for lawyers practicing in multiple districts to keep up with the differing requirements. Commentary to the 2000 Changes to the Rules of Procedure, 192 F.R.D. at 384-85.

To address these problems, the 2000 changes to Rule 26(a)(1) narrowed the disclosure of potential witnesses and documents and things to those that "the disclosing party may use to support its claims or defenses, unless solely for impeachment." The phrase "use to support its claims or defenses" was intended to encompass "any use at a pretrial conference, to support a motion, or at trial," or the use of a document as an exhibit in a discovery deposition. Commentary to the 2000 Rule Changes, 192 F.R.D. at 385. Further, the changes deleted the provision that allowed district courts to opt-out of the disclosure requirement except in a limited number of categories of cases. Commentary to the 2000 Rule Changes, 192 F.R.D. at 385.

The 2000 rule changes, however, did allow a court to make case-specific findings that the Rule 26(a)(1) initial disclosures need not be made, particularly if objections to making them were filed by one or more parties. Likewise, the changes permitted the parties to a case to stipulate that the initial disclosures would not be made.

Rule 26(a)(2) Expert Disclosures: In addition to the Rule 26(a)(1) initial disclosures, the 1993 changes adopted Rule 26(a)(2), which requires extensive disclosures about the opinions of experts retained, or regularly employed by a party, to provide opinion testimony at trial. These disclosures, extensively discussed at chapter 35, Expert Disclosures—Treating Physician or Other Hybrid Fact/Expert Witness, and chapter 34, Timing and Supplementation of Expert Disclosures, *supra,* differentiated between so-called "hybrid expert witnesses" and "retained experts." Hybrid experts were fact witnesses, by virtue of their involvement in the events that led to the litigation, who also possessed qualifications that would entitle them under FRE 702 to give opinion testimony about matters involving scientific, technical, or specialized information. Retained experts were those hired to give expert testimony or employees of a party whose duties as an employee regularly involved giving expert testimony. Rule 26(a)(2), Commentary to the 1993 Rule Changes, 146 F.R.D. at 633-35.

As to the former, Rule 26(a)(2)(A) only required the disclosure of the name of a hybrid expert. As to the latter, Rule 26(a)(2) required the disclosure of detailed information regarding the opinions to be expressed and the basis and reasons therefor, as well as the data or other information considered in forming the opinions, and the qualifications, compensation, and publications of the expert.

Rule 26(a)(3) Pretrial Disclosures: Rule 26(a)(3) disclosures, due not later than 30 days before trial unless otherwise ordered by the court, required each party to identify the following, except if offered solely for impeachment: (1) the name, address, and telephone number of each witness, separately designating those expected to be presented from those to be called only if the need arises; (2) the designation of the witnesses whose testimony was expected to be presented by deposition, referencing the transcript portions intended to be offered into evidence; and (3) an "appropriate" identification of each document or other exhibit, including summaries of other evidence, separately identifying those expected to be used from those that may be used if the need arises.

Evidence expected to be used "solely for impeachment purposes" is not subject to these discovery requirements. Rule 26(a)(1) (which contains the same language), Rule 26(a)(3), and the Rules commentary do not define that phrase. Obviously, the idea that impeachment is the process of diminishing the credibility of a witness is familiar enough to need no formal explanation. The difficulty is that in addition to the three methods of impeachment expressly authorized by the Rules of Evidence (FRE 608, impeachment by character trait of untruthfulness or by prior conduct probative of untruthfulness; FRE 609, impeachment by prior qualifying conviction; and FRE 613, impeachment by prior inconsistent statement), there are three common law methods of impeachment that may be used: impeachment by evidence of motive, bias, or interest; impeachment by showing diminished capacity to perceive, remember, or relate; and impeachment by specific contradiction. *Behler v. Hanlon,* 199 F.R.D. 553, 556 (D. Md. 2001), *citing* 4 Jack B. Weinstein & Margaret A. Berger, *Weinstein's Federal Evidence* § 607.03[2][a] (2d ed.1997).

Of these methods, the last, impeachment by specific contradiction, poses particular problems in the context of Rules 26(a)(1) and (3), as impeachment by contradiction involves introducing as substantive evidence extrinsic, noncollateral facts that contradict what a prior witness said. The impeachment is achieved if the extrinsic contradictory evidence is more credible or of greater weight than the testimony of the witness who testified to the contrary. However, since the extrinsic contradictory evidence is offered for a substantive purpose, it is not used *solely* to impeach, and therefore would not be excluded from the disclosure requirement of Rules 26(a)(1) and (3) and the automatic exclusion of Rule 37(c)(1) if not disclosed. It also must be remembered that Rules 26(a)(1) and (3) exempt disclosure of *impeachment* evidence, not *rebuttal* evidence.

Rule 26(a)(3) also imposed on a party receiving pretrial disclosures a duty to advise the producing party within 14 days of any objections to the introduction of the proposed evidence. Failure to give such notice waived all objections other than those pursuant to FRE 402 and 403, absent good cause shown.

The Rule 26(a)(3) pretrial disclosures were intended to impose "an additional duty to disclose, without any request, information customarily needed in final preparation for trial." Commentary to 1993 Rule Changes 146 F.R.D. at 635. They intentionally were timed to be very close to trial "to eliminate the time and expense in making these disclosures of evidence and objections in those cases that settle shortly before trial, while affording a reasonable time for final preparation for trial in those cases that do not settle." *Id.* at 637.

Rule 26(a)(4) provided that unless the court requires otherwise, "all disclosures under Rules 26(a)(1) through (3) must be made in writing, signed, and served." The signature constitutes the important certifications described in Rule 26(g), discussed *infra* at chapter 44 (Sanctions for Bad Faith Discovery Requests: The Requirement of a Signature on Discovery Requests, Responses, and Objections).

Rule 26(e)(1) (Supplementation of Rule 26(a) Disclosures): Finally, the 1993 changes to Rule 26(e) imposed a requirement that the Rule 26(a) disclosures be supplemented at "appropriate intervals" during the discovery process if a disclosing party learned that a prior disclosure was incomplete or incorrect in some material respect. Although the rule did not define what was meant by "appropriate intervals," the commentary to the rule stated that "[t]he obligation to supplement disclosures and discovery responses applies whenever a party learns that its prior disclosures or responses are in some material respect incomplete or incorrect." A party is not obliged, however, to provide supplemental or corrective information that has been otherwise made known in writing or during the discovery process, as when a previously undisclosed witness is identified during a deposition or an expert deponent corrects information contained in an earlier report." Commentary to the 1993 Rule Changes, 146 F.R.D. at 641.

The deadline for supplementation of the Rule 26(a)(2)(B) retained expert disclosures, unless otherwise set by the court, is not later than the deadline for making the Rule 26(a)(3) pretrial disclosures—ordinarily not later than 30 days before trial. Rule 26(e)(1).

Rule 37(c) Sanctions: The outcome in the example is governed by Rule 37(c), which is the mechanism for enforcing Rule 26(a) disclosures and addressing unwarranted refusals to admit when served with Rule 36 requests for admission. Any party that fails to disclose information required to be disclosed by Rule 26(a) and 26(e)(1) without substantial justification is precluded from using the information as evidence at trial, in any motion, or at a hearing unless the failure to disclose was harmless. *Samos Imex Corp. v. Nextel Communications, Inc.*, 194 F.3d 301 (1st Cir. 1999); *Jones v. Lincoln Elect. Co.*, 188 F.3d 709 (7th Cir. 1999); *Sullivan v. Glock*, 175 F.R.D. 497, 503 (D. Md. 1997). "This automatic sanction provides a strong inducement for disclosure of material that the disclosing party would expect to use as evidence, whether at a trial, at a hearing, or on a motion, such as under Rule 56 [summary judgment]." Commentary to the 1993 Rule Changes, 146 F.R.D. at 691.[1]

The two exceptions to the automatic exclusion rule—"substantial justification" for the failure to disclose and "harmlessness"—are not defined, but the commentary provides illustrations that include the inadvertent failure to disclose under Rule 26(a)(1) the name of a witness known to all parties; the failure to list as a trial witness in a Rule 26(a)(3) pretrial disclosure a person listed by another party as a witness; or the lack of knowledge of a pro se litigant of the Rule 26(a) requirements to disclose information. Commentary to the 1993 Rule Changes, 146 F.R.D. at 691.

Beyond such circumstances, courts have fashioned multifactor tests to determine if a failure to disclose was substantially justified or harmless. *See*

---

1. Two further points should be noted: First, Rule 37(a)(3) states that an evasive or incomplete discovery disclosure or response is treated as a failure to disclose or respond. Second, as the Rule 26(a) and 26(e) disclosures do not require the disclosure of information intended to be used solely for impeachment purposes, the Rule 37(c) automatic exclusion is inapplicable to purely impeachment information. Commentary to the 1993 Rule Changes, 146 F.R.D. at 691.

Southern States Rack & Fixture, Inc. v. Sherwin-Williams Co., 318 F.3d 592, 597 (4th Cir. 2003) ("We therefore hold that in exercising its broad discretion to determine whether a nondisclosure of evidence is substantially justified or harmless for purposes of a Rule 37(c)(1) exclusion analysis, a district court should be guided by the following factors: (1) the surprise to the party against whom the evidence would be offered; (2) the ability of that party to cure the surprise; (3) the extent to which allowing the evidence would disrupt the trial; (4) the importance of the evidence; and (5) the nondisclosing party's explanation for its failure to disclose the evidence."); *Woodworker's Supply, Inc. v. Principal Mut. Life Ins. Co.*, 170 F.3d 985 (10th Cir. 1999) (adopting a four-factor test for substantial justification or harmless error evaluations: (1) the prejudice or surprise to the party against whom the evidence would be offered; (2) the ability of that party to cure the prejudice; (3) the extent to which introducing the evidence would disrupt the trial; and (4) whether the failure to disclose was willful or in bad faith); and *United States v. $9,041,598.68*, 163 F.3d 238, 252 (5th Cir. 1998) (adopting a four-factor test for evaluating substantial justification or harmlessness under Rule 37(c)(1): "(1) the importance of the witness's testimony, (2) the prejudice to the opposing party of allowing the witness to testify; (3) the possibility of curing such prejudice by granting a continuance; and (4) the explanation, if any, for the party's failure to identify the witness").

In addition to, or in lieu of, the exclusionary sanction, a court may impose "other appropriate sanctions," including attorneys' fees and costs, provided that the offending party has an opportunity to be heard. Such other sanctions include any of the sanctions allowed by Rule 37(b)(2)(A)-(C). *See Newman v. GHS Osteopathic Inc.*, 60 F.3d 153 (3d Cir. 1995).

Rule 37(c)(2) provides for sanctions against a party that improperly fails to admit the genuineness of any document or the truth of a Rule 36 request. The party that served the Rule 36 request may recover its reasonable expenses, including attorneys' fees, if it proves the genuineness of the document or truth of the fact at trial. Under Rule 37(c)(2), the court must impose the sanctions unless it finds that: (1) the request to admit was objectionable; (2) the admission sought was of no substantial importance; (3) the party failing to admit had a reasonable ground to believe that it would prevail on the matter at trial; or (4) there is any other good reason for the failure to admit.

In the example, the documents that plaintiff's counsel disclosed on the eve of trial (which he intends to use substantively—not merely for impeachment) should have been disclosed in plaintiff's Rule 26(a)(1) initial disclosures and Rule 26(a)(3) pretrial disclosures as well as in response to defendant's Rule 34 document production requests. Likewise, disclosure should have been made in a Rule 26(e) supplementation of disclosures or discovery responses. As Rules 26(a)(1) and (3) were violated, the automatic exclusion called for by Rule 37(c)(1) will prevent plaintiff from using the documents at trial, at a hearing, or in support of any motion unless the court determines that the failure to disclose was substantially justified or harmless. Here, it seems unlikely that the plaintiff can show "harmlessness" because the evidence concerns an important issue and the trial is near. Unless the court is willing to postpone the trial and reopen discovery, the prejudice to defendant cannot easily be overcome. Whether the plaintiff can establish substantial justification for the failure to disclose turns on the reasons for the prior nondisclosure—including when he or his client first became aware of the material. If the explanation is weak, and if the court believes that there was bad faith or willful misconduct, plaintiff will lose.

Practice Tips

To minimize the risk of Rule 37(c) sanctions, consider the following:

1. Carefully check the scheduling order as soon as it is issued to determine the deadlines for making Rule 26(a)(1)-(3) disclosures and the deadline for Rule 26(e) supplementation. If the scheduling order does not set dates, consider asking that they be set—especially the Rule 26(e) supplementation deadline. Keep in mind that if the court refuses to set dates, the rules themselves establish "default" deadlines for each disclosure. Read the rules and determine those default dates.
2. Periodically review the Rule 26(a) disclosures and other discovery responses to determine whether they require supplementation. Remember that supplementation can be informal, Rule 26(e)(1), but it is wise to do it in writing. This will facilitate later proof that the supplementation, in fact, took place.
3. When reviewing your Rule 26(a)(3) pretrial disclosures, make sure that designations of exhibits and witnesses are proper. The

---

rule requires designation of the evidence that a party expects to use and a separate designation for evidence that may be used if the need arises. Keep in mind that the only exception to this disclosure is evidence used solely as impeachment. If you withhold evidence on that basis, remember that it will not be admitted for substantive purposes.

4. Carefully review your opponent's Rule 26(a)(3) pretrial disclosures and make sure that if you have any evidentiary objections (other than objections based on FRE 402 and 403), you give notice to the other side within 14 days. Otherwise, your objections will be waived, absent a showing of good cause.

5. At trial, make sure that you have a copy of your written discovery responses and Rule 26(a)(1)-(3) disclosures as well as any Rule 26(e) supplements. These papers frequently are not filed with the court, Rule 5(d), and if a dispute arises over whether certain evidence was or was not disclosed, it will be helpful to be able to point quickly to your prior disclosure.

6. If you are the subject of a motion to preclude evidence under Rule 37(c)(1), be prepared to address each of the factors identified in the controlling case law in the jurisdiction where the case is pending to demonstrate that (a) the disclosure was made, (b) disclosure was not required, (c) there was substantial justification for not disclosing, or (d) any failure to disclose was harmless.

44. SANCTIONS FOR BAD FAITH DISCOVERY REQUESTS: THE REQUIREMENT OF A SIGNATURE ON DISCOVERY REQUESTS, RESPONSES, AND OBJECTIONS

Plaintiff Technicorp sued its biggest competitor, Defense Solutions, Inc. (DSI), as well as Schultz, a former Technicorp vice president who quit his job to work at DSI. Technicorp alleged that DSI wrongfully induced Schultz to switch jobs in violation of his covenant not to compete, and that DSI planned to use Technicorp trade secrets that Schultz brought with him to DSI in violation of his confidentiality agreement with Technicorp. Technicorp sought injunctive relief and damages against both defendants.

The court issued an expedited discovery order, and counsel for Technicorp promptly served Rule 33 and 34 discovery requests seeking virtually all of DSI's hard-copy and electronically stored research and development, financial, marketing, and personnel records. The discovery requests sought access to DSI's computer hard drives for purposes of searching for deleted records and e-mail communications. Hurriedly prepared, the discovery requests were unsigned.

Counsel for DSI wrote to counsel for Technicorp, objecting to the discovery on the grounds of burdensomeness and overbreadth. She described the large amount of time and exorbitant cost needed to comply with the requests, and attached an affidavit from her client particularizing that burden and expense. She also proposed compromise discovery. Further, she suggested that the lawyers confer by telephone in an effort to come to an agreement. Finally, she sought more time to respond to the requests.

Technicorp's lawyer called, but no agreement was reached. Counsel for Technicorp refused to narrow the scope of discovery, saying, "Look, your client started this thing by stealing Schultz. DSI should have considered the consequences before doing that—why do you think I filed this lawsuit? Just to teach you a lesson!" Counsel for DSI pointed out that it was improper to file a lawsuit and pursue discovery for punitive purposes. Counsel for Technicorp replied, "So what—Rule 11 doesn't apply to discovery. And, by the way, we expect your responses within 30 days. My client specifically instructed me—no extensions!" He then hung up the phone. Counsel for DSI wrote a letter memorializing the conversation and then told her client that they would have to meet the 30-day deadline.

Unfortunately, DSI missed the deadline. One day later, Technicorp filed a motion to compel discovery under Rule 37(a); it made no effort to resolve the dispute informally. DSI opposed the motion on the grounds that the discovery requests were overbroad and burdensome and were served for an improper, punitive purpose. DSI also noted that it was under no obligation to respond at all because the discovery was unsigned. How should the court rule?

Comment: While Rule 11 does not apply to discovery, Rule 26(g), which serves the same function, does. Rule 26(g)(1) provides that Rule 26(a)(1) preliminary disclosures and Rule 26(a)(3) pretrial disclosures must be signed by an attorney or unrepresented party, and that the signature constitutes a certification that the disclosure is complete and correct at the time made to the best of the signer's knowledge, information, and belief formed after reasonable inquiry.

Rule 26(g)(2) imposes the same signature requirement on discovery requests, responses, and objections. On such items, a signature constitutes a certification that, to the best of the signer's knowledge, information, and belief formed after reasonable inquiry, the document is: (a) consistent with the Federal Rules of Civil Procedure, warranted by existing law or a good faith argument for extension, modification, or reversal of existing law; (b) not interposed for an improper purpose, such as to harass, cause unnecessary delay, or needlessly increase litigation cost; and (c) not unreasonable, unduly burdensome, or expensive, given: (i) the needs of the case; (ii) the discovery already had; (iii) the amount in controversy; and (iv) the importance of the issues at stake in the litigation. If the document is not so signed, it shall be stricken unless promptly signed after notice of defect. Absent a signature on the proponent's document, the responding party is not required to take any action. Sanctions, including reasonable attorney's fees and costs, are mandatory if there is a violation unless the court finds substantial justification for such violation. Sanctions may be imposed against the offending attorney and/or party, in response to a motion or on the court's own initiative.

The signature requirement and sanctions provisions of Rule 26(g) were adopted in 1983 as a result of concerns about the increase in abusive discovery tactics. The commentary to the 1983 rule changes explains their function:

> Rule 26(g) imposes an affirmative duty to engage in pretrial discovery in a responsible manner that is consistent with the spirit and purposes of Rules 26 through 37. In addition, Rule 26(g) is designed to curb discovery abuse by explicitly encouraging the

imposition of sanctions. The subdivision provides a deterrent to both excessive discovery and evasion by imposing a certification requirement that obliges each attorney to stop and think about the legitimacy of a discovery request, a response thereto, or an objection. The term "response" includes answers to interrogatories and to requests to admit as well as responses to production requests. Commentary to the 1983 Amendments to the Federal Rules of Civil Procedure, 97 F.R.D. 165, 218.

The drafters stressed that the signature requirement and sanction provisions were intended to impress upon counsel and litigants that "they must be obliged to act responsibly and avoid abuse," and that Rule 26(g) was intended to parallel the requirements of Rule 11. *Id.* at 218-19. The committee notes also provide guidance on the extent of the duties imposed on counsel and parties as to a certification made by signature:

> Although the certification duty requires the lawyer to pause and consider the reasonableness of his request, response or objection, it is not meant to discourage or restrict necessary and legitimate discovery. The rule simply requires that the attorney make a reasonable inquiry into the factual basis of his response, request or objection. The duty to make a 'reasonable inquiry' is satisfied if the investigation undertaken by the attorney and the conclusions drawn therefrom are reasonable under the circumstances. It is an objective standard similar to the one imposed by Rule 11. . . . Ultimately, what is reasonable is a matter for the court to decide on the totality of the circumstances. *Id.* at 219.

The commentary further notes that Rule 26(g) does not require a signing attorney to certify the truthfulness of the *client's* factual responses to a discovery request. Rather, the signature certifies that the lawyer has made a reasonable effort to assure that the client has provided all the information and documents available to him that are responsive to the discovery demand. *Id.*

Finally, the commentary explains the rationale for Rule 26(g) sanctions:

Concern about discovery abuse has led to widespread recognition that there is a need for more aggressive judicial control and supervision [of the discovery process]. . . . Thus the premise of Rule 26(g) is that imposing sanctions on attorneys who fail to meet the rule's standards will significantly reduce abuse by imposing disadvantages therefor. . . . [The Rule] makes explicit the authority judges now have to impose appropriate sanctions and requires them to use it. *Id.* at 220.

Courts have made extensive use of Rule 26(g) in policing abusive discovery tactics. *Imperial Chemicals Indus., PLC v. Barr Laboratories*, 126 F.R.D. 467 (S.D.N.Y. 1989). In *St. Paul Reinsurance Co., Ltd. v. Commercial Fin. Corp.*, 198 F.R.D. 508 (N.D. Iowa 2000), Chief Judge Bennett observed that while the federal rules contemplate that discovery will be broad and liberal, they are premised on the assumption that discovery "requests are tendered in good faith and are not unduly burdensome." *Id.* at 511. When a party objects to a Rule 34 document request on the grounds of relevancy and burdensomeness, it "bears the burden of establishing lack of relevancy or undue burden," which requires a showing that "'the requested documents either do not come within the broad scope of relevance defined pursuant to Fed. R. Civ. P. 26(b)(1) or else are of such marginal relevance that the potential harm occasioned by discovery would outweigh the ordinary presumption in favor of discovery.'" *Id.* (citations omitted). The court further observed that when responding to interrogatories the "'mere statement by a party that the interrogatory [or request for production] was "overly broad, burdensome, oppressive, and irrelevant" is not adequate to preserve a successful objection.'" *Id.* (citations omitted). Rather, the resisting party "'must show specifically how . . . each interrogatory [or request for production] is not relevant or how each question is overly broad, burdensome, or oppressive.'" *Id.* (citations omitted). The showing must be made by affidavit or other evidence that demonstrates the burden, and not simply by argument of counsel. *Id.*[1]

---

1. To be sure, in objecting to Rule 33 or Rule 34 requests, many lawyers simply state general objections without providing the detail required in *St. Paul*—and suffer no judicial sanction for it. The trend among many courts seems to be in the direction of *St. Paul*, however, and counsel should be aware that their former practices may not suffice in the future. *See generally* chapter 5, *supra*, and chapter 46, *infra*.

In determining whether sanctions are warranted, the court in *St. Paul* employed an objective standard to assess whether the signer of the certificate made a reasonable inquiry before submitting the discovery request, response, or objection. *Id.* at 516, n.3. Factors considered were: (1) the number and complexity of the issues; (2) the location, nature, number, and availability of potentially relevant witnesses or documents; (3) the extent of past working relationships between the attorney and the client, particularly in related or similar litigation; and (4) the time available to conduct an investigation. *Id.* (citations omitted). A finding that the discovery request, response, or objection was submitted for an improper purpose need not be predicated upon a showing of bad faith. *Id.*

The decision whether to impose sanctions under Rule 26(g) parallels the analysis used in determining whether to impose sanctions under Rule 11. *Id.* at 516, n.4. Sanctions may include an order requiring the offending lawyer or party to pay the opponent's attorneys' fees and costs, but a monetary award is not the exclusive sanction; the court has discretion to impose whatever sanctions are appropriate "in light of the particular circumstances." *Id.*, at 515 (citations omitted). In *St. Paul*, the court required plaintiffs' counsel to write an article in an appropriate law journal, explaining why it was improper to make the type of objections he had asserted in that case.

See also: *Or. RSA No. 6 v. Castle Rock Cellular of Or. Ltd. P'ship*, 76 F.3d 1003 (9th Cir. 1996) (Rule 26(g) permits sanctions to be imposed against a counsel or party for improper discovery requests or responses. An objective standard is employed by the court. In addition, a court has the inherent authority to sanction a lawyer or party for a discovery violation that is a willful abuse of the judicial process, but sanctions under a court's inherent authority require a finding of subjective bad faith.); *Project 74 Allentown, Inc. v. Frost*, 143 F.R.D. 77 (E.D. Pa. 1992) (extensive discussion of Rule 26(g), its commentary, and applicable case law. The court imposed Rule 26(g) sanctions sua sponte. In imposing sanctions, the court considered the inexperience of the misbehaving lawyer as a mitigating, but not excusing, factor); *Apex Oil Co. v. Belcher Co. of New York*, 855 F.2d 1009 (2d Cir. 1988) (discussing the effect of the certification requirement of Rule 26(g), noting that while it is similar to the objective standard employed by Rule 11, Rule 26(g) imposes "a more stringent certification requirement than Rule 11," which is necessary because a "'discovery request, response, or objection usually deals with more specific subject matter than motions or papers [governed by Rule 11].'" *Id.*, at 1014 (citations omitted)); *Poole v. Textron,*

Inc., 192 F.R.D. 494 (D. Md. 2000) (discussion of propriety of Rule 26(g) sanctions, standards for imposing such sanctions, nature of sanctions available for multiple discovery violations involving responses to document production requests, and failure appropriately to designate a corporate representative under Rule 30(b)(6)).

The example illustrates the scope of Rule 26(g). Because the discovery requests were not signed, the defendant was not required to answer them; the motion to compel could be denied on that ground alone. Further, it appears that the discovery was served, at least in part, for the improper purpose of harassing and causing needless litigation cost to the defendant. Although a court may not sanction that behavior if the discovery is otherwise pertinent, the court is not likely to be charitably disposed toward the attorney. And, if the lawyer's position is otherwise subject to challenge, it may tip the balance against him. Thus, the unreasonable position taken by plaintiff's counsel in response to defense counsel's attempt to compromise in an effort to resolve the dispute without involving the court as required by Rule 37(a), and plaintiff's refusal to grant an extension of time for answers, could well result in denial of the plaintiff's motion to compel.

Plaintiff's counsel may argue that his failure to sign the discovery requests insulates him from sanctions (as the certifications required by the signature requirement of Rule 26(g) were not triggered), but this argument should fail for several reasons. By filing the motion to compel, plaintiff's counsel has subjected himself to Rule 11 sanctions because that rule governs motions. Further, sanctions could be imposed under the court's inherent authority if it found, after a hearing, that the discovery was served for an improper purpose. Finally, the court could sanction plaintiff's counsel under 28 U.S.C. § 1927.

Practice Tips

In initiating or responding to discovery, counsel should consider:

1. Is it within the scope of Rule 26(b)(1)? Rule 26(b)(1) permits discovery of unprivileged facts that are relevant to the claims and defenses raised by the pleadings. Many lawyers continue to rely on the former standard (narrowed by the December 2000 amendments to the rules), which allowed discovery of unprivileged facts relevant to the subject matter of the litigation. *Thompson v. HUD,*

199 F.R.D. 168, 170 (D. Md. 2001); *Shapo v. Engle*, No. 98 C 7909, 2001 WL 204804, at *2 (N.D. Ill. Mar.1, 2001).

2. Have you considered the Rule 26(b)(2) risk/benefits factors? In 1993 Rule 26(b)(2) was modified to "enable the court to keep tighter rein on the extent of discovery. The information explosion of recent decades has greatly increased both the potential cost of wide-ranging discovery and the potential for discovery to be used as an instrument for delay or oppression . . . . The revisions in Rule 26(b)(2) were intended to impose additional restrictions on the scope and extent of discovery . . . ." *Thompson, supra,* at 170 (citing the commentary to the 1993 changes to Rule 26(b)(2), 146 F.R.D. 401, 638). *See Sanyo Laser Products Inc. v. Arista Records, Inc.,* 214 F.R.D. 496, 500 (S.D. Ind. 2003) ("The change, while meaningful, is not dramatic, and broad discovery remains the norm. The revised rule simply provides one additional justification for the Court to put the brakes on discovery that strays from the claims or defenses being asserted."). As changed, Rule 26(b) states that the court shall limit the frequency or extent of the use of discovery methods if it determines that: (1) the discovery sought is unreasonably cumulative, obtainable from another more convenient, less burdensome, or less expensive source; (2) the party seeking discovery has had ample opportunity to obtain the information already through discovery; or (3) the burden or expense of the proposed discovery outweighs its likely benefit, taking into consideration (a) the needs of the case, (b) the amount in controversy, (c) the parties' resources, and (d) the importance of the proposed discovery in resolving the issues in the case.

    The *Thompson* court further noted that, in attempting to persuade a court to order discovery to which objection has been made with particularity, it is unhelpful for counsel simply to assert the "right" to discovery of relevant information without justifying it under the Rule 26(b)(2) cost/benefit factors. *Id.,* at 170-71. Thus, while it may be appropriate to draft discovery requests broadly at the outset of a case, if the responding party can make a showing under Rule 26(b)(2) that the discovery sought is overbroad or burdensome, counsel should discuss narrowing the scope of discovery or adopting a phased discovery approach. *Id.,* at 171. Therefore, a lawyer should consider the Rule 26(b)(2) factors before initiating the discovery. In the example, plaintiff's counsel should have made a good faith effort to modify the discovery requests objected to, or at the least, explained why the discovery was proper despite the objections, as well as why it was not interposed for an improper purpose.

3. Was the discovery interposed for a proper purpose? The certification requirement of Rule 26(g) prohibits serving a discovery request for an improper purpose. All discovery requests impose some level of burden or expense, so the mere fact that these consequences will accompany otherwise proper requests does not prohibit the discovery. However, in the example, the comments of plaintiff's counsel allow the defendant to argue that the discovery was propounded, at least in part, for the purpose of harassment. If a reviewing court believes that this was what motivated the discovery, it may be more likely to impose sanctions. Therefore, before initiating discovery, think about what you will say if opposing counsel objects on the basis of burden and undue expense, and in giving your response, do not take positions that could suggest you are motivated by an improper purpose.

4. Has the party serving the discovery complied with the rules of civil procedure, any local rules of court, discovery guidelines of the court, scheduling orders, or other orders of the court? Most courts have local rules that may further restrict the scope of permissible discovery. Also, many courts have adopted discovery guidelines that also are intended to govern how discovery is conducted. *See*, *e.g.*, Discovery Guidelines for the United States District Court for the District of Maryland, Appendix A, Local Rules, United States District Court for the District of Maryland. Local Rule 26.5, United States District Court for the District of Massachusetts. Discovery requests, responses, or objections that do not comply with applicable rules, local rules, guidelines, or court orders are a recipe for disaster. Check such rules and guidelines early and carefully.

5. Has enough effort been made to obtain responsive information to legitimate discovery requests? The Rules' 30-day response time frequently is too short to allow for meaningful responses. In such circumstances, the wrong way to react is to ignore the deadlines until pressed to respond by the threat of a motion to compel, or to file a "response" that is nothing but pro forma objections. Neither is acceptable. The better, and common, practice is to seek agreement on reasonable extensions of discovery response times from the other side. Receipt of such an extension, however, imposes the concomitant obligation to provide a meaningful response. *Jayne H. Lee v. Flagstaff Indust. Corp.*, 173 F.R.D. 651 (D. Md. 1997).

   Whatever the response time, an attorney must act promptly to coordinate with the client to identify the responsive information. If more time is required than what is allowed by the rules or agreed to by counsel, the lawyer should tell opposing counsel in writing and propose an alternate schedule. It may make sense to offer a partial production within the required time with prompt supplementation thereafter. If a lawyer can demonstrate good faith and reasonable efforts to respond to discovery, the chance that a court will impose sanctions if a dispute later develops is substantially reduced. Remember: Clients often fail to understand the importance of these rules. Part of a lawyer's job is to stress their importance.

6. Are the discovery responses provided complete and unevasive? Rule 37(a)(3) states: "[A]n evasive or incomplete disclosure, answer, or response is to be treated as a failure to disclose, answer, or respond." Few lawyers fully appreciate the importance of this rule. All too frequently, "answers" to interrogatories and document production requests provide less than what was sought or are patently evasive. If the request is objectionable in whole, the response should be a clear, non-boilerplate objection that demonstrates with particularity why it is objectionable. If only part of the request is objectionable, the responding attorney should object to the offensive portion and answer the rest fully and unevasively.

7. Have objections been made timely and properly? Absent court order or stipulation, a late response may prevent the responding party from raising objections. *See Byrd v. Reno*, No. CIV.A.96-2375CKK, 1998 WL 429676, at *4 (D.D.C. Feb. 12, 1998) ("Without a showing of good cause, defendant's failure to respond to the interrogatories ordinarily compels the conclusion that the untimely objection is waived."). In the words of Rule 33(b)(4), "[a]ll grounds for an objection to an interrogatory shall be stated with specificity. Any ground not stated in a timely objection is waived unless the party's failure to object is excused by the court for good cause shown." *Lee v. Flagstaff Indust. Corp.*, 173 F.R.D. 651, 653 (D. Md. 1997) ("[a] party who ignores the 30 day deadline for responding to interrogatories risks the imposition of immediate sanctions from the court, and loses the right to object . . . unless the court excuses the failure to timely answer."). Further, objections stated in a conclusory, boilerplate fashion are inadequate. *St. Paul Reinsurance Co., Ltd. v. Commercial Fin. Corp.*, 198 F.R.D. 508 (N.D. Iowa 2000); *Marens v. Carrabba's Italian Grill, Inc.*, 196 F.R.D. 35 (D. Md. 2000); *Coker v. Duke & Co.*, 177 F.R.D. 682, 686 (M.D. Ala. 1998); *Jackson v. Montgomery Ward & Co.*, 173 F.R.D. 524, 528-29 (D. Nev. 1997); *Kelling v. Bridgestone/Firestone, Inc.*, 157 F.R.D. 496, 497 (D. Kan. 1994); *Eureka Fin. Corp. v. Hartford Accident and Indem. Co.*, 136 F.R.D. 179, 182-83 (E.D. Cal. 1991). *See also* Rule 26(b)(5): Claims of privilege or work product "shall describe the nature of the documents, communications, or things not produced or disclosed in a manner that, without revealing information itself privileged or protected, will enable other parties to assess the applicability of the privilege or protection"; Rule 33(b)(4): "[a]ll grounds for an objection to an interrogatory shall be stated with specificity"; and chapters 5 (Interrogatories—Sufficiency of Objections), 8 (Document Requests—Numerosity, Propriety, Timing, and Sufficiency of Objections), 11 (Privilege Logs), and 18 (Asserting Privileges During Deposition), *supra*, regarding the proper way to assert a privilege when objecting to discovery.

As these cases demonstrate, courts increasingly are impatient with vague, uninformative objections to discovery, and are quite willing to rule that improperly stated objections do not provide a valid reason to resist discovery, and result in waiver of objections that otherwise could have been made. Counsel should therefore avoid boilerplate objections, object only when there is a specifically articulable basis for doing so, and then provide to the party seeking the discovery (as well as the court if a motion to compel is filed) the specific facts supporting each distinct objection. Facts, including affidavits, should be provided to justify the objection.

8. If objecting to discovery requests, consider offering as a compromise solution some portion of what was requested or some other less objectionable form of discovery instead of simply refusing to provide any information.

"[W]hen confronted with a difficult scope of discovery dispute, the parties should confer, and discuss the Rule 26(b)(2) factors, in an effort to reach an acceptable compromise, or narrow the scope of their disagreement. For example, if the plaintiff seeks discovery of information going back 20 years, and the defendant objects on the grounds of burden, a possible solution may be to agree first to produce information going back five years. Then, depending on the results of a review of the more recent information, if more extensive disclosure can be justified, based on the results of the initial, more limited, less burdensome examination, it should be produced. Similarly, if the burden and expense of searching for and producing all documents that fall within the scope of a broad Rule 34 request is objected to, the party objecting might agree to spend up to a stated amount of time looking for the records, and producing them for inspection, with the understanding that if, following review of the documents produced, the requesting party can justify a request for more under the Rule 26(b)(2) factors, it would be produced, perhaps under a cost sharing or shifting agreement . . . ."
Thompson v. HUD, 199 F.R.D. 168, 172 (D. Md. 2001).

All too often, litigants view discovery requests as an "all or nothing" proposition, which they seldom are. A party that objects to a discovery request but then proposes a lesser but meaningful response as a compromise is in a better position if opposing counsel files a motion to compel. By contrast, an attorney who merely objects and produces nothing may face a skeptical court when seeking to justify his approach, and if unsuccessful in defending his or her actions, risks imposition of sanctions, attorneys' fees, or costs.

Finally, the court's comments in *Project 74 Allentown Inc. v. Frost, supra,* regarding the dilemma faced by young attorneys instructed by more senior lawyers to initiate discovery requests that violate Rule 26(g), should be taken to heart. Courts understand that in such cases the junior attorney has been placed in a difficult situation, but that will not prevent the imposition of sanctions. *See further* ABA Model Rules of Professional Conduct, Rule 5.2 (notwithstanding the professional obligation of experienced attorneys, subordinate attorneys also are required to adhere to ethical guidelines). Most likely it will be considered as a mitigating factor in determining the sanctions. Experienced attorneys thus have a professional obligation to ensure that the junior lawyers whom they supervise know how to conduct discovery properly, and an equally important obligation not to place those attorneys in jeopardy by insisting that they propound discovery requests in a fashion that could be sanctioned by the court.

45. MOTION TO COMPEL DISCOVERY

Plaintiff was fired from his job. He brought an age discrimination suit in federal court in the District of Columbia against his former employer, a large nationwide company with many offices. Plaintiff's discovery included an Interrogatory 12 and a Document Request 12 seeking information "relating to the termination of employment of any employee over the age of 40" from all divisions of the company throughout the United States.

Defendant obtained a 30-day extension to respond, memorialized in a letter to plaintiff's counsel. When the extension expired without responses, plaintiff's counsel filed a motion to compel and for sanctions. She did not contact defense counsel before filing the motion. Defense counsel opposed the motion and simultaneously filed discovery responses. The response to both Interrogatory 12 and Document Request 12 was: "This request is over-broad, burdensome, not calculated to lead to the production of admissible evidence, and defendant therefore refuses to answer it."

In his opposition to the motion to compel, defense counsel acknowledged that the answers were filed 10 days after the extension expired, but explained that the delay was unavoidable because the associate working on the case had broken her leg and was hospitalized. Defense counsel further stated that he did not realize that the discovery answers were overdue until the weekend after the accident, while he was reviewing the associate's files. Responses were filed the following Tuesday, and so any delay was the product of excusable neglect. Furthermore, the defendant's lawyer noted, the plaintiff had suffered no prejudice, and if plaintiff's counsel had called or written first, the dispute could have been avoided without bothering the court. Moreover, the motion was moot because responses were filed.

Substantively, defense counsel argued that Interrogatory 12 and Document Request 12 were grossly overbroad, citing cases from circuits other than the District of Columbia Circuit. He also argued, without reference to any affidavit or other supporting facts, that the time required to provide complete responses to the discovery requests would be prohibitive and expensive. Therefore plaintiff not only was not entitled to the discovery, but further, should be sanctioned for having filed a frivolous motion.

In plaintiff's reply, his lawyer noted that the complaint alleged that plaintiff's termination was part of defendant's systematic nationwide policy to purge older workers; counsel cited many cases from circuits other than the District of Columbia Circuit to the effect that Interrogatory 12 and Document Request 12 were proper, given plaintiff's entitlement to evidence that might help prove discriminatory motive. Moreover, she argued that because the defendant's discovery responses were late, all objections were waived. They were waived for the further reason that defendant had failed to particularize any claims of burden. Finally, defendant's explanation for the late responses was no justification for the delay. Plaintiff asked for monetary sanctions and an order precluding the defendant from offering evidence at trial to contest the allegation that the defendant had systematically discriminated against workers over the age of 40 throughout the country.

Plaintiff's reply brief was filed three days ago, and no decision has been issued by the district court. Eager to schedule the deposition of defendant's corporate designee, plaintiff's counsel needs the information sought in Interrogatory and Document Request 12 to prepare. Accordingly, she faxes a letter to the district judge's law clerk and leaves her three voice mail messages stressing the urgency of this dispute and asking when a ruling will be received. Defense counsel, who was copied with the faxed letter, writes a five-page letter to the court reiterating what he has said in his opposition brief and also leaves a voice mail message with the judge's law clerk urging a prompt decision.

How should the court rule?

Comment: The starting point for analyzing the example is Rule 37(a), which governs the filing of motions to compel. Rule 37(a) applies if a party fails to make a Rule 26(a) disclosure; a deponent fails to answer a proper question at a deposition; a corporation or other party-entity fails to make a proper Rule 30(b)(6) designation; or a party fails to answer an interrogatory or document production request. A party filing the motion to compel must include a certification of good faith efforts to resolve the dispute without the need to involve the court.

If the motion is granted, or if the discovery that is sought is provided subsequent to the filing of the motion, the rule provides that, after giving the noncompliant party an opportunity to be heard, the court shall impose as a sanction reasonable expenses and attorneys' fees, absent a finding that (i) the motion was filed without first making a good faith effort to obtain the discovery without involving the court; (ii) the opposing party's nondisclosure, response, or objection was substantially justified; or (iii) the imposition of sanctions would be unjust. Here, the fact that plaintiff's counsel did not try to resolve the dispute before filing the motion will likely mean that the court will not award costs and attorneys' fees to the plaintiff even if he prevails. (Note, however, that filing the discovery response after the opposing party has incurred the expense of preparing and filing a motion to compel is no defense against the imposition of sanctions.)

If the court denies the motion, it may enter a protective order limiting or barring the discovery sought. Further, after affording the moving party an opportunity to be heard and absent a finding that the motion was substantially justified or that an award of sanctions would be unjust, the court may require the moving party and/or its attorney to pay the opposing party reasonable expenses and attorneys' fees. Finally, if the court grants the motion in part and denies it in part, reasonable attorneys' fees may be apportioned after the parties have been heard. The right to be heard does not mean the right to a hearing (although the court may order a hearing at its discretion), but simply the right to file written submissions. Commentary to the 1993 Changes to Rule 37, 146 F.R.D. at 690.

Turning to the example, it is obvious that plaintiff's counsel failed to make a good faith effort to resolve the dispute without involving the court. She was therefore unable to include such required certification in her motion. Such failure alone has led courts to deny motions to compel. *Nwachukwu v. Karl*, 223 F. Supp. 2d 60, 71 n.7 (D.D.C. 2002); *Murphy v. Barberino Bros., Inc.*, 208 F.R.D. 483 (D. Conn. 2001); *Burton v. R.J. Reynolds Tobacco Co.*, 203 F.R.D. 624 (D. Kan. 2001); *Doe v. Nat'l Hemophilia Found.*, 194 F.R.D. 516 (D. Md. 2000); *Alexander v. F.B.I.*, 186 F.R.D. 185 (D.D.C. 1999). And, even if the court *does* address the merits of the dispute, it will not overlook the fact that both counsel have violated the cardinal rule of discovery motions practice: Never involve the court unless you can show that you have made reasonable efforts to resolve the dispute first.

On the merits of the dispute, both sides have valid arguments. The defense has a point about the overbreadth and burden of this discovery—plaintiff has propounded discovery requests that require a nationwide search of records, potentially from the company's founding date to the present. The request appears excessive, although a court surely will find that the plaintiff is entitled to some part of what he has requested.

The problem for the defense attorney is that he filed late discovery responses and failed to explain in detail why the discovery sought was overbroad and burdensome. This may prevent him from winning on what otherwise could have been meritorious objections. Although it is not unusual for lawyers to respond initially to interrogatories and document requests by making broadly phrased objections that lack particularized facts to justify them, it is clear from the requirements of the Rules and, with increasing frequency, the cases interpreting them, that such practice is unwise and likely will be unsuccessful.

Rule 33(b)(4) states that "[a]ll grounds for an objection to an interrogatory shall be stated with specificity. Any ground not stated in a timely objection is waived, unless the party's failure to object is excused by the court for good cause shown." In a case similar to the example, the United States District Court for the District of Maryland held that a party that had obtained an extension of time in which to respond to interrogatories and document requests, but failed to meet the agreed-upon extension, waived all of its objections. *Jayne H. Lee v. Flagstaff Indust.*, 173 F.R.D. 651 (D. Md. 1997); *see also Safeco Ins. Co. of Am. v. Rawstrom,* 183 F.R.D. 668 (C.D. Cal. 1998); *Joseph v. Gen. Eng'g Co.*, 2002, No. Civ. 2000/48, WL 31618810, at *1 (D. V.I. April 15, 2002) ("The law is well settled that a party's failure to object to interrogatories within thirty (30) days of service thereof is considered a waiver of any objections they might have had."); *Disantis v. Smith of Phila.*, No. Civ. A87-05151987, 1987 WL 28357, at *1 (E.D. Pa.) (*citing Bohlin v. Brass Rail, Inc.*, 20 F.R.D. 224 (S.D.N.Y. 1957), "Regardless of how outrageous or how embarrassing the questions may be, the defendants have long since lost their opportunity to object to the questions . . ."); *Fretz v. Keltner*, 109 F.R.D. 303, 309 (D. Kan. 1985).

Unlike Rule 33, Rule 34 does not specifically say that a late response to a request for production of documents waives otherwise proper objections. However, the commentary to the rule states that "[t]he procedure provided in Rule 34 [regarding the timing and content of a response to a document production request] is essentially the same as that in Rule 33 . . . and the discussion in the . . . [comment] appended to that rule is relevant to Rule 34 as well." Commentary to the 1970 Revisions to Rule 34, 48 F.R.D. at 527. The commentary to Rule 33(b) states that "[p]aragraph (4) is added to make clear that objections must be specifically justified, and that unstated or untimely grounds for objection ordinarily are waived." Commentary to the 1993 Revisions to Rule 33, 146 F.R.D. at 676.

Similarly, courts repeatedly caution that boilerplate claims of overbreadth, burden, or excessive expense fail to meet the requirement to particularize objections to discovery requests, thereby waiving them. *See* chapter 44 *supra*. In the example, defense counsel has put himself in a very poor tactical position by failing to provide sufficient details to establish a factual basis for his claims of unfair burden.

There is no bright line test for how much detail is required in objecting to discovery. In some instances, the discovery requests' overbreadth and burdensomeness will be apparent. In others, more factual detail will be needed to establish overbreadth and burdensomeness. As a rule of thumb, the objecting lawyer should simply try to provide as much specificity as possible, such as time and cost estimates. Any other relevant information—for example, that the information sought is stored in remote locations and archives—would also be helpful. In providing such explanations, affidavits are not required at the initial stage of objection.

Apart from his tardiness in responding and his failure to particularize his objections, defense counsel has made what is probably an even bigger tactical mistake. While plaintiff's demand seems excessive, defendant unwisely has taken an "all or nothing approach." He refused to offer any compromise. It is foolish to think that the court will not allow the plaintiff some discovery about the termination of other employees, given the allegation of a systematic plan to fire older workers. By offering nothing, defendant has set himself up for failure.

A far better approach would have been to object, providing particular information to demonstrate the burden but offering as a compromise a lesser amount of information covering the region at issue for a reasonable period of time (e.g., information and records for the past five years from the Washington, D.C., regional office). *See, e.g., Thompson v. HUD*, 199 F.R.D. 168, 172 (D. Md. 2001). Indeed, the commentary to the rules expressly encourages this approach: "[I]f, for example, an interrogatory seeking information about numerous facilities or products is deemed objectionable, but an interrogatory seeking information about a lesser number of facilities or products would not have been objectionable, the interrogatory should be answered as to the latter even though an objection is raised as to the balance of the facilities or products." Commentary to the 1993 Revisions to Rule 33, 146 F.R.D. at 676.

Lawyers must recognize that Rule 37 sanctions, unlike Rule 11 sanctions, are required unless limited exceptions are satisfied. The three circumstances listed in Rule 37 that excuse a court from imposing sanctions are: (i) substanatial justification for the violation; (ii) unfairness; and (iii) lack of prejudice to the party denied the discovery. The court's discretion not to sanction is preserved, but the rule is structured to make sanctions the norm, and a decision not to sanction is the exception.

In the example, however, it is an open question whether the court would accept defense counsel's explanation for the late filing (his associate's broken leg) as "substantial justification" for the tardy response and decline to impose sanctions. This phrase is not defined in the rule, but the commentary suggests a common-sense approach: "Expenses ordinarily should be awarded unless a court finds that the losing party acted justifiably in carrying his point to court." Commentary to the 1970 Revisions to Rule 33, 48 F.R.D. at 540. *See also Pierce v. Underwood*, 487 U.S. 552, 565 (1988) ("substantially justified" as used in Rule 37(a)(4) does not mean "substantial to a high degree," but instead is satisfied by the existence of a "genuine dispute," or "justified to a degree that could satisfy a reasonable person"). But remember this: Judges are human beings. Each will have a different view of "common sense" in differing cases. You cannot be sure what reception you will get, and such uncertainty is a reason to be cautious.

Factors that determine whether sanctions will be imposed are: (1) the extent to which the parties attempted to work out the dispute without court intervention; (2) the egregiousness of the violation, and whether it was willful or done in bad faith, as opposed to being caused by a lack of experience or knowledge of the rules; (3) the level of experience of counsel; (4) whether the moving party has suffered any prejudice or expense; (5) the explanation offered by the party against whom the motion was filed; (6) whether the moving party also acted improperly or unreasonably; and (7) the equities of the case, including the financial resources of the parties.

In the example, plaintiff's counsel requested as a sanction an order precluding the defendant from offering certain rebuttal evidence at trial. She will not get that relief, because Rule 37(a) does not permit the court to award such sanctions, which are reserved for more egregious discovery violations such as a refusal to obey a court's discovery order, Rule 37(b), or failure to make Rule 26(a) disclosures. *See* Rule 37(c) and chapter 43, *supra*.

Motions to compel discovery responses where none have been filed, or to compel responsive responses when deficient answers have been given, are the most frequent disputes that the court is called upon to resolve. Usually, the motions focus on allegedly deficient interrogatory responses and document production responses. These disputes usually involve whether the requests were overbroad and burdensome or beyond the scope of discovery as defined by Rule 26(b)(1), and whether a party has properly asserted privilege in accordance with Rule 26(b)(5). Courts do not need a great deal of information to resolve these routine questions. What is likely to help the court is: (1) information regarding the claims and defenses raised in the pleadings, as this defines the proper scope of discovery; (2) the exact text of the interrogatory or document production request propounded; (3) the exact text of the allegedly deficient response; and (4) any cases directly on point from that district court, or the circuit where the district court is located.

Unfortunately, despite the fact that parties have a shared interest in resolving their dispute promptly—which would be facilitated by focused and succinct memoranda—more often than not they file long, ponderous memoranda with pages of string cites to cases from other circuits or districts (as illustrated by the example). This type of briefing usually offers little of value to help the court resolve the dispute. Such sloppy advocacy exasperates the court and delays a decision.[1] Perhaps this happens because discovery disputes seem to be relegated to less experienced lawyers, who mistakenly feel that overkill is helpful. A far better approach is to draft a short, focused motion or opposition citing the fewest cases possible and making sure that those cited are from the jurisdiction where the case is pending.

Beyond such basics, and with a little imagination, counsel can take steps that will greatly assist the court in promptly resolving these discovery disputes. One approach that has been used successfully in the United States District Court for the District of Maryland is for the moving party to prepare a chart containing columns for the following information: (1) the number of the interrogatory/document request in dispute, and a very succinct description of what was requested; (2) the moving party's argument why the relief requested should be granted, with citation to a limited number of cases supporting their argument (rarely more than five); (3) the opposing party's argument in response to the moving party's argument, again citing only a few

---

1. This practice is so common that the Federal Judicial Center and the Judicial Conference of the United States Courts have suggested to judges that they consider issuing orders setting limits on the length of memoranda that may be submitted in connection with routine discovery disputes, and limits on the number of cases that may be cited. *See* MANUAL FOR COMPLEX LITIGATION 3d ed. 64-65 (Federal Judicial Center 1995); CIVIL LITIGATION MANAGEMENT MANUAL 35 (Judicial Conference of the United States 2001).

cases supporting the position; and (4) a column for the court's ruling. That chart would look like this:

Interrog./RPD no. w/brief description	Moving party's argument w/authority	Opposing party's argument w/authority	Court's ruling

The moving party prepares the chart on a disk and forwards it to the opposing party who enters his or her information into the disk and then files it with the court. The only exhibits filed are the interrogatories or document production requests at issue and the response. Upon receipt, the court can decide whether to permit the moving party to respond to the opposing party's submission, or, if that seems unnecessary, to enter its ruling in the final column, and the chart is then filed with the clerk as a court ruling, with copies to counsel. Use of this technique has resulted in rulings on motions to compel within one or two days of filing.

Obviously, this approach requires cooperation among counsel and the court, but that is often easy to obtain, because both parties, as well as the court, want to resolve the dispute quickly. Although this particular technique works best for disputes involving the sufficiency of answers to interrogatories and responses to document production requests, comparable techniques are applicable to other discovery disputes: scheduling telephone hearings with the court to resolve motions once they are briefed; agreement to limit the number of pages for memoranda relating to discovery disputes and restrict the number of cases cited; and agreement to shorten the time for briefing discovery disputes.

Practice Tip

Consider the following when preparing to file or respond to motions to compel discovery:

1. Never file a motion to compel unless a genuine, good faith effort has been made to resolve the dispute without court intervention.
2. Avoid taking "all or nothing" positions on the dispute—be prepared to compromise. For example, if the plaintiff seeks information that you believe is overbroad and burdensome, but the court likely will conclude that some of the information is discoverable, offer to provide what the court might order. If the plaintiff refuses and files a motion to compel, your willingness to offer some dis-

covery will go a long way with the court. Even if it rules that you must provide more information than you proposed, if your compromise offer was reasonable it may result in a decision not to award sanctions. Similarly, if the court agrees that your position was reasonable and that the moving party's was not, it is far more likely to award sanctions against the moving party. If you are the moving party, remember that if the court rules against you it may impose sanctions for filing a motion that was not substantially justified. Accordingly, make sure that your position is reasonable.

3. Try to anticipate how the court will rule when deciding whether to file a motion to compel or a response to such a motion. Check to see if the judge assigned to your case has decided similar disputes in the past or if other judges on that court have done so. If your position is out of line with how that court has previously ruled, rethink your approach.

4. When drafting a motion or response, be professional. Exaggerated claims of bad faith or improper motive aimed at your opponent do not help your argument. Ad hominem attacks are distractions, and usually are evidence that the party taking the shots has nothing better to say.

5. Make your brief brief. Avoid string cites. Do not cite authority from another jurisdiction unless there is no case on point in your court. If this is the situation, say so; then the court knows that you tried to find controlling authority from that court.

6. At the first hint that there may be a discovery dispute, identify the most efficient and quickest way to resolve it, and discuss it with opposing counsel. Write to the court to request a discovery conference to establish procedures to resolve disputes quickly.

7. Do not spend too much time researching and drafting discovery motions. Courts are loath to award excessive fees. The involvement of many lawyers, excessive conferences, and repetitive entries for "reviewing and revising" the motion will not be well received.

8. Senior lawyers have a duty to work with less experienced lawyers who handle discovery disputes to make sure that they learn how to manage such situations properly.

46. MOTION FOR PROTECTIVE ORDER

Plaintiff Snack Attack, Inc. sued defendant Commercial Foods, Inc. in federal court for antitrust violations. Snack Attack maintains vending machines in office buildings. It purchases one of its most popular products, "Nutrisnak," from Commercial. Snack Attack alleged that Commercial charges higher prices for Nutrisnak sold to smaller vendors such as Snack Attack than it charges for the same product when sold to national and international vendors. Snack Attack sought treble damages, attorneys' fees, and injunctive relief. Commercial denied liability; it argued that the cost difference between Nutrisnak sold to Snack Attack and that sold to larger vendors is justified by the fact that it is less expensive to produce the larger lots ordered by big companies, and some of those savings are passed on to the customer.

Snack Attack subsequently served Rule 34 document requests, seeking, among other things, all of Commercial's records for the last 25 years relating to the cost of manufacturing all of its snack products including Nutrisnak. Snack Attack also sought production of records for the last 25 years relating to Commercial's income, earnings, and expenses for its consumer foods division, as well as information relating to Commercial's customers for the last 25 years, including copies of all contracts between Commercial and food vendors.

Commercial, in a timely response, objected to production of the documents described, on the grounds of burden, expense, and irrelevance, and on the further ground that the information is confidential and includes trade secrets. Commercial submitted an affidavit from its assistant CFO estimating the amount of time that it would take to locate, review, and produce the documents, as well as the costs of production. As an alternative, Commercial offered a more limited scope of production related to the costs of manufacturing Nutrisnak and contracts with other Nutrisnak vendors in Snack Attack's region. Commercial took the position, however, that if Snack Attack did not agree to this limitation, none of the disputed documents would be produced. As to the undisputed areas of production sought by Snack Attack, Commercial agreed to produce the originals for copying on a date certain. Commercial did not file a motion for a protective order.

Snack Attack's lawyer called Commercial's lawyer, refused the offer of a limited production, and asked him to reconsider Commercial's position. Counsel for Commercial declined. Snack Attack thereupon filed a motion to compel under Rule 37(a) seeking all of the documents that it had requested.

Commercial filed an opposition reiterating its objections. Snack Attack filed a reply memorandum arguing that despite the fact that Commercial had filed a timely Rule 34 response, it was also required to file a motion for a protective order, which it had not done. Thus, argued Snack Attack, Commercial's objections were waived.

How should the court rule?

Comment: This dispute is governed primarily by Rule 26(c) and secondarily by Rule 26(b). Rule 26(c) states that a party or person from whom discovery or a Rule 26(a) disclosure is sought may move for an order protecting him from annoyance, embarrassment, oppression, or undue burden or expense associated with the discovery or disclosure. The motion must be based on "good cause shown" and accompanied by a certificate that the moving party has conferred or attempted to confer in good faith with its opponent in an effort to resolve the dispute.

The rule gives eight examples of appropriate relief: (1) an order that the disclosure or discovery not be had; (2) an order that the disclosure or discovery be had only under terms and conditions stated, including a designation of time or place; (3) an order that the disclosure or discovery may be had only by a different method than the one selected by the party seeking it; (4) an order that certain matters not be inquired into, or that the scope of the disclosure or discovery be limited to certain matters; (5) an order that discovery be conducted with no one present except designated persons; (6) an order that a deposition, after being sealed, be opened only by order of the court; (7) an order that a trade secret or other confidential research, development, or commercial information not be revealed or be revealed only in a designated way; and (8) an order that the parties simultaneously file specified documents or information in sealed envelopes to be opened as directed by the court.

The rule also permits any further order "which justice requires." The Rule 26(b)(2) cost-benefit balancing factors, discussed in chapter 44, *supra*, are helpful in evaluating whether the discovery sought warrants a protective order. Rule 26(b)(2) recognizes the relationship between the cost/benefit factors and motions for protective orders, stating that the court, in ordering relief under Rule 26(b)(2), "may act upon its own initiative after reasonable notice or pursuant to a motion under Rule 26(c)." Rule 26(b)(2).

Rule 26(c) does not say whether a motion for protective order must be filed in response to Rule 33 or 34 discovery requests that require written responses stating the basis for any objections. Most lawyers, in their initial responses, usually provide only a brief description of their objections. If the interrogating lawyer is dissatisfied with the objections, they may become the basis for discussion and negotiation among counsel. The objecting lawyer may expand on his objections in follow-up correspondence. Often, however, a detailed account of the grounds for objection is not provided until efforts to compromise have failed and the interrogating lawyer files a motion to compel.

Lawyers should be aware, nonetheless, that this conventional practice has been rejected by some courts, which require much more from a party when it files its objections to Rule 33 or 34 requests. In *Brittain v. Stroh Brewery Co.*, 136 F.R.D. 408 (M.D.N.C. 1991), for example, the court held that the "obligation to timely move for a protective order applies equally to written discovery requests as to protective orders for oral depositions." *Id.* at 413. *Concur: United States v. I.B.M. Corp.*, 70 F.R.D. 700 (S.D.N.Y. 1976) (motion for a protective order must be served before the date set for production of documents); *United States v. I.B.M. Corp.*, 79 F.R.D. 412 (S.D.N.Y. 1978). Although conceding that a rigid application of this requirement could inundate federal courts with motions for protective orders filed contemporaneously with written discovery responses, the *Brittain* court suggested a procedure that would mitigate this problem—the party objecting to written discovery requests would file responses that detailed the objections, as well as a proposed protective order. The parties would attempt to agree on a protective order, but if they were unsuccessful, the objecting party would file its motion. *Id.*; *Parkway Gallery Furniture, Inc. v. Kittinger/Pennsylvania House Group, Inc.*, 121 F.R.D. 264 (M.D.N.C. 1988).

To be sure, not all courts agree with this rigorous approach. In *Nelson v. Capital One Bank*, 206 F.R.D. 499, 500 (N.D. Cal. 2001), the court stated:

> [T]he party responding to *written* discovery may either 'object properly or seek a protective order'. . . . It would make little sense to hold that in order to preserve objections to written discovery, the responding party must file written objections rather than moving for a protective order. If she merely files objections, the propounding party is forced to file a motion to compel. Filing a motion for protective order rather than serving objections puts the disputed matters at issue as quickly, indeed probably more quickly, than precipitating a motion to compel. Both mechanisms give timely notice to the pro-

pounding party of the respondent's objections. (Citations omitted, emphasis in original.)

Similarly, a respected commentator suggests that a party responding to Rule 33 or 34 requests may raise objections in its written response and need not, but may, also file a motion for protective order. Wright, Miller & Marcus, *Federal Practice and Procedure* 2d ed., § 2035 (1994). The difference in approaches underscores the need to determine which procedure is followed in the court in which the case is pending. If there is no definitive authority, it would be prudent to serve both responses to the discovery requests, as well as a motion for protective order, prior to the due date for the discovery. At the least, specific, detailed reasons should be provided, and boilerplate generalizations avoided, when objections are stated. *See* chapter 5, *supra*.

If a motion for protective order is filed, "[t]he burden of showing good cause rests with the party requesting the protective order. The party must make a particular request and a specific demonstration of facts in support of the request as opposed to a conclusory or speculative statement about the need for a protective order and the harm which would be suffered without one." *Britain,* 136 F.R.D. at 412; *Gulf Oil v. Bernard,* 452 U.S. 89, 102 n.16 (1981) (protective order must be based on a "clear record" and "specific findings" supporting the relief sought); and *Deines v. Vermeer Mfg. Co.,* 133 F.R.D. 46, 48 (D. Kan. 1990) (conclusory statements are insufficient to meet a party's "heavy burden of showing good cause for a protective order").

In satisfaction of the requirement that sufficient facts be included in the motion so that the court "only grant[s] as narrow a protective order as necessary under the facts," the *Brittain* court stated that affidavits from persons with knowledge of the facts constituting good cause and in camera submissions may be helpful. *Brittain, supra,* at 412; *Reliance Ins. Co. v. Barron's,* 428 F. Supp. 200 (S.D.N.Y. 1977); *Merit Indust. Inc. v. Feuer,* 201 F.R.D. 382, 384-85 (E.D. Pa. 2001) ("It has been said that 'good cause' [for a protective order] is established on a showing that disclosure will work a clearly defined and serious injury to the party seeking closure. The injury must be shown with specificity. Broad allegations of harm, unsubstantiated by specific examples or articulated reasoning, do not support a good cause showing.") (citations omitted); *Pansy v. Borough of Stroudsburg,* 23 F.3d 772, 786 (3d Cir. 1994) (party filing motion for protective order has burden of demonstrating good cause with specific showing that disclosure will cause a clearly defined, serious injury).

Relying on the text of earlier versions of Rule 26(c), the *Brittain* court held that the rule contained an "implicit condition" that a party seeking a protective order has a duty to file it "seasonably" or "promptly," which the court concluded was "prior to the date set for producing the discovery." *Id.* at 413. *Accord: Seminara v. City of Long Beach*, 68 F. 3d 481 (9th Cir. 1995); *Gov't of Virgin Isl. v. Knight*, 989 F. 2d 619, 627 (3d Cir. 1993); *United States v. Portland Cement Co.*, 338 F.2d 798 (10th Cir. 1964); *Drexel Heritage Furnishings, Inc. v. Furniture USA, Inc.*, 200 F.R.D. 255, 259 (M.D.N.C. 2001); *Nestle Foods Corp. v. Aetna Cas. & Sur. Co.*, 129 F.R.D. 483, 487 (D. N.J. 1990); and *Truxes v. Rolan Elect. Co.*, 314 F. Supp. 752, 759 (D. P.R. 1970). Thus, a motion for a protective order filed on or after the deadline for producing the requested discovery is untimely unless excused for "good cause such as a lack of sufficient time or opportunity to obtain the order." *Brittain, supra*, at 413.

In the example, the defendant filed timely answers and noted its objections, but did not seek a motion for protective order beforehand. If the court follows *Brittain*, defendant will be deemed to have waived its objections, absent good cause for its failure to file a motion for protective order. That the defendant particularized its objections with affidavits (as opposed to making generalized objections) and further proposed a more limited production (as opposed to simply offering no documents at all) may persuade the court that defendant's objections should be heard on the merits. If the court concludes that defendant's objections have merit, at least in part, and that the plaintiff has been overbroad it its demand for documents and unreasonable in its refusal to compromise, it is less likely that defendant will be penalized for having failed to seek a protective order in the first instance.

Practice Tips

1. Before filing a motion for protective order, always make a good faith effort to resolve the dispute. It is especially important to make a particularized showing that the discovery objected to is annoying, embarrassing, oppressive, unduly burdensome, or expensive. In doing so, it is prudent to address the Rule 26(b)(2) balancing factors and to offer a compromise if that is possible. If this approach is taken, it is much more likely that the court will conclude that the moving party has acted in good faith, and

it increases the likelihood that the court will grant all, or at least part, of the relief requested.

2. Promptly review all discovery requests received, and determine whether, and if so when, local practice requires that a motion for protective order (in addition to objections) should be filed if informal attempts to resolve objections are unsuccessful. At a minimum, if unable to obtain a negotiated resolution of the dispute, make sure that your objections or, if required, motion for protective order, are filed before the deadline for serving written discovery responses under Rules 33 and 34, or before the date of any deposition noted. Timing is important, because a party objecting to requested discovery cannot file a Rule 26(c) motion before exhausting good faith efforts to resolve the dispute without court intervention, yet at the same time, cannot afford to wait too long for fear of a judicial finding that the motion was untimely filed.

3. If you propound discovery to which the opposing party objects, be reasonable in your response to the objections. Do not reject out of hand proposals to compromise, and document your willingness to try to work out the dispute. Failure to negotiate in good faith may factor prominently in the court's decision to grant the motion. Further, if you reject a proposed compromise, make sure that you respond dispassionately in writing, with no ad hominem attacks, explaining the basis for your rejection of the proposal. This will enable you to document your professionalism and good faith if a motion for protective order is filed.

47. RULE 37(d) SANCTIONS FOR FAILURE OF A PARTY TO ATTEND ITS OWN DEPOSITION OR RESPOND TO INTERROGATORIES OR DOCUMENT PRODUCTION REQUESTS

The plaintiff sued an automobile manufacturer for injuries sustained when the driver's airbag deployed without warning while he was driving. Plaintiff claims that the airbag deployment system was defectively designed, manufactured, or installed. Suit is pending in federal court, based on diversity jurisdiction.

After receiving the court's scheduling order, plaintiff's counsel served interrogatories and document requests and noted a Rule 30(b)(6) deposition of the defendant. The deposition notice listed 25 categories for which defendant was to designate a witness. In response, defense counsel wrote to plaintiff's counsel objecting to all but four categories. Defense counsel did not file a Rule 26(c) motion for a protective order, however. Ten days before the deposition date, defense counsel produced the documents requested by the plaintiff.

On the day specified in the Rule 30(b)(6) notice, the defendant produced a witness who testified fully and nonevasively on the four topics to which defense counsel had not objected. The deponent was questioned about any efforts she had undertaken to learn information responsive to the remaining 21 topics in the notice; the witness said that she had made no efforts.

During the deposition, plaintiff's counsel informed defense counsel that defendant's interrogatory answers were two days overdue, to which defense counsel responded, "Duly noted," and nothing more. Plaintiff's counsel said, "Is that all you have to say?," to which defense counsel retorted, "You got it."

The next day, plaintiff's counsel filed a motion for sanctions under Rule 37(d). The motion sought entry of a default judgment against the defendant for failing to answer the interrogatories and for failing to produce a designee regarding the other 21 topics identified in the deposition notice.

In response, defense counsel argued that the interrogatories were overbroad, argumentative, and burdensome. He also contended that his interrogatory answers would only be a few days late, and that was because he was waiting for an affidavit from a representative of the defendant to particularize the factual basis for the objections. In fact, he said, the affidavit was expected within five business days and the answers would be filed within one week. As for the failure to produce a witness for the disputed 21 topics, he pointed out that he had written to plaintiff's counsel stating his objections and advising that he would not produce a witness for the objectionable topics. He went on to say that the burden was thus on plaintiff's counsel to file a motion to compel, and having failed to do so, plaintiff had waived any opposition to defendant's objections to the topics.

The dispute is fully briefed. How should the court rule?

Comment: Rule 37(d) states that if a party, officer, director, or managing agent of a party, or a person designated under Rule 30(b)(6) to testify on behalf of a party, fails to: (1) appear for the deposition after properly having been served a deposition notice; or (2) serve answers or objections to interrogatories that properly have been served; or (3) serve a written response to a Rule 34 production request that properly has been served, such party or designee may be sanctioned by the court. The court is authorized to impose "such orders as are just," including the severe sanctions identified at Rule 37(b)(2)(A)-(C). *See* chapter 44, *supra*.

A motion for sanctions under Rule 37(d) for failure to respond to interrogatories or document production requests must be accompanied by a certification of a good faith attempt to resolve the dispute. If the motion is granted, the court may order the noncompliant party to pay the reasonable attorneys' fees and costs of the moving party unless the failure to respond was substantially justified or an award of expenses would be unjust. Finally, the rule states that a failure to act as described in subsection (d) "may not be excused on the ground that the discovery sought is objectionable unless the party failing to act has a pending motion for a protective order as provided by Rule 26(c)." That is, unlike the situation in chapter 46, where the objecting party filed discovery responses and objections, Rule 37(d) contemplates the situation where no responses whatsoever have been served. In that case, any objections that could have been raised will not excuse the failure to provide the discovery unless there was a motion for a protective order filed and pending at the time the discovery was due.

Rule 37(d) appears to overlap with Rule 37(a)(2), which also permits a court to sanction a party that fails to provide proper interrogatory answers or respond appropriately to document production requests. The rules, however, are different in scope. Rule 37(a)(2)(B) addresses the failure to answer "*an* interrogatory" or "*a* request for inspection," which implies that written responses were filed, but the respondent refused to provide a specific response to one or more of the requests. In contrast, Rule 37(d) addresses the wholesale failure of a party to serve *any* responses to Rule 33 or 34 requests, or the failure of the party (or its representative) to attend its own deposition.

This distinction is evidenced by the different sanctions available under the two rules. A Rule 37(a)(2) violation is remedied by an order under Rule 37(a) for appropriate discovery responses, attorneys' fees, and costs. A Rule 37(d) violation, which is more egregious, exposes the miscreant to Rule 37(b)(2) sanctions, which could include a finding of contempt, without the need to file a motion to compel. As a rule, if a party files written responses to Rule 33 and 34 requests that purport to answer and/or object, if the propounding party is dissatisfied with the adequacy of the responses, his remedy is to file a motion to compel under Rule 37(a)(2). On the other hand, the remedy for a failure to file any responses is a motion under Rule 37(d).

Courts generally restrict imposition of the harshest sanctions for Rule 37(d) violations, however, to situations where there is extreme misconduct such as: (1) a total failure to respond to discovery requests; (2) willful or bad faith failure to provide discovery; or (3) failure to obey prior discovery orders of the court. *See, e.g., Haverson v. Campbell Soup Co.*, 374 F.2d 810, 812 (7th Cir. 1967) (holding that the "extreme sanctions" of Rule 37(d) may be imposed for failure to respond to interrogatories "only when a party willfully fails to serve answers to properly served interrogatories"); *Sigliano v. Mendoza* , 642 F.2d 309, 310 (9th Cir. 1981) ("Dismissal is a proper sanction under Rule 37(d) for a serious or total failure to respond to discovery even without a prior order."); *J.M. Cleminshaw Co. v. City of Norwich*, 93 F.R.D. 338, 345 (D. Conn. 1981) ("Rule 37(d) may not be invoked for 'anything less than a serious or total failure to respond to interrogatories' or requests for production. Where the party resisting discovery has responded by objecting to certain interrogatories or requests for production, or has served responses that the party seeking discovery considers to be evasive or incomplete, then 'the proper remedy is to move for an order compelling answers or production under Rule 37(a).'"); *United States v. Certain Real Prop. Located at Route 1, Bryant, Ala.,* 126 F.3d 1314, 1317 (11th Cir. 1997) ("The decision to dismiss a claim or enter default judgment [as a discovery sanction] 'ought to be a last resort—ordered only if noncompliance with discovery orders is due to willful or bad faith disregard for those orders.'" The court also noted that although Rule 37(d) does not require a prior court order as a prerequisite for imposition of case dispositive sanctions, "judicial interpretation" of the rule may require a prior court order before a case may be ended as a result of discovery failures.).

Rule 37(d)'s required certification of an effort to resolve the discovery dispute is meant to prevent knee-jerk motions for sanctions where the delinquent party has simply missed the deadline. If a communication to opposing counsel likely will produce a prompt agreement to provide the overdue responses within a reasonable time, it makes no sense to file the motion only to have the opposing attorney file a response saying that the dispute is moot because the answers have been or shortly will be provided. While the judge still may impose monetary sanctions against the party that failed to file timely responses prior to the filing of the motion, if it concludes that the motion would not have been necessary had the moving party attempted to resolve the dispute without the court's involvement, it may well not award the moving party costs and attorneys' fees. Likewise, if the moving party makes a good faith, albeit unsuccessful, attempt to resolve the dispute before filing, this will support an argument for more severe sanctions, as it evidences willful or bad faith failure by the respondent to meet its discovery obligations.

Rule 37(d) sanctions also are applicable if a party, its representative, or designee under Rule 30(b)(6) fails to appear for a deposition. "Failing to appear," it is important to note, includes situations where a Rule 30(b)(6) witness in fact does appear and is sworn, but is unprepared to address the topics listed in the deposition notice:

> [I]n reality if a Rule 30(b)(6) witness is unable to give useful information he is no more present for the deposition than would be a deponent who physically appears for the deposition but sleeps through it. Indeed, we believe that the purpose behind Rule 30(b)(6) undoubtedly is frustrated in the situation in which a corporate party produces a witness who is unable and/or unwilling to provide the necessary factual information on the entity's behalf. . . . Thus, we hold that when a witness is designated by a corporate party to speak on its behalf pursuant to Rule 30(b)(6) "[p]roducing an unprepared witness is tantamount to a failure to appear" that is sanctionable under Rule 37(d).

Black Horse Lane Assoc. v. Dow Chemical Corp., 228 F.3d 275, 304 (3d Cir. 2000); *Resolution Trust Corp. v. Southern Union Co. Inc.,* 985 F.2d 196, 197 (5th Cir. 1993) ("When a corporation or association designates a person to testify on its behalf, the corporation appears vicariously through that agent. If that agent is not knowledgeable about relevant facts, and the principal has failed to designate an available, knowledgeable, and readily identifiable witness, then the appearance is, for all practical purposes, no appearance at all".).

Not all courts read Rule 37(d) this harshly. One has concluded that when a corporation actually produces a witness for a Rule 30(b)(6) deposition, but he or she is unprepared or refuses to testify on the topics listed in the notice, "[t]he proper procedure is first to obtain an order from the court as authorized by Rule 37(a), directing him to be sworn and testify." *Salahuddin v. Harris,* 782 F.2d 1127, 1131 (2d Cir. 1986); *Pioche Mines Consol., Inc. v. Dolman,* 333 F.2d 257, 269 (9th Cir. 1964), *cert. denied,* 380 U.S. 956 (1965).

Finally, Rule 37(d) requires a party that receives discovery requests that it views as improper to do more than simply tell the adverse party that it objects. "The failure to act described in this subdivision may not be excused on the ground that the discovery sought is objectionable unless the party failing to act has a pending motion for a protective order as provided by Rule 26(c)." Rule 37(d). The commentary to the rule notes that "[t]he last sentence . . . [of Rule 37(d)] is revised to clarify that it is the pendency of a motion for protective order that may be urged as an excuse for a violation of subdivision (d). If a party's motion has been denied, the party cannot argue that its subsequent failure to comply would be justified." Commentary to the 1993 Rule Changes, 146 F.R.D. 692. The commentary further cautions, "[I]t should be noted that the filing of a motion under Rule 26(c) is not self-executing—the relief authorized under that rule depends on obtaining the court's order to that effect." *Id.*

Courts have underscored the importance of filing a motion for protective order. *See Byrnes v. JetNet Corp.* 111 F.R.D. 68 (M.D.N.C. 1986) (requiring a party objecting to a deposition notice and document subpoena to file a motion for a protective order to preserve the objection); *In re Air Crash Disaster at Detroit Metro.,* 130 F.R.D. 627, 631 (E.D. Mich. 1989); *Brittain v. Stroh Brewery Co.* 136 F.R.D. 408 (M.D.N.C. 1991) (the party resisting written discovery requests or a deposition notice has an affirmative obligation to file a motion for a protective order, not simply object and wait for a motion to compel to be filed); and *Mason C. Day Excavating v. Lumberman's Mut. Cas. Co.,* 143 F.R.D. 601 (D. N.C. 1992) (a party opposing a Rule 34 request on the basis of privilege must also move for a protective order); 8 C. Wright & A. Miller, *Federal Practice and Procedure,* § 2116, at 426-27 (West 1970 & Supp. 1988); *see also* chapter 46, *supra.*

In the example, defense counsel did not file a motion for a protective order relating to his objections to 21 of the topics listed in the Rule 30(b)(6) deposition notice. He runs the risk that the court will rule that the production of a witness who was not prepared to give meaningful testimony as to these topics was tantamount to a failure to produce a deponent. If the court finds that Rule 37(d) was violated, it will also determine which sanctions are appropriate. If the court is convinced that defense counsel acted in bad faith or willfully, and that all or at least most of the 21 disputed topics are legitimate areas of testimony for a Rule 30(b)(6) witness, it may impose severe sanctions under Rule 37(b)(2)(A)-(C). Alternatively, if the court finds no improper motive underlying the failure to produce a knowledgeable witness, or if the court concludes that all or many of the topics are objectionable, it is more likely to order only that the defendant produce a witness prepared to address the nonobjectionable topics and pay costs and attorneys' fees.

What about the plaintiff's motion for sanctions for defendant's failure to provide timely Rule 33 answers? The plaintiff's lawyer should have tried harder to resolve the dispute without court intervention. The court probably will conclude that plaintiff's counsel did not make a good faith effort to resolve the dispute. By not taking adequate pre-motion steps to resolve the dispute, plaintiff's counsel runs the risk that the court will not impose sanctions. Instead, the court can be expected to order responsive answers to interrogatories within a stated time.

Practice Tips

1. A party that receives interrogatories, document production requests, or a deposition notice must carefully evaluate how to preserve any objections. The most conservative course is to serve timely written objections to the Rule 33 and 34 discovery, together with a motion for a protective order under Rule 26(c), if informal attempts to resolve the dispute are unsuccessful. In practice, however, it is unusual for an attorney to file both written responses containing objections plus a motion for protective order, even though some courts expect this to be done. *See* chapter 46, *supra*. The cardinal rule is—file responses to Rule 33 and 34 requests, and appear at properly noticed depositions, unless you have previously filed a motion for a protective order. Otherwise, you risk Rule 37(d) sanctions.

2. A party that receives a Rule 30(b)(6) designee deposition notice should promptly and carefully review each topic listed. Any objections should be communicated to the initiating party, and a motion for a protective order should be filed if the parties cannot resolve the dispute on their own. It is not sufficient to simply object to some or all of the topics and then not produce a witness for the deposition, or produce a witness not prepared to address all topics listed.

3. A party that files a Rule 37(d) motion seeking severe sanctions under Rule 37(b)(2) must show the court why such penalties are appropriate. Saying that discovery was not provided is insufficient. Sanctions depend on a showing of factors, such as: (a) evidence that the delinquent party acted in bad faith or willfully (such as destroying documents after receipt of a Rule 34 request); (b) prejudice to the party seeking the discovery (for example, an inability to examine an allegedly defective product because it was destroyed by plaintiff's expert during testing); (c) an explanation of why the discovery that was sought, but not provided, legitimately was discoverable, and why there was no valid basis for objecting to it; (d) the efforts taken by the moving party to obtain the discovery without court intervention; and (e) the importance of the information sought to the moving party's case. Remember that courts generally are reluctant to impose case-determinative sanctions. Do not seek the harshest penalties except in extreme cases.

48. NONPRODUCTION, SPOLIATION, DISCOVERY VIOLATIONS, AND ADVERSE INFERENCE

Mrs. Smith's husband drowned in an indoor pool at a resort. She sued the owner-operator for negligence, basing her claim on the lack of a safety line to separate the shallow end of the pool from the deep end, the absence of a lifeguard and other emergency aid, and the poor design and maintenance of the pool, including a steep slope, inaccurate depth markers, and dim lighting. Two years after the accident and more than a year after the complaint was filed, the defendant redesigned and substantially modified the pool. The plaintiff contended that this conduct constituted "spoliation of evidence" and asked that the court sanction the defendant by striking its answer and granting her summary judgment.

How should the court rule?

Comment: Spoliation is destroying, significantly altering, or failing to preserve property for another's use as evidence in pending or reasonably foreseeable litigation. A party on notice that evidence is relevant has a duty to preserve it. See *Turner v. Hudson Transit Lines, Inc.*, 142 F.R.D. 68, 78 (S.D.N.Y. 1991). Courts have the power to sanction litigants for spoliation of evidence under Fed. R. Civ. P. 37(b) and under their inherent powers to control litigation. *West v. Goodyear Tire & Rubber Co.*, 167 F.3d 776, 779 (2d Cir. 1999). The court must determine the appropriate sanction based on (1) the relative fault of the litigant against whom sanctions are sought, and (2) the degree of prejudice suffered by the movant due to the destruction or loss of the evidence at issue. "Destruction of potentially relevant evidence obviously occurs along a continuum of fault—ranging from innocence through the degrees of negligence to intentionality. The resulting penalties vary correspondingly." *Welsh v. United States*, 844 F.2d 1239, 1246 (6th Cir. 1998). Sanctions can include dismissal of a suit or striking an answer. However, dismissal (or its analogue, striking an answer) should be imposed only in extraordinary circumstances. *John B. Hull, Inc. v. Waterbury Petroleum Prods.*, 845 F.2d 1172, 1176 (2d Cir. 1998).

The example is based on *Townes v. Cove Haven, Inc.*, 2003 WL 22861921 (S.D.N.Y. Dec. 2, 2003) (not reported). There, the court denied the motion for sanctions. Although the defendant had certainly altered the evidence, there was no showing that its conduct was malicious or in bad faith. The length of time between the accident and the reconstruction suggested as much;

a finding of "malice" would have been more likely if the reconstruction had seemed to be an immediate reaction to the accident or the suit. In fact, the defendant's preservation of the pool for two years after the accident gave the plaintiff ample time to preserve the evidence. Any detriment to her arose mostly out of her lawyer's dilatory handling of the case. "The scope of the duty to preserve evidence is not boundless. A potential spoliator need only do what is reasonable." *Id.*, quoting *Kolanovic v. Gida*, 77 F. Supp. 2d 595, 602 (D.N.J. 1999). The defendant acted reasonably in preserving the pool for as long as it did; "[T]he doctrine of spoliation does not require [the resort] to retain on their property indefinitely what Plaintiff alleges to be a negligent condition." *Townes, supra* *4.

In *Residential Funding Corp. v. DeGeorge Financial Corp.*, 306 F.3d 1999 (2d Cir. 2002), the court considered the standard for determining whether failure to comply with discovery requests warranted sanctions. The court observed that an adverse inference instruction is usually employed in cases involving spoliation or destruction of evidence. Where an adverse inference instruction is sought because evidence is not produced in time for trial (for whatever reason, including spoliation), the party seeking the instruction must show that: (1) its opponent had control over the evidence and had an obligation to produce it; (2) the party that failed to timely produce the evidence had a culpable state of mind; and (3) a reasonable trier of fact could find that the missing evidence would support a claim or defense.

The culpable conduct in *Residential Funding* was the responding party's negligent foot-dragging in producing relevant e-mails. The court held that the defendant's sluggishness in producing the requested documents supported an inference that the e-mails not produced in time for trial were harmful to the defendant, warranting an adverse inference instruction. *See* Gregory P. Joseph, "Electronics Spoliation," *National Capital Law Journal,* Dec. 9, 2002 ("*Residential Funding* holds that negligent delay—not destruction, merely delay—in producing electronic data is sanctionable.").

When does the duty to preserve evidence arise? One court has said that the duty arises:

[n]ot only during litigation but also . . . before the litigation when a party reasonably should know that the evidence may be relevant to anticipated litigation. . . . If a party cannot fulfill this duty to preserve because he does not own or control the evidence, he still has

an obligation to give the opposing party notice of access to the evidence or of the possible destruction of the evidence if the party anticipates litigation involving that evidence.

Silvestri v. G. M. Corp., 271 F.3d 583, 591 (4th Cir. 2001) (internal citations omitted); *Kronisch v. United States*, 150 F.3d 112, 126 (2d Cir. 1998); *Andersen v. Schwartz*, 687 N.Y.S.2d. 232, 234-35 (N.Y. Sup. Ct. 1999); *Fujitsu Ltd. v. Federal Express Corp.*, 247 F.3d 423, 436 (2d Cir. 2001); *Zubulake v. UBS Warburg LLC*, 2003 WL 22410619 at *2 (S.D.N.Y. Oct. 22, 2003); *Perez-Velasco v. Suzuki Motor Co., Ltd.*, 266 F. Supp. 2d 266, 269 (D.P.R. 2003).

In the context of discovery of electronically stored information, one court recently held that this duty does not encompass all repositories of electronic information, such as backup tapes or rarely accessed archival data, but does encompass information relevant to the "key players" in the litigation. *Zubulake, supra.* Once that duty to preserve is triggered, the party must put a "litigation hold" on the pertinent information. A failure to do so or to produce the material in a timely fashion in response to a proper discovery request may subject that party to an adverse inference instruction. *Id.* at *4.

Indeed, no aspect of discovery has been more controversial recently than discovery of electronically stored information, because new technology has created new problems relating to the retrieval, storage, deleting, and the expense associated with electronically stored information. *See generally* chapter 9 (Discovery of Electronically Stored Information), *supra*, and Appendix D.

Counsel should also bear in mind that altering or failing to preserve evidence in pending or reasonably foreseeable litigation could violate ethical guidelines. Rule 3.4 of the Rules and Professional Responsibility, American Bar Association Model Rules of Professional Conduct, "Fairness to Opposing Party and Counsel" (2003), provides that counsel shall not unlawfully obstruct another party's access to evidence or destroy evidence. The ABA's Civil Discovery Standards (August 1999 and August 2004 Proposed Amendment), Standard No. 10, titled "Preservation of Documents," emphasizes that when counsel learns that litigation is probable, she should inform the client of its duty to preserve potentially relevant documents and consequences resulting if documents are not properly preserved.

Practice Tip

A party that engages in negligent, sluggish conduct that allows or causes evidence to be destroyed does so at its own peril. In the case of a responding party that negligently permits evidence to be destroyed, sanctions will be imposed. The intentional or grossly negligent destruction or nonproduction of relevant evidence could lead to the most severe sanctions. However, an inquiring party that waits too long to gather evidence may have no remedy if the evidence is gone or altered.

All lawyers should be thoroughly familiar with the applicable rules in the jurisdictions in which they practice.

49. SANCTIONS FOR FAILURE TO COMPLY WITH COURT-ORDERED DISCOVERY

Gourmet Catering, Inc. has sued its insurer, AllSafe, Inc., for failure to pay a business interruption claim filed by Gourmet. Gourmet seeks recovery of $250,000 in property loss caused by a fire that broke out in its kitchen, as well as $350,000 in lost profits for the time necessary to repair the damage and re-open for business. The suit is pending in federal court.

During discovery, AllSafe served interrogatories and document requests on Gourmet asking for information about the details and amount of Gourmet's claimed damages. AllSafe believed that Gourmet's responses were evasive and vague and attempted to resolve the issue informally without success. AllSafe thereafter filed a Rule 37(a) motion to compel production of responsive answers. The motion was granted; the court ordered Gourmet to furnish amended Rule 33 and 34 responses within 30 days and directed that they be complete and unevasive as required by Rule 37(a)(3). The court cautioned that a failure to comply with the order could subject Gourmet to sanctions, including case-dispositive ones.

The 30 days passed, and, although amended answers were filed, Gourmet still failed to explain in detail how it calculated its property loss and lost profit damages. AllSafe has filed a motion seeking monetary sanctions and an order preventing Gourmet from recovering any damages at trial. In response, Gourmet has argued that this relief would be tantamount to dismissing its claim. Gourmet contends that the sanction sought is too harsh and argues that any failure to provide detailed information should be addressed at trial after Gourmet has had a chance to present its case in chief.

How should the court rule?

Comment: Rule 37(b) allows a court to sanction a party that fails to comply with a previous court order regarding discovery. The court may issue such orders as are just, including: (a) that matters that were within the scope of the prior court order or other designated facts shall be taken to be established for the purpose of the lawsuit; (b) refusing to allow the disobedient party to support or oppose designated claims or defenses, or prohibiting that party from introducing designated matters into evidence at trial; (c) striking pleadings or parts of pleadings, or staying further proceedings in the case until the order is obeyed, or dismissing the action, or any part of it, or rendering a default judgment against the disobedient party; or (d) issuing an order holding the disobedient party in contempt (except as to an order concerning a Rule 35 physical or mental examination).

Rule 37(b) also provides that in lieu of or in addition to any of the sanctions just listed, the court shall require the disobedient party or his or her attorney, or both, to pay the reasonable expenses, including attorneys' fees, caused by the failure, unless the court finds that the failure was substantially justified or that circumstances make the imposition of monetary sanctions unjust. These are the same standards discussed at chapter 45 (Motion to Compel Discovery) regarding the imposition of attorneys' fees and costs associated with discovery disputes.

Because a Rule 37(b) motion, by definition, may be filed only based on failure to comply with a prior court order, the moving party need not certify that a good faith effort has been made to try to resolve the dispute. The rule makes the imposition of the very severe sanctions listed in section 37(b)(2)(A)-(E) *permissive*, recognizing that they are potentially case-determinative. However, imposition of reasonable costs and attorneys' fees against the recalcitrant party is *mandatory*, unless the court finds the failure to obey the earlier order was substantially justified or it would be unjust to do so.

Neither Rule 37(b) nor its commentary identifies factors that a court should use when considering sanctions. However, the cases are clear that the most serious sanctions, such as the entry of a default judgment or preclusion of evidence, are not automatic simply because a party fails to obey a discovery order. The Fourth Circuit has a four-factor test for imposition of Rule 37(b)(2) sanctions: (1) whether the noncomplying party acted in bad faith; (2) the degree of prejudice to the party seeking sanctions; (3) the need for deterrence; and (4) whether less drastic sanctions would be effective. *Southern States Rack and Fixture, Inc. v. Sherwin-Williams Co.*, 318 F.3d 592, 597 (4th Cir. 2003); *Anderson v. Found. for Advancement, Educ. & Employment of Am. Indians*, 155 F.3d 500 (4th Cir. 2001); and *Wilson v. Volkswagen of Am. Inc.*, 561 F.2d 494, 505-06 (4th Cir. 1977).

Other courts have held that it is reversible error for a trial court to impose Rule 37(b)(2)(A)-(E) sanctions absent some showing of bad faith, willfulness, or prejudice. *Dorsey v. Academy Moving & Storage, Inc.*, 423 F.2d 858, 860 (5th Cir. 1970) ("The sanctions available under Rule 37(b) . . . are predicated upon the presence of such factors as willful disobedience, gross indifference to the right of the adverse party, deliberate callousness or gross negligence. The sanctions are not predicated upon a party's failure to satisfy the requirements of a production order when the failure 'was due to inability fostered neither by its own conduct nor by circumstances within its control.'" (internal citations omitted)); *Mid-America Tablewares, Inc. v. Mogio Trading Co. Ltd.*, 100 F.3d 1353 (7th Cir. 1996) (Rule 37(b)(2) sanctions were properly denied where violation of prior discovery order did not prejudice moving party's trial preparation); *Wendt v. Host International, Inc.*, 125 F.3d 806, 814 (9th Cir. 1997) (articulating five-factor test for imposing sanction of evidence preclusion for violation of discovery obligations: (1) the public's interest in expeditious resolution of litigation; (2) the court's need to manage its docket; (3) the risk of prejudice to the party seeking preclusion sanctions; (4) the public policy favoring disposition of cases on their merits; and (5) availability of less drastic sanctions); and *Bonds v. District of Columbia*, 93 F.3d 801, 808 (D.C. Cir. 1996) (It was error for the trial court to issue Rule 37(b)(2) sanctions precluding defendant from calling any fact witnesses at trial for failure to properly provide interrogatory response. "In determining whether a severe sanction is justified, the district court may consider the resulting prejudice to the other party, any prejudice to the judicial system, and the need to deter similar misconduct in the future.").

In the example, Gourmet failed to provide sufficient Rule 33 or 34 discovery on its damages as ordered by the court. In deciding whether to impose Rule 37(b)(2) sanctions, the court's primary concern will be whether this failure was willful or in bad faith—or instead, was the product of a lesser failing. For example, if the failure was a deliberate refusal, harsh sanctions are likely. If, instead, the failure was caused by excusable neglect, such as forgetting to provide the discovery due to overwork, or unavoidable circumstances like illness, lesser sanctions are more likely. The court will also be concerned with the real possibility of prejudice to the defendant at trial, as Gourmet has the burden of proving its damages, which are substantial, by a preponderance of evidence.

On balance, if additional damages information sought by Gourmet can be readily produced, if trial is not imminent, and if Gourmet did not act in bad faith, the court is not likely to issue an order precluding Gourmet from introducing damages evidence at trial. Regardless of the severity of the court's sanctions under Rule 37(b)(2), however, it likely will tax costs and attorneys' fees against Gourmet.

Practice Tips

In the example, AllSafe cannot simply cite the court's earlier order, demonstrate that it was ignored, and expect the court to impose Rule 37(b)(2)(A)-(E) sanctions as a matter of course. Rather, a moving party must carefully address each of the factors discussed above and be prepared to explain in detail how it has suffered prejudice, why lesser sanctions would be inappropriate, and, if known, how the disobedient party's conduct amounted to bad faith. This should be done in a straightforward manner with no ad hominem attack. It is particularly important for the moving party to explain why it cannot obtain the substantial equivalent of the information ordered from other discovery provided in the case. Further, if the moving party asks the court to preclude the disobedient party from asserting or opposing claims or defenses, it must provide specific references to the pleadings that raised the claims or defenses and demonstrate why the discovery that was not produced as ordered is relevant to them.

A lawyer opposing a Rule 37(b) motion should focus on the factors discussed, but from a different perspective. General, unsupported statements that the failure to answer was not a result of bad faith or willfulness have no value. Rather, there must be a particularized explanation, including affidavits and exhibits, of his client's failure to comply with the earlier order.

For example, if the failure to comply was caused by a fire that destroyed the documents that were to be produced, an affidavit setting this out, supplemented by the fire department report and photographs, would show the court why compliance was impossible. If electronically stored information that has been deleted could not be produced, as ordered by the court, an affidavit from the technician who tried to recapture the information explaining what had been done and why it was not successful, as well as an explanation that the deletion was not done improperly, would help to demonstrate that noncompliance was not willful or in bad faith.

Next, the defending party should address in similar detail the issue of prejudice to the moving party and explain how any potential prejudice could be cured. It is especially helpful if the defending party can point to other material that it has provided that contains the same information that was ordered to be produced (or its substantial equivalent). In doing so, however, it is unwise simply to attach to the opposition memorandum voluminous documents, interrogatory answers, and deposition transcripts: Few courts will want to wade through such a mass of material to determine whether the moving party in fact has received equivalent information. Rather, counsel should demonstrate in the clearest way possible the specific information that he contends fairly met the moving party's discovery request at issue. For example, if a party failed to answer an interrogatory asking for the identity of witnesses to an event, but during the defendant's deposition she identified those witnesses, attach an excerpt of the deposition transcript showing this and highlight it in yellow so that the court readily can see it. If it is necessary to attach voluminous exhibits, highlight the exact text that you want the court to read.

50. CHART SUMMARIZING DISCOVERY SANCTIONS

Rule	Summary	Sanction
R 26(g): Signature & Certification	R 11 sanctions are inapplicable to discovery, R 11(d). R 26(g) serves the same function for the discovery process as R 11. It addresses two aspects of discovery: (1) R 26(a)(1) & (3) Disclosures: Requires the signature of attorney/unrepresented party on the initial and pretrial disclosures provided for by R 26(a)(1) & (3). Signature constitutes a certification that, to best of signer's knowledge, information, & belief, formed after *reasonable inquiry*, the disclosure is *complete & correct* at the time made [see R 26(e) for requirement to supplement disclosures]. (2) Discovery Requests, Responses, & Objections: R 26(g) requires all discovery requests, responses & objections to be signed by attorney/unrepresented party. Signature constitutes certification that to best of signer's knowledge, information, & belief, formed after *reasonable inquiry*, the request/response/objection is: (a) consistent w/ the FRCP, warranted by existing law or good faith argument for extension/modification /reversal of existing law; (b) not interposed for improper purpose (i.e., to harass or cause unnecessary delay/needless increase in litigation cost; and (c) not unreasonable, unduly burdensome, or expensive, given: (i) needs of the case; (ii) the	For violations of R 26(g) court SHALL impose appropriate sanctions, including award of reasonable attorney's fees & expenses, UNLESS court finds that there was substantial justification for the violation. Court may impose sanctions on motion or on own initiative. Court may sanction party who made certification and/ or party on whose behalf it was made. Note: Commentary to R 26(g) states that this rule, in conjunction with R 37(a)(4) & (c)(1), is intended to be used by court to sanction for violations of disclosure/discovery rules.

Rule	Summary	Sanction
	discovery already had; (iii) the amount in controversy; & (iv) the importance of the issues at stake in the litigation. A failure to sign means the defective discovery request, response, or objection *shall be stricken* unless promptly signed after notice of defect. Importantly, failure to sign means responding party *NOT required to take any action* with respect to request, response, or objection until it is signed.	
R 37(a): Motion for Order Compelling Discovery	Applies when: (1) a party fails to make a R 26(a) disclosure; (2) a deponent fails to answer a question; (3) a corporation or other entity fails to make a R 30(b)(6) designation; (4) a party fails to answer an interrogatory; (5) a party fails to allow inspection of documents/things as requested under R 34. Moving party MUST include a certification of good faith efforts to resolve the dispute w/o court action. Moving party may seek order compelling disclosure/ discovery and request appropriate sanctions. Note: R 37(a)(3) states that an evasive or incomplete disclosure, answer, or response is treated as a failure to disclose, answer, or respond.	(1) If the motion is granted or if the disclosure or requested discovery is provided after the motion is filed, the court SHALL: (a) afford noncompliant party an opportunity to be heard; (b) require deponent/party/attorney whose conduct prompted filing of motion to pay the moving party reasonable expenses & attorney's fees incurred in filing motion, UNLESS court finds : (a) motion was filed *w/o making good faith effort to obtain disclosure/ discovery w/o court action;* or (b) opposing party's nondisclosure, response, or objection was substantially justified; or (c) imposing sanctions would be unjust.

Rule	Summary	Sanction
		(2) If motion is denied, court may enter R 26(c) protective order and SHALL: (a) afford moving party *opportunity to be heard*; (b) require moving party/ attorney or both to pay opposing party/ deponent *reasonable expenses & attorney's fees* incurred in opposing motion, UNLESS court finds: (i) making the motion was substantially justified; or (ii) other circumstances make award of sanctions unjust. (3) If motion granted in part/ denied in part, court MAY: (a) enter R 26(c) protective order; (b) *apportion* reasonable expenses incurred regarding the motion among parties/persons in a just manner, provided the court gives parties/persons an opportunity to be heard.
R 37(b): Sanctions on Failure to Comply w/ Order Directing Disclosure or Discovery	Applicability: (1) If party/ officer/director/managing agent of party or person designated under R 30(b)(6) fails to obey order to provide/permit discovery issued under R 37(a), or R 35 discovery (mental or physical examination); (2) if party fails to obey order entered by court under R 26(f) (directing parties to have conference to plan discovery), the court MAY make	In lieu of/addition to the orders designated by R 37(b)(2) (A)-(E), court SHALL require party disobeying order or attorney advising that party or both to pay reasonable expenses / attorneys' fees caused by failure to obey, UNLESS court finds failure was: (1) substan-

Rule	Summary	Sanction
	such orders as are just, including: (a) ordering that designated facts shall be taken as established for purposes of action in accordance with claim of party obtaining discovery; (b) order that disobedient party may not oppose designated claims or defenses, or prohibit that party from introducing designated matters into evidence; (c) order striking pleadings or parts of pleadings, or staying further proceedings until order is obeyed, or dismissing the action or proceeding, in whole or part, or rendering a default judgment against disobedient party; (d) in lieu of/addition to above, issue order treating as contempt the failure to obey prior order, EXCEPT the failure to obey an order under R 35 to submit to physical/mental examination; (e) where party failed to comply with order under R 35, to produce another person for examination, any of the actions in (a)-(c) above, unless failing party shows it was unable to do so.	tially justified, or (2) award of expenses would be unjust.
R 37(c): Failure to Disclose; False/ Misleading Disclosure; Refusal to Admit	Applicability: (1) party fails w/o substantial justification to: (a) provide R 26(a) disclosures (initial, expert, and/or pretrial); (b) provide R 26(e)(1) & (2) disclosure (supplemental disclosures when prior disclosures and/or retained expert deposition testimony is incomplete or incorrect); (2) fails to admit genuineness of document or truth of matter requested	(1) Sanctions for failure w/o substantial justification to make discovery disclosures under R 26(a) & (e)(1) & (2): (a) noncompliant party may not be permitted to use as evidence at trial/ hearing/motion any witness/information that should have been

Rule	Summary	Sanction
	under R 36 (request for admission of fact/genuineness of documents). Note: R 37(a)(3) provides that incomplete/evasive discovery disclosures, answers, or responses are tantamount to a failure to answer or respond.	disclosed and was not, UNLESS failure to disclose was harmless; (b) in addition to/lieu of (a), court may, on motion & after providing *reasonable opportunity to be heard*, impose other *appropriate sanctions* including: (i) payment of *reasonable expenses/attorneys' fees*; (ii) *sanctions allowed by R 37(b)(2)(A)-(C)* (orders relating to ability to offer evidence, assert claims or defenses, issuing default judgments); (iii) *inform jury of failure of party to make required disclosures.* (2) Sanctions for failure to admit genuineness of documents/truth of facts: (a) if, after party refused to admit genuineness of documents/truth of facts, the party that requested the admission proves the genuineness/truth of the matter, that party may apply to the court for an order requiring adverse party to pay reasonable expenses/attorneys' fees incurred in making the proof. Court SHALL make the order unless it finds the R 36 request was (a) *objectionable*; (b) the admission sought was of *inconse-*

Rule	Summary	Sanction
		quential matter; (c) the party failing to admit had *reasonable ground to believe he/she might prevail* on the matter; (d) there was other *good reason* for failing to admit.
R 37(d): Sanctions for a party's failure to attend own deposition or to serve answers to interrogatories or a request for inspection	Applicability: If a party, officer/director/managing agent of a party, or a person designated under R 30(b)(6) or R 31(a) fails: (1) to *appear for a deposition* after proper service of notice of deposition; (2) to *serve answers/objections to properly served interrogatories*; or (3) to *serve proper response to a properly served Rule 34 request for inspection*. Party filing motion with court must certify *good faith attempt to resolve* dispute w/o court involvement if motion involves failure to serve proper R 33 and R 34 responses.	Court may make such orders as are just, including: (1) action authorized by R 36(b)(2)(A)-(C) (order designating facts/matters as having been established, precluding proof of claims/defenses, striking pleadings, dismissing action, or entering a default judgment); (2) in lieu of/addition to (1) above, court SHALL require party/or attorney advising that party or both to pay reasonable expenses/attorneys' fees UNLESS court finds: (a) failure was substantially justified; or (b) sanctions would be unjust.
R 37(g): Failure to participate in framing of discovery plan under R 26(f)	Applicability: Failure of party/attorney to participate in good faith in development & submission of discovery plan required by R 26(f).	Following opportunity to be heard, court may require party/attorney or both to pay other party the reasonable expenses/attorneys' fees caused by the failure.
28 U.S.C. § 1927	Provides that an attorney "who so multiplies the proceedings in	28 U.S.C. § 1927 does not require a showing of

Rule	Summary	Sanction
	any case unreasonably and vexatiously may be required by the court to satisfy personally the excess costs, expenses, and attorneys' fees reasonably incurred because of such conduct."	bad faith or willfulness, and may be used concurrently with other sanctions. *Chambers, supra*, at 49-50; *Ausherman, infra*, at 442.
Inherent Authority of the Court	The court has the inherent authority to sanction an attorney for misconduct regarding the handling of a case, including discovery abuses. *Chambers v. NASCO*, 501 U.S. 32 (1991); *U.S. v. Shaffer Equipment Co.*, 11 F.3d 450 (4th Cir. 1993); *Oregon RSA No. 6 v. Castle Rock Cellular of Oregon Ltd. Partnership*, 76 F.3d 1003 (9th Cir. 1996); *Ausherman v. Bank of America*, 212 F. Supp. 2d 435 (D. Md. 2002).	Courts are cautious in using their inherent authority to impose discovery sanctions. Imposing sanctions for discovery abuse under the court's inherent authority requires a showing of bad faith or a willful violation of a court order.
Rule of Professional Conduct 3.2	This rule provides that a lawyer "shall make reasonable efforts to expedite litigation consistent with the interests of the client." The comment to the rule notes that dilatory tactics "bring the administration of justice into disrepute. . . . It is not a justification that [dilatory conduct] . . . is tolerated by the bench and bar. The question is whether a competent lawyer acting in good faith would regard the course of action as having some substantial purpose."	If a court believes that an attorney has violated Rule 3.2 in connection with discovery practice, it may refer the matter to the appropriate bar disciplinary committee.

Appendix A

Federal Rules of Civil Procedure: Rules 26-37; Rule 45

RULE 26. GENERAL PROVISIONS GOVERNING DISCOVERY; DUTY OF DISCLOSURE

(a) Required Disclosures; Methods to Discover Additional Matter.

    (1) Initial Disclosures. Except in categories of proceedings specified in Rule 26(a)(1)(E), or to the extent otherwise stipulated or directed by order, a party must, without awaiting a discovery request, provide to other parties:

        (A) the name and, if known, the address and telephone number of each individual likely to have discoverable information that the disclosing party may use to support its claims or defenses, unless solely for impeachment, identifying the subjects of the information;

        (B) a copy of, or a description by category and location of, all documents, data compilations, and tangible things that are in the possession, custody, or control of the party and that the disclosing party may use to support its claims or defenses, unless solely for impeachment;

        (C) a computation of any category of damages claimed by the disclosing party, making available for inspection and copying as under Rule 34 the documents or other evidentiary material, not privileged or protected from disclosure, on which such computation is based, including materials bearing on the nature and extent of injuries suffered; and

        (D) for inspection and copying as under Rule 34 any insurance agreement under which any person carrying on an insurance business may be liable to satisfy part or all of a judgment which may be entered in the action or to indemnify or reimburse for payments made to satisfy the judgment.

(**E**) The following categories of proceedings are exempt from initial disclosure under Rule 26(a)(1):

   (**i**)   an action for review on an administrative record;

   (**ii**) a petition for habeas corpus or other proceeding to challenge a criminal conviction or sentence;

   (**iii**) an action brought without counsel by a person in custody of the United States, a state, or a state subdivision;

   (**iv**) an action to enforce or quash an administrative summons or subpoena;

   (**v**) an action by the United States to recover benefit payments;

   (**vi**) an action by the United States to collect on a student loan guaranteed by the United States;

   (**vii**) a proceeding ancillary to proceedings in other courts; and

   (**viii**) an action to enforce an arbitration award.

These disclosures must be made at or within 14 days after the Rule 26(f) conference unless a different time is set by stipulation or court order, or unless a party objects during the conference that initial disclosures are not appropriate in the circumstances of the action and states the objection in the Rule 26(f) discovery plan. In ruling on the objection, the court must determine what disclosures—if any—are to be made, and set the time for disclosure. Any party first served or otherwise joined after the Rule 26(f) conference must make these disclosures within 30 days after being served or joined unless a different time is set by stipulation or court order. A party must make its initial disclosures based on the information then reasonably available to it and is not excused from making its disclosures because it has not fully completed its investigation of the case or because it challenges the sufficiency of another party's disclosures or because another party has not made its disclosures.

(**2**) **Disclosure of Expert Testimony.**

   (**A**) In addition to the disclosures required by paragraph (1), a party shall disclose to other parties the identity of any person who may be used at trial to present evidence under Rules 702, 703, or 705 of the Federal Rules of Evidence.

   (**B**) Except as otherwise stipulated or directed by the court, this disclosure shall, with respect to a witness who is retained or specially employed to provide expert testimony in the case or whose duties as an employee of the party regularly involve giving expert testimony, be accompanied by a written report prepared and signed by the witness. The report shall contain a complete statement of all opinions to be expressed and the basis and reasons therefor; the data or other information considered by the witness in forming the opinions; any exhibits to be used as a summary of or support for the opinions; the qualifications of the witness, including a list of all publications authored by the witness within the preceding ten years; the compensation to be paid for the study and testimony; and a listing of any other cases in which the witness has testified as an expert at trial or by deposition within the preceding four years.

(C) These disclosures shall be made at the times and in the sequence directed by the court. In the absence of other directions from the court or stipulation by the parties, the disclosures shall be made at least 90 days before the trial date or the date the case is to be ready for trial or, if the evidence is intended solely to contradict or rebut evidence on the same subject matter identified by another party under paragraph (2)(B), within 30 days after the disclosure made by the other party. The parties shall supplement these disclosures when required under subdivision (e)(1).

(3) Pretrial Disclosures. In addition to the disclosures required by Rule 26(a)(1) and (2), a party must provide to other parties and promptly file with the court the following information regarding the evidence that it may present at trial other than solely for impeachment:

(A) the name and, if not previously provided, the address and telephone number of each witness, separately identifying those whom the party expects to present and those whom the party may call if the need arises;

(B) the designation of those witnesses whose testimony is expected to be presented by means of a deposition and, if not taken stenographically, a transcript of the pertinent portions of the deposition testimony; and

(C) an appropriate identification of each document or other exhibit, including summaries of other evidence, separately identifying those which the party expects to offer and those which the party may offer if the need arises.

Unless otherwise directed by the court, these disclosures must be made at least 30 days before trial. Within 14 days thereafter, unless a different time is specified by the court, a party may serve and promptly file a list disclosing (i) any objections to the use under Rule 32(a) of a deposition designated by another party under Rule 26(a)(3)(B), and (ii) any objection, together with the grounds therefor, that may be made to the admissibility of materials identified under Rule 26(a)(3)(C). Objections not so disclosed, other than objections under Rules 402 and 403 of the Federal Rules of Evidence, are waived unless excused by the court for good cause.

(4) **Form of Disclosures.** Unless the court orders otherwise, all disclosures under Rules 26(a)(1) through (3) must be made in writing, signed, and served.

(5) **Methods to Discover Additional Matter.** Parties may obtain discovery by one or more of the following methods: depositions upon oral examination or written questions; written interrogatories; production of documents or things or permission to enter upon land or other property under Rule 34 or 45(a)(1)(C), for inspection and other purposes; physical and mental examinations; and requests for admission.

(b) **Discovery Scope and Limits.** Unless otherwise limited by order of the court in accordance with these rules, the scope of discovery is as follows:

(1) **In General.** Parties may obtain discovery regarding any matter, not privileged, that is relevant to the claim or defense of any party, including the existence, description, nature, custody, condition, and location of any books, documents, or other tangible things and the identity and location of persons having knowledge of any discoverable matter. For good cause, the court may order discovery of any matter relevant to the subject matter involved in the action. Relevant information need not be admissible at the trial if the discovery appears reasonably calculated to lead to the discovery of admissible evidence. All discovery is subject to the limitations imposed by Rule 26(b)(2)(i), (ii), and (iii).

(2) **Limitations.** By order, the court may alter the limits in these rules on the number of depositions and interrogatories or the length of depositions under Rule 30. By order or local rule, the court may also

limit the number of requests under Rule 36. The frequency or extent of use of the discovery methods otherwise permitted under these rules and by any local rule shall be limited by the court if it determines that: (i) the discovery sought is unreasonably cumulative or duplicative, or is obtainable from some other source that is more convenient, less burdensome, or less expensive; (ii) the party seeking discovery has had ample opportunity by discovery in the action to obtain the information sought; or (iii) the burden or expense of the proposed discovery outweighs its likely benefit, taking into account the needs of the case, the amount in controversy, the parties' resources, the importance of the issues at stake in the litigation, and the importance of the proposed discovery in resolving the issues. The court may act upon its own initiative after reasonable notice or pursuant to a motion under Rule 26(c).

(3) **Trial Preparation: Materials.** Subject to the provisions of subdivision (b)(4) of this rule, a party may obtain discovery of documents and tangible things otherwise discoverable under subdivision (b)(1) of this rule and prepared in anticipation of litigation or for trial by or for another party or by or for that other party's representative (including the other party's attorney, consultant, surety, indemnitor, insurer, or agent) only upon a showing that the party seeking discovery has substantial need of the materials in the preparation of the party's case and that the party is unable without undue hardship to obtain the substantial equivalent of the materials by other means. In ordering discovery of such materials when the required showing has been made, the court shall protect against disclosure of the mental impressions, conclusions, opinions, or legal theories of an attorney or other representative of a party concerning the litigation.

A party may obtain without the required showing a statement concerning the action or its subject matter previously made by that party. Upon request, a person not a party may obtain without the required showing a statement concerning the action or its subject matter previously made by that person. If the request is refused, the person may move for a court order. The provisions of Rule 37(a)(4) apply to the award of expenses incurred in relation to the motion. For purposes of this paragraph, a statement previously made is (A) a written statement signed or otherwise adopted or approved by the person making it, or (B) a stenographic, mechanical, electrical, or other recording, or a transcription thereof, which is a substantially verbatim recital of an oral statement by the person making it and contemporaneously recorded.

(4) **Trial Preparation: Experts.**

(A) A party may depose any person who has been identified as an expert whose opinions may be presented at trial. If a report from the expert is required under subdivision (a)(2)(B), the deposition shall not be conducted until after the report is provided.

(B) A party may, through interrogatories or by deposition, discover facts known or opinions held by an expert who has been retained or specially employed by another party in anticipation of litigation or preparation for trial and who is not expected to be called as a witness at trial, only as provided in Rule 35(b) or upon a showing of exceptional circumstances under which it is impracticable for the party seeking discovery to obtain facts or opinions on the same subject by other means.

(C) Unless manifest injustice would result, (i) the court shall require that the party seeking discovery pay the expert a reasonable fee for time spent in responding to discovery under this subdivision; and (ii) with respect to discovery obtained under subdivision (b)(4)(B) of this rule the court shall require the party seeking discovery to pay the other party a fair portion of the fees and expenses reasonably incurred by the latter party in obtaining facts and opinions from the expert.

(5) **Claims of Privilege or Protection of Trial Preparation Materials.** When a party withholds information otherwise discoverable under these rules by claiming that it is privileged or subject to protection as trial preparation material, the party shall make the claim expressly and shall describe the nature of the documents, communications, or things not produced or disclosed in a manner that, without revealing information itself privileged or protected, will enable other parties to assess the applicability of the privilege or protection.

(c) **Protective Orders.** Upon motion by a party or by the person from whom discovery is sought, accompanied by a certification that the movant has in good faith conferred or attempted to confer with other affected parties in an effort to resolve the dispute without court action, and for good cause shown, the court in which the action is pending or alternatively, on matters relating to a deposition, the court in the district where the deposition is to be taken may make any order which justice requires to protect a party or person from annoyance, embarrassment, oppression, or undue burden or expense, including one or more of the following:

(1) that the disclosure or discovery not be had;

(2) that the disclosure or discovery may be had only on specified terms and conditions, including a designation of the time or place;

(3) that the discovery may be had only by a method of discovery other than that selected by the party seeking discovery;

(4) that certain matters not be inquired into, or that the scope of the disclosure or discovery be limited to certain matters;

(5) that discovery be conducted with no one present except persons designated by the court;

(6) that a deposition, after being sealed, be opened only by order of the court;

(7) that a trade secret or other confidential research, development, or commercial information not be revealed or be revealed only in a designated way; and

(8) that the parties simultaneously file specified documents or information enclosed in sealed envelopes to be opened as directed by the court.

If the motion for a protective order is denied in whole or in part, the court may, on such terms and conditions as are just, order that any party or other person provide or permit discovery. The provisions of Rule 37(a)(4) apply to the award of expenses incurred in relation to the motion.

(d) Timing and Sequence of Discovery. Except in categories of proceedings exempted from initial disclosure under Rule 26(a)(1)(E), or when authorized under these rules or by order or agreement of the parties, a party may not seek discovery from any source before the parties have conferred as required by Rule 26(f). Unless the court upon motion, for the convenience of parties and witnesses and in the interests of justice, orders otherwise, methods of discovery may be used in any sequence, and the fact that a party is conducting discovery, whether by deposition or otherwise, does not operate to delay any other party's discovery.

(e) Supplementation of Disclosures and Responses. A party who has made a disclosure under subdivision (a) or responded to a request for discovery with a disclosure or response is under a duty to supplement or correct the disclosure or response to include information thereafter acquired if ordered by the court or in the following circumstances:

(1)   A party is under a duty to supplement at appropriate intervals its disclosures under subdivision (a) if the party learns that in some material respect the information disclosed is incomplete or incorrect and if the additional or corrective information has not otherwise been made known to the other parties during the discovery process or in writing. With respect to testimony of an expert from whom a report is required under subdivision (a)(2)(B) the duty extends both to information contained in the report and to information provided through a deposition of the expert, and any additions or other changes to this information shall be disclosed by the time the party's disclosures under Rule 26(a)(3) are due.

(2)   A party is under a duty seasonably to amend a prior response to an interrogatory, request for production, or request for admission if the party learns that the response is in some material respect incomplete or incorrect and if the additional or corrective information has not otherwise been made known to the other parties during the discovery process or in writing.

(f) Conference of Parties; Planning for Discovery. Except in categories of proceedings exempted from initial disclosure under Rule 26(a)(1)(E) or when otherwise ordered, the parties must, as soon as practicable and in any event at least 21 days before a scheduling conference is held or a scheduling order is due under Rule 16(b), confer to consider the nature and basis of their claims and defenses and the possibilities for a prompt settlement or resolution of the case, to make or arrange for the disclosures required by Rule 26(a)(1), and to develop a proposed discovery plan that indicates the parties' views and proposals concerning:

(1)   what changes should be made in the timing, form, or requirement for disclosures under Rule 26(a), including a statement as to when disclosures under Rule 26(a)(1) were made or will be made:

(2)   the subjects on which discovery may be needed, when discovery should be completed, and whether discovery should be conducted in phases or be limited to or focused upon particular issues;

(3) what changes should be made in the limitations on discovery imposed under these rules or by local rule, and what other limitations should be imposed; and

(4) any other orders that should be entered by the court under Rule 26(c) or under Rule 16(b) and (c).

The attorneys of record and all unrepresented parties that have appeared in the case are jointly responsible for arranging the conference, for attempting in good faith to agree on the proposed discovery plan, and for submitting to the court within 14 days after the conference a written report outlining the plan. A court may order that the parties or attorneys attend the conference in person. If necessary to comply with its expedited schedule for Rule 16(b) conferences, a court may by local rule (i) require that the conference between the parties occur fewer than 21 days before the scheduling conference is held or a scheduling order is due under Rule 16(b), and (ii) require that the written report outlining the discovery plan be filed fewer than 14 days after the conference between the parties, or excuse the parties from submitting a written report and permit them to report orally on their discovery plan at the Rule 16(b) conference.

(g) Signing of Disclosures, Discovery Requests, Responses, and Objections.

(1) Every disclosure made pursuant to subdivision (a)(1) or subdivision (a)(3) shall be signed by at least one attorney of record in the attorney's individual name, whose address shall be stated. An unrepresented party shall sign the disclosure and state the party's address. The signature of the attorney or party constitutes a certification that to the best of the signer's knowledge, information, and belief, formed after a reasonable inquiry, the disclosure is complete and correct as of the time it is made.

(2) Every discovery request, response, or objection made by a party represented by an attorney shall be signed by at least one attorney of record in the attorney's individual name, whose address shall be stated. An unrepresented party shall sign the request, response, or objection and state the party's address. The signature of the attorney or party constitutes a certification that to the best of the signer's knowledge, information, and belief, formed after a reasonable inquiry, the request, response, or objection is:

(A) consistent with these rules and warranted by existing law or a good faith argument for the extension, modification, or reversal of existing law;

(B) not interposed for any improper purpose, such as to harass or to cause unnecessary delay or needless increase in the cost of litigation; and

(C) not unreasonable or unduly burdensome or expensive, given the needs of the case, the discovery already had in the case, the amount in controversy, and the importance of the issues at stake in the litigation.

If a request, response, or objection is not signed, it shall be stricken unless it is signed promptly after the omission is called to the attention of the party making the request, response, or objection, and a party shall not be obligated to take any action with respect to it until it is signed.

(3)   If without substantial justification a certification is made in violation of the rule, the court, upon motion or upon its own initiative, shall impose upon the person who made the certification, the party on whose behalf the disclosure, request, response, or objection is made, or both, an appropriate sanction, which may include an order to pay the amount of the reasonable expenses incurred because of the violation, including a reasonable attorney's fee.

RULE 27. DEPOSITIONS BEFORE ACTION OR PENDING APPEAL

(a) Before Action.

(1)   **Petition.** A person who desires to perpetuate testimony regarding any matter that may be cognizable in any court of the United States may file a verified petition in the United States district court in the district of the residence of any expected adverse party. The petition shall be entitled in the name of the petitioner and shall show: 1, that the petitioner expects to be a party to an action cognizable in a court of the United States but is presently unable to bring it or cause it to be brought, 2, the subject matter of the expected action and the petitioner's interest therein, 3, the facts which the petitioner desires to establish by the proposed testimony and the reasons for desiring

to perpetuate it, 4, the names or a description of the persons the petitioner expects will be adverse parties and their addresses so far as known, and 5, the names and addresses of the persons to be examined and the substance of the testimony which the petitioner expects to elicit from each, and shall ask for an order authorizing the petitioner to take the depositions of the persons to be examined named in the petition, for the purpose of perpetuating their testimony.

(2) Notice and Service. The petitioner shall thereafter serve a notice upon each person named in the petition as an expected adverse party, together with a copy of the petition, stating that the petitioner will apply to the court, at a time and place named therein, for the order described in the petition. At least 20 days before the date of hearing the notice shall be served either within or without the district or state in the manner provided in Rule 4(d) for service of summons; but if such service cannot with due diligence be made upon any expected adverse party named in the petition, the court may make such order as is just for service by publication or otherwise, and shall appoint, for persons not served in the manner provided in Rule 4(d), an attorney who shall represent them, and, in case they are not otherwise represented, shall cross-examine the deponent. If any expected adverse party is a minor or incompetent the provisions of Rule 17(c) apply.

(3) Order and Examination. If the court is satisfied that the perpetuation of the testimony may prevent a failure or delay of justice, it shall make an order designating or describing the persons whose depositions may be taken and specifying the subject matter of the examination and whether the depositions shall be taken upon oral examination or written interrogatories. The depositions may then be taken in accordance with these rules; and the court may make orders of the character provided for by Rules 34 and 35. For the purpose of applying these rules to depositions for perpetuating testimony, each reference therein to the court in which the action is pending shall be deemed to refer to the court in which the petition for such deposition was filed.

(4) Use of Deposition. If a deposition to perpetuate testimony is taken under these rules or if, although not so taken, it would be admissible in evidence in the courts of the state in which it is taken, it may be used in any action involving the same subject matter subsequently brought in a United States district court, in accordance with the provisions of Rule 32(a).

(b) Pending Appeal. If an appeal has been taken from a judgment of a district court or before the taking of an appeal if the time therefor has not expired, the district court in which the judgment was rendered may allow the taking of the depositions of witnesses to perpetuate their testimony for use in the event of further proceedings in the district court. In such case the party who desires to perpetuate the testimony may make a motion in the district court for leave to take the depositions, upon the same notice and service thereof as if the action was pending in the district court. The motion shall show (1) the names and addresses of persons to be examined and the substance of the testimony which the party expects to elicit from each; (2) the reasons for perpetuating their testimony. If the court finds that the perpetuation of the testimony is proper to avoid a failure or delay of justice, it may make an order allowing the depositions to be taken and may make orders of the character provided for by Rules 34 and 35, and thereupon the depositions may be taken and used in the same manner and under the same conditions as are prescribed in these rules for depositions taken in actions pending in the district court.

(c) Perpetuation by Action. This rule does not limit the power of a court to entertain an action to perpetuate testimony.

RULE 28. PERSONS BEFORE WHOM DEPOSITIONS MAY BE TAKEN

(a) Within the United States. Within the United States or within a territory or insular possession subject to the jurisdiction of the United States, depositions shall be taken before an officer authorized to administer oaths by the laws of the United States or of the place where the examination is held, or before a person appointed by the court in which the action is pending. A person so appointed has power to administer oaths and take testimony. The term officer as used in Rules 30, 31 and 32 includes a person appointed by the court or designated by the parties under Rule 29.

(b) In Foreign Countries. Depositions may be taken in a foreign country (1) pursuant to any applicable treaty or convention, or (2) pursuant to a letter of request (whether or not captioned a letter rogatory), or (3) on notice before a person authorized to administer oaths in the place where the examination is held, either by the law thereof or by the law of the United States, or (4) before a person commissioned by the court, and a person so commissioned shall have the power by virtue of the commission to administer any necessary oath and take testimony. A commission or a letter of request shall be issued on application and notice and on terms that are just and appropriate. It is not requisite to the issuance of a commission or a letter of request that the taking of the deposition in any other manner is impracticable or inconvenient; and both a commission and a letter of request may be issued in proper cases. A notice or commission may designate the person before whom the deposition is to be taken either by name or descriptive title. A letter of request may be addressed "To the Appropriate Authority in [here name the country]." When a letter of request or any other device is used pursuant to any applicable treaty or convention, it shall be captioned in the form prescribed by that treaty or convention. Evidence obtained in response to a letter of request need not be excluded merely because it is not a verbatim transcript, because the testimony was not taken under oath, or because of any similar departure from the requirements for depositions taken within the United States under these rules.

(c) **Disqualification for Interest.** No deposition shall be taken before a person who is a relative or employee or attorney or counsel of any of the parties, or is a relative or employee of such attorney or counsel, or is financially interested in the action.

RULE 29. STIPULATIONS REGARDING DISCOVERY PROCEDURE

Unless otherwise directed by the court, the parties may by written stipulation (1) provide that depositions may be taken before any person, at any time or place, upon any notice, and in any manner and when so taken may be used like other depositions, and (2) modify other procedures governing or limitations placed upon discovery, except that stipulations extending the time provided in Rules 33, 34, and 36 for responses to discovery may, if they would interfere with any time set for completion of discovery, for hearing of a motion, or for trial, be made only with the approval of the court.

RULE 30. DEPOSITIONS UPON ORAL EXAMINATION

(a) When Depositions May Be Taken; When Leave Required.

(1)   A Party may take the testimony of any person, including a party, by deposition upon oral examination without leave of court except as provided in paragraph (2). The attendance of witnesses may be compelled by subpoena as provided in Rule 45.

(2)   A party must obtain leave of court, which shall be granted to the extent consistent with the principles stated in Rule 26(b)(2), if the person to be examined is confined in prison or if, without the written stipulation of the parties,

(A) a proposed deposition would result in more than ten depositions being taken under this rule or Rule 31 by the plaintiffs, or by the defendants, or by third-party defendants;

(B) the person to be examined already has been deposed in the case; or

(C) a party seeks to take a deposition before the time specified in Rule 26(d) unless the notice contains a certification, with supporting facts, that the person to be examined is expected to leave the United States and be unavailable for examination in this country unless deposed before that time.

(b) Notice of Examination: General Requirements; Method of Recording; Production of Documents and Things; Deposition of Organization; Deposition by Telephone.

(1)   A party desiring to take the deposition of any person upon oral examination shall give reasonable notice in writing to every other party to the action. The notice shall state the time and place for taking the deposition and the name and address of each person to be examined, if known, and, if the name is not known, a general description sufficient to identify the person or the particular class or group to which the person belongs. If a subpoena duces tecum is to be served on the person to be examined, the designation of the materials to be produced as set forth in the subpoena shall be attached to, or included in, the notice.

(2)   The party taking the deposition shall state in the notice the method by which the testimony shall be recorded. Unless the court orders otherwise, it may be recorded by sound, sound-and-visual, or stenographic means, and the party taking the deposition shall bear the cost of the recording. Any party may arrange for a transcription to be made from the recording of a deposition taken by nonstenographic means.

(3) With prior notice to the deponent and other parties, any party may designate another method to record the deponent's testimony in addition to the method specified by the person taking the deposition. The additional record or transcript shall be made at that party's expense unless the court otherwise orders.

(4) Unless otherwise agreed by the parties, a deposition shall be conducted before an officer appointed or designated under Rule 28 and shall begin with a statement on the record by the officer that includes (A) the officer's name and business address; (B) the date, time, and place of the deposition; (C) the name of the deponent; (D) the administration of the oath or affirmation to the deponent; and (E) an identification of all persons present. If the deposition is recorded other than stenographically, the officer shall repeat items (A) through (C) at the beginning of each unit of recorded tape or other recording medium. The appearance or demeanor of deponents or attorneys shall not be distorted through camera or sound-recording techniques. At the end of the deposition, the officer shall state on the record that the deposition is complete and shall set forth any stipulations made by counsel concerning the custody of the transcript or recording and the exhibits, or concerning other pertinent matters.

(5) The notice to a party deponent may be accompanied by a request made in compliance with Rule 34 for the production of documents and tangible things at the taking of the deposition. The procedure of Rule 34 shall apply to the request.

(6) A party may in the party's notice and in a subpoena name as the deponent a public or private corporation or a partnership or association or governmental agency and describe with reasonable particularity the matters on which examination is requested. In that event, the organization so named shall designate one or more officers, directors, or managing agents, or other persons who consent to testify on its behalf, and may set forth, for each person designated, the matters on which the person will testify. A subpoena shall advise a non-party organization of its duty to make such a designation. The persons so designated shall testify as to matters known or reasonably available to the organization. This subdivision (b)(6) does not preclude taking a deposition by any other procedure authorized in these rules.

(7) The parties may stipulate in writing or the court may upon motion order that a deposition be taken by telephone or other remote electronic means. For the purposes of this rule and Rules 28(a), 37(a)(1), and 37(b)(1), a deposition taken by such means is taken in the district and at the place where the deponent is to answer questions.

(c) Examination and Cross-Examination; Record of Examination; Oath; Objections. Examination and cross-examination of witnesses may proceed as permitted at the trial under the provisions of the Federal Rules of Evidence except Rules 103 and 615. The officer before whom the deposition is to be taken shall put the witness on oath or affirmation and shall personally, or by someone acting under the officer's direction and in the officer's presence, record the testimony of the witness. The testimony shall be taken stenographically or recorded by any other method authorized by subdivision (b)(2) of this rule. All objections made at the time of the examination to the qualifications of the officer taking the deposition, to the manner of taking it, to the evidence presented, to the conduct of any party, or to any other aspect of the proceedings shall be noted by the officer upon the record of the deposition; but the examination shall proceed, with the testimony being taken subject to the objections. In lieu of participating in the oral examination, parties may serve written questions in a sealed envelope on the party taking the deposition and the party taking the deposition shall transmit them to the officer, who shall propound them to the witness and record the answers verbatim.

(d) Schedule and Duration; Motion to Terminate or Limit Examination.
(1) Any objection during a deposition must be stated concisely and in a non-argumentative and non-suggestive manner. A person may instruct a deponent not to answer only when necessary to preserve a privilege, to enforce a limitation directed by the court, or to present a motion under Rule 30(d) (4).

(2) Unless otherwise authorized by the court or stipulated by the parties, a deposition is limited to one day of seven hours. The court must allow additional time consistent with Rule 26(b)(2) if needed

for a fair examination of the deponent or if the deponent or another person, or other circumstance, impedes or delays the examination.

(3) If the court finds that any impediment, delay, or other conduct has frustrated the fair examination of the deponent, it may impose upon the persons responsible an appropriate sanction, including the reasonable costs and attorney's fees incurred by any parties as a result thereof.

(4) At any time during a deposition, on motion of a party or of the deponent and upon a showing that the examination is being conducted in bad faith or in such manner as unreasonably to annoy, embarrass, or oppress the deponent or party, the court in which the action is pending or the court in the district where the deposition is being taken may order the officer conducting the examination to cease forthwith from taking the deposition, or may limit the scope and manner of the taking of the deposition as provided in Rule 26(c). If the order made terminates the examination, it may be resumed thereafter only upon the order of the court in which the action is pending. Upon demand of the objecting party or deponent, the taking of the deposition must be suspended for the time necessary to make a motion for an order. The provisions of Rule 37(a)(4) apply to the award of expenses incurred in relation to the motion.

(e) Review by Witness; Changes; Signing.

If requested by the deponent or a party before completion of the deposition, the deponent shall have 30 days after being notified by the officer that the transcript or recording is available in which to review the transcript or recording and, if there are changes in form or substance, to sign a statement reciting such changes and the reasons given by the deponent for making them. The officer shall indicate in the certificate prescribed by subdivision (f)(1) whether any review was requested and, if so, shall append any changes made by the deponent during the period allowed.

(f) Certification and Delivery by Officer; Exhibits; Copies.

(1) The officer must certify that the witness was duly sworn by the officer and that the deposition is a true record of the testimony given by the witness. This certificate must be in writing and accompany the record of the deposition. Unless otherwise ordered by the court, the officer must securely seal the deposition in an envelope or package indorsed with the title of the action and marked "Deposition of [here insert name of witness]" and must promptly send it to the attorney who arranged for the transcript or recording, who must store it under conditions that will protect it against loss, destruction, tampering, or deterioration. Documents and things produced for inspection during the examination of the witness must, upon the request of a party, be marked for identification and annexed to the deposition and may be inspected and copied by any party, except that if the person producing the materials desires to retain them the person may (A) offer copies to be marked for identification and annexed to the deposition and to serve thereafter as originals if the person affords to all parties fair opportunity to verify the copies by comparison with the originals, or (B) offer the originals to be marked for identification, after giving to each party an opportunity to inspect and copy them, in which event the materials may then be used in the same manner as if annexed to the deposition. Any party may move for an order that the original be annexed to and returned with the deposition to the court, pending final disposition of the case.

(2) Unless otherwise ordered by the court or agreed by the parties, the officer shall retain stenographic notes of any deposition taken stenographically or a copy of the recording of any deposition taken by another method. Upon payment of reasonable charges therefor, the officer shall furnish a copy of the transcript or other recording of the deposition to any party or to the deponent.

(3) The party taking the deposition shall give prompt notice of its filing to all other parties.

(g) Failure to Attend or to Serve Subpoena; Expenses.

(1) If the party giving the notice of the taking of a deposition fails to attend and proceed therewith and another party attends in person or by attorney pursuant to the notice, the court may order the party giving the notice to pay to such other party the reasonable expenses incurred by that party and that party's attorney in attending, including reasonable attorney's fees.

(2) If the party giving the notice of the taking of a deposition of a witness fails to serve a subpoena upon the witness and the witness because of such failure does not attend, and if another party attends in person or by attorney because that party expects the deposition of that witness to be taken, the court may order the party giving the notice to pay to such other party the reasonable expenses incurred by that party and that party's attorney in attending, including reasonable attorney's fees.

RULE 31. DEPOSITIONS UPON WRITTEN QUESTIONS

(a) Serving Questions; Notice.

(1) A party may take the testimony of any person, including a party, by deposition upon written questions without leave of court except as provided in paragraph (2). The attendance of witnesses may be compelled by the use of subpoena as provided in Rule 45.

(2) A party must obtain leave of court, which shall be granted to the extent consistent with the principles stated in Rule 26(b)(2), if the person to be examined is confined in prison or if, without the written stipulation of the parties.

　(A) a proposed deposition would result in more than ten depositions being taken under this rule or Rule 30 by the plaintiffs, or by the defendants, or by third-party defendants;

　(B) the person to be examined has already been deposed in the case; or

　(C) a party seeks to take a deposition before the time specified in Rule 26(d).

(3) A party desiring to take a deposition upon written questions shall serve them upon every other party with a notice stating (1) the name and address of the person who is to answer them, if known, and if the name is not known, a general description sufficient to identify the person or the particular class or group to which the person belongs, and (2) the name or descriptive title and address of the officer before whom the deposition is to be taken. A deposition upon written questions may be taken of a public or private corporation or a partnership or association or governmental agency in accordance with the provisions of Rule 30(b)(6).

(4) Within 14 days after the notice and written questions are served, a party may serve cross questions upon all other parties. Within 7 days after being served with cross questions, a party may serve redirect questions upon all other parties. Within 7 days after being served with redirect questions, a party may serve recross questions upon all other parties. The court may for cause shown enlarge or shorten the time.

(b) **Officer to Take Responses and Prepare Record.** A copy of the notice and copies of all questions served shall be delivered by the party taking the deposition to the officer designated in the notice, who shall proceed promptly, in the manner provided by Rule 30(c), (e), and (f), to take the testimony of the witness in response to the questions and to prepare, certify, and file or mail the deposition, attaching thereto the copy of the notice and the questions received by the officer.

(c) **Notice of Filing.** When the deposition is filed the party taking it shall promptly give notice thereof to all other parties.

RULE 32. USE OF DEPOSITIONS IN COURT PROCEEDINGS

(a) **Use of Depositions.** At the trial or upon the hearing of a motion or an interlocutory proceeding, any part or all of a deposition, so far as admissible under the rules of evidence applied as though the witness were then present and testifying, may be used against any party who was present or represented at the taking of the deposition or who had reasonable notice thereof, in accordance with any of the following provisions:

   (1) Any deposition may be used by any party for the purpose of contradicting or impeaching the testimony of deponent as a witness, or for any other purpose permitted by the Federal Rules of Evidence.

   (2) The deposition of a party or of anyone who at the time of taking the deposition was an officer, director, or managing agent, or a person designated under Rule 30(b)(6) or 31(a) to testify on behalf of a public or private corporation, partnership or association or governmental agency which is a party may be used by an adverse party for any purpose.

   (3) The deposition of a witness, whether or not a party, may be used by any party for any purpose if the court finds:

   (A) that the witness is dead; or

   (B) that the witness is at a greater distance than 100 miles from the place of trial or hearing, or is out of the United States, unless it appears that the absence of the witness was procured by the party offering the deposition; or

(C) that the witness is unable to attend or testify because of age, illness, infirmity, or imprisonment; or

(D) that the party offering the deposition has been unable to procure the attendance of the witness by subpoena; or

(E) upon application and notice, that such exceptional circumstances exist as to make it desirable, in the interest of justice and with due regard to the importance of presenting the testimony of witnesses orally in open court, to allow the deposition to be used.

A deposition taken without leave of court pursuant to a notice under Rule 30(a)(2)(C) shall not be used against a party who demonstrates that, when served with the notice, it was unable through the exercise of diligence to obtain counsel to represent it at the taking of the deposition; nor shall a deposition be used against a party who, having received less than 11 days notice of a deposition, has promptly upon receiving such notice filed a motion for a protective order under Rule 26(c)(2) requesting that the deposition not be held or be held at a different time or place and such motion is pending at the time the deposition is held.

(4) If only part of a deposition is offered in evidence by a party, an adverse party may require the offeror to introduce any other part which ought in fairness to be considered with the part introduced, and any party may introduce any other parts.

Substitution of parties pursuant to Rule 25 does not affect the right to use depositions previously taken; and, when an action has been brought in any court of the United States or of any State and another action involving the same subject matter is afterward brought between the same parties or their representatives or successors in interest, all depositions lawfully taken and duly filed in the former action may be used in the latter as if originally taken therefor. A deposition previously taken may also be used as permitted by the Federal Rules of Evidence.

(b) Objections to Admissibility. Subject to the provisions of Rule 28(b) and subdivision (d)(3) of this rule, objection may be made at the trial or hearing to receiving in evidence any deposition or part thereof for any reason which would require the exclusion of the evidence if the witness were then present and testifying.

(c) Form of Presentation. Except as otherwise directed by the court, a party offering deposition testimony pursuant to this rule may offer it in stenographic or nonstenographic form, but, if in nonstenographic form, the party shall also provide the court with a transcript of the portions so offered. On request of any party in a case tried before a jury, deposition testimony offered other than for impeachment purposes shall be presented in nonstenographic form, if available, unless the court for good cause orders otherwise.

(d) Effect of Errors and Irregularities in Depositions.

   (1) As to Notice. All errors and irregularities in the notice for taking a deposition are waived unless written objection is promptly served upon the party giving the notice.

   (2) As to Disqualification of Officer. Objection to taking a deposition because of disqualification of the officer before whom it is to be taken is waived unless made before the taking of the deposition begins or as soon thereafter as the disqualification becomes known or could be discovered with reasonable diligence.

   (3) As to Taking of Deposition.

     (A) Objections to the competency of a witness or to the competency, relevancy, or materiality of testimony are not waived by failure to make them before or during the taking of the deposition, unless the ground of the objection is one which might have been obviated or removed if presented at that time.

     (B) Errors and irregularities occurring at the oral examination in the manner of taking the deposition, in the form of the questions or answers, in the oath or affirmation, or in the conduct of parties, and errors of any kind which might be obviated, removed, or cured if promptly presented, are waived unless seasonable objection thereto is made at the taking of the deposition.

     (C) Objections to the form of written questions submitted under Rule 31 are waived unless served in writing upon the party propounding them within the time allowed for serving the succeeding cross or other questions and within 5 days after service of the last questions authorized.

(4) **As to Completion and Return of Deposition.** Errors and irregularities in the manner in which the testimony is transcribed or the deposition is prepared, signed, certified, sealed, indorsed, transmitted, filed, or otherwise dealt with by the officer under Rules 30 and 31 are waived unless a motion to suppress the deposition or some part thereof is made with reasonable promptness after such defect is, or with due diligence might have been, ascertained.

RULE 33. INTERROGATORIES TO PARTIES

(a) **Availability.** Without leave of court or written stipulation, any party may serve upon any other party written interrogatories, not exceeding 25 in number including all discrete subparts, to be answered by the party served or, if the party served is a public or private corporation or a partnership or association or governmental agency, by any officer or agent, who shall furnish such information as is available to the party. Leave to serve additional interrogatories shall be granted to the extent consistent with the principles of Rule 26(b)(2). Without leave of court or written stipulation, interrogatories may not be served before the time specified in Rule 26(d).

(b) **Answers and Objections.**

(1) Each interrogatory shall be answered separately and fully in writing under oath, unless it is objected to, in which event the objecting party shall state the reasons for objection and shall answer to the extent the interrogatory is not objectionable.

(2) The answers are to be signed by the person making them, and the objections signed by the attorney making them.

(3) The party upon whom the interrogatories have been served shall serve a copy of the answers, and objections if any, within 30 days after the service of the interrogatories. A shorter or longer time may be directed by the court or, in the absence of such an order, agreed to in writing by the parties subject to Rule 29.

(4) All grounds for an objection to an interrogatory shall be stated with specificity. Any ground not stated in a timely objection is waived unless the party's failure to object is excused by the court for good cause shown.

(5) The party submitting the interrogatories may move for an order under Rule 37(a) with respect to any objection to or other failure to answer an interrogatory.

(c) **Scope; Use at Trial.** Interrogatories may relate to any matters which can be inquired into under Rule 26(b)(1), and the answers may be used to the extent permitted by the rules of evidence.

An interrogatory otherwise proper is not necessarily objectionable merely because an answer to the interrogatory involves an opinion or contention that relates to fact or the application of law to fact, but the court may order that such an interrogatory need not be answered until after designated discovery has been completed or until a pre-trial conference or other later time.

(d) **Option to Produce Business Records.**

Where the answer to an interrogatory may be derived or ascertained from the business records of the party upon whom the interrogatory has been served or from an examination, audit or inspection of such business records, including a compilation, abstract or summary thereof, and the burden of deriving or ascertaining the answer is substantially the same for the party serving the interrogatory as for the party served, it is a sufficient answer to such interrogatory to specify the records from which the answer may be derived or ascertained and to afford to the party serving the interrogatory reasonable opportunity to examine, audit or inspect such records and to make copies, compilations, abstracts or summaries. A specification shall be in sufficient detail to permit the interrogating party to locate and to identify, as readily as can the party served, the records from which the answer may be ascertained.

RULE 34. PRODUCTION OF DOCUMENTS AND THINGS AND ENTRY UPON LAND FOR INSPECTION AND OTHER PURPOSES

(a) **Scope.** Any party may serve on any other party a request (1) to produce and permit the party making the request, or someone acting on the requestor's behalf, to inspect and copy, any designated documents (including writings, drawings, graphs, charts, photographs, phonorecords, and other data compilations from which information can be obtained, translated, if necessary, by the respondent through detection devices into reasonably usable form), or to inspect and copy, test, or sample any tangible things which constitute or contain matters within the scope of Rule 26(b) and which are in the possession, custody or control of the party upon whom the request is served; or (2) to permit entry upon designated land or other property in the possession or control of the party upon whom the request is served for the purpose of inspection and measuring, surveying, photographing, testing, or sampling the property or any designated object or operation thereon, within the scope of Rule 26(b).

(b) Procedure. The request shall set forth, either by individual item or by category, the items to be inspected and describe each with reasonable particularity. The request shall specify a reasonable time, place, and manner of making the inspection and performing the related acts. Without leave of court or written stipulation, a request may not be served before the time specified in Rule 26(d).

The party upon whom the request is served shall serve a written response within 30 days after the service of the request. A shorter or longer time may be directed by the court or, in the absence of such an order, agreed to in writing by the parties, subject to Rule 29. The response shall state, with respect to each item or category, that inspection and related activities will be permitted as requested, unless the request is objected to, in which event the reasons for the objection shall be stated. If objection is made to part of an item or category, the part shall be specified and inspection permitted of the remaining parts. The party submitting the request may move for an order under Rule 37(a) with respect to any objection to or other failure to respond to the request or any part thereof, or any failure to permit inspection as requested. A party who produces documents for inspection shall produce them as they are kept in the usual course of business or shall organize and label them to correspond with the categories in the request.

(c) Persons Not Parties. A person not a party to the action may be compelled to produce documents and things or to submit to an inspection as provided in Rule 45.

RULE 35. PHYSICAL AND MENTAL EXAMINATIONS OF PERSONS

(a) Order for Examination. When the mental or physical condition (including the blood group) of a party or of a person in the custody or under the legal control of a party, is in controversy, the court in which the action is pending may order the party to submit to a physical or mental examination by a suitably licensed or certified examiner or to produce for examination the person in the party's custody or legal control. The order may be made only on motion for good cause shown and upon notice to the person to be examined and to all parties and shall specify the time, place, manner, conditions, and scope of the examination and the person or persons by whom it is to be made.

(b) Report of Examiner.

(1) If requested by the party against whom an order is made under Rule 35(a) or the person examined, the party causing the examination to be made shall deliver to the requesting party a copy of the detailed written report of the examiner setting out the examiner's findings, including results of all tests made, diagnoses and conclusions, together with like reports of all earlier examinations of the same condition. After delivery the party causing the examination shall be entitled upon request to receive from the party against whom the order is made a like report of any examination, previously or thereafter made, of the same condition, unless, in the case of a report of examination of a person not a party, the party shows that the party is unable to obtain it. The court on motion may make an order against a party requiring delivery of a report on such terms as are just, and if an examiner fails or refuses to make a report the court may exclude the examiner's testimony if offered at trial.

(2) By requesting and obtaining a report of the examination so ordered or by taking the deposition of the examiner, the party examined waives any privilege the party may have in that action or any other involving the same controversy, regarding the testimony of every other person who has examined or may thereafter examine the party in respect of the same mental or physical condition.

(3) This subdivision applies to examinations made by agreement of the parties, unless the agreement expressly provides otherwise. This subdivision does not preclude discovery of a report of an examiner or the taking of a deposition of the examiner in accordance with the provisions of any other rule.

RULE 36. REQUESTS FOR ADMISSION

(a) **Request for Admission.** A party may serve upon any other party a written request for the admission, for purposes of the pending action only, of the truth of any matters within the scope of Rule 26(b)(1) set forth in the request that relate to statements or opinions of fact or of the application of law to fact, including the genuineness of any documents described in the request. Copies of documents shall be served with the request unless they have been or are otherwise furnished or made available for inspection and copying. Without leave of court or written stipulation, requests for admission may not be served before the time specified in Rule 26(d).

Each matter of which an admission is requested shall be separately set forth. The matter is admitted unless, within 30 days after service of the request, or within such shorter or longer time as the court may allow or as the parties may agree to in writing, subject to Rule 29, the party to whom the request is directed serves upon the party requesting the admission a written answer or objection addressed to the matter, signed by the party or by the party's attorney. If objection is made, the reasons therefor shall be stated. The answer shall specifically deny the matter or set forth in detail the reasons why the answering party cannot truthfully admit or deny the matter. A denial shall fairly meet the substance of the requested admission, and when good faith requires that a party qualify an answer or deny only a part of the matter of which an admission is requested, the party shall specify so much of it as is true and qualify or deny the remainder. An answering party may not give lack of information or knowledge as a reason for failure to admit or deny unless the party states that the party has made reasonable inquiry and that the information known or readily obtainable by the party is insufficient to enable the party to admit or deny. A party who considers that a matter of which an admission has been requested presents a genuine issue for trial may not, on that ground alone, object to the request; the party may, subject to the provisions of Rule 37(c), deny the matter or set forth reasons why the party cannot admit or deny it.

The party who has requested the admissions may move to determine the sufficiency of the answers or objections. Unless the court determines that an objection is justified, it shall order that an answer be served. If the court determines that an answer does not comply with the requirements of this rule, it may order either that the matter is admitted or that an amended answer be served. The court may, in lieu of these orders, determine that final disposition of the request be made at a pretrial conference or at a designated time prior to trial. The provisions of Rule 37(a)(4) apply to the award of expenses incurred in relation to the motion.

(b) Effect of Admission. Any matter admitted under this rule is conclusively established unless the court on motion permits withdrawal or amendment of the admission. Subject to the provision of Rule 16 governing amendment of a pre-trial order, the court may permit withdrawal or amendment when the presentation of the merits of the action will be subserved thereby and the party who obtained the admission fails to satisfy the court that withdrawal or amendment will prejudice that party in maintaining the action or defense on the merits. Any admission made by a party under this rule is for the purpose of the pending action only and is not an admission for any other purpose nor may it be used against the party in any other proceeding.

RULE 37. FAILURE TO MAKE DISCLOSURE OR COOPERATE IN DISCOVERY; SANCTIONS

(a) Motion For Order Compelling Disclosure or Discovery. A party, upon reasonable notice to other parties and all persons affected thereby, may apply for an order compelling disclosure or discovery as follows:

   (1) Appropriate Court. An application for an order to a party shall be made to the court in which the action is pending. An application for an order to a person who is not a party shall be made to the court in the district where the discovery is being, or is to be, taken.

   (2) Motion.

     (A) If a party fails to make a disclosure required by Rule 26(a), any other party may move to compel disclosure and for appropriate sanctions. The motion must include a certification that the movant has in good faith conferred or attempted to confer with the party not making the disclosure in an effort to secure the disclosure without court action.

     (B) If a deponent fails to answer a question propounded or submitted under Rules 30 or 31, or a corporation or other entity fails to make a designation under Rule 30(b)(6) or 31(a), or a party fails to answer an interrogatory submitted under Rule 33, or if a party, in response to a request for inspection submitted under Rule 34, fails to respond that inspection will be permitted as requested or fails to permit inspection as requested, the discovering party may move for an order compelling an answer, or a designation, or an order compelling inspection in accordance with the request. The motion must include a certification that the movant has in good faith conferred or attempted to confer with the person or party failing to make the discovery in an effort to secure the information or material without court action. When taking a deposition on oral examination, the proponent of the question may complete or adjourn the examination before applying for an order.

(3) **Evasive or Incomplete Disclosure, Answer, or Response.** For purposes of this subdivision an evasive or incomplete disclosure, answer, or response is to be treated as a failure to disclose, answer, or respond.

(4) **Expenses and Sanctions.**

(A) If the motion is granted or if the disclosure or requested discovery is provided after the motion was filed, the court shall, after affording an opportunity to be heard, require the party or deponent whose conduct necessitated the motion or the party or attorney advising such conduct or both of them to pay to the moving party the reasonable expenses incurred in making the motion, including attorney's fees, unless the court finds that the motion was filed without the movant's first making a good faith effort to obtain the disclosure or discovery without court action, or that the opposing party's nondisclosure, response, or objection was substantially justified, or that other circumstances make an award of expenses unjust.

(B) If the motion is denied, the court may enter any protective order authorized under Rule 26(c) and shall, after affording an opportunity to be heard, require the moving party or the attorney filing the motion or both of them to pay to the party or deponent who opposed the motion the reasonable expenses incurred in opposing the motion, including attorney's fees, unless the court finds that the making of the motion was substantially justified or that other circumstances make an award of expenses unjust.

(**C**) If the motion is granted in part and denied in part, the court may enter any protective order authorized under Rule 26(c) and may, after affording an opportunity to be heard, apportion the reasonable expenses incurred in relation to the motion among the parties and persons in a just manner.

(b) Failure to Comply With Order.

(**1**) **Sanctions by Court in District Where Deposition is Taken.** If a deponent fails to be sworn or to answer a question after being directed to do so by the court in the district in which the deposition is being taken, the failure may be considered a contempt of that court.

(**2**) **Sanctions by Court in Which Action is Pending.** If a party or an officer, director, or managing agent of a party or a person designated under Rule 30(b)(6) or 31(a) to testify on behalf of a party fails to obey an order to provide or permit discovery, including an order made under subdivision (a) of this rule or Rule 35, or if a party fails to obey an order entered under Rule 26(f), the court in which the action is pending may make such orders in regard to the failure as are just, and among others the following:

(**A**) An order that the matters regarding which the order was made or any other designated facts shall be taken to be established for the purposes of the action in accordance with the claim of the party obtaining the order;

(**B**) An order refusing to allow the disobedient party to support or oppose designated claims or defenses, or prohibiting that party from introducing designated matters in evidence;

(**C**) An order striking out pleadings or parts thereof, or staying further proceedings until the order is obeyed, or dismissing the action or proceeding or any part thereof, or rendering a judgment by default against the disobedient party;

(**D**) In lieu of any of the foregoing orders or in addition thereto, an order treating as a contempt of court the failure to obey any orders except an order to submit to a physical or mental examination;

(**E**) Where a party has failed to comply with an order under Rule 35(a) requiring that party to produce another for examination, such orders as are listed in paragraphs (A), (B), and (C) of this subdivision, unless the party failing to comply shows that that party is unable to produce such person for examination.

In lieu of any of the foregoing orders or in addition thereto, the court shall require the party failing to obey the order or the attorney advising that party or both to pay the reasonable expenses, including attorney's fees, caused by the failure, unless the court finds that the failure was substantially justified or that other circumstances make an award of expenses unjust.

(c) Failure to Disclose; False or Misleading Disclosure; Refusal to Admit.

(1) A party that without substantial justification fails to disclose information required by Rule 26(a) or 26(e)(1), or to amend a prior response to discovery as required by Rule 26(e)(2), is not, unless such failure is harmless, permitted to use as evidence at a trial, at a hearing, or on a motion any witness or information not so disclosed. In addition to or in lieu of this sanction, the court, on motion and after affording an opportunity to be heard, may impose other appropriate sanctions. In addition to requiring payment of reasonable expenses, including attorney's fees, caused by the failure, these sanctions may include any of the actions authorized under Rule 37(b)(2)(A), (B), and (C) and may include informing the jury of the failure to make the disclosure.

(2) If a party fails to admit the genuineness of any document or the truth of any matter as requested under Rule 36, and if the party requesting the admissions thereafter proves the genuineness of the document or the truth of the matter, the requesting party may apply to the court for an order requiring the other party to pay the reasonable expenses incurred in making that proof, including reasonable attorney's fees. The court shall make the order unless it finds that (A) the request was held objectionable pursuant to Rule 36(a), or (B) the admission sought was of no substantial importance, or (C) the party failing to admit had reasonable ground to believe that the party might prevail on the matter, or (D) there was other good reason for the failure to admit.

(d) Failure of Party to Attend at Own Deposition or Serve Answers to Interrogatories or Respond to Request for Inspection. If a party or an officer, director, or managing agent of a party or a person designated under Rule 30(b)(6) or 31(a) to testify on behalf of a party fails (1) to appear before the officer who is to take the deposition, after being served with a proper notice, or (2) to serve answers or objections to interrogatories submitted under Rule 33, after proper service of the interrogatories, or (3) to serve a written response to a request for inspection submitted under Rule 34, after proper service of the request, the court in which the action is pending on motion may make such orders in regard to the failure as are just, and among others it may take any action authorized under subparagraphs (A), (B), and (C) of subdivision (b)(2) of this rule. Any motion specifying a failure under clause (2) or (3) of this subdivision shall include a certification that the movant has in good faith conferred or attempted to confer with the party failing to answer or respond in an effort to obtain such answer or response without court action. In lieu of any order or in addition thereto, the court shall require the party failing to act or the attorney advising that party or both to pay the reasonable expenses, including attorney's fees, caused by the failure unless the court finds that the failure was substantially justified or that other circumstances make an award of expenses unjust.

The failure to act described in this subdivision may not be excused on the ground that the discovery sought is objectionable unless the party failing to act has a pending motion for a protective order as provided by Rule 26(c).

(e) [Abrogated]

(f) [Repealed. Pub.L. 96-481, Title II, § 205(a), Oct. 21, 1980, 94 Stat. 2330]

(g) Failure to Participate in the Framing of a Discovery Plan. If a party or a party's attorney fails to participate in good faith in the development and submission of a proposed discovery plan as required by Rule 26(f), the court may, after opportunity for hearing, require such party or attorney to pay to any other party the reasonable expenses, including attorney's fees, caused by the failure.

RULE 45. SUBPOENA

(a) Form; Issuance.
   (1) Every subpoena shall
      (A) state the name of the court from which it is issued; and
      (B) state the title of the action, the name of the court in which it is pending, and its civil action number; and
      (C) command each person to whom it is directed to attend and give testimony or to produce and permit inspection and copying of designated books, documents or tangible things in the possession, custody or control of that person, or to permit inspection of premises, at a time and place therein specified; and
      (D) set forth the text of subdivisions (c) and (d) of this rule.
      A command to produce evidence or to permit inspection may be joined with a command to appear at trial or hearing or at deposition, or may be issued separately.
   (2) A subpoena commanding attendance at a trial or hearing shall issue from the court for the district in which the hearing or trial is to be held. A subpoena for attendance at a deposition shall issue from the court for the district designated by the notice of deposition as the district in which the deposition is to be taken. If separate from a subpoena commanding the attendance of a person, a subpoena for production or inspection shall issue from the court for the district in which the production or inspection is to be made.
   (3) The clerk shall issue a subpoena, signed but otherwise in blank, to a party requesting it, who shall complete it before service. An attorney as officer of the court may also issue and sign a subpoena on behalf of
      (A) a court in which the attorney is authorized to practice; or
      (B) a court for a district in which a deposition or production is compelled by the subpoena, if the deposition or production pertains to an action pending in a court in which the attorney is authorized to practice.

(b) Service.
   (1) A subpoena may be served by any person who is not a party and is not less than 18 years of age. Service of a subpoena upon a person named therein shall be made by delivering a copy thereof to such person and, if the person's attendance is commanded, by tendering

to that person the fees for one day's attendance and the mileage allowed by law. When the subpoena is issued on behalf of the United States or an officer or agency thereof, fees and mileage need not be tendered. Prior notice of any commanded production of documents and things or inspection of premises before trial shall be served on each party in the manner prescribed by Rule 5(b).

(2) Subject to the provisions of clause (ii) of subparagraph (c)(3)(A) of this rule, a subpoena may be served at any place within the district of the court by which it is issued, or at any place without the district that is within 100 miles of the place of the deposition, hearing, trial, production, or inspection specified in the subpoena or at any place within the state where a state statute or rule of court permits service of a subpoena issued by a state court of general jurisdiction sitting in the place of the deposition, hearing, trial, production, or inspection specified in the subpoena. When a statute of the United States provides therefor, the court upon proper application and cause shown may authorize the service of a subpoena at any other place. A subpoena directed to a witness in a foreign country who is a national or resident of the United States shall issue under the circumstances and in the manner and be served as provided in Title 28, U.S.C. § 1783.

(3) Proof of service when necessary shall be made by filing with the clerk of the court by which the subpoena is issued a statement of the date and manner of service and of the names of the persons served, certified by the person who made the service.

(c) Protection of Persons Subject to Subpoenas.

(1) A party or an attorney responsible for the issuance and service of a subpoena shall take reasonable steps to avoid imposing undue burden or expense on a person subject to that subpoena. The court on behalf of which the subpoena was issued shall enforce this duty and impose upon the party or attorney in breach of this duty an appropriate sanction, which may include, but is not limited to, lost earnings and a reasonable attorney's fee.

(2)

(A) A person commanded to produce and permit inspection and copying of designated books, papers, documents or tangible things, or inspection of premises need not appear in person at the place of production or inspection unless commanded to appear for deposition, hearing or trial.

(B) Subject to paragraph (d)(2) of this rule, a person commanded to produce and permit inspection and copying may, within 14 days after service of the subpoena or before the time specified for compliance if such time is less than 14 days after service, serve upon the party or attorney designated in the subpoena written objection to inspection or copying of any or all of the designated materials or of the premises. If objection is made, the party serving the subpoena shall not be entitled to inspect and copy the materials or inspect the premises except pursuant to an order of the court by which the subpoena was issued. If objection has been made, the party serving the subpoena may, upon notice to the person commanded to produce, move at any time for an order to compel the production. Such an order to compel production shall protect any person who is not a party or an officer of a party from significant expense resulting from the inspection and copying commanded.

(3)

(A) On timely motion, the court by which a subpoena was issued shall quash or modify the subpoena if it

    (i) fails to allow reasonable time for compliance;

    (ii) requires a person who is not a party or an officer of a party to travel to a place more than 100 miles from the place where that person resides, is employed or regularly transacts business in person, except that, subject to the provisions of clause (c)(3)(B)(iii) of this rule, such a person may in order to attend trial be commanded to travel from any such place within the state in which the trial is held, or

    (iii) requires disclosure of privileged or other protected matter and no exception or waiver applies, or

    (iv) subjects a person to undue burden.

(B) If a subpoena

    (i) requires disclosure of a trade secret or other confidential research, development, or commercial information, or

    (ii) requires disclosure of an unretained expert's opinion or information not describing specific events or occurrences in dispute and resulting from the expert's study made not at the request of any party, or

(iii) requires a person who is not a party or an officer of a party to incur substantial expense to travel more than 100 miles to attend trial, the court may, to protect a person subject to or affected by the subpoena, quash or modify the subpoena or, if the party in whose behalf the subpoena is issued shows a substantial need for the testimony or material that cannot be otherwise met without undue hardship and assures that the person to whom the subpoena is addressed will be reasonably compensated, the court may order appearance or production only upon specified conditions.

(d) Duties in Responding to Subpoena.

(1) A person responding to a subpoena to produce documents shall produce them as they are kept in the usual course of business or shall organize and label them to correspond with the categories in the demand.

(2) When information subject to a subpoena is withheld on a claim that it is privileged or subject to protection as trial preparation materials, the claim shall be made expressly and shall be supported by a description of the nature of the documents, communications, or things not produced that is sufficient to enable the demanding party to contest the claim.

(e) Contempt. Failure by any person without adequate excuse to obey a subpoena served upon that person may be deemed a contempt of the court from which the subpoena issued. An adequate cause for failure to obey exists when a subpoena purports to require a non-party to attend or produce at a place not within the limits provided by clause (ii) of subparagraph (c)(3)(A).

Appendix B

Discovery Guidelines of the United States District Court for the District of Maryland

GUIDELINE 1: CONDUCT OF DISCOVERY

a. The purpose of these Guidelines is to facilitate the just, speedy, and inexpensive conduct of discovery in all civil cases before the Court, and these Guidelines will be construed and administered accordingly with respect to all attorneys, parties, and non-parties involved in discovery of civil cases before this Court.

b. Compliance with these Guidelines will be considered by the Court in resolving discovery disputes, including whether sanctions should be awarded pursuant to Fed. R. Civ. P. 37.

c. Attorneys are expected to behave professionally and with courtesy towards all involved in the discovery process, including but not limited to opposing counsel, parties and non-parties.

d. Whenever possible, attorneys are expected to communicate with each other in good faith throughout the discovery process to resolve disputes without the need for intervention by the Court. In the event that such good faith efforts are unsuccessful, the disputes should be referred promptly to the Court for resolution.

e. To the extent that any part of these Guidelines is considered by the Court to conflict with any Federal Rule of Civil Procedure, Local Rules of this Court, or order of this Court in a particular case, then the conflicting rule or order should be considered to be governing.

GUIDELINE 2: STIPULATIONS SETTING DISCOVERY DEADLINES

Subject to approval by the Court, attorneys are encouraged to enter into written discovery stipulations to supplement the Court's scheduling order.

GUIDELINE 3: EXPERT WITNESS FEES

a. Unless counsel agree that each party will pay its own experts, the party taking an expert witness's deposition ordinarily pays the expert's fee for the time spent in deposition and related travel. See L.R. 104.11.a. Accordingly, counsel for the party that designated the expert witness should try to assure that the fee charged by the expert to the party taking the deposition is fair and reasonable. In the event a dispute arises as to the reasonableness or other aspects of an expert's fee, counsel should promptly confer and attempt in good faith to resolve the dispute without the involvement of the Court. If counsel are unsuccessful, the expert's deposition shall proceed on the date noted, unless the Court orders otherwise, and the dispute respecting payment shall be brought to the Court's attention promptly. The factors that may be considered in determining whether a fee is reasonable include, but are not limited to: (1) the expert's area of expertise; (2) the expert's education and training; (3) the fee being charged to the party who designated the expert; and (4) the fees ordinarily charged by the expert for non-litigation services, such as office consultations with patients or clients.

b. Recognizing that a treating physician may be considered both a fact witness and an expert, the Court has chosen to impose a specific limitation on the fee a treating physician may charge to either party. It is implicit in L.R. 104.11.b, which requires counsel to estimate the hours of deposition time required, that the physician may charge a fee for the entire time he or she reserved in accordance with the estimate, even if counsel conclude the deposition early. Further, unless the physician received notice at least two business days in advance of a cancellation, the physician is entitled to be paid for any time reserved that cannot reasonably be filled. Every effort should be made to schedule depositions at a time convenient for the witness, and to use videotaped de bene esse depositions rather than requiring the physician's presence at trial. Note that the Rule does not limit the reasonable fee a treating physician may charge if required to testify in Court.

GUIDELINE 4: SCHEDULING DEPOSITIONS

a. Attorneys are expected to make a good faith effort to coordinate deposition dates with opposing counsel, parties, and non-party deponents, prior to noting a deposition.

b. Before agreeing to a deposition date, an attorney is expected to attempt to clear the date with his/her client if the client is a deponent, or wishes to attend the deposition, and with any witnesses the attorney agrees to attempt to produce at the deposition without the need to have the witness served with a subpoena.

c. An agreed upon deposition date is presumptively binding. An attorney seeking to change an agreed upon date has a duty to coordinate a new date before changing the agreed date.

GUIDELINE 5: DEPOSITION QUESTIONING, OBJECTIONS AND PROCEDURE

a. An attorney should not intentionally ask a witness a question that misstates or mischaracterizes the witness's previous answer.

b. During the taking of a deposition, it is presumptively improper for an attorney to make objections which are not consistent with Fed. R. Civ. P. 30(d)(1). Objections should be stated as simply, concisely and non-argumentatively as possible to avoid coaching or making suggestions to the deponent, and to minimize interruptions in the questioning of the deponent (for example: "objection, leading"; "objection, asked and answered"; "objection, compound question"; "objection, form"). If an attorney desires to make an objection for the record during the taking of a deposition that reasonably could have the effect of coaching or suggesting to the deponent how to answer, then the deponent, at the request of any of the attorneys present, or, at the request of a party if unrepresented by an attorney, shall be excused from the deposition during the making of the objection.

c. An attorney should not repeatedly ask the same or substantially identical question of a deponent if the question already has been asked and fully and responsively answered by the deponent. Upon objection by counsel for the deponent, or by the deponent if unrepresented, it is presumptively improper for an attorney to continue to ask the same or substantially identical question of a witness unless the previous answer was evasive or incomplete.

d. It is presumptively improper to instruct a witness not to answer a question during the taking of a deposition unless under the circumstances permitted by Fed. R. Civ. P. 30(d)(1). However, it is also presumptively improper to ask questions clearly beyond the scope of discovery permitted by Fed. R. Civ. P. 26(b)(1), particularly of a personal nature, and continuing to do so after objection shall be evidence that the deposition is being conducted in bad faith or in such a manner as unreasonably to annoy, embarrass, or oppress the deponent or party, which is prohibited by Fed. R. Civ. P. 30(d)(3).

e. If requested to supply an explanation as to the basis for an objection, the objecting attorney should do so, consistent with Guideline 5(b) above.

f. While the interrogation of the deponent is in progress, neither an attorney nor the deponent should initiate a private conversation except for the purpose of determining whether a privilege should be asserted. To do so otherwise is presumptively improper.

g. During breaks in the taking of a deposition, no one should discuss with the deponent the substance of the prior testimony given by the deponent during the deposition. Counsel for the deponent may discuss with the deponent at such time whether a privilege should be asserted or otherwise engage in discussion not regarding the substance of the witness's prior testimony.

h. Unless otherwise ordered by the Court, the following persons may, without advance notice, attend a deposition: individual parties; a representative of non-individual parties; and expert witnesses of parties. Except for the persons identified above, counsel shall notify other parties not later than five (5) business days before the taking of a deposition if counsel desires to have a non-party present during a deposition. If the parties are unable to agree to the attendance of this person, then the person shall not be entitled to attend the deposition unless the party desiring to have the person attend obtains a Court order permitting him/her to do so. Unless ordered by the Court, however, a dispute regarding who may attend a deposition shall not be grounds for delaying the deposition. All persons present during the taking of a deposition should be identified on the record before the deposition begins.

i. Except for the person recording the deposition in accordance with Fed. R. Civ. P. 30(b), during the taking of a deposition no one may record the testimony without the consent of the deponent and all parties in attendance, unless otherwise ordered by the Court.

GUIDELINE 6: ASSERTIONS OF PRIVILEGE AT DEPOSITIONS

a. When a claim of privilege is asserted during a deposition, and information is not provided on the basis of such assertion:

i. In accordance with Fed. R. Civ. P. 26(b)(5), the person asserting the privilege shall identify during the deposition the nature of the privilege (including work product) that is being claimed.

ii. After a claim of privilege has been asserted, the person seeking disclosure shall have reasonable latitude during the deposition to question the witness to establish other relevant information concerning the assertion of privilege, including: (i) the applicability of the particular privilege being asserted; (ii) any circumstances which may constitute an exception to the assertion of the privilege; (iii) any circumstances which may result in the privilege having been waived; and (iv) any circumstances that may overcome a claim of qualified privilege. In accordance with Fed. R. Civ. P. 26(b)(5), the party asserting the privilege, in providing the foregoing information, shall not be required to reveal the information which is itself privileged or protected from disclosure.

GUIDELINE 7: MAKING A RECORD OF IMPROPER CONDUCT DURING A DEPOSITION

Upon request of any attorney, party unrepresented by an attorney, or the deponent if unrepresented by an attorney, the person recording the deposition in accordance with Fed. R. Civ. P. 30(b) shall enter on the record a description by the requesting person of conduct of any attorney, party, or person attending the deposition which violates these guidelines, the Federal Rules of Civil Procedure, or the Local Rules of this Court.

GUIDELINE 8: DELAY IN RESPONDING TO DISCOVERY REQUESTS

a. Interrogatories, Requests for Production of Documents, and Requests for Admission of Facts and Genuineness of Documents.

The Federal Rules of Civil Procedure designate the time prescribed for responding to interrogatories, requests for production of documents, and requests for admission of facts and genuineness of documents. Nothing contained in these guidelines modifies the time limits prescribed by the Federal Rules of Civil Procedure. Attorneys shall make good faith efforts to respond to discovery requests within the time prescribed by those rules.

Absent exigent circumstances, attorneys seeking additional time to respond to discovery requests shall contact opposing counsel as soon as practical after receipt of the discovery request, but not later than three days before the response is due. In multiple party cases, the attorney wanting additional time shall contact the attorney for the party propounding the discovery.

A request for additional time which does not conflict with a scheduling deadline imposed by the Federal Rules of Civil Procedure, the Local Rules of this Court, or a Court order should not be unreasonably refused. If a request for additional time is granted, the requesting party shall promptly prepare a writing which memorializes the agreement, which shall be served on all parties but need not be submitted to the Court for approval.

Unless otherwise provided by the Local Rules of this Court, no stipulation which modifies a Court-imposed deadline shall be deemed effective unless and until the Court approves the stipulation.

b. Depositions.

Unless otherwise ordered by the Court or agreed upon by the parties, eleven days notice shall be deemed to be "reasonable notice" within the meaning of Fed. R. Civ. P. 30(b)(1), for the noting of depositions.

GUIDELINE 9: INTERROGATORIES, REQUESTS FOR PRODUCTION OF DOCUMENTS, ANSWERS TO INTERROGATORIES, AND WRITTEN RESPONSES TO DOCUMENT REQUESTS

a. A party may object to an interrogatory, document request, or part thereof, while simultaneously providing partial or incomplete answers to the request. If a partial or incomplete answer is provided, the answering party shall state that the answer is partial or incomplete.

b. No part of an interrogatory or document request should be left unanswered merely because an objection is interposed to another part of the interrogatory or document request.

c. In accordance with Fed. R. Civ. P. 26(b)(5), where a claim of privilege is asserted in objecting to any interrogatory, document request, or part thereof, and information is not provided on the basis of such assertion:

    i. The party asserting the privilege shall, in the objection to the interrogatory, document request, or part thereof, identify with specificity the nature of the privilege (including work product) that is being claimed;

    ii. The following information should be provided in the objection, if known or reasonably available, unless divulging such information would cause disclosure of the allegedly privileged information;

        a. For oral communications:

      i. the name of the person making the communication and the names of persons present while the communication was made, and, where not apparent, the relationship of the persons present to the person making the communication;

     ii. the date and place of the communication; and

   iii. the general subject matter of the communication.

  b. For documents:

      i. the type of document;

     ii. the general subject matter of the document;

   iii. the date of the document; and

   iv. such other information as is sufficient to identify the document, including, where appropriate, the author, addressee, custodian, and any other recipient of the document, and, where not apparent, the relationship of the author, addressee, custodian, and any other recipient to each other.

iii. Within twenty days after the receipt of the information contained in paragraph (ii), the party seeking disclosure of the information withheld may serve a motion to compel in accordance with L.R. 104.8.

d. In addition to paper copies, parties are encouraged, but not required, to exchange discovery requests and responses on computer disk in an ASCII or other commonly-accepted format, if requested, in order to reduce the clerical effort required to prepare responses and motions.

Appendix C

Standard Interrogatories in the United States District Court for the District of Maryland

STANDARD INTERROGATORIES

IN THE UNITED STATES DISTRICT COURT

FOR THE DISTRICT OF MARYLAND

_____,	*	
Plaintiff	*	
v.	*	Civil Action No.:
_____,	*	
Defendant	*	_____

* *

INTERROGATORIES

Pursuant to Fed. R. Civ. P. 33, and L.R. 104, _____, by its undersigned attorneys, propounds these Interrogatories, to which _____ shall respond separately and fully, in writing and under oath, within the time prescribed by the Federal Rules of Civil Procedure, in accordance with the Instructions and Definitions set forth here-inafter.

INSTRUCTIONS

1. These instructions and definitions should be construed to require answers based upon the knowledge of, and information available to, the responding party as well as its agents, representatives, and, unless privileged, attorneys. It is intended that the following discovery requests will not solicit any material protected either by the attorney/client privilege or work product doctrine which was created by, or developed by, counsel for the responding party after the date on which this litigation was commenced. If any inquiry is susceptible of a construction which calls for the production of such material, that material need not be provided and no privilege log pursuant to Fed. R. Civ. P. 26(b)(5) or Discovery Guideline 9(a) will be required as to such material.

2. These Interrogatories are continuing in character, so as to require that supplemental answers be filed seasonably if further or different information is obtained with respect to any interrogatory.

3. Pursuant to Discovery Guideline 9(b), no part of an interrogatory should be left unanswered merely because an objection is interposed to another part of the interrogatory. Pursuant to Discovery Guideline 9(a), if a partial or incomplete answer is provided, the responding party shall state that the answer is partial or incomplete.

4. Pursuant to Discovery Guideline 9(c), in accordance with Fed. R. Civ. P. 26(b)(5), where a claim of privilege is asserted in objecting to any interrogatory or part thereof, and information is not provided on the basis of such assertion:

   A. In asserting the privilege, the responding party shall, in the objection to the interrogatory, or part thereof, identify with specificity the nature of the privilege (including work product) that is being claimed;

B. The following information should be provided in the objection, if known or reasonably available, unless divulging such information would cause disclosure of the allegedly privileged information,

    (1) For oral communications:

        a. the name of the person making the communication and the names of persons present while the communication was made, and, where not apparent, the relationship of the persons present to the person making the communication;

        b. the date and place of the communication; and

        c. the general subject matter of the communication.

    (2) For documents:

        a. the type of document,

        b. the general subject matter of the document,

        c. the date of the document, and

        d. such other information as is sufficient to identify the document, including, where appropriate, the author, addressee, custodian, and any other recipient of the document, and where not apparent, the relationship of the author, addressee, custodian, and any other recipient to each other.

5. If the responding party elects to specify and produce business records in answer to any interrogatory, the specification shall be in sufficient detail to permit the interrogating party to locate and identify, as readily as the responding party can, the business records from which the answer may be ascertained.

6. If, in answering these interrogatories, the responding party encounters any ambiguities when construing a question, instruction, or definition, the responding party's answer shall set forth the matter deemed ambiguous and the construction used in answering.

DEFINITIONS

Notwithstanding any definition below, each word, term, or phrase used in these Interrogatories is intended to have the broadest meaning permitted under the Federal Rules of Civil Procedure.

1. *Concerning*: The term "concerning" means relating to, referring to, describing, evidencing, or constituting.

2. *Communication*: The term "communication" means the transmittal of information by any means.

3. *Document*: The terms "document" and "documents" are defined to be synonymous in meaning and equal in scope to the usage of the term "documents" in Fed. R. Civ. P. 34(a) and include(s) the term "writing". Unless the producing party demonstrates undue burden or other grounds sufficient to meet the requirements of Fed. R. Civ. P. 26(c), electronic mail is included within the definition of the term "document". The terms "writings", "recordings", and "photographs" are defined to be synonymous in meaning and equal in scope to the usage of those terms in Fed. R. Evid. 1001. A draft or non-identical copy is a separate document within the meaning of the term "document".

4. *Identify (with respect to persons)*: When referring to a person, to "identify" means to state the person's full name, present or last known address, and, when referring to a natural person, additionally, the present or last known place of employment. If the business and home telephone numbers are known to the answering party, and if the person is not a

party or present employee of a party, said telephone numbers shall be provided. Once a person has been identified in accordance with this subparagraph, only the name of the person need be listed in response to subsequent discovery requesting the identification of that person.

5. *Identify (with respect to documents)*: When referring to documents, to "identify" means to state the: (i) type of document; (ii) general subject matter; (iii) date of the document; and, (iv) author(s), addressee(s), and recipient(s) or, alternatively, to produce the document.

6. *Occurrence/Transaction*: The terms "occurrence" and "transaction" mean the events described in the Complaint and other pleadings, as the word "pleadings" is defined in Fed. R. Civ. P. 7(a).

7. *Parties*: The terms "plaintiff" and "defendant" (including, without limitation, third-party plaintiff, third-party defendant, counter claimant, cross-claimant, counter-defendant, and cross-defendant), as well as a party's full or abbreviated name or a pronoun referring to a party, mean that party and, where applicable, its officers, directors, and employees. This definition is not intended to impose a discovery obligation on any person who is not a party to the litigation or to limit the Court's jurisdiction to enter any appropriate order.

8. *Person*: The term "person" is defined as any natural person or any business, legal or governmental entity or association.

9. *You/Your*: The terms "you" or "your" include the person(s) to whom these requests are addressed, and all of that person's agents, representatives and attorneys.

10. The present tense includes the past and future tenses. The singular includes the plural, and the plural includes the singular. "All" means "any and all"; "any" means "any and all." "Including" means "including but not limited to." "And" and "or" encompass both "and" and "or." Words

in the masculine, feminine or neuter form shall include each of the other genders.

STANDARD INTERROGATORIES TO A PLAINTIFF

STANDARD INTERROGATORY NO. 1: Identify all persons who are likely to have personal knowledge of any fact alleged in the complaint, and state the subject matter of the personal knowledge possessed by each such person.

STANDARD INTERROGATORY NO. 2: Identify all persons who have a subrogation interest in any claim set forth in the complaint, and state the basis and extent of such interest.

STANDARD INTERROGATORY NO. 3: Itemize and show how you calculate any damages claimed by you in this action, whether economic, non-economic, punitive or other.

STANDARD INTERROGATORIES TO A DEFENDANT

STANDARD INTERROGATORY NO. 4: If you contend that the Defendant is improperly identified, state Defendant's correct identification.

STANDARD INTERROGATORY NO. 5: Identify any persons or entities whom Defendant contends are persons needed for just adjudication within the meaning of Fed. R. Civ. P. 19, but who have not been named by Plaintiff.

STANDARD INTERROGATORY NO. 6: Identify all persons who are likely to have personal knowledge of any fact alleged in the complaint or in your answer to the complaint, and state the subject matter of the personal knowledge possessed by each such person.

STANDARD INTERROGATORY NO. 7: If you have knowledge of any person carrying on an insurance business that might be liable to satisfy part or all of a judgment that might be entered in this action or to indemnify or reimburse the payments made to satisfy the judgment, identify that person and state the applicable policy limits of any insurance agreement under which the person might be liable.

STANDARD INTERROGATORIES TO ANY PARTY

STANDARD INTERROGATORY NO. 8: For each witness identified by you in connection with the disclosures required by Fed. R. Civ. P. 26(a)(2)(A), provide a complete statement of the opinions to be expressed and basis and reasons therefor.

STANDARD INTERROGATORY NO. 9: For each witness you have retained or specially employed to provide expert testimony in this case, or employed by you whose duties regularly involve giving expert testimony and whom you expect to testify at trial, provide a complete statement of the opinions to be expressed and the basis and reasons therefor.

STANDARD INTERROGATORY NO. 10: State the facts concerning the matters alleged in [paragraph _____ of your Complaint] [paragraph _____ of your Answer to the Complaint] [your affirmative defense no. ___].

STANDARD INTERROGATORY NO. 11: If you contend that _____, state the facts concerning such contention.

Appendix D

American Bar Association Civil Discovery Standards and August 2004 Amendments

VIII. TECHNOLOGY

AMENDMENTS

SECTION OF LITIGATION
American Bar Association

CIVIL DISCOVERY STANDARDS
August, 1999

PREFACE

These Standards are intended as guidelines to assist the parties, counsel and the court in civil discovery. They are based on the premise that discovery can be costly and inefficient if it is conducted (or resisted) without a clear set of goals or a careful, reasoned plan. The Standards recognize the interrelated roles of the court and the parties and counsel in fairly and efficiently managing discovery, and therefore include suggested practices to guide both judges and the parties. Each Standard is intended (i) to eliminate unnecessary effort and expense, (ii) to restrict the opportunities for misusing the discovery process, both offensively and defensively, and (iii) where possible, to encourage a cooperative rather than adversarial approach to discovery. Attorneys should select the means and the methods of discovery which maximize the possibility that these intended goals will be achieved.

The Standards do not provide definitions. Words are used according to their ordinary legal meaning. In particular, the definition of what is "relevant" and the permissible scope of discovery will be governed by the rule or rules in the relevant jurisdiction.

The Standards also are not a restatement of the law, nor are they intended to replace existing law or rules. They seek, instead, to address practical aspects of the discovery process that may not be covered by the rules or other law in a given jurisdiction or may be covered only in part. In the event of a conflict or inconsistency between existing substantive law or procedural rules and these Standards, the existing law or rules of the jurisdiction will govern. Counsel should therefore always review each court's rules and governing law to see whether a particular issue has been settled.

I. JUDICIAL MANAGEMENT AND PARTY INVOLVEMENT

1. Discovery Conferences and Plan.

    a. Discovery Plan. As a general practice, the court should (i) direct or encourage (as appropriate under the governing rules) the parties to develop a reasonable, comprehensive discovery plan and (ii) promptly set a scheduling conference where they will submit a proposed case management plan, including discovery, for the court's approval.
    b. Scheduling Conference. As a general practice, the court should set a scheduling conference promptly after all counsel have appeared (or after an unrepresented party has had a reasonable opportunity to obtain counsel) to consider the items listed in the following section. Lead counsel, or counsel with decision-making authority, should be required to participate either in person or by telephone. At or promptly following the conference, the court should enter an order governing the further conduct of the case, including discovery.
    c. Before the Scheduling Conference. Before the scheduling conference, the parties should confer, in person if possible but at least by telephone, to try to agree on a proposed discovery plan that may address:

        i. Discovery.

            A. The scope and timing of discovery, including any substantive or numerical limits on discovery and whether bifurcation or staging of discovery would help to reduce expense and make discovery more effective;
            B. Whether the parties are prepared to make any voluntary disclosures;
            C. The possibility of informal production of documents or other information;
            D. The number, identity, location, date and length of any fact witness depositions;
            E. Expert discovery, including the timing and dates for identifying experts and exchanging expert reports and, if an expert's deposition is to be taken, its location, date and length; and

F. Any other remaining issues, including difficulties in obtaining access to or retrieving documents or other information, document or deposition discovery of third parties, privilege claims and ways to resolve them, and any other potential area of dispute.

ii. Other Scheduling.

A. Deadlines for the staging and completion of discovery;
B. When dispositive motions on all or part of the case should be filed, briefed (and/or argued) and decided;
C. Deadlines for amending the pleadings or joining additional parties;
D. When to have settlement discussions; whether some form of alternative dispute resolution might be useful and, if so, what kind and when to have it;
E. Dates for exchanging lists of trial witnesses and exhibits;
F. Whether the parties will consent to trial by a magistrate judge (or similar judicial officer) and, if so, which one;
G. Whether a trial date or range of dates should be set and, if appropriate, the date(s) for one or more preliminary or final pretrial conferences;
H. In a jury trial, when proposed jury instructions should be submitted;
I. In a bench trial, if and when proposed findings and conclusions should be submitted;
J. Whether trial briefs should be submitted and, if so, when; and
K. Any other appropriate issues.

iii. Joint Submission. The parties should prepare and submit to the court prior to the conference a joint submission reflecting their agreement and any areas of disagreement to be resolved at the court's scheduling conference or a subsequent conference.

d. The Court's Discovery Plan. At or shortly after the scheduling conference, the court should enter an order adopting a case management plan agreed to by the parties, if it is reasonable, and rule on any other pending matters, including those items on which the parties have not reached agreement. If the parties have been able to agree on a proposed case management plan, they should promptly advise the court, which can then decide whether it needs to have a scheduling conference or can simply enter an order adopting the parties' proposed plan. The court should retain plenary authority to modify its order if circumstances warrant.

Comment

Subsections (a)-(d). In Rand Corporation, Institute for Civil Justice, An Evaluation of Judicial Case Management Under the Civil Justice Reform, *Effects of Early Judicial Case Management* 51-59 (1996) and *Discovery Management, Further Analysis of the Civil Justice Reform Act, Evaluation Data* 67 (1998) (collectively the "Rand Report"), the Rand Report concluded that the time from a case's start to its disposition was significantly reduced by early judicial management. The Rand Report also found that judicial control of discovery reduced the amount of time lawyers and their clients would be required to spend on a case.

This Standard therefore recommends that both the parties and the court take an active, early role in addressing discovery matters. For example, where appropriate, the court should encourage voluntary discovery or disclosures between the parties. The Standard also suggests that, as a general rule, the court should encourage, and preferably direct, the parties to develop an overall discovery plan for the court's approval at a scheduling conference as soon as possible at the start of the case.

The volume and types of cases in some courts and other practical considerations may make it difficult or even impossible to adopt all of the procedures suggested here. Some cases also may not require detailed case management plans or pretrial orders. The courts and the parties are nevertheless encouraged to use them where practicable, particularly in complex cases, and where they would help to reduce the costs and time incurred in litigation.

Many of the practices outlined in this Standard are found in Fed. R. Civ. P. 16 and 26(f) and similar provisions in various state court rules, e.g., Va. Sup. Ct. R. 4:13; Tex. R. Civ. P. 190.1 - 190.4, and guidelines, e.g., Discovery Guidelines of the Maryland State Bar Ass'n, reprinted in Md. R. Civ. P., Ch. 400, preface (1998) ("*Md. Discovery Guidelines*"). They are also consistent with Guideline 4 of the National Conference of State Trial Judges, adopted by the ABA in August 1998:

> The court shall promptly schedule a supervised discovery conference at which counsel shall submit a reasonable and comprehensive discovery plan, subject to court approval, which shall designate the time, place and the most cost effective manner of discovery; the dates for exchange of expected trial witnesses; the dates and sequence for disclosure of experts and written reports containing their opinions; and the deadline for completion of all discovery.

Some courts require pretrial conferences if requested by the parties or the court. In Arizona, experience has shown that these procedures reduce the number of pretrial disputes and streamline the trial process by making the parties work together. *See* Robert D. Myers, *MAD Track: An Experiment in Terror,* 25 Ariz. St. L.J. 11, 27 (1993). In some courts—for example, Michigan—a pretrial conference is not required if the parties can agree on a discovery plan and pretrial schedule by themselves to be adopted in a court scheduling order. *See* Mich. Ct. R. MCK 2.401(B). In other courts, the parties are given broad latitude to guide the course of discovery. *E.g.,* Va. Sup. Ct. R. 4:4.

The court may formalize these practices by rule or standing order, or by less formal means such as pretrial orders, notices or letters to the parties.

Subsection (c). This subsection describes specific matters the parties should address in a proposed discovery plan, which will of course depend upon the nature of the case. The guiding principle should be to arrive at a plan that reduces unnecessary time and expense without compromising the substantive or procedural rights of any party. Where a case is particularly complex or if a judicial decision on one or more facts or issues in the case may be dispositive and/or would encourage a settlement, the parties and the court should consider conducting discovery in stages. There may also be cases where judicial efficiency would be served by bifurcating discovery of the liability and damages issues, or putting some limitations on discovery pending initial settlement discussions or the filing of dispositive motions.

The Advisory Committee Notes to the 1993 amendments to Fed. R. Civ. P. 26(f) (requiring a "meeting" to develop a proposed discovery plan) state that "it is desirable that the parties' proposals regarding discovery be developed through a process where they meet in person . . . . The revised rule directs that in all cases not exempted by local rule or special order the litigants must meet in person and plan for discovery." Other court and local rules, on the other hand, require only a "conference" rather than an in-person "meeting." *E.g.,* U.S.D.C. -D. Mass. Local Rule 16.1(B) ("[u]nless otherwise ordered by the judge, counsel for the parties shall . . . confer no later than fourteen (14) days before the date for the scheduling conference"). This Standard recommends that the court approve, by local rule or order, telephone conferences as satisfying the meet and confer requirements. In-person conferences are not required in a great many cases.

Subsection (d). Each case should have a discovery plan, even if it is highly informal or the parties simply agree to have no discovery. The amount of discovery and complexity of the plan will depend on the size and complexity of each case. *E.g.,* U.S.D.C. - C.D. Cal. Local Rule 6.4.1; Tex. R. Civ. P. 190. The court should consider whether efficiency can be gained through the adoption of forms for discovery plans and for case management plans.

2. Resolving Discovery Disputes.

    a. Prompt, Informal Contact with the Court. The court should hear and decide discovery disputes as soon as reasonably possible after they arise. The court should consider ways to resolve these disputes that do not require a formal written motion or in-person hearing. Any resulting ruling should be made a matter of record.

        i.   Depositions. Where the parties (and/or a nonparty witness) are unable to resolve a dispute in a deposition, unless the court has by rule or otherwise directed that they not do so, they should call the court and ask for a telephone conference. If appropriate, and if the court is available, the court should consider resolving the matter at that time. If the dispute is not resolved by the telephone conference, the court should consider other ways to resolve the issue promptly and with minimal time and expense,

including having a discovery dispute conference (discussed below), before having the parties file formal discovery motions or
papers and holding a hearing.

    ii.   Other Discovery. Where the parties (and/or a nonparty witness
or subpoena recipient) are unable to resolve any other discovery
dispute, unless the court has by rule or otherwise directed that
they not do so, the party seeking relief should notify the court,
either by telephone or by short letter, outlining the nature of the
dispute and attaching any pertinent materials. If the notification
is by telephone, all other parties should also be given the opportunity to be on the line. If the notification is by letter, the opposing party (and/or affected witness or subpoena recipient) should
be allowed to submit a short letter in response attaching any
pertinent materials. The court should then resolve the matter
promptly, either by a telephone call, by a letter-ruling, by an
order or by calling an informal discovery conference to hear the
parties further.

    iii. The Parties Should First Confer. Before any informal contact
with the court, the parties should confer in good faith, either in
person or by telephone, to try to resolve the dispute. Any letter
sent to the court on a discovery dispute should outline the efforts to resolve the dispute.

    iv. Informal Discovery Conference. The court may hold an infor-
mal conference, either in person or by telephone, to try to resolve any discovery dispute.

b. No Discovery Motions Before Attempting to Resolve the Issue
Informally.

    i.   Most Issues. The court normally should not permit a formal dis-
covery motion unless the court and the parties have not been
able to resolve or narrow the dispute informally. The court may,
and at the request of any party should, memorialize a ruling in
writing.

    ii. Some Issues May Not Be Appropriate For Informal Resolution.
Some discovery issues ordinarily would not be appropriate for
informal resolution. These may include attorney-client privilege
or work-product claims, the adequacy of a party's discovery re-

sponses or production, or the scope of appropriate discovery in a particular case. The court may by rule or otherwise exempt these or similar issues from the requirement that the parties first present them informally to the court.

c.   Formal Discovery Motions. A party that is dissatisfied with a ruling does not, by complying with this standard, waive its right to file a formal discovery motion.

    i.   The Parties Should First Confer. Before filing a discovery motion, the parties should confer in good faith to attempt to resolve the dispute, narrow the issues needing formal adjudication and agree on a schedule so that the matter may be resolved by the court as promptly and efficiently as possible.

    ii.   Motions to Compel and/or for Sanctions. A party seeking an award of attorney fees or other form of sanction for an alleged discovery or disclosure violation should include as part of its motion:

        A.   The facts and circumstances that support the motion;

        B.   The efforts made by the moving party to obtain compliance with the rule, obligation or order that allegedly has been violated;

        C.   What sanctions are being sought and why they are appropriate;

        D.   Whether attorney fees or other costs or expenses are requested and, if so, a description of the time and expenses directly caused by the alleged violation.

    iii.   Prompt Ruling by the Court. The court should rule on any pending discovery motion as soon as reasonably practicable. This may be by letter or memorandum ruling before the time set for hearing, from the bench at the hearing or as soon as possible after the hearing. It is often more valuable to the parties to have a prompt ruling than an elaborate one.

Comment

Subsection (a). The practices in this Standard are patterned after U.S.D.C. - E.D.N.Y. Local Civil Rule 37.3. They stem from a concern that discovery disputes often create unnecessary expense for the parties and can be an inefficient use of scarce court resources. In many cases, discovery disputes can be resolved more quickly and efficiently by informal approaches than by fullblown motion practice. A large number of discovery disputes are not casedispositive and delaying a ruling on them will simply add time and expense to the case. Local rules in a number of federal and state courts provide for prompt access to and rulings by the court as soon as problems first appear. *See* James G. Carr & Craig T. Smith, *Depositions and the Court*, 32 Tort & Ins. L.J. 635, 648- 49 n.70 (1997); U.S.D.C. - E.D. Va. Local Rules 7, 37.

Although these Standards favor informal resolution of discovery disputes, they do not contemplate or permit *ex parte* communications with the court. Except in highly unusual cases, all calls, letters or conferences should be attended by or copied to all counsel (and any self-represented party) of record.

Subsections (b)-(c). It has now become widely accepted that the parties should first attempt to resolve discovery (as well as other) issues informally in good faith before seeking the court's assistance. *E.g.,* U.S.D.C. -C.D. Cal. Local Rule 7.15.1; U.S.D.C. - E.D. Va. Local Rule 37(e); Cal. Civ. Proc.Code §§ 2025(g) (depositions), 2031(l) (documents).

A ruling by a court, although it may arise informally, is nonetheless a ruling and should be viewed as a final court order or determination. Depending on the jurisdiction, such a ruling may be challenged by a motion for reconsideration.

The adequacy of a party's discovery responses or production, as well as the appropriate scope of discovery, may be resolved by the court informally. The determination in each particular case as to which discovery issues are appropriate for informal resolution remains within the discretion of the court.

The requirements for supporting a motion to compel and/or for sanctions are based on U.S.D.C. - N.D. Cal. Local Rule 37-1(e); *see also* U.S.D.C.

- C.D. Cal. Local Rule 7.15.2; U.S.D.C. - E.D. Va. Local Rule 37. California also requires that the motion specifically identify each party or attorney against whom sanctions are sought. Cal. Civ. Proc. Code § 2023(b), (c); Blumenthal v. Superior Court of Marin County, 163 Cal. Rptr. 39, 40 (Ct. App. 1980).

These Standards primarily seek to establish general principles that should help reduce time and expense required of the parties and the court for discovery disputes. They are, however, not intended to restrict the court's broad discretion to fashion particular methods to resolve discovery disputes efficiently. They are not intended to operate to deprive a party of its right to have a record of the court's discovery rulings or to file a motion for reconsideration if a party can demonstrate that with additional time and an opportunity for the formal presentation of additional information, a different result might be appropriate.

If a motion for attorneys' fees is being made, it should be supported by contemporaneous time records and affidavits containing such relevant information as hourly rates and attorney experience.

3. Sanctions for Failure to Comply with Discovery Obligations. To obtain the benefits of early judicial management and control of discovery, the court should consider whether to impose appropriate sanctions for noncompliance with discovery obligations, including the failure to participate in preparing a discovery plan, unless the court finds good cause for the party's failure to do so.

Comment

To achieve the benefits of these Standards, parties and their counsel must comply with their obligations and must not abuse the discovery process. Although sanctions are not the primary or favored device for solving discovery problems, they must be perceived by counsel and the parties as the likely consequence of noncompliance with or abuse of discovery. Studies indicate that a major problem is the perception by counsel that judges are unwilling to resolve discovery disputes and are reluctant to impose meaningful sanctions for discovery violations. *E.g.,* Susan Keilitz et al., *Attorneys' Views of Civil Discovery*, 32 Judges' J., Spring 1993, at 2. *See also* ABA Court Delay

Reduction Committee of the National Conference of State Trial Judges, *Discovery Guidelines Reducing Cost and Delay*, Guideline 6, 36 Judges' J. Spring 1997, at 9.

This Standard therefore creates a presumption that sanctions will be imposed for discovery violations, with the burden shifting to the noncomplying party to demonstrate why they are not warranted. This is consistent with the discovery guidelines of the National Conference of State Trial Judges adopted by the ABA in August 1998: "When a party fails to comply with its disclosure obligations the court has a duty to impose appropriate sanctions." It also accords with the provisions in Fed. R. Civ. P. 16(f), 26(g)(3), 37(b)(2), and many state court rules, *e.g.,* Ariz. R. Civ. P. 16(C)(5); Cal. Civ. Proc. Code §§ 2025-2031; Va. Sup. Ct. R. 4:12(b)(2), and local federal court rules, *e.g.,* U.S.D.C. - E.D. Va. Local Rule 37(G), (H).

Noncompliance applies to a complete failure to respond to a discovery request, the failure to comply with a court's discovery order, or an obvious disregard for compliance with the spirit of discovery rules, i.e., bad faith. Such noncompliance would include in the appropriate case of an obvious disregard for compliance not only the outright failure to do something, but also an inadequate or inappropriate response. *E.g.*, Traxler v. Ford Motor Co., 576 N.W.2d 398 (Mich. 1998) (sanctions imposed for evasive discovery responses). And it would include propounding unnecessary and/or oppressive discovery requests. *See* U.S.D.C. - E.D. Va. Local Rule 37(G); Tex. R. Civ. P. 215.3.

The type and scope of sanction will depend on the nature of the violation. The court should impose sanctions proportionately, taking into consideration any pattern of improper behavior, any aggravating or mitigating circumstances, notice and knowledge. Sanctions might include *(a)* entering specified findings of fact or admissions against a party; *(b)* excluding or limiting a party's evidence; *(c)* striking part or all of a party's claims or defenses; *(d)* entering full or partial default on one or all of the party's claims; and *(e)* requiring a party or counsel to pay the other side's counsel fees and expenses caused by the default or failure.

4. Alternative Discovery Management. Consistent with the demands on the court, the need for a prompt resolution of any potential disputes or issues, the parties' resources and the nature of the case, the court may assign discovery disputes to a magistrate judge, similar judicial officer, referee or a specially appointed master, with the cost to be borne initially by one or more of the parties and/or taxed as costs at the end of the case. Any decisions by the magistrate judge or master should be subject to timely review by the court.

Comment

Many cases will not require significant court supervision, much less having a magistrate judge or someone other than a trial judge supervise discovery. On the other hand, the delegation of discovery disputes to a magistrate judge (or similar officer) or special master may be appropriate, particularly if a case is large or complex, or if for practical reasons the court is unable to provide the time and attention to discovery issues that are necessary for the case to proceed on a reasonable timetable. If this is so, the parties and the court would be well advised to consider having someone other than the trial judge become involved in overseeing discovery from the outset. *See* N.Y. C.P.L.R. 3104 (upon motion or court initiative, referee may be designated to supervise disclosure). The court should, however, always weigh each party's economic resources and its ability to bear the additional cost of having discovery issues decided in the first instance by someone other than a judicial officer.

Continued court involvement should be the norm in cases that require ongoing pre-trial supervision. *See* James S. Kakalik et al., *An Evaluation of Judicial Case Management Under the Civil Justice Reform Act* 89 (1996) (finding that although early judicial management of cases decreased the time to disposition, the assignment of discovery matters to a magistrate judge did not result in any significant decrease).

II. THE PARTIES' DISCOVERY OBLIGATIONS

5. Tailoring Discovery Requests and Responses to the Needs of the Case.

a. Preparing Discovery Requests. A party should tailor discovery requests to the needs of each case. This means that the content of the requests should apply to the case, and the form of discovery requested should be the one best suited to obtain the information sought. A party should weigh in each case which discovery methods will achieve the discovery goals of *(i)* obtaining usable information and *(ii)* obtaining it as efficiently and inexpensively as possible for everyone concerned.

b. Responding to Discovery Requests. A party responding to a discovery request should see that the response *(i)* fairly meets and complies with the discovery request and *(ii)* does not impose unnecessary burdens or expense on the requesting party.

Comment

Both the federal and many state court rules of civil procedure call for counsel or a self-represented party to certify, implicitly if not explicitly, that his or her discovery requests and responses are appropriate and not propounded or interposed for an improper purpose, including imposing unnecessary burdens or expense on the other side. *E.g.,* Fed. R. Civ. P. 26(g); Va. Sup. Ct. R. 4:1(f).

Beyond these requirements, the parties should also consider what is the most appropriate way to obtain or furnish the requested information. Most court rules provide for various forms of discovery. Depending on the case, some information can best be obtained through interrogatories, while other information can best be obtained through document requests, requests for admission or depositions. Some cases may call for limited interrogatories. Others may require more extensive ones. In some cases, the same information can be obtained more readily (and easily) by taking one or more depositions or simply asking for selected documents, rather than spending hours crafting interrogatories, which then require the other side to spend even more time framing responses.

Although discovery is an integral part of the adversary process, and a lawyer has no duty to help prepare an opponent's case but does have a duty to vigorously represent the client, at times a party can and should provide requested information in a way that minimizes time and expense for everyone concerned, including the court. This is explicit in rules such as Fed. R. Civ. P. 26(c), 33(d) and 34(b) and similar state court provisions, e.g., Tex. R. Civ. P. 192.4, 192.6(b), and it is also implicit in the overriding spirit of the discovery process itself. *Cf.* Fed. R. Civ. P. 1 ("[These rules] shall be construed and administered to secure the just, *speedy, and inexpensive* determination of every action." (Emphasis added.)).

III. INTERROGATORIES

6. Propounding Interrogatories.

   a. Use of Interrogatories. The ease of propounding numerous interrogatories and the often substantial burden placed upon the party with the obligation to respond imposes a duty upon an attorney who chooses this form of discovery to consider, as to each question posed and as to the set of interrogatories as a whole, (a) whether the information sought is the type that the responding party can efficiently provide through this form of discovery and (b) whether depositions or other discovery forms should be employed as the more appropriate and more efficient method of obtaining the information sought.
   b. The Framing of Interrogatories. Interrogatories should be concise, focused, objective and unambiguous. They should not be argumentative or used for cross-examination, nor should they impose unreasonable burdens on the responding party.
   c. Form Interrogatories. The court, together with advisory panels or bar organizations, should consider developing form interrogatories that presumptively will be deemed appropriate forms of inquiry.

Comment

Subsection (a). This section is modeled on U.S.D.C. - S.D.N.Y. Civil Rule 33.3(b). It is a more specific statement of the general rule that any discovery mechanism should be used only when it is the most efficient and economical means to obtain the desired information. The Standard emphasizes that an attorney should consider efficiency and economy not only as to the set of interrogatories as a whole but as to each interrogatory posed and not only from that attorney's own perspective but also, to the extent possible, from the perspective of the party with the obligation to respond.

The underlying policy—that interrogatories should not be used to impose unnecessary or unreasonable burdens on the responding party—also supports the numerical limits in the current federal rule and many state rules. While interrogatories generally are the least expensive form of discovery to prepare, they can be costly to answer and used as a means of harassment. *See, e.g.,* Fed. R. Civ. P. 33(a), 1993 Advisory Committee Notes. This Standard is also consistent with the provision in Fed. R. Civ. P. 26(b)(2) that any discovery device "*shall* be limited by the court if it determines that . . . the discovery sought is unreasonably cumulative or duplicative, or is obtainable from some other source that is more convenient, less burdensome, or less expensive." (Emphasis added.)

Subsection (b). These requirements are based, in part, on the principles underlying Standard 5 above, including the premise that one party should avoid imposing unreasonable burdens on a responding party. They also stem from a practical concern that discovery should not be an exercise in semantics or grammatical construction. Interrogatories that are clear and concise leave less room for the responding party to object or to provide vague and evasive answers. Interrogatories that do not seek objective facts invite artfully drafted responses and generalities that are apt to be of little use to the proponent. In addition, a party who serves a large number of onerous interrogatories may have a hard time arguing against responding to an equally burdensome set of interrogatories from the other side.

Subsection (c). A number of courts and/or bar organizations have developed pattern or form interrogatories that are presumptively deemed to be appropriately worded to obtain discoverable information. *E.g.,* Md. R. 2-421(a), Md. R. Appendix, Form Interrogatories (1998).

7. Responding to Interrogatories.

   a. Interpreting Interrogatories. Interrogatories should be interpreted reasonably, in good faith and according to the meaning the plain language of the interrogatories would naturally import.
   b. Interrogatory Responses. A party and counsel should ordinarily be viewed as having complied with their obligation to respond to interrogatories if they have:

     i.   Responded to the interrogatories within the time set by the governing rule, stipulation or court-ordered extension;

    ii.   Made reasonable inquiry, including a review of documents likely to have information necessary to respond to the interrogatories;

   iii.   Given specific objections to those interrogatories they have objected to;

   iv.   Provided responsive answers to any interrogatories not objected to.

c.   Objecting to Interrogatories.

     i.   Matching Objections to Interrogatories. Specific objections should be matched to specific interrogatories. General or blanket objections should be used only when they apply to every interrogatory.

    ii.   Narrowing the Scope of a Response. When an answer is narrowed by one or more objections, this fact and the nature of the information withheld should be made clear in the response itself.

d.   When Responses Should Be Served. Answers and objections to interrogatories are presumptively due on the date specified by the requesting party unless that date conflicts with a court order or the discovery rules themselves. When the parties agree on additional time to respond to certain interrogatories or subparts, but not all of them, responses to the other interrogatories and subparts should be provided by the original deadline unless otherwise agreed or ordered.

Comment

Subsection (a). A responding party should resist the temptation to impose strained interpretations on interrogatories that are clearly not what was intended and that thwart the legitimate inquiries of the opposing party. *E.g.,* James Wm. Moore et al., *Moore's Federal Practice* § 33.101, at 33-67 (Daniel R. Coquillette et al. eds., 3d ed. 1999) ("A sufficient answer [to an interrogatory] generally entails a conscientious and good faith effort to comprehend the question and to answer it explicitly."). Forced interpretations and evasive answers also lead to disputes that unnecessarily lengthen discovery and, where motions follow, are an inappropriate use of judicial resources.

Subsection (b). Fed. R. Civ. P. 26(g) and many state rules, e.g., Va. Sup. Ct. R. 4:1(g), contain a certification requirement with respect to all written discovery responses. These rules impose on counsel and parties an affirmative duty of reasonable inquiry into both law and fact. Gregory P. Joseph,*Sanctions: The Federal Law of Litigation Abuse* (2d ed. 1994). A certification inviolation of the rule, made without substantial justification, provokes a mandatorysanction. *See* Fed. R. Civ. P. 26(g)(3); Va. Sup. Ct. R. 4:1(g).

This Standard attempts to guide courts and the parties as to what is expected in responding to interrogatories, and is patterned on a proposal of the Defense Research Institute submitted to the Discovery Subcommittee of the Advisory Committee on Civil Rules in August 1997.

Subsection (c)(i). In objecting to interrogatories, the practice of making boilerplate objections at the outset of the response and incorporating them *in toto* into the specific numbered responses generally is not acceptable. *Cf.* Tex. R. Civ. P. 193.2(e) (an objection that is "obscured by numerous unfounded objections" will be deemed waived unless the court excuses it for good cause). The responding party should make plain exactly which objections apply to exactly which interrogatories. The response to each interrogatory should identify the particular language or characteristics of the interrogatory that is being objected to. *E.g.,* Tex. R. Civ. P. 193.2(a) ("The party must state specifically the legal or factual basis for the objection and the extent to which the party is refusing to comply with the request."); *see also* Obiajulu v. City of Rochester, Dep't of Law, 166 F.R.D. 293, 295 (W.D.N.Y. 1996) ("pat, generic, non-specific objections, intoning the same boilerplate language, are inconsistent with both the letter and the spirit of the [discovery rules]").

Subsection (c)(ii). The practice of answering an interrogatory "subject to these objections" or "without waiving these objections" often leaves the requesting party unsure as to whether the full answer is being provided or only a portion of it. To prevent this uncertainty, the responding party should expressly state either that (i) the information being provided is the entire answer or (ii) the information being provided is responsive only to that portion of the interrogatory to which no objection is asserted.

Subsection (d). Fed. R. Civ. P. 33(b)(3) and many state court rules provide that answers and objections to interrogatories ordinarily are to be provided within "x" number of days after the interrogatories were served. The court is always free to set a different deadline. Where a party needs additional time to gather the information to answer one or more of the interrogatories or subparts, the parties may agree to a later deadline as long as it does not conflict with a court order (including a discovery cut-off date). The propounding party should be agreeable to a reasonable request for more time. Unless the propounding party agrees to a different date, however, the responding party should serve its answers and objections to any interrogatories and subparts that do not require additional time by the original deadline. There is no justification for delaying the progress that the propounding party can make with initial responses while the responding party is collecting the information needed to answer the balance.

8.   Contention Interrogatories. Interrogatories that generally require the responding party to state the basis of particular claims, defenses or contentions made in pleadings or other documents should be used sparingly and, if used, should be designed to target claims, defenses or contentions that the propounding attorney reasonably suspects may be the proper subjects of early dismissal or resolution or, alternatively, to identify and to narrow the scope of claims, defenses and contentions made where the scope is unclear.

Comment

Contention interrogatories are expressly authorized by Fed. R. Civ. P. 33(c) and similar state rules, e.g., Tex. R. Civ. P. 194.2(c). Contention interrogatories, like all forms of discovery, can be susceptible to abuse. Among other things, they can be used as an attempt to tie up the opposing party rather than to obtain discovery. The legitimate purpose of contention interrogatories is to narrow the issues for trial, not to force the opposing side to marshal all its evidence on paper. *See* Tex. R. Civ. P. 194.2(c) cmt. (contention interrogatories "are not properly used to require a party to marshal evidence or brief legal issues").

The potential for overreaching is particularly present when interrogatories seeking the detailed underpinnings of the opposing party's allegations are served early in the case. Although, when used with discretion, interrogatories served near the outset of the case can be useful in narrowing the issues to define the scope of necessary discovery, contention interrogatories ordinarily are more appropriate after the bulk of discovery has already taken place. At that point, the party on whom the interrogatories are served should have the information necessary to give specific, useful responses. *See, e.g.,* Fed. R. Civ. P. 33(c); Va. Sup. Ct. R. 4:8(e).

9. Supplementation of Interrogatory Responses. A party should timely supplement or correct any answer provided in its original response if it acquires new material information or otherwise learns that the answer is incomplete or incorrect in some material respect and if the parties to whom the original response was due do not have written notice or other notice through discovery of the additional or corrective material information.

Comment

This Standard, which is based on Fed. R. Civ. P. 26(e) and analogous state court provisions such as N.Y. C.P.L.R. 3101(h) and Tex. R. Civ. P. 193.5, establishes a reasonable requirement if the goals of discovery are to be achieved. Supplementation should be made promptly, and particularly when a case is approaching a discovery cut-off, pre-trial conference or trial date. In determining whether newly discovered information is material, both the party and counsel should consider the effect on the party's case if favorable information were to be precluded at trial or, conversely, the consequence of a bar on any evidence to rebut information that would appear to favor the other side.

Depending on the circumstances, the court may consider sanctions or remedies other than exclusion of evidence for a party's failure to timely supplement an interrogatory answer.

IV. DOCUMENT PRODUCTION

10. The Preservation of Documents. When a lawyer who has been retained to handle a matter learns that litigation is probable or has been com-

menced, the lawyer should inform the client of its duty to preserve potentially relevant documents and of the possible consequences of failing to do so.

Comment

This Standard is derived from various sources, including court decisions that imply a duty to preserve potentially relevant material from the discovery rules or a court's inherent powers. *E.g.,* Figgie Int'l v. Alderman, 698 So. 2d 563, 567 (Fla. Dist. Ct. App. 1997); Hirsch v. General Motors Corp., 628 A.2d 1108 (N.J. Super. Ct. Law Div. 1993); Turner v. Hudson Transit Lines, Inc., 142 F.R.D. 68, 72 (S.D.N.Y. 1991); Struthers Patent Corp. v. Nestle Co., 558 F. Supp. 747, 765 (D.N.J. 1981) (quoting Bowmar Instrument Corp. v. Texas Instruments, Inc., 25 Fed. R. Serv. 2d (Callaghan) 423, 427 (N.D. Ind. 1977) (improper for a party, "with knowledge that [a] lawsuit would be filed, [to] wilfully destroy[] documents which it knew or should have known would constitute evidence relevant to [the] case")).

Other cases recognize "spoliation of evidence" as an independent tort. *E.g.,* Hazen v. Municipality of Anchorage, 718 P.2d 456 (Alaska 1986); Bondu v. Gurvich, 473 So. 2d 1307 (Fla. Dist. Ct. App. 1984); Smith v. Superior Court, 198 Cal. Rptr. 829 (Ct. App. 1984). Because of its importance and the significant penalties that can be imposed for its violation, *Computer Assocs. Int'l, Inc. v. American Fundware, Inc.,* 133 F.R.D. 166 (D. Colo. 1990) (default), an attorney should make certain that the client is fully aware of the duty and the potential consequences of failing to comply with it.

The point at which the duty to preserve materials arises is not the same in all cases. Although the language of Fed. R. Civ. P. 37 and similar state rules suggests that sanctions may be levied only when the document destruction conflicts with a court order (issued in the course of the case), this limitation has not been widely followed. The more common rule is that the duty is triggered when a party becomes aware that litigation has commenced, and arises even earlier where the party has notice that litigation is likely to take place. *E.g.,* Turner v. Hudson Transit Lines, Inc., 142 F.R.D. 68, 73 (S.D.N.Y. 1991).

For the duty to attach before a suit has been filed, however, the litigation must be probable, not merely possible. *E.g.*, Iowa Ham Canning, Inc. v. Handtmann, Inc., 870 F. Supp. 238, 245 (N.D. Ill. 1994) (the requisite knowledge for imposing sanctions is not the "potential" for litigation, but the "contemplation" or "anticipation" of litigation).

In addition to notifying a client of its duty to preserve documents once litigation has been filed or appears imminent, counsel should instruct the client as to what documents or types of documents it needs to preserve. The client should be told to preserve any documents that are directly at issue, as well as other documents that the opposing party would be entitled to obtain in discovery. *E.g.*, Wm. T. Thompson Co. v. General Nutrition Corp., 593 F. Supp. 1443, 1455 (C.D. Cal. 1984).

The duty to preserve documents is an affirmative one that requires the party and its counsel to ensure that necessary steps are taken when potentially relevant documents might otherwise be destroyed. For example, corporate officers and corporate counsel who have notice of discovery obligations should communicate these obligations to relevant employees. If documents are destroyed, it is no defense that the employees responsible did not know of the duty to preserve them, so long as the company itself had notice. *E.g.*, National Ass'n of Radiation Survivors v. Turnage, 115 F.R.D. 543 (N.D. Cal. 1987).

By the same token, a party that is on notice of the potential relevance (and therefore discoverability) of documents may not destroy them simply by following a preexisting document retention and disposal policy. Once the duty to preserve documents comes into play, producible documents should be preserved even if they ordinarily would not be preserved in the normal course of business. *E.g.*, Shaffer v. RWP Group, 169 F.R.D. 19 (E.D.N.Y. 1996).

11. What to Do When a Document Request Is Received.

    a. Advising the Client. On receiving a document request, counsel should promptly confer with the client and take reasonable steps to ensure that the client (i) understands what documents are being requested, (ii) has adopted a reasonable plan to obtain the documents in a timely manner and (iii) is actually implementing that plan.

    b.   Interpreting Document Requests. A document request should be interpreted reasonably, in good faith, and according to the meaning the plain language of the requests would naturally import.

Comment

Subsection (a). Counsel should take an active role in ensuring that a client properly complies with a document request. Counsel should develop or oversee the client's development of a plan that will achieve a timely and complete production, and should take whatever follow-up steps are necessary to ensure that the plan is effectively carried out. In particular, counsel should look for areas where the plan may have broken down. For example, where a person who is likely to have responsive documents has not provided anything in response, an attorney should confirm that someone has contacted that person to verify that an appropriate search was made. In the final analysis, as in many areas of discovery compliance, counsel must accept the client's word as to what searches have been made and what documents have been found. It is the lawyer's responsibility, however, to guide the client in devising and implementing a procedure that satisfies its obligations under the discovery rules. *E.g.*, Meeropol v. Meese, 790 F.2d 942, 950-51 (D.C. Cir. 1986) (*FOIA* case: "[I]n determining whether an agency has discharged its responsibilities 'the issue to be resolved is not whether there might exist any other documents possibly responsive to the request, but rather whether the <u>search</u> for those documents was <u>adequate</u>.'") (quoting Weisberg v. United States Dep't of Justice, 745 F.2d 1476, 1485 (D.C. Cir. 1984)).

Subsection (b). Both counsel and the party who receives a document request should bear in mind that the propounding party may have drafted it without knowing what specific documents or types of documents the other side possesses. While objections may be asserted where this gap in the propounding party's knowledge has produced vague or overbroad requests, requests for production should not be interpreted "in an artificially restrictive or hypertechnical manner to avoid disclosure of information fairly covered by the discovery request." Fed. R. Civ. P. 37(a) 1993 Advisory Committee Notes; *see also* 7 James Wm. Moore et al., *Moore's Federal Practice* § 34.11[3], at 34-30 (Daniel R. Coquillette et al. eds., 3d ed. 1999) (the "degree of specificity required [in document requests] may depend on the extent of the requesting party's knowledge with respect to the documents sought"); Sellon v. Smith, 112 F.R.D. 9 (D. Del. 1986) (party may not adopt an unreasonably narrow interpretation of document requests); Washington State Physicians Ins. Exch. & Ass'n v. Fisons Corp., 858 P.2d 1054 (Wash. 1993) (en banc) (candor and reason are required in discovery; misleading responses, even if technically accurate, are improper).

12. Responding to a Document Request.

   a. Response to a Request for Production. A party and counsel ordinarily should be viewed as having complied with its duty to respond to a document request by:

      i. Responding to the requests within the time set by the governing rule, stipulation or court-ordered extension;
      ii. Making specific objections to those requests they have objected to;
      iii. Physically producing the documents themselves (or copies) or specifically identifying those documents that are being or will be produced and/or specifying precisely where the documents can be found and when they can be reviewed;
      iv. Specifically stating if no documents have been found to respond to a given request; and
      v. Making a reasonable inquiry of those persons and a reasonable search of those areas likely to have responsive documents.

   b. Matching Objections to Requests. Specific objections should be matched to specific requests. General or blanket objections ordinarily should be used only when they apply to every request.
   c. Producing Documents Subject to Objection. When the scope of the document production is narrowed by one or more objections, this fact and the nature of the documents withheld should be made explicit.
   d. Where Production Is Limited by Interpretation. Where a party objects to a request as overbroad when a narrower version of the request would not be in dispute, the documents responsive to the narrower version ordinarily should be produced without waiting for a resolution of the dispute over the scope of the request. When a

production is limited by a party's objection, the producing party should clearly describe the limitation in its response.

Comment

Subsection (a). Fed. R. Civ. P. 26(g) and many state rules, e.g., Va. Sup. Ct. R. 4:1(g), contain a certification requirement for all written discovery responses. These rules impose an affirmative duty on counsel and parties of reasonable inquiry into both law and fact. Gregory P. Joseph, *Sanctions: The Federal Law of Litigation Abuse* (2d ed. 1994). A certification in violation of the rule, made without substantial justification, calls for a mandatory sanction. *See* Fed. R. Civ. P. 26(g)(3); Va. Sup. Ct. R. 4:1(g).

This Standard is an attempt to provide guidance to courts, counsel and the parties as to what is expected in responding to a request for production of documents, and is patterned on Tex. R. Civ. P. 196.2 and a proposal of the Defense Research Institute submitted to the Discovery Subcommittee of the Advisory Committee on Civil Rules in August 1997. *Cf.* Standard 7(b) above.

Subsections (a)(ii), (b). The responding party should make plain exactly which objections are applicable to exactly which requests. The response to each request should also identify the particular language or characteristic of the request that is the basis of the objection. *E.g.*, Obiajulu v. City of Rochester, Dep't of Law, 166 F.R.D. 293, 295 (W.D.N.Y. 1996) ("[P]at, generic, non-specific objections, intoning the same boilerplate language, are inconsistent with both the letter and the spirit of the [discovery rules]. An objection to a document request must clearly set forth the specifics of the objection and how that objection relates to the documents being demanded.").

Subsections (a)(iii), (c). The practice of producing documents "subject to these objections" or "without waiving these objections" often leaves the party who served the requests unclear as to whether all responsive documents or only a subset is being provided. In addition, withholding documents after asserting such a response can be a violation of the discovery rules, including the certification requirement of the attorney who signs the response. *E.g.*, Washington State Physicians Ins. Exch. & Ass'n v. Fisons Corp., 858 P.2d 1054, 1081 (Wash. 1993) (en banc) (awarding sanctions where key documents were withheld after response stated that "[w]ithout waiver of these objections and subject to these limitations, [defendant] will produce documents responsive to this request").

To prevent these problems, whenever documents are produced at the same time that an objection has been made to a request, including a claim of privilege, the response to the request should expressly state either that (i) all responsive documents are being produced or (ii) the documents provided are only those to which the stated objection does not apply. *See* Tex. R. Civ. P. 193.2. Otherwise the requesting party may unknowingly file an unnecessary motion to overrule the objection.

Subsection (d). In many situations where a party objects to a request as overbroad it does not dispute that the opposing party is entitled to at least some portion of the documents requested. If so, the responding party should ordinarily produce any documents that have not been objected to, notwithstanding its objection to producing others. It is improper to withhold documents that are clearly called for by a request simply because the responding party objects to producing some of the documents that have been asked for. For example, a party may object to a request as overbroad in failing to restrict the request to a particular time frame. The party should make clear in its written response that it objects to the request as written, and that the documents it is producing are limited to the specified period that it does not object to. There may, however, be situations where all parties would save time and money by deferring a comprehensive search for documents until the issue of what documents have to be produced has been resolved. This would be particularly appropriate if it would avoid multiple, expensive searches through a large universe of potentially responsive documents.

13. When and Where Documents Should Be Produced.

    a. The Date Set by the Party Asking for Documents. The requesting party should set a realistic date for document production, one that gives the responding party enough time to obtain, review and organize the documents after submitting its written response to the request.

    b. By the Responding Party. If the responding party objects to the date and/or place of production set by the requesting party, the responding party's response should give a reasonable alternative date and/or place for production, to which it will be bound without further request unless the parties stipulate or the court orders otherwise. Unless otherwise specified by the requested party, documents should be produced on a "rolling" basis when they become available.

c. Where Documents Should Be Produced. Documents presumptively should be produced for inspection at the place where they are regularly kept and in their original form. The parties may agree otherwise or, for good cause, the court may order otherwise.

Comment

Subsection (a). Fed. R. Civ. P. 34(b) and many state rules provide that a request for production of documents specify a "reasonable time [and] place" for producing the documents. This should be self-evident. In practice, however, the requesting party often will unilaterally set the same date for the written response as for the production itself. In many cases the production will follow the written response. It may be virtually impossible to produce a large volume of documents that must be obtained from many sources within the time provided for the written response. Although production may follow the written response, a proper written response cannot be prepared without first reviewing the relevant documents.

The better practice is for the requesting party to consult and try to agree with the responding party on a deadline that allows a reasonable time to complete the production.

Subsection (b). Although most court rules typically require that a written response specifying what documents will be produced, and which requests will be objected to, be served within a particular number of days, they do not dictate when, other than the date initially specified, the responding party has to actually produce the documents. The responding party should try to reach an agreement with the propounding party on a reasonable date for production.

Generally, documents should then be produced on a rolling basis, because in most cases there is no justification for withholding documents that are ready for production.

Where documents are not voluminous and objections have not been raised, the documents should be copied and produced simultaneously with the written response to the request.

Subsection (c). Fed. R. Civ. P. 34(b) and similar state court rules state that the request for production "shall specify a reasonable . . . place" for making documents available for inspection. What is reasonable will depend on the nature of the request. The presumption should be that they will be produced where they are normally kept. *E.g.*, Bercow v. Kidder, Peabody & Co., 39 F.R.D. 357 (S.D.N.Y. 1965); Niagara Duplicator Co. v. Shackleford, 160 F.2d 25 (D.C. Cir. 1947). In practice, counsel for the responding party may make them available at his or her counsel's office or some other convenient location.

The rules contemplate that the producing party will make the originals available for the other side to inspect and copy. The parties may agree to supply copies in the first instance, subject to the requesting party's right to examine the originals. *See* Tex. R. Civ. P. 196.3(b). The parties should also attempt to reach agreement on who will pay for the copying costs.

14. How Documents Should Be Produced.

    a. Where Voluminous Amounts of Documents Are Involved. Where a request for production may call for a large number of responsive documents, the parties should confer to try to agree on the most efficient and cost-effective way to have the documents produced and reviewed.

    b. Organization of Production. Documents should be produced either as they are kept in the usual course of business or to correspond to the categories in the request.

Comment

Subsection (a). In cases involving productions of a large number of documents, cooperation between the parties may help to reduce the costs to both sides of the production and review. For example, where a request calls for many documents that are largely redundant on a particular issue, the parties may agree to the production of a smaller number of sample documents. Alternatively, the parties may agree to produce the documents in installments until sufficient information has been obtained. The parties may also save significant expense by agreeing to defer production of certain types of documents pending resolution of issues in the case that might eliminate the need for the documents.

Efficiencies in the mechanics of production also should be explored. For example, as discussed in Standard 30 below, documents may be "scanned" and then data-coded into a digital visual format, which may allow all parties to review and retrieve information from them much more easily and inexpensively than by some other method. The parties can also agree on how to share or allocate the costs of doing so.

Subsection (b). Although Fed. R. Civ. P. 34(b) and many state court rules, e.g., N.Y. C.P.L.R. 3122(c), Tex. R. Civ. P. 193.5, require production of documents either as they are kept in the usual course of business or organized and labeled to correspond to the categories in the request, in practice these provisions are often ignored. This not only is required by the rules, but also constitutes the best practice even where it is not covered by a rule.

15. Supplementation of Document Production. A party should timely produce any responsive documents discovered after the original production if the newly discovered documents would make the original production incomplete or incorrect in a material respect.

Comment

This Standard, based on Fed. R. Civ. P. 26(e) and analogous state provisions such as Va. Sup. Ct. R. 4:1(e) and Tex. R. Civ. P. 193.5, is necessary to achieve the basic purpose of discovery. Supplementation should be made promptly, particularly when the case is approaching a discovery cut-off date, a final pre-trial conference or trial itself. In determining whether a newly discovered document is material, a party and counsel should consider the effect on the party's case if a favorable document were to be precluded at trial or, conversely, the consequence of a bar on any evidence to rebut the contents of a document that would appear to favor the other side. As with the failure to serve supplementary interrogatory answers, the court will have discretion to determine what remedy, including the exclusion of evidence or adverse inferences, is appropriate for a party's failure to supplement its production of requested documents.

V. DEPOSITIONS

16. General Procedures for Depositions.

    a. Scheduling a Deposition. Before noticing a deposition, unless there are extraordinary circumstances, a party should try to consult all other parties to agree on the date(s) and place for the deposition, taking into account the convenience of all counsel, the parties and the person to be deposed. A deposition notice should be served a reasonable period of time in advance of the date set for the deposition.

    b. Objections to a Deposition. An objection to the date or place of a deposition should be made promptly after a notice of deposition is received. If an objection is made promptly, in most cases meaning within three business days of receipt of the notice, the deposition should ordinarily be stayed until the parties agree on or the court sets a date or place for it.

    c. Length of the Deposition. The court may consider, either by rule, order or as part of a case management plan, whether it would be appropriate to place a presumptive limit on the length of some or all of the depositions in specific types of cases or the particular case before it.

    d. Who Should Be Permitted to Attend a Deposition. The parties, a deponent's spouse or one other member of the deponent's immediate family, a designated representative of a party that is not a natural person, the attorney(s) (including one or more legal assistants) for a party or the witness and any expert retained by a party ordinarily should be permitted to attend a deposition.

    e. Pertinent Documents Should Be Produced Before a Deposition. A party seeking production of documents in connection with or that will be used in a deposition should, whenever reasonably possible, schedule the deposition to allow for the production of documents in advance.

    f. Where Depositions Should Be Taken: Presumptions. A defendant may take a plaintiff's deposition where the suit has been brought; a plain-

366 Discovery Problems and Their Solutions

tiff may take a defendant's deposition where the defendant resides or, if the defendant is a corporate or associational entity, where it has its principal place of business; and the deposition of a nonparty witness may be taken where he or she resides or works. Subject to the preceding requirements, a deposition ordinarily will be taken at the office of the attorney noticing the deposition. The deposing party and/or the witness may agree on another location taking into account the convenience of the witness, counsel and the parties.

Comment

Subsection (a). Fed. R. Civ. P. 30(b)(1) and similar state court rules, e.g., Va. Sup. Ct. R. 4:5(b)(1), do not specify any minimum number of days between service of notice and the date noticed for a deposition, but merely state that it shall be "reasonable." Before noticing a deposition (or scheduling any other date or deadline), counsel should almost always consult with and try to accommodate the schedules and pre-existing commitments of other counsel, the parties and any nonparty witnesses. *See* ABA Guidelines for Conduct Nos. 14, 15 (Aug. 1998); Seventh Circuit Standards of Civility, Nos. 14, 15 (1992); Md. Discovery Guidelines 4, 7; Va. State Bar Principles of Professional Courtesy, Art. III(d); D.C. Bar Voluntary Standards for Civility in Professional Conduct, No. 8 (1996).

There will be rare occasions (for example, expedited discovery in aid of a preliminary injunction motion) when prior consultation may not be possible. Even then, a party should try to accommodate a reasonable request for some other date or time. If the court has to become involved in what is essentially a housekeeping matter, it is a strong indication that the courtesy expected among counsel has broken down.

Subsection (b). The federal and many state rules are silent on the effect of an objection to the date or place of a deposition. Fed. R. Civ. P. 37(d) and similar state rules provide for sanctions where a party does not attend at its own noticed deposition and the party's failure to attend is not excused unless that party has filed a motion for a protective order. Some courts, however, have taken the position that the objecting party must actually obtain a protective order to be excused from attending a deposition. For obvious practical reasons, particularly where a deposition is set on relatively short notice, an objection should act as a stay of the deposition to give the parties time to agree or obtain a court ruling on the issue rather than precipitate a formal motion for protective order.

Subsection (c). A number of state and local federal court rules now provide presumptive limits on the length of a single deposition. *E.g.,* Tex. R. Civ. P. 199.5(c) (six hours); Ariz. R. Civ. 30(d) (four hours).

Subsection (d). Fed. R. Civ. P. 30(c) excludes from its operation Fed. R. Evid. 615 (providing for the exclusion of witnesses). State provisions such as Va. Sup. Ct. R. 4:5(c) merely state that "[e]xamination and crossexamination may proceed as permitted at trial" and therefore also do not address who can attend. Depositions normally are held in nonpublic settings, such as an attorney's or the deponent's office. Even depositions taken at a courthouse are not normally viewed as being in a public forum. *E.g.,* Seattle Times Co. v. Rhinehart, 467 U.S. 20, 33 (1984) (pre-trial depositions are not public components of a civil trial); Amato v. City of Richmond, 157 F.R.D. 26, 27 (E.D. Va. 1994), *cert. denied*, 519 U.S. 862 (1996) (press not permitted to attend depositions); Kimberlin v. Quinlan, 145 F.R.D. 1 (D.D.C. 1992) (same); Times Newspapers, Ltd. (of Great Britain) v. McDonnell Douglas Corp., 387 F. Supp. 189, 197 (C.D. Cal. 1974) (same); *but see* Avirgan v. Hull, 118 F.R.D. 252 (D.D.C. 1987) (order denying motion to preclude the press from attending a deposition).

Except in extraordinary cases, a deposition, unlike a trial, should not be considered a "public" proceeding. The attendees at a deposition presumptively should be limited to those persons who have a direct relationship to the case itself that gives them a legitimate reason for being there to hear, firsthand, what the witness has to say. Tex. R. Civ. P. 199.5(d)(3). In addition, if the person's presence will not otherwise be disruptive or objectionable, one member of the deponent's family may also be permitted to attend. This latter allowance is intended to take into account those circumstances in which the mere presence of a deponent's spouse or a caretaker child or other close family member in a purely supportive role might be considered helpful. It would not include other persons who have no other relationship to the case. It would include a party, counsel to a party and counsel to the witness, as well as any expert who can assist in questioning or understanding the testimony of the witness. *Id.* Fed. R. Civ. P. 26(c)(5), 45(c)(1) and 45(c)(3)(B) and similar state provisions authorize a party or the witness to seek a protective order to further limit attendance at the deposition. *E.g.,* Galella v. Onassis, 487 F.2d 986, 997 (2d Cir. 1973). Tex. R. Civ. P. 199.5(a)(3) takes a slightly different approach, and requires advance notice if a party intends to have anyone other than the parties, counsel, etc., attend—presumably to allow the other side or the deponent to object and/or file for a protective order.

This Standard leaves open the issue of who should have the burden of moving to enlarge or restrict the attendees at a deposition if it becomes an issue. *See* Fed. R. Civ. P. 30(c), 1993 Advisory Committee Note (the rule 28 "does not attempt to resolve issues concerning attendance by others, such as members of the public or press").

Subsection (e). Producing documents just before or during a deposition usually generates only delay and aggravation to both the witness (who is asked either to wait while examining counsel reviews the documents for the first time or to return later to complete the deposition) and the attorney seeking the documents, who faces a Hobson's choice of either undertaking a less-thanthorough review or adjourning the session to a later time or date. Whenever possible, the parties should agree to have any requested documents made available long enough before the deposition so that they can be reviewed and the deposition can go forward at a reasonable pace. Fed. R. Civ. P. 26(c) and 30(d) and similar state law provisions are available if an examining attorney unduly delays the deposition by insisting on examining a large volume of documents during a deposition.

In appropriate cases and subject to the examining party's right to determine how to frame questions to the deponent, the parties also may consider having the witness review specified documents before the deposition or during a recess so that everyone does not have to wait during the deposition itself while the witness painstakingly peruses each exhibit he or she is questioned about.

Subdivision (f). The plaintiff should normally attend his or her deposition in the place where the suit is pending on the theory that the plaintiff chose the forum. Sonitrol Distributing Corp. v. Security Controls, Inc., 113 F.R.D. 160 (E.D. Mich. 1986). A defendant, who usually has had no role in deciding where the suit was filed, should normally be allowed to have his or her deposition taken where he or she resides or works. Salter v. Upjohn Co., 593 F.2d 649, 651 (5th Cir. 1979) (The deposition of a corporation "'should ordinarily be taken at its principal place of business,' especially when . . . the corporation is the defendant. 8 C.Wright & A.Miller, Federal Practice & Procedure § 2112 at 410 (1970)[.]'"); Pinkham v. Paul, 91 F.R.D. 613, 615 (D. Me. 1981); *but see* Dollar Sys., Inc. v. Tomlin, 102 F.R.D. 93, 94 (M.D. Tenn. 1984) (defendant that contractually agreed to the forum cannot complain about having to give a deposition there). Depositions of nonparty witnesses also normally should be taken where they reside or do business. *See* 8A Charles Alan Wright et al., *Federal Practice and Procedure* § 2112 (2d ed. 1994). While the parties are encouraged to agree on a reasonable place to take a deposition, the normal rule is that, subject to the basic principles described above, the examining attorney is allowed to pick the site, which is often his or her own office.

In agreeing on another location for a deposition, taking into account the convenience of the witness, counsel and the parties, the factor of "expense" should be considered. For example, if numerous plaintiff-party witnesses are located outside the forum where the litigation is occurring, it may be far less costly (and therefore convenient) for an attorney for each party to travel to where the witnesses are located, rather than requiring each of the witnesses to travel to, and to be housed in, the forum where the case is being litigated. Moreover, in such cases (as in all appropriate cases), the court may exercise its discretion to require a departure from the normal presumption and should encourage the parties to negotiate these issues voluntarily.

17. Objections and Comments During a Deposition.

   a. Form of Objections. Where the court's rules provide that all deposition objections are preserved for further ruling and the testimony is subject to the objection, any objection ordinarily should be made concisely and in a non-argumentative and non-suggestive manner. In most cases, a short-form objection such as "leading," "argumentative," "form," "asked and answered" or "non-responsive" will suffice.

   b. Appropriate Remedies for Deposition Misconduct. In addition to imposing sanctions against a party and/or its attorney for misconduct during a deposition, the court should, consistent with the applicable rules of evidence, consider whether deposition misconduct warrants allowing portions of a deposition transcript or other evidence to be admitted at trial on the issue of the witness' credibility during that deposition.

Comment

Subsection (a). Fed. R. Civ. P. 30(d)(1) provides that "[a]ny objection to evidence during a deposition shall be stated concisely and in a nonargumentative and non-suggestive manner." Many state rules are similar, and numerous cases from both federal and state court have stressed that only simple straightforward objections are appropriate. Tex. R. Civ. P. 199.5(e) is explicit: "Objections to questions during the oral deposition are limited to 'Objection, leading' and 'Objection, form.' Objections to testimony during the oral deposition are limited to 'Objection, nonresponsive.'"

Subsection (b). To give added teeth to these commands, where counsel and/or the witness violates them, the jury should be permitted to have this evidence before it. By the same token, if the examining attorney engages in oppressive conduct, the jury should also be allowed to consider this evidence in determining the merits of the case.

18. Conferring with the Witness.

    a. During the Deposition.

        i. An attorney for a deponent should not initiate a private conference with the deponent during the taking of the deposition except to determine whether a privilege should be asserted or to enforce a court-ordered limitation on the scope of discovery. Subject to the provisions of subparagraph (a)(ii) and (b) below, a deponent and the attorney may confer during any recess in a deposition.

       ii. An attorney for a deponent should not request or take a recess while a question is pending except to determine whether a privilege should be asserted or to ascertain whether the answer to the question would go beyond a court-ordered limitation on discovery.

    iii. In objecting to or seeking to clarify a pending question, an attorney for a deponent should not include any comment that coaches the witness or suggests an answer.

    iv. Any discussion among counsel about the subject matter of the examination should at the request of the examining attorney occur only when the deponent has been excused from the deposition room.

    v. An attorney shall not instruct or permit another attorney or any other person to violate the guidelines set forth in sections a(i)-a(iv) with respect to that attorney's client.

b.   During a Recess.

    i. During a recess, an attorney for a deponent may communicate with the deponent; this communication should be deemed subject to the rules governing the attorney-client privilege.

    ii. If, as a result of a communication between the deponent and his or her attorney, a decision is made to clarify or correct testimony previously given by the deponent, the deponent or the attorney for the deponent should, promptly upon the resumption of the deposition, bring the clarification or correction to the attention of the examining attorney.

    iii. The examining attorney should not attempt to inquire into communications between the deponent and the attorney for the deponent that are protected by the attorney-client privilege. The examining attorney may inquire as to the circumstances that led to any clarification or correction, including inquiry into any matter that was used to refresh the deponent's recollection.

Comment

Subsection (a). Conferences between a witness and the witness's attorney during a deposition, while at times perhaps appropriate to clarify a question or prevent abuse, can be used to prevent forthright, uncoached answers from the witness. Except for conferences necessary to determine whether the attorney-client or other privilege should be asserted, an attorney for a deponent ordinarily should not initiate a private conference with the deponent during the deposition. *E.g.*, U.S.D.C. - S.D. Ind. Gen. Rule 30.1(c);

U.S.D.C. - D. Or. Local Rule 230-5(d); Tex. R. Civ. P. 199.5(d). This Standard is not intended to prevent a witness from requesting the opportunity to consult with counsel; however, counsel should be mindful of the obligation to avoid the suggesting of answ ers or other abuse of the consultation right. Moreover, the Standard is not intended to restrict an attorney's intervention when the attorney has a good faith concern thatthe witness is unable to continue the deposition.

For the same reason, an attorney for the witness (or for any party) should not be permitted to take a recess while a question is pending. The only exception is to clarify an issue to determine whether the attorney-client (or some other) privilege should be asserted.

Counsel should not as part of an objection make a "speaking objection" or include commentary that would suggest an answer to the witness. Fed. R. Civ. P. 30(c) provides that the deposition should proceed "with the testimony being taken subject to the objections," reserving a ruling on any objection to when the deposition is used in court. *See also* Tex. R. Civ. P. 199.5(d), (e); Va. Sup. Ct. R. 4:5(c); Ethicon Endo-Surgery v. United States Surgical Corp., 160 F.R.D. 98, 99 (S.D. Ohio 1995); American Directory Serv. Agency v. Beam, 131 F.R.D. 635, 642-43 (D.D.C. 1990) (Magistrates Report), *adopted*, 131 F.R.D. 15, 18-19 (D.D.C. 1990). There is therefore normally no reason to object to a question with anything more than a brief description of the nature of the objection or, as Fed. R. Civ. P. 30(d)(1) puts it, "concisely and in a non-argumentative and non-suggestive manner."

There may, however, be times when a discussion among counsel can clarify or shorten some or all of the line of questioning. If this occurs, and if the examining attorney requests it, the witness should be excused from the deposition while counsel discuss the issue.

Subsection (b). Some decisions have taken the position that, so long as the deposition has not been completed, there should be no communication between the deponent and counsel. *E.g.*, Hall v. Clifton Precision, 150 F.R.D. 525, 531-32 (E.D. Pa. 1993); Standing Order of Hon. G. Ross Anderson, Jr., U.S.D.C. - D.S.C., ¶ 5 (Dec. 18, 1993); Cascella v. GDV, Inc., No. 5899, 1981 WL 15129 (Del. Ch. Jan. 15, 1981).

To afford every person an unrestricted right to obtain the advice of his or her counsel, the bar against conferring with counsel should not apply (i) when the conference is initiated by the witness and (ii) whenever there is a recess from the actual taking of deposition testimony. *E.g.,* Odone v. Croda Int'l PLC, 170 F.R.D. 66, 68-69 (D.D.C. 1997). The witness and counsel should therefore be able to confer during a recess, either during the day or between deposition sessions, without having to risk a finding that the attorney-client privilege does not apply.

If a conference during a recess between the witness and the witness's attorney results in a decision to correct or clarify previous testimony, the correction or clarification should be promptly placed in the record when the deposition resumes. If the deposition has been completed when the decision to make a correction or clarification is made, the correction should promptly be brought to the examining attorney's attention. *Cf.* Fed. R. Civ. P. 30(e) ("if there are changes in form or substance," the deponent must "sign a statement reciting such changes and the reasons given by the deponent for making them"); *see* Lugtig v. Thomas, 89 F.R.D. 639, 641 (N.D. Ill. 1981) (outlining the requirements of the rule).

Where a substantive correction is made, it may be appropriate to resume or re-open the deposition so that the examining attorney can question the deponent in person about the change. *Id.* In any further deposition the examining attorney may inquire as to the circumstances that led to the change, including any matter that was used to refresh or alter the witness's recollection, but the examining attorney may not inquire into areas protected by the attorneyclient privilege.

19. Designations by an Organization of Someone to Testify on Its Behalf.

   a. Requested Areas of Testimony. A notice or subpoena to an entity, association or other organization should accurately and concisely identify the designated area(s) of requested testimony, giving due regard to the nature, business, size and complexity of the entity being asked to testify. The notice or subpoena should ask the recipient to provide the name(s) of the designated person(s) and the areas that each person will testify to by a reasonable date before the deposition is scheduled to begin.

b. Designating the Best Person to Testify for the Organization. An entity, association or other organization responding to a deposition notice or subpoena should make a diligent inquiry to determine what individual(s) is (are) best suited to testify.

c. More Than One Person May Be Necessary. When it appears that more than one individual should be designated to testify without duplication on the designated area(s) of inquiry, each such individual should be identified, a reasonable period of time before the date of the deposition, as a designated witness along with a description of the area(s) to which he or she will testify.

d. Reasonable Interpretation Is Required. Both in preparing and in responding to a notice or subpoena to an entity, association or other organization, a party or witness is expected to interpret the designated area(s) of inquiry in a reasonable manner consistent with the entity's business and operations.

e. If in Doubt, Clarification Is Appropriate. A responding party or witness that is unclear about the meaning and intent of any designated area of inquiry should communicate in a timely manner with the requesting party to clarify the matter so that the deposition may go forward as scheduled.

f. Duty to Prepare the Witness. Counsel for the entity should prepare the designated witness to be able to provide meaningful information about any designated area(s) of inquiry.

g. If an Officer, etc., Lacks Knowledge. Whenever an officer, director or managing agent of an entity is served with a deposition notice or subpoena that contemplates giving testimony on a subject about which he or she has no knowledge or information, that individual may submit, reasonably before the date noticed for the deposition, an affidavit or declaration under penalty of perjury so stating and identifying a person within the entity having knowledge of the subject matter. The noticing party should then consider whether to proceed with the deposition of the officer, director or managing agent initially noticed or subpoenaed.

h. Consideration for an Organization's Senior Management. Where information is being sought from an organization, counsel ordinarily should not seek in the first instance to take the deposition of the organization's senior management if someone else in the organization can be expected to have more direct and firsthand knowledge or information.

Comment

Subsection (a). The use of organizational designations under Fed. R. Civ. P. 30(b)(6) and similar state rules imposes responsibilities on both the examining and the defending party. The examining party should designate the areas of inquiry with reasonable particularity so that the defending party will have enough information to identify the person(s) whose testimony can be taken to provide an adequate and complete response. *E.g.*, United States v. Taylor, 166 F.R.D. 356, 360 (M.D.N.C. 1996); Mitsui & Co. (U.S.A.) v. Puerto Rico Water Resources Auth., 93 F.R.D. 62, 66 (D.P.R. 1981); Cal. Civ. Proc. Code § 2025(d).

Subsections (b), (c). The defending party should then identify the person or persons who are in the best position to testify on these areas. *E.g.*, Protective Nat'l Ins. Co. v. Commonwealth Ins. Co., 137 F.R.D. 267 (D. Neb. 1989); *see also* 7 James Wm. Moore et al., *Moore's Federal Practice* § 30.25[3], at 30-53 (Daniel R. Coquillette et al. eds., 3d ed. 1999). If this means that more than one person should testify to cover the requested areas adequately, the defending party should designate each person and identify the area(s) he or she will cover. Marker v. Union Fidelity Life Ins. Co., 125 F.R.D. 121, 126 (M.D.N.C. 1989). Both sides are expected to interpret the designated areas in a reasonable manner, taking into account the business and operations of the entity. Any issues of interpretation that remain unclear should be clarified in a timely manner so that the deposition can proceed as scheduled.

Fed. R. Civ. P. 30(b)(6) and similar state provisions typically call for a designated person to consent to testify on behalf of the entity. Sometimes the person who would seem to have the most knowledge on the subject, and would therefore be the logical person to designate, will not agree to testify. *E.g.*, Mitsui & Co. (U.S.A.) v. Puerto Rico Water Resources Auth., 93 F.R.D. 62 (lower-level employee's deposition is normally not considered to be that of the corporation). *But see* Cal. Civ. Proc. Code § 2025(d) (requiring that the most qualified individual among an entity's "officers, directors, managing agents, employees, or agents" must be produced; the individual's consent is not optional).

Subsection (f). Fed. R. Civ. P. 30(b)(6) and similar state provisions, e.g., Va. Sup. Ct. R. 4:5(b)(6), also provide that the designated person "shall testify as to matters known or reasonably available to the organization." A number of decisions have construed this language to impose an obligation on the defending party to prepare the designated person so that he or she will be able to give "knowledgeable and binding" answers. *E.g.*, United States v. Taylor, 166 F.R.D. at 361; Marker v. Union Fidelity Life Ins. Co., 125 F.R.D. at 126; Cal. Civ. Proc. Code § 2025(d) (designee shall testify "to the extent of any information known or reasonably available to the deponent"); Robert I. Weil & Ira A. Brown, Jr., *California Practice Guide: Civil Procedure Before Trial* ¶ 8:475 (1998) (a designee who does not have personal knowledge "is supposed to find out from those who do!"). This would require counsel to review with the witness materials that he or she may not previously have seen but that are part of the organizational "mind," so that the witness will be in a position to answer "fully, completely, [and] unevasively" all questions on the designated subject matter. Mitsui & Co. (U.S.A.) v. Puerto Rico Water Resources Auth., 93 F.R.D. at 67.

Subsections (g), (h). A number of court decisions have held that it is improper to try to take the deposition of a company's or organization's senior executives if they are not the best persons within the organization to provide the information being sought. *See, e.g.*, Baine v. General Motors Corp., 141 F.R.D. 332, 334-36 (M.D. Ala. 1991); Crown Cent. Petroleum Corp. v. Garcia, 904 S.W.2d 125 (Tex. 1995); Liberty Mut. Ins. Co. v. Superior Court, 13 Cal. Rptr. 2d 363 (Ct. App. 1992).

VI. EXPERTS

The following Standards on experts are intended for those jurisdictions where the practice or procedure is not otherwise governed by statute or rule.

20. Disclosure of Expert Witnesses.

   a. What "Experts" Should Be Disclosed. Each party should disclose the identity of any person who may be used at trial to present evidence as an expert witness. This includes an expert witness retained by another party (such as a codefendant's expert) who may be used by the disclosing party. It does not include a "hybrid" witness, such as a treating physician, who was not specially retained for the litigation and will provide both fact and expert testimony.

b. When Experts Should Be Disclosed. The identity of every expert should be disclosed at least 90 days before the trial date or the date the case is to be ready for trial.

c. The Sequence of Expert Disclosure. The plaintiff usually should disclose its expert first, followed by the defendant's disclosure of its expert, followed by plaintiff's disclosure of any rebuttal expert. Each party should be permitted at least 20 days between each disclosure.

Comment

Subsection (a). Public policy favors pretrial disclosure of any experts a party plans to use as well as their opinions and the grounds for their opinions. Fed. R. Civ. P. 26(a)(2), 26(b)(4); Tex. R. Civ. P. 195.3. At least in the Federal Rules, however, not all experts have to be identified. Fed. R. Civ. P. 26(a)(2)(B) requires written reports only from retained experts and from employee experts who give expert testimony as part of their regular duties, but does not expressly require written reports from employees who are called on to give expert testimony only in the case at hand. *Compare* Cal. Civ. Proc. Code § 2034(a)(2), (f)(2)(B) (requiring an expert witness statement from any employee of a party but that the statement for all experts provide only a "brief narrative statement of the general substance of the testimony that the expert is expected to give").

The better practice is to identify and provide a written report from any person who will be called upon to provide expert opinion testimony, regardless of whether the person regularly provides expert testimony. 3M v. Signtech USA, No. 4-96-1262, 1997 U.S. Dist. LEXIS 21738, at *2 (D. Minn. Nov. 24, 1997) (while the wording of Fed. R. Civ. P. 26(a)(2)(B) seemingly does not embrace employees who are not "retained or specially employed to provide expert testimony in the case or whose duties . . . [do not] regularly involve giving expert testimony," it is inconsistent with the purposes of that rule to exempt an employee from the report requirement merely because he does not "regularly" give testimony).

The Standard makes an exception to the expert disclosure requirement for "hybrid" witnesses, typically treating physicians, who were not specially retained for the litigation and are providing both fact and expert testimony. *E.g.*, Sprague v. Liberty Mut. Ins., 177 F.R.D. 78, 80 (D.N.H. 1998) (no report required from treating physician); Paxton v. Stewart, 80 Cal. Rptr. 2d 179 (Ct. App. 1998), *rev. granted* (same; but treating physician is limited to testimony based on personal observation and cannot testify on liability issues); District of Columbia v. Mitchell, 533 A.2d 629, 652 (D.C. 1987) (same); Turgut v. Levine, 556 A.2d 720 (Md. Ct. Spec. App. 1989); *but see* Salas v. United States, 165 F.R.D. 31, 33 (W.D.N.Y. 1995) (doctor must submit an expert report when his opinion goes beyond facts developed during treatment); Plunkett v. Spaulding, 60 Cal. Rptr. 2d 377, 380 (Ct. App. 1997) (expert witness statement when a doctor goes beyond factual testimony to address the standard of care); 6 James Wm. Moore et al., *Moore's Federal Practice* § 26.23[2][b][iii], at 26-74 to - 75 & nn.29-30.1 (Daniel R. Coquillette et al. eds., 3d ed. 1999) (collecting cases).

Because the identity and opinion of a "hybrid" fact-and-expert witness normally will be disclosed or discoverable using the other discovery mechanisms, failure to designate a fact witness as an expert should not result in surprise to the opposing party.

Subsections (b), (c). Some jurisdictions call for simultaneous disclosure of experts and their opinions by both sides, followed by simultaneous rebuttal or reply reports. *See, e.g.,* Fed. R. Civ. P. 26(a)(2)(A), (B); Robert I. Weil & Ira A. Brown, Jr., *California Practice Guide: Civil Procedure Before Trial* (1997) (explaining that the rationale for simultaneous disclosure in California as provided in Cal. Civ. Proc. Code § 2034 is fairness to both parties).

The better practice, at least in most cases, is to have the party with the burden of proof provide its expert report first, followed by the opposing party's report, and any rebuttal or surrebuttal reports in turn after that. *See* U.S.D.C. - E.D. Va. Local Rule 26(D); Tex. R Civ. P. 195.2. The plaintiff presumably will have framed its case before filing suit, and should be expected to have a reasonably good idea of how it will prove it by the time an expert report is due. Although an argument can be made that the defendant should also have a good grasp on the issues by then, as a practical matter the defendant will normally not know what the plaintiff's expert is going to say until it receives the expert's report.

An expert should be identified and, as provided in Standard 21 below, his or her report given to the other side enough in advance so that it can be analyzed and, if the opposing party wants one, the expert's deposition can be taken before the final pretrial conference and/or trial.

21. Written Reports From Each Testifying Expert.

    a. When the Report Should Be Disclosed. At the same time a party discloses the identity of its expert, it should also furnish to the other side a written report signed by the expert.

    b. What the Report Should Contain. The expert's report should contain:

        i. A complete statement of each opinion the expert will give;

        ii. The basis and reason(s) for that opinion;

        iii. The data or information the expert is relying on in formulating the opinion and a description of where this data or information can be found if it is not part of the record or has not been produced in discovery;

        iv. Any exhibit(s) to be used as a summary of or support for the opinion;

        v. The expert's qualifications, including a list of any publication written by the expert in the last ten years;

        vi. The compensation paid or to be paid to the expert;

        vii. A list of any cases, including each case's name, court, docket number and the name, address and telephone number of each counsel of record, in which the expert has testified at trial or in deposition in the last four years; and

        viii. If not provided in response to subsection (v) above, the expert's current résumé and bibliography, if any.

    c. When a Non-Testifying Consultant Becomes a Testifying Expert. A testifying expert who was initially retained as a non-testifying consultant and who prepared a written report in a consultant capacity should disclose the written report to the opposing party in the same manner and subject to the same requirements as any other testifying expert.

d.   Supplementation of an Expert's Opinion.

i.   Ordinarily an expert's report, as well as his or her deposition testimony, should be final and complete when given, and not subject to later revision or amendment. The parties may stipulate that an expert's opinion can be supplemented within a reasonable specified time before trial.

ii.   In the absence of stipulation, a party wishing to supplement an expert's opinion less than 30 days before trial or a discovery cut-off or other date set by the court should first obtain leave of court. Factors that a court should consider in determining whether or not to allow supplementation include:

A.   The good faith of the party seeking to supplement the opinion;

B.   hether the information was available to that party and/or the expert at an earlier date;

C.   Unfair prejudice to any party; and

D.   Whether it would result in an unfair delay of the trial.

iii.   A party that is permitted to supplement its expert's opinion less than 30 days before trial or a discovery cutoff date should promptly make the expert available for deposition.

e.   No Waiver of Attorney Work Product. The provision in section 21(b)(iii) above that an expert's report describe "the data or information the expert is relying on in formulating [his or her] opinion" does not require the disclosure of communications that would reveal an attorney's mental impressions, opinions or trial strategy protected under the attorney work product doctrine. The report should disclose, however, any data or information, including that coming from counsel, that the expert is relying on in forming his or her opinion. In jurisdictions where this issue has not been addressed or decided, the parties should either stipulate how to treat this issue or seek a ruling from the court at the earliest practical time as to its view on the scope of protection for this information.

f.   Failure to Provide a Report or Opinion. The court should consider whether a party's failure to disclose the identity of its expert or to provide the expert's written report or a deposition within a reasonable period of time before trial or by a date set for doing so should preclude that party from *(i)* calling the expert at trial or *(ii)* introducing that part of the expert's opinion that was not timely disclosed.

g.   Sanctions: Factors to Consider. Among the factors a court should consider in assessing what sanctions, if any, should be imposed for a party's failure to identify an expert or to provide the expert's report in timely fashion are:

  i.   The party's good or bad faith in the matter;
  ii.   Whether or not the failure was due to circumstances beyond the party's control;
  iii. Whether there has been unfair surprise or prejudice to the opposing side; and
  iv.   Whether the failure will unreasonably delay the trial or any other key events in the case.

Comment

Subsection (a). See Comment above for Standard 20(a). Unlike the federal rule, this Standard requires that reports be provided by any person, other than a "hybrid" fact-opinion expert, who will give expert testimony at trial. In jurisdictions where there is no requirement that all experts furnish written reports containing the information listed in this Standard, it would be prudent to serve interrogatories that ask for this information.

Subsection (b). This Standard is modeled on the disclosure and discovery requirements in Fed. R. Civ. P. 26(a)(2)(B) and similar state rules, e.g., Tex. R. Civ. P. 194.2(f). *Compare* Cal. Civ. Proc. Code § 2034(f) (which requires less detailed information); Castaneda v. Bornstein, 43 Cal. Rptr. 2d 10, 17 (Ct. App. 1995) (expert should not be excluded for failure to disclose the "general substance" of testimony).

Subsection (d). A party has a duty to supplement its expert's disclosure whenever it learns that the disclosure is incomplete or incorrect in some material respect. This duty applies to changes in the opinions in the expert's report, as well as those the expert gives in deposition. While supplementation should be made promptly after the deficiency has been discovered, the

Standard sets a 30-day deadline before trial or a discovery cutoff after which a party must obtain the court's permission to make the change. *Accord* Fed. R. Civ. P. 26(e), (a)(3).

Subsection (e). Other than court-appointed experts, which are *sui generis*, an expert is retained to provide testimony to assist one side in the case. The expert is entitled to have the benefit of the theories, however tentative or preliminary they may be, of the counsel that has retained the expert. Experts logically come within the "zone of privacy for strategic litigation planning" that is the rationale for the attorney work product doctrine. *See* United States v. Adlman, 68 F.3d 1495, 1501 (2d Cir. 1995) (construing Fed. R. Civ. P. 26(b)(3) in an unrelated context). Counsel should be able to explore counsel's theories or ideas about the litigation with an expert without the worry that the discussion is tantamount to disclosure to the other side.

At least in federal practice, however, there is a split of authority as to whether communications to an expert of an attorney's "core" or "opinion" work product are immune from disclosure after the 1993 amendments to Rule 26.

For cases holding that all work product is now discoverable under Fed. R. Civ. P. 26(a)(2)(B), see, e.g., *Musselman v. Phillips*, 176 F.R.D. 194 (D. Md. 1997); *Barna v. United States*, No. 95 C 6552, 1997 U.S. Dist. LEXIS 10853 (N.D. Ill. July 23, 1997); *B.C.F. Oil Ref. v. Consolidated Edison Co.*, 171 F.R.D. 57, 66 (S.D.N.Y. 1997); *Karn v. Ingersoll Rand*, 168 F.R.D. 633, 639-40 (N.D. Ind. 1996).

For cases holding otherwise, see, e.g., *Magee v. Paul Revere Life Ins. Co.*, 172 F.R.D. 627, 642 (E.D.N.Y. 1997); *Haworth, Inc. v. Herman Miller, Inc.*, 162 F.R.D. 289 (W.D. Mich. 1995); *All W. Pet Supply Co. v. Hill's Pet Prods. Div.*, 152 F.R.D. 634 (D. Kan. 1993); see also Gregory P. Joseph, *Emerging* Expert Issues Under the 1993 Disclosure Amendments to the Federal Rules of *Civil Procedure,* 164 F.R.D. 97, 101-04 (1996) (collecting cases, and outlining reasons why the continuing recognition of protection for opinion work product is appropriate after recent amendments to Rule 26).

Particularly where an expert is acting as a consultant, the expert's report is likely to reflect counsel's mental processes and legal theories. The court may, however, assess whether there is "substantial need" for using the report to impeach the expert that would outweigh the policy of protecting work product. National Steel Prods. Co. v. Superior Court, 210 Cal. Rptr. 535, 543 (Ct. App. 1985).

An attorney's mental impressions, theories and strategies—archetypal "work product"—that have been conveyed to an expert should not have to be disclosed if the expert is not relying on them in his or her testimony. The ability to have untrammeled access to the process by which an expert has formulated his or her final opinion(s) in the case is outweighed by (1) the undesirability of placing substantial barriers to a full and free exchange of ideas and theories between counsel and the expert; (2) the fact that the expert has been retained to advise and assist one side in an adversary trial system; (3) the added, unnecessary expense of having to retain two experts— one to testify and the other to consult—if a lawyer wants to maintain the confidentiality of his or her work product, and (4) the ability of counsel to obtain and cross-examine the expert on anything the expert is actually relying on in his or her opinion.

If there is no controlling contrary case law in a particular jurisdiction, counsel should assume that there is a reasonable possibility that any communication with the expert will be fair game for inquiry by the other side. 8 Charles Alan Wright et al., *Federal Practice and Procedure* § 2031.1, at 442 (2d ed. 1994 & Supp. 1999) ("It appears that counsel should now expect that any written or tangible data provided to testifying experts will have to be disclosed."). Until there is a clear legal rule, the best way to deal with the issue is to try to obtain an agreement from all the parties to the case on how they will treat the issue or seek a ruling from the court on it.

Although a stipulation that there will be no waiver by sharing work product with an expert would probably protect the information in the particular case, there is no guarantee that it would protect it against nonparties in another setting. *E.g.*, Bank Brussels Lambert v. Crédit Lyonnais (Suisse) S.A., 160 F.R.D. 437, 448 (S.D.N.Y. 1995) (the test is whether disclosure is done in a way that "substantially increases the likelihood that the work product will fall into the hands of the adversary").

Subsection (f). This Standard is modeled on Fed. R. Civ. P. 37(c)(1). The Standard creates a presumption that an expert will not be permitted to give trial testimony that has not first been disclosed in either a report or a deposition. *But see* Martinez v. City of Poway, 15 Cal. Rptr. 2d 644, 646 (Ct. App. 1993) (if an expert declaration has been submitted the expert cannot be excluded based on the inadequacy of the information in the declaration). The Standard also recognizes the court's discretion to use other remedies than an absolute bar on the expert's testimony.

Subsection (g). This subsection identifies factors that are among those to be considered in determining whether or not a failure to identify an expert or to provide a report in a timely fashion should result in some form of sanction and, if so, what form. The list is not exclusive and a court should consider any other factors that would promote the interests of justice.

22. Expert Depositions.

   a. Timing. If requested by the other side, a party's testifying expert should be made available for deposition promptly after the expert's report has been given to the other side. Where no expert report is required (for example, where a treating physician will testify as a "hybrid" fact-expert witness), an expert should be made available for deposition promptly after discovery of the facts underlying the expert's testimony has been completed.
   b. When and Where. Subject to the general principles in Standard 16(f), each party should make its expert available for deposition at a reasonably convenient time and place for the witness, the parties and counsel.
   c. Supplying Underlying Information. Reasonably in advance of an expert's deposition, each party should identify or, to the extent not otherwise readily available to the other side, make available all of the materials or information that the expert is specifically relying on or specifically using in formulating his or her opinion. These materials or information ordinarily should be given to the other side no less than five days before the deposition, except where an earlier deadline is set by rule, order, stipulation or a discovery request. The identification and/or other disclosure of such materials in an expert's

report will be sufficient to satisfy the requirements of this Standard. This Standard does not require the disclosure of that part of a communication that would reveal an attorney's mental impressions, opinions or trial strategy protected under the work product doctrine.

Comment

Making experts available for deposition as of right has become the standard practice in many jurisdictions, either formally by rule or informally by general agreement. *But see* N.Y. C.P.L.R. 3101(d)(1)(iii) (deposition of an expert may be obtained only by court order upon showing of special circumstances). Usually, an expert should be available for deposition just like any other witness who will testify at trial.

For the deposition to be effective, the other side must be given, in advance, access to the information or materials the expert is relying or basing his or her opinion on. Fed. R. Civ. P. 26(b)(4)(C) and similar state rules, e.g., Va. Sup. Ct. R. 4:1(b)(4), call for the party that takes an opposing side's expert's deposition to pay for the time spent in the deposition. *Contra* Tex. R. Civ. P. 195.7 (the party that retains an expert pays for all of the expert's fees). These rules are silent as to travel costs. In line with a general presumption that depositions ordinarily will take place in or near the forum court, it is expected that ordinarily the party that retains an expert will pay the expert's fees and expenses in traveling to the site of the deposition.

23. Motions to Preclude or Limit Expert Testimony.

    a. When the Motion Should Be Filed. A motion challenging all or part of the admissibility of proposed expert testimony should be filed at the earliest practical time and, at the latest, sufficiently in advance of the date set for a final pretrial order or conference so that the court can rule on the motion as part of or before the entry of the final pretrial order. This would include any motion to bar an expert for failure to meet the jurisdiction's standards for the admissibility of expert testimony.

    b. Parties Should Confer Before Filing a Motion. As with discovery in general, before filing a motion on the admissibility of expert testimony a party should make a good faith attempt to resolve or narrow the dispute with the other side.

Comment

This Standard seeks to have the basic issue of the admissibility of an expert's testimony settled, if possible, before discovery has closed and/or a final pretrial order is entered. It is intended to prevent last-minute claims that a party's expert should not be permitted to testify for one reason or another, including the claimed failure of the expert's testimony to satisfy the applicable evidentiary standard.

In *Daubert v. Merrell Dow Pharms.*, 509 U.S. 579 (1993), the U.S. Supreme Court rejected the *Frye* "generally accepted" test for the admissibility of expert scientific evidence and embraced a "scientifically reliable" standard in accordance with Fed. R. Evid. 702. *Compare* Frye v. United States, 293 F. 1013 (D.C. Cir. 1923). Some states have followed *Daubert*'s lead, while others have adhered to a test that more closely resembles *Frye*. State v. Porter, 698 A.2d 739, 742 (Conn. 1997) (adopting *Daubert* standard), *cert. denied*, 118 S. Ct. 1384 (1998); E.I. du Pont de Nemours & Co. v. Robinson, 923 S.W.2d 549 (Tex. 1995) (same); *but see* State v. Isley, 936 P.2d 275, 279 (Kan. 1997) (*Frye* test applicable in Kansas); Brim v. State, 695 So. 2d 268, 271-72 (Fla. 1997) (rejecting *Daubert* and maintaining "the higher standard of reliability as dictated by *Frye*"); People v. Leahy, 882 P.2d 321 (Cal. 1994) (retaining the *Kelly/Frye* standard and rejecting *Daubert* for California). In *General Elec. Co. v. Joiner*, 522 U.S. 136 (1997), the Supreme Court held that the standard of appellate review of a federal trial court's "gatekeeping" decision on the admissibility of scientific evidence is whether the trial court abused its discretion. Given the difficulty of overturning an evidentiary ruling on appeal in state or federal court, motions challenging an expert's testimony under the standard of *Daubert*, *Frye* or similar cases should be filed promptly and, at the latest, sufficiently before a discovery cut-off or final pretrial conference or order to give the other party time to develop an alternative for trial if its expert is barred from testifying. The trial court always retains discretion to exclude or limit expert testimony if it is cumulative or if its probative value is outweighed by its potential prejudice. Fed. R. Evid. 403; United States v. Carswell, 922 F.2d 876, 879 (D.C. Cir. 1991); E.I. du Pont de Nemours & Co. v. Robinson, 923 S.W.2d 549, 557 (Tex. 1995);

Anthony's Pier Four, Inc. v. HBC Assocs., 583 N.E.2d 806, 825 (Mass. 1991).

VII. CLAIMS OF PRIVILEGE

24. **What Constitutes Privileged Information.** Information or a document is "privileged" if it is protected from disclosure by any recognized legal privilege, including without limitation any privilege established by the United States or a State Constitution, statute, rule or common law.

Comment

These Standards apply to discovery from a party or nonparty. They apply to information sought by any form of discovery.

25. **How a Privilege Should Be Asserted.**

   a. **In Response to a Written Discovery Request.** Unless otherwise provided by Standard 26, as soon as reasonably practicable, and in any event no later than the date that the discovery response is due under applicable discovery rules, a party should identify in writing each document or communication the other side has requested in discovery that the party claims is privileged. A discovery response that does not include this identification due to the voluminous nature of the documents or the attorney's lack of particularized identifying information as of the response due date should assert the applicable privilege as to each inquiry to which the privilege relates and give a date within a reasonable time by which the identity of the writing or other communication asserted to be privileged will be furnished. That date will be binding on the responding party unless modified by stipulation or court order.

   b. **During a Deposition.** Unless the basis for the claim of privilege is apparent from the question itself, a party that objects to answering a deposition question based on a claim of privilege should, if possible at that time and without revealing the privileged information, state the basis for the claim of privilege on the record. If requested by the examining party, the objecting party should provide in writing as soon as practicable any additional nonprivileged factual information supporting the claim of privilege.

c. Further Inquiry to Test a Claim of Privilege. The examining party should be able to question a party or witness at the deposition or by interrogatories and, if appropriate, to conduct other reasonable inquiries to ascertain whether the information in question is or should remain privileged. An appropriate inquiry could include questions designed to ascertain:

    i. The applicability of the particular privilege being claimed;
    ii. Any circumstances that may be deemed a waiver or exception to the privilege being claimed; and
    iii. Any other circumstances that may overcome a claim of privilege.

Comment

Subsections (a), (b). Fed. R. Civ. P. 26(b)(5) and 45(d), similar state provisions and federal and state case law require that a party or other person who asserts a privilege must claim it expressly at or before the time that a response or answer to a question would be required. *See generally* Tex. R. Civ. P. 193.2, 193.3. As a practical matter, particularly where large amounts of documents are involved or a number of locations have to be searched, it may not be reasonable to expect a party to provide detailed information about all of the documents claimed as privileged at the time the party's initial response to a discovery request or disclosure requirement is due. If this is the case, it would be appropriate to describe generally the class or type of documents being claimed as privileged and to state that a more detailed listing and supporting information will be given at a specified future date.

Subsection (c). A party that has asked for documents or information must be able to inquire into the factual basis of a claimed privilege against producing or disclosing them, including whether the privilege has been waived or, if it is qualified, whether an exception or exemption would apply. As with discovery in general, the inquiry should be reasonable and use the mechanism best suited to obtain the kind of information that may legitimately be sought.

26. Information Supporting a Claim of Privilege. Except as provided by Standard 27, the following information ordinarily should be provided to support a claim of privilege unless doing so would disclose the privileged information itself.

a. For a Document.

    i. The type of document (e.g., letter, memo), its length and a description of any enclosures or accompanying documents claimed to be privileged. Any enclosure or accompanying document that is not claimed to be privileged in and of itself should be produced unless it would somehow disclose the information claimed to be privileged or result in a waiver of the privilege.

    ii. Its general subject matter.

    iii. The date on the document and/or when it was created; if there is no specific date, a best estimate of when it was created.

    iv. Its author(s), including for each his or her last known address.

    v. Each addressee and/or recipient, including his or her last known address, and, if not apparent, his or her relationship to the author(s).

    vi. The type of privilege (e.g., attorney-client privilege, work product, etc.) being claimed.

b. For an Oral or Other Non-Written Communication.

    i. The name of the person making the communication, any person present when the communication was made and for each his or her last known address.

    ii. The date and place it was made.

    iii. Its general subject matter.

    iv. The type of privilege (e.g., attorney-client privilege, work product, etc.) being claimed.

c. Deleted or Redacted Information. Any deleted, redacted or withheld portion of a document or communication should be clearly identified as deleted and redacted on the ground of privilege and the same information described above should be provided to support the claim of privilege. If some, but not all, of the information on a document or in a communication is withheld on the ground that it is not relevant or not responsive to a discovery request, this fact should also be clearly stated along with the grounds for not producing it.

Comment

Most courts require that a party must provide enough information about documents or information claimed as privileged so that the requesting party can assess the claim and, if a motion is filed, the court can then rule on it. *E.g.,* Fed. R. Civ. P. 26(b)(5); *see also* Cal. Civ. Proc. Code § 2031(f)(3) (items not produced and the basis for objection must be identified "with particularity"); Wellpoint Health Networks, Inc. v. Superior Court, 68 Cal. Rptr. 2d 844, 857 (Ct. App. 1997) (privilege log must be sufficiently specific to make a determination of the validity of the privilege claim); Tex. R. Civ. P. 193.3(b) (same).

Many court rules and decisions require a "privilege log" that gives a document-by-document basis for the privilege(s) claimed for each withheld document. *E.g.,* U.S.D.C. - S.D.N.Y. Civil Rule 26.2(a)(2)(A) (type, subject matter, date, author(s), addressee(s) and relationship of author(s) and addressee(s)); U.S.D.C. - E.D.N.Y. Standing Order on Effective Discovery, Rule 21 (requiring similar information for depositions and document productions); N.Y. C.P.L.R. 3122(b); William W Schwarzer et al., *Federal Civil Procedure Before Trial* § 11:34.1-.4 (1997) (suggesting similar information for a privilege log); United States v. Construction Prods. Research, 73 F.3d 464, 473 (2d Cir.), *cert. denied,* 519 U.S. 927 (1996) (a "party asserting the privilege must establish the essential elements of the privilege"; a cursory description of individual documents is insufficient); Eureka Fin. Corp. v. Hartford Accident. & Indem. Co., 136 F.R.D. 179, 182 (E.D. Cal. 1991) (privilege waived where "blanket objections" did not specifically identify each document and the basis for the claimed privilege); *Wellpoint Health Networks,* 68 Cal. Rptr. 2d 844.

These requirements also are appropriate given that the burden normally rests with the party claiming a privilege to support it. *E.g.,* Construction Prods. Research, 73 F.3d at 473; Clarke v. American Commerce Nat'l Bank, 974 F.2d 127, 129 (9th Cir. 1992).

27. Alternatives to Supplying Detailed Information. If it would be overly burdensome, expensive and/or time-consuming to prepare a detailed listing of the information called for in Standard 26, the parties and the court should consider whether the information can be supplied in some other way or, given the demands and circumstances of the case, it can be re-

duced or eliminated for some or all of the documents or communications in question, including whether:

a. a categorical or general description of the material in question would be sufficient;
b. the existence of particular privileged communications, as opposed to their content, is material to the litigation;
c. the likely probative value of the material in question justifies the expense and burden of providing detailed information; and
d. the expense of providing detailed information should be shared or paid by the party requesting that it be done.

Comment

The 1993 Advisory Committee Notes to Fed. R. Civ. P. 26(b)(5) acknowledge that providing detailed descriptions may be "unduly burdensome when voluminous documents are claimed to be privileged or protected, particularly if the items can be described by categories." The Advisory Committee Notes add that, if this is the case, a party can seek a protective order under Fed. R. Civ. P. 26(c).

Where individual identification of privileged materials may be unduly burdensome or expensive, the parties and/or the court should consider reasonable alternatives. In cases involving numerous communications, documents and files, the parties may agree that communications within certain categories or within certain given time periods may be generally described rather than individually identified. The parties or other persons from whom discovery is sought have an obligation to confer in good faith to try to devise a workable solution. This could include, for example, exempting documents of certain types or within specified date ranges from having to be included on a privilege log; requiring only certain information to be provided about certain categories of documents; or asking the court to appoint an independent third person or special master to review the materials *in camera*.

The parties also can agree that no privilege will be waived by producing documents *en masse* but that all claims of privilege would be preserved until the requesting party actually designates the particular documents to be copied or tries to use them in the case. As noted above in connection with Standard 21, however, a stipulation may not preserve the claim of privilege against nonparties in another setting and the parties would be advised to obtain a court order to this effect. *E.g.*, Bank Brussels Lambert v. Crédit Lyonnais (Suisse) S.A., 160 F.R.D. 437, 448 (S.D.N.Y. 1995) (the test is whether disclosure is done in a way that "substantially increases the likelihood that the work product will fall into the hands of the adversary").

28. Inadvertent Disclosure of Privileged Information. The parties should consider stipulating in advance that the inadvertent disclosure of privileged information ordinarily should not be deemed a waiver of that information or of any information that may be derived from it.

Comment

The law among various jurisdictions differs on the effect of an inadvertent production of privileged communications. The better practice, consistent with most jurisdictions' ethical rules governing attorneys, is that an inadvertent disclosure of privileged information ordinarily should not be deemed a waiver, either of that information or any information that can be derived from it. *See* Tex. R. Civ. P. 193.3(d) ("[a] party who produces material or information without intending to waive a claim of privilege does not waive that claim under these rules," provided it promptly seeks to rectify the issue; the requesting party must then return the material uncopied pending a court ruling); ABA Formal Op. 92-368 (1992) (a lawyer who receives privileged materials through error should not read them and should return them).

To avoid any uncertainty, particularly in those jurisdictions that do not follow this principle, the parties would be advised to obtain a stipulation and/or court order that the inadvertent production of privileged documents will not constitute a waiver, and that these documents will be immediately returned uncopied to the producing party if the inadvertent disclosure is promptly brought to the receiving party's attention after their disclosure has come to light. *See* Federal Judicial Center, *Manual for Complex Litigation 3d* § 21.431 (1995) (parties may so stipulate or court may so order). This avoids unfairness or overreaching and provides the parties with the assurance that inadvertent errors of counsel, the client or their personnel will not prejudice them or their case.

VIII. TECHNOLOGY

29. Preserving and Producing Electronic Information.

    a. Duty to Preserve Electronic Information.

        i. A party's duty to take reasonable steps to preserve potentially relevant documents, described in Standard 10 above, also applies to information contained or stored in an electronic medium or format, including a computer word-processing document, storage medium, spreadsheet, database and electronic mail.

       ii. Unless otherwise stated in a request, a request for "documents" should be construed as also asking for information contained or stored in an electronic medium or format.

      iii. Unless the requesting party can demonstrate a substantial need for it, a party does not ordinarily have a duty to take steps to try to restore electronic information that has been deleted or discarded in the regular course of business but may not have been completely erased from computer memory.

    b. Discovery of Electronic Information.

        i. A party may ask for the production of electronic information in hard copy, in electronic form or in both forms. A party may also ask for the production of ancillary electronic information that relates to relevant electronic documents, such as information that would indicate *(a)* whether and when electronic mail was sent or opened by its recipient(s) or *(b)* whether and when information was created and/or edited. A party also may request the software necessary to retrieve, read or interpret electronic information.

       ii. In resolving a motion seeking to compel or protect against the production of electronic information or related software, the court should consider such factors as *(a)* the burden and expense of the discovery; *(b)* the need for the discovery; *(c)* the complexity of the case; *(d)* the need to protect the attorney-client or attorney work product privilege; *(e)* whether the information or the software needed to access it is proprietary or constitutes confidential business information; *(f)* the breadth of the discovery request; and *(g)* the resources of each party. In complex cases and/or ones involving large volumes of electronic information, the court may want to consider using an expert to aid or advise the court on technology issues

iii. The discovering party generally should bear any special expenses incurred by the responding party in producing requested electronic information. The responding party should generally not have to incur undue burden or expense in producing electronic information, including the cost of acquiring or creating software needed to retrieve responsive electronic information for production to the other side.

iv. Where the parties are unable to agree on who bears the costs of producing electronic information, the court's resolution should consider, among other factors:

(a) whether the cost of producing it is disproportional to the anticipated benefit of requiring its production;

(b) the relative expense and burden on each side of producing it;

(c) the relative benefit to the parties of producing it; and

(d) whether the responding party has any special or customized system for storing or retrieving the information.

v. The parties are encouraged to stipulate as to the authenticity and identifying characteristics (date, author, etc.) of electronic information that is not selfauthenticating on its face.

Comment

Subsection (a). Fed. R. Civ. P. 34(a) and various state rules, e.g., Va. Sup. Ct. R. 4:9(a), provide that the term "documents" includes "data compilations from which information can be obtained [or] translated, if necessary, by the respondent through detection devices into reasonably usable form." *See also* Fed. R. Civ. P. 34(a), 1970 Advisory Committee Note. The 1993 amendment to Fed. R. Civ. P. 26 also makes "data compilations" subject to mandatory disclosure. Tex. R. Civ. P. 196.4 also calls for the production of data or information in electronic or magnetic form, but only if it is specifically requested.

This Standard makes it clear that (a) information contained or stored in an electronic medium or format should be produced pursuant to a "document" request and (b) a party has the same duty when it is aware of potential or pending litigation to take reasonable steps to preserve potentially relevant electronic information as it does to preserve "hard" copies of documents.

Subsection (a)(iii). Attempting to retrieve previously deleted electronic information can be time-consuming and costly. Just as a party ordinarily has no duty to create documents, or to re-create or retrieve previously discarded ones, to respond to a document request, it should not have to go to the time and expense to resurrect or restore electronic information that was deleted in the ordinary course of business. *E.g.,* Tex. R. Civ. P. 196.4 (duty to produce applies only to electronic data that is "reasonably available to the responding party in its ordinary course of business"); Strasser v. Yalamanchi, 669 So. 2d 1142 (Fla. Dist. Ct. App. 1996) (plaintiff may search defendant's computer for purged information only if the plaintiff shows the likelihood of retrieving it and there is no less intrusive way to obtain it; any search must have defined parameters of time and scope and ensure that the defendant's information remains confidential and its computer and databases are not harmed).

Subsection (b). The Standard contemplates that whether and, if so, how much electronic information is subject to discovery, along with the allocation of the cost of producing it, depends on the factors specific to each case. *See, e.g.,* Tex. R. Civ. P. 196.4 (if objected to, no out-of-the-ordinary efforts to retrieve electronic information are required unless the court orders them; if it does so, the requesting party must pay for them); In re Brand Name Prescription Drugs Antitrust Litig., No. 94-C-897, MDL 997, 1995 U.S. Dist. LEXIS 8281 (N.D. Ill. June 13, 1995) (weighing whether to compel a company to retrieve and produce electronic mail messages at its expense); Anti-Monopoly, Inc. v. Hasbro, Inc., No. 94 Civ 2120, 1995 U.S. Dist. LEXIS 16355, at *4 (S.D.N.Y. Nov. 3, 1995) (neither the fact that material was available in hard copy nor the need for the responding party to create the computerized data necessarily precluded production of the information in computerized form); PHE, Inc. v. Department of Justice, 139 F.R.D. 249,

257 (D.D.C. 1991) (requiring production of computerized records where no program existed to obtain the requested information because the response would require "little effort" and "modest additional expenditures"); National Union Elec. Corp. v. Matsushita Elec. Indus. Co., 494 F. Supp. 1257, 1262 (E.D. Pa. 1980) (requiring production of information on computer-readable magnetic tape in addition to hard copy; the discovering parties were required to pay for making the tapes); In re Air Crash Disaster at Detroit Metro. Airport, 130 F.R.D. 634, 635-36 (E.D. Mich. 1989) (party required to produce simulation data on computer-readable tape in addition to hard copy); Armstrong v. Executive Office of the President, 1 F.3d 1274, 1280 (D.C. Cir. 1993) (printouts were not acceptable substitute because they did not reveal various information such as directories, distribution lists, acknowledgments of receipts and similar materials); *see also* Federal Judicial Center, *Manual for Complex Litigation, 3d* § 21.446 (1995).

An issue arises when responsive information required to be produced is part of a much larger database and no software exists to retrieve only the responsive information. A large database, e.g., the transaction history for every customer of a business, should not be made available as if it was a single "document." The parties should confer in this situation and attempt to agree on what will be produced, the format and who will bear the cost of extracting the information.

30. Using Technology to Facilitate Discovery.

    a. In appropriate cases, the parties may agree or the court may direct that some or all discovery materials be produced, at least in the first instance, in an electronic format and how the expenses of doing so will be allocated among the parties.

    b. Upon request, a party serving written discovery requests or responses should provide the other party or parties with a diskette or other electronic version of the requests or responses.

Comment

In appropriate cases, technology can streamline and reduce the costs of discovery, pretrial and trial itself for all parties and the court. Hard copies of documents and other information can be scanned into an electronic format, saved in digital form and then retrieved in short order using sophisticated search methods. The cost is constantly going down, but is still relatively expensive. Electronic storage and retrieval is therefore not appropriate in many cases. In cases where the stakes or issues or the volume of documents call for it, the parties and the court should seriously consider whether putting some or all of the relevant documents into an electronic format would help in managing the case and reducing expenses for the parties. *See* Federal Judicial Center, *Manual for Complex Litigation, 3d* § 21.444 (1995).

Many court rules require that responses to discovery requests be preceded by the full text of each request. *E.g.,* U.S.D.C. - C.D. Cal. Local Rule 8.2.3; U.S.D.C. - D.D.C. Local Rule 207(d); N.Y. C.P.L.R. 3133(b). Other courts require that each numbered discovery request leave space for an answer, so that the responding party can simply fill in the information, copy the combined request-and-answer, and send it back to the requesting party. *E.g.,* Va. Sup. Ct. R. 4:8(b). Given that most discovery requests are now prepared on a computer, the responding party should be able to ask the requesting party to give it a diskette containing the requests to use in preparing its response.

Amendments to Civil Discovery Standards
August 2004

IV. DOCUMENT PRODUCTION

10. The Preservation of Documents. When a lawyer who has been retained to handle a matter learns that litigation is probable or has been commenced, the lawyer should inform the client of its duty to preserve potentially relevant documents in the client's custody or control and of the possible consequences of failing to do so. The duty to produce may be, but is not necessarily, coextensive with the duty to preserve. Because the Standards do not have the force of law, this Standard does not attempt to create, codify or circumscribe any preservation duty. Any such duty is created by governing state or federal law. This Standard is, instead, an admonition to counsel that it is counsel's responsibility to advise the client as to whatever duty exists, to avoid spoliation issues.

2004 Comment

The addition of the phrase "in the client's custody or control" in the first sentence is not substantive. It is intended as a reminder to counsel that documents in the control, as well as the custody, of a client should also be the subject of counsel's advice with respect to document preservation. This includes, for example, documents in the control of senior executives of a corporation.

The second sentence is added to indicate that the duty to preserve data prior to litigation may be different from the duties imposed either by agreement or court order once litigation has commenced. The duty to preserve, whatever its scope, will vary significantly over time, becoming more pronounced as litigation becomes more likely and once litigation is, in fact, commenced. Litigants often will be required to produce that which they had no duty to preserve.

The <u>third</u> sentence is added to clarify that the Standards do not have the force of law and do not purport to create any duty. All duties are created by governing state or federal law.

VIII. TECHNOLOGY

29. Electronic Information.

a.   ~~Duty to Preserve~~ Identifying-Electronic Information. <u>In identifying electronic data that parties may be called upon, in appropriate circumstances, to preserve or produce, counsel, parties and courts should consider:</u>

   <u>i.</u>   A party's duty to take reasonable steps to preserve potentially relevant documents, described in Standard 10 above, also applies to information contained or stored in an electronic medium or format, including a computer word-processing document, storage medium, spreadsheet, database and electronic mail<u>: The following types of data:</u>

   <u>ii.</u>   <u>A.</u>   <u>Email (including attachments);</u>
   <u>B.</u>   <u>Word processing documents;</u>
   <u>C.</u>   <u>Spreadsheets;</u>
   <u>D.</u>   <u>Presentation documents;</u>
   <u>E.</u>   <u>Graphics;</u>
   <u>G.</u>   <u>Animations;</u>
   <u>H.</u>   <u>Images;</u>
   <u>I.</u>   <u>Audio, video and audiovisual recordings; and</u>
   <u>J.</u>   <u>Voicemail.</u>

   ii.   The following platforms in the possession of the party or a third person under the control of the party (such as an employee or outside vendor under contract):

    A. <u>Databases;</u>
    B. <u>Networks;</u>
    C. <u>Computer systems, including legacy systems (hardware and software);</u>
    D. <u>Servers;</u>
    E. <u>Archives;</u>
    F. <u>Back up or disaster recovery systems;</u>
    G. <u>Tapes, discs, drives, cartridges and other storage media;</u>
    H. <u>Laptops;</u>
    I. <u>Personal computers;</u>
    J. <u>Internet data;</u>
    K. <u>Personal digital assistants;</u>
    L. <u>Handheld wireless devices;</u>
    M. <u>Mobile telephones;</u>
    N. <u>Paging devices; and</u>
    O. <u>Audio systems, including voicemail.</u>

  iii. <u>Whether potentially producible electronic data may include data that have been deleted but can be restored.</u>

  ~~ii.~~ ~~Unless otherwise stated in a request, a request for "documents" should be construed as also asking for information contained or stored in an electronic medium or format.~~

  ~~iii.~~ ~~Unless the requesting party can demonstrate a substantial need for it, a party does not ordinarily have a duty to take steps to try to restore electronic information that has been deleted or discarded in the regular course of business but may not have been completely erased from computer memory.~~

b. Discovery of Electronic Information.

  i. <u>Document requests should clearly state whether electronic data is sought. In the absence of such clarity, a request for "documents" should ordinarily be construed as also asking for information contained or stored in an electronic medium or format.</u>

  ii. A party ~~may ask~~<u>should specify whether</u> ~~for the production of~~ electronic information <u>should be produced</u> in hard copy, ~~in electronic form or in both forms. A party may also ask for the production of,~~ <u>in electronic form or, in an appropriate case, in both forms. A party requesting information in electronic form should also consider:</u>

    A. <u>Specifying the format in which it prefers to receive the data, such as:</u>

      I. Its native (original) format, or

      II. A searchable format.

B. Asking for the production of metadata associated with the responsive data — *i.e.,* ancillary electronic information that relates to ~~relevant~~responsive electronic ~~documents~~data, such as information that would indicate ~~(a)~~ whether and when the responsive electronic ~~mail was sent or opened by its recipient(s) or (b) whether and when information~~data was created ~~and/or~~, edited, sent, received and/or opened. ~~A party also may request~~

C. Requesting the software necessary to retrieve, read or interpret electronic information.

D. Inquiring as to how the data are organized and where they are stored.

A party who produces information in electronic form ordinarily need not also produce hard copy to the extent that the information in both forms is identical or the differences between the two are not material.

~~ii.~~ iii. In resolving a motion seeking to compel or protect against the production of electronic information or related software, or to allocate the costs of such discovery, the court should consider such factors as:

A. The burden and expense of the discovery, considering among other factors the total cost of production in absolute terms and as compared to the amount in controversy;

B. The need for the discovery, including the benefit to the requesting party and the availability of the information from other sources;

C. The complexity of the case and the importance of the issues;

D. The need to protect the attorney-client privilege or attorney work product ~~privilege,~~ including the burden and expense of a privilege review by the producing party and the risk of inadvertent disclosure of privileged or protected information despite reasonable diligence on the part of the producing party;

E. The need to protect trade secrets, and proprietary or confidential information;

F. Whether the information or the software needed to access it is proprietary or constitutes confidential business information;

G. The breadth of the discovery request;

H. Whether efforts have been made to confine initial production to tranches or subsets of potentially responsive data;

I. The extent to which production would disrupt the normal operations and processing routines of the responding party;

J. Whether the requesting party has offered to pay some or all of the discovery expenses;

K The relative ability of each party to control costs and its incentive to do so;

L. The resources of each party as compared to the total cost of production; and (g) the resources of each party.

M. Whether responding to the request would impose the burden or expense of acquiring or creating software to retrieve potentially responsive electronic data or otherwise require the responding party to render inaccessible electronic information accessible, where the responding party would not do so in the ordinary course of its day-to-day use of the information;

N. Whether responding to the request would impose the burden or expense of converting electronic information into hard copies, or converting hard copies into electronic format;

O. Whether the responding party stores electronic information in a manner that is designed to make discovery impracticable or needlessly costly or burdensome in pending or future litigation, and not justified by any legitimate personal, business, or other non-litigation related reason; and

P. Whether the responding party has deleted, discarded or erased electronic information after litigation was commenced or after the responding party was aware that litigation was probable and, if so, the responding party's state of mind in doing so.

In complex cases and/or ones cases involving large volumes of electronic information, the court may want to consider using an expert to aid or advise the court on technology issues

iii. The discovering party generally should bear any special expenses incurred by the responding party in producing requested electronic information. The responding party should generally not have to incur undue burden or expense in producing electronic information, including the cost of acquiring or creating software needed to re-

~~trieve responsive electronic information for production to the other~~
~~side~~.
iv. ~~Where the parties are unable to agree on who bears the costs of~~
~~producing electronic information, the court's resolution should con-~~
~~sider, among other factors:~~
  ~~(a) whether the cost of producing it is disproportional to the antici-~~
  ~~pated benefit of requiring its production;~~
  ~~(b) the relative expense and burden on each side of producing it;~~
  ~~(c) the relative benefit to the parties of producing it; and~~
  (d) whether the responding party has any special or customized system for storing or retrieving the information.
~~v~~iv. The parties are encouraged to stipulate as to the authenticity and
identifying characteristics (date, author, etc.) of electronic information that is not self-authenticating on its face.

2004 Comment
Subdivision(a)

Subdivision (a)(i). Standard 29(a)(i) is principally designed to provide
a checklist to assist counsel in identifying types of electronic data as to which
the duty to preserve may apply, once that duty has been triggered under
applicable law. *See, e.g., Super Film of Am., Inc. v. UCB Films, Inc.*, 219
F.R.D. 649, 657 (D. Kan. 2004) (for purposes of Federal Rule of Civil Procedure 26, "[c]omputerized data and other electronically-recorded information includes, but is not limited to: voice mail messages and files, back-up
voice mail files, e-mail messages and files, backup e-mail files, **deleted** e-
mails, **data** files, program files, backup and archival tapes, temporary files,
system history files, web site information stored in textual, graphical or audio format, web site log files, cache files, cookies, and other electronically-
recorded information") (citation and quotations omitted).

This Standard is not intended to suggest that electronic discovery is appropriate in all cases. There may be many cases in which electronic discovery is not warranted, in light of the amount in controversy or any number of
other reasons.

The deletion of the former first sentence of subdivision (a)(i) is intended
to clarify that the Standards do not create or codify law but rather defer to
governing substantive law. The purpose of the list provided in subdivision
(a)(i) is to assist counsel in protecting client interests under whatever strictures may be imposed by governing law. It is not to suggest that every item

in the list is applicable in every case or that counsel has any duty to instruct a client to preserve any, much less every, item on the list. All duties are dictated by governing state or federal law and not by this or any other of these Standards.

Subdivision (a)(ii). Just as subdivision (a)(i) provides a checklist of the types of electronic data that counsel should bear in mind, Standard 29(a)(ii) provides a checklist of platforms and places where such data may be found. As with subdivision (a)(i), subdivision (a)(ii) does not create a preservation duty. Rather, it is another reference tool intended to be consulted once the duty to preserve electronic data has accrued under local law.

Subdivision (a)(iii). Standard 29(a)(iii) is simply a reminder that, as is well established in the case law, when a preservation duty has been triggered, it may be found to apply to "deleted" information remaining on the hard drive of the computer. *Zubulake v. UBS Warburg LLC*, 217 F.R.D. 309, 313 n.19 (S.D.N.Y. 2003) ("The term 'deleted' is sticky in the context of electronic data. 'Deleting' a file does not actually erase that data from the computer's storage devices. Rather, it simply finds the data's entry in the disk directory and changes it to a 'not used' status — thus permitting the computer to write over the 'deleted' data. Until the computer writes over the 'deleted' data, however, it may be recovered by searching the disk itself rather than the disk's directory. Accordingly, many files are recoverable long after they have been deleted — even if neither the computer user nor the computer itself is aware of their existence. Such data is referred to as 're-sidual data.'")(internal quotations and citation omitted).

Former Subdivision (a)(ii). Former subdivision (a)(ii) has been moved to subdivision (b), where it conceptually belongs, as new subdivision (b)(i), with minor modification.

Former Subdivision (a)(iii). Former subdivision (a)(iii) has been deleted. As drafted, it appeared to create or codify a proposition of law, which is not the proper function of a Standard. Moreover, the law is evolving swiftly in the area of electronic discovery and, as stated, the deleted language is not necessarily good law. *See, e.g., Zubulake v. UBS Warburg LLC*, 217 F.R.D. 309, 324 (S.D.N.Y. 2003) ("because the cost-shifting analysis is so fact-intensive, it is necessary to determine what data may be found on the inaccessible media. Requiring the responding party to restore and produce responsive documents from a small sample of the requested backup tapes is a sensible approach in most cases").

Subdivision(b)

Subdivision (b)(i). The second sentence of subdivision (b)(i) is the former subdivision (a)(ii), with the addition of a connecting dependent clause and the insertion of the modifier "ordinarily," the latter in recognition of the fact that there may be unusual circumstances in which the state presumption is obviously inapt. The new first sentence is added as a "best practices" reminder to counsel.

Subdivision (b)(ii). Subdivision (b)(ii) restates and expands the former subdivision (b)(i). The substantive additions are to remind counsel, first, that they have the option of specifying the format in which they wish to receive the desired data and, second, that they may want to inquire as to how the data were organized and where they were stored, since this information may be lost in electronic production.

Subdivision (b)(iii). Subdivision (b)(iii) combines the former subdivisions (b)(ii) and (b)(iv) in recognition of the fact that the factors applied by the courts in resolving motions to compel (or resist production) and motions to allocate costs are largely the same. Additionally, subdivision (b)(iii) expands the former subdivisions (b)(ii) and (b)(iv) to capture additional factors that experience and the developing case law have identified as pertinent to the court's decision. Among the authorities relied on in the recitation of factors in this subdivision are: Federal Judicial Center, MANUAL FOR COMPLEX LITIGATION § 11.446 (4th ed. 2004); 7 MOORE'S FEDERAL PRACTICE §§ 37a.30-33 (3d ed. 2004); *Zubulake v. UBS Warburg LLC*, 217 F.R.D. 309 (S.D.N.Y. 2003); *Zubulake v. UBS Warburg LLC*, 216 F.R.D. 280 (S.D.N.Y. 2003); *Computer Associates International, Inc. v. Quest Software, Inc.*, No. 02-C-4721, 2003 WL 21277129 (N.D. Ill. June 3, 2003); *Medtronic Sofamor Danek, Inc. v. Michelson,* No. 01-2373-M1V, 2003 WL 21468573 (W.D. Tenn. May 13, 2003); *Dodge, Warren, & Peters Ins. Servs. v. Riley*, 130 Cal. Rptr. 2d 385 (Cal. App. 2003); *Byers v. Illinois State Police*, 2002 WL 1264004 (N.D. Ill. June 3, 2002); *Southern Diagnostic Assocs. v. Bencosme*, 833 So.2d 801 (Fla. App. 2002); *Murphy Oil USA, Inc. v. Fluor Daniel, Inc.*, 2002 WL 246439 (E.D. La. Feb. 19, 2002); *Rowe Entertainment, Inc. v. William Morris Agency,* 205 F.R.D. 421 (S.D.N.Y. Jan 16, 2002); *In re CI Host, Inc.*, 92 S.W. 3d 514 (Tex. 2002); *In re Bristol-Meyers Squibb Secs. Litig.*, 205 F.R.D. 437 (D.N.J. 2002); *McPeek v. Ashcroft*, 202 F.R.D. 31 (D.D.C. Aug. 1, 2001); *McCurdy Group, LLC v. American Biomedical Group, Inc.,* Nos. 00-6183, 00-6332, 2001 WL 536974 (10th Cir. May 21, 2001).

Subdivision (b)(iv). Subdivision (b)(iv) is the former subdivision (b)(v) unchanged.

Former Subdivision (b)(ii). Former subdivision (b)(ii), together with former subdivision (b)(iv), is contained within new subdivision (b)(iii).

Former Subdivision (b)(iii). Former subdivision (b)(iii) has been deleted. As drafted, it appeared to create or codify a proposition of law, which is not the proper function of a Standard. Moreover, the law is evolving swiftly in the area of electronic discovery and, as stated, the deleted language is not necessarily good law. *See, e.g., Zubulake v. UBS Warburg LLC*, 217 F.R.D. 309, 324 (S.D.N.Y. 2003).

Former Subdivision (b)(iv). Former subdivision (b)(iv), together with former subdivision (b)(ii), is contained within new subdivision (b)(iii).

30. Using Technology to Facilitate Discovery.
    a. In appropriate cases, the parties may agree or the court may direct that some or all discovery materials that have not been stored in electronic form should nonetheless be produced, at least in the first instance, in an electronic format and how the expenses of doing so will be allocated among the parties.
    b. ~~Upon request,~~ aA party serving written discovery requests or responses should provide the other party or parties with ~~a diskette or other~~an electronic version of the requests or responses unless the parties have previously agreed that no electronic version is required.

2004 Comment

Subdivision (a). This change is not substantive but merely clarifying. If the data sought in discovery already exist in electronic form, there is no need for a court order requiring their production in that format. This subdivision is directed at the production in electronic format of data not currently stored electronically. The amendment makes that clear.

Subdivision (b). Subdivision (b) has been amended to interpose a presumption where previously a request was suggested. As amended, this subdivision affirmatively recommends that counsel provide adversaries with discovery requests or responses in electronic format unless the parties have previously agreed to the contrary. Because the Standard is purely precatory, it imposes no duty. Rather, it recommends a practice for counsel to consider.

31. Discovery Conferences.
   a. At the initial discovery conference, the parties should confer about any electronic discovery that they anticipate requesting from one another, including:
      i. The subject matter of such discovery.
      ii. The time period with respect to which such discovery may be sought.
      iii. Identification or description of the party-affiliated persons, entities or groups from whom such discovery may be sought.
      iv. Identification or description of those persons currently or formerly affiliated with the prospective responding party who are knowledgeable of the information systems, technology and software necessary to access potentially responsive data.
      v. The potentially responsive data that exist, including the platforms on which, and places where, such data may be found as set forth in Standard 29 (a).
      vi. The accessibility of the potentially responsive data, including discussion of software, hardware or other specialized equipment that may be necessary to obtain access.
      vii. Whether potentially responsive data exist in searchable form.
      viii. Whether potentially responsive electronic data will be requested and produced:
         A. In electronic form or in hard copy, and
         B. If in electronic form, the format in which the data exist or will be produced
      ix. Data retention policies applicable to potentially responsive data.
      x. Preservation of potentially responsive data, specifically addressing (A) preservation of data generated subsequent to the filing of the claim, (B) data otherwise customarily subject to destruction in ordinary course, and (C) metadata reflecting the creation, editing, transmittal, receipt or opening of responsive data.
      xi. The use of key terms or other selection criteria to search potentially responsive data for discoverable information.
      xii. The identity of unaffiliated information technology consultants whom the litigants agree are capable of independently extracting, searching or otherwise exploiting potentially responsive data.
      xiii. Stipulating to the entry of a court order providing that production to other parties, or review by a mutually-agreed indepen-

dent information technology consultant, of attorney-client privileged or attorney work-product protected electronic data will not effect a waiver of privilege or work product protection.

xiv. The appropriateness of an inspection of computer systems, software, or data to facilitate or focus the discovery of electronic data.

xv. The allocation of costs.

b. At any discovery conference that concerns particular requests for electronic discovery, in addition to conferring about the topics set forth in subsection (a), the parties should consider, where appropriate, stipulating to the entry of a court order providing for:

i. The initial production of tranches or subsets of potentially responsive data to allow the parties to evaluate the likely benefit of production of additional data, without prejudice to the requesting party's right to insist later on more complete production.

ii. The use of specified key terms or other selection criteria to search some or all of the potentially responsive data for discoverable information, in lieu of production.

iii. The appointment of a mutually-agreed, independent information technology consultant pursuant to Standard 32(a) to:

A. Extract defined categories of potentially responsive data from specified sources, or

B. Search or otherwise exploit potentially responsive data in accordance with specific, mutually-agreed parameters.

2004 Comment

The Federal Rules of Civil Procedure require a discovery conference at the outset of every case and prior to the filing of any discovery motion. Practices vary district by district. State court practice varies state by state, but a conference early in the case is sensible in connection with electronic discovery, regardless of whether it is compelled. Standard 31 focuses on effective use of discovery conferences to address electronic discovery issues.

Subdivision (a). Subdivision (a) focuses on the initial discovery conference. It specifies several categories of electronic discovery related matters that the parties should confer about at an initial discovery conference. It is intended to assist counsel and the court by providing a detailed array of potentially relevant issues to address. These include:

- Subject matter
- Relevant time period
- Identification of the party-affiliated persons or entities from whom electronic discovery may be sought
- Identification of those persons (including former employees) who are knowledgeable of the information systems, technology and software necessary to access potentially responsive data
- The universe of potentially responsive data that exist, including the platforms on which, and places where, such data may be found (including databases, networks, systems, servers, archives, back up or disaster recovery systems, tapes, discs, drives, cartridges and other storage media, laptops, PCs, Internet data, and PDAs)
- Accessibility issues, such as the software that may be necessary to access data
- Whether potentially responsive data exist in searchable form
- Whether potentially responsive electronic data will be requested and produced in electronic form or in hard copy
- Data retention policies
- Preservation issues, including preservation of data generated subsequent to the filing of the claim
- Possible use of key terms or other selection criteria to scour massive amounts of data for relevant information

Anticipating the privilege-related issues addressed in Standard 32, subdivision (a)(xii) suggests that the parties discuss whether they can agree on the names of unaffiliated information-technology consultants who would be capable of serving them jointly, either in a privately-retained or court-appointed capacity. In the same vein, subdivision (a)(xiii) proposes that the parties consider whether it would be desirable for them to stipulate to entry of a court order along the lines discussed in Standard 32(b) or (c).

Subdivision (b). Subdivision (b) focuses on discovery conferences relating to outstanding discovery requests (in common parlance, the "meet-and-confer"). It recognizes that there are additional issues for the parties to consider once discovery demands have been served and specific issues are on the table. Subdivision (b) anticipates a number of the privilege-related initiatives contained in Standard 32, recommending that the parties consider stipulating to a court order providing for:

- Initial production, on a without-prejudice basis, of subsets of electronic data to allow the parties to evaluate the likely benefit of production of additional data;
- The use of search terms or other selection criteria in lieu of production; or
- The appointment of an independent consultant pursuant to Standard 32

32. Attorney-Client Privilege and Attorney Work Product. To ameliorate attorney-client privilege and work product concerns attendant to the production of electronic data, the parties should consider, where appropriate, stipulating to the entry of a court order:

    a. Appointing a mutually-agreed, independent information technology consultant as a special master, referee, or other officer or agent of the court such that extraction and review of privileged or otherwise protected electronic data will not effect a waiver of privilege or other legal protection attaching to the data.

    b. Providing that production to other parties of attorney-client privileged or attorney work-product protected electronic data will not effect a waiver of privilege or work product protection attaching to the data. In stipulating to the entry of such an order, the parties should consider the potential impact that production of privileged or protected data may have on the producing party's ability to maintain privilege or work-product protection vis-à-vis third parties not subject to the order.

    c. Providing that extraction and review by a mutually-agreed independent information technology consultant of attorney-client privileged or attorney work-product protected electronic data will not effect a waiver of privilege or work product protection attaching to the data.

    d. Setting forth a procedure for the review of the potentially responsive data extracted under subdivision (a), (b), or (c). The order should specify that adherence to the procedure precludes any waiver of privilege or work product protection attaching to the data. The order may contemplate, at the producing party's option:

        i. Initial review by the producing party for attorney-client privilege or attorney work product protection, with production of the

> > unprivileged and unprotected data to follow, accompanied with a privilege log, or
> ii. Initial review by the requesting party, followed by:
> > A. Production to the producing party of all data deemed relevant by the requesting party, followed by
> > B. A review by the producing party for attorney-client privilege or attorney work product protection. Before agreeing to this procedure, the producing party should consider the potential impact that it may have on the producing party's ability to maintain privilege or work-product protection attaching to any such data if subsequently demanded by non-parties.
> > The court's order should contemplate resort to the court for resolution of disputes concerning the privileged or protected nature of particular electronic data.

> e. Prior to receiving any data, any mutually-agreed independent information technology consultant should be required to provide the court and the parties with an affidavit confirming that the consultant will keep no copy of any data provided to it and will not disclose any data provided other than pursuant to the court's order or parties' agreement. At the conclusion of its engagement, the consultant should be required confirm under oath that it has acted, and will continue to act, in accordance with its initial affidavit.

> f. If the initial review is conducted by the requesting party in accordance with subsection (d)(ii), the requesting party should provide the court and the producing party an affidavit stating that the requesting party will keep no copy of data deemed by the producing party to be privileged or work product, subject to final resolution of any dispute by the court, and will not use or reveal the substance of any such data unless permitted to do so by the court.

2004 Comment

Standard 32 deals with privilege and work product (collectively, "privilege") concerns. It applies in the common situation in which electronic data must be extracted for production by an information technology (IT) expert not employed by the producing party. This scenario by definition raises a risk of waiver because privileged documents are being exposed to persons outside the privilege. Standard 32 sets forth three methods to ameliorate the risk of waiver. Each would be implemented by entry of a stipulated court order.

Subdivision (a). Subdivision (a) suggests that the parties consider having the court appoint a mutually-agreed IT consultant as a special master, referee, or other officer of the court, so that the consultant's extraction and review of privileged electronic data will not effect a waiver. This approach would allow the third party consultant to pull and have access to privileged material (which may be included in any mass extraction of data) without risk that the holder of the privilege will have effected a waiver by permitting the third party to review them. Following extraction, the parties are then free to specify whatever protocol they prefer with respect to review of the data. This is addressed in subdivision (d).

Subdivision (b). Subdivision (b) addresses what is sometimes known as the "quick peek" approach to electronic discovery. Under the quick-peek scenario envisioned by subdivisions (b) and (d)(ii), the requesting party may have sufficient resources to perform or pay for the extraction, and the producing party may be inclined to allow its opponent to incur all expenses associated with doing so. At the same time, the producing party has no interest in waiving privilege. The parties therefore agree that the data will be turned over to the requesting party without review by the producing party; the requesting party will identify which documents it is interested in, and the producing party will then conduct a privilege review. Subdivision (b) captures the court order necessary to permit this procedure to proceed.

Under subdivision (b), the parties stipulate to an order providing that production of privileged electronic data will not effect a waiver. Note that this is different from the customary agreed order, which provides that *inadvertent* production will not effect a waiver, because parties using the subdivision (b) approach may know or be fairly certain that privileged material is contained in the mass of data to be extracted. Like that order, however, there is some question as to the effectiveness of such an order vis-à-vis a third party who subsequently seeks the disclosed data. Accordingly, there is an appropriate caution in the text of this subdivision and in subdivision (d)(ii).

Subdivision (c). Subdivision (c) is similar to subdivision (a) in that it envisions the use of an agreed third-party consultant. Under subdivision (c), unlike subdivision (a), that consultant is not appointed as a special master or other court officer. The court, for example, may not be inclined to appoint the consultant as a master or the parties may prefer to control the consultant directly. Subdivision (c) is also similar to subdivision (b) in that it envisions the entry of an order providing that review of intentionally-produced privileged data will not effect a waiver. But the reviewing party under subdivision (c) is an agreed-on consultant, not the opposition. As under both subdivisions (a) and (b), under subdivision (c) the parties are free to specify whatever protocol they prefer with respect to review of the data, following extraction. This is addressed in subdivision (d).

As observed in the comment to subdivision (b), *supra*, in current practice, there is no assurance that a stipulated order providing that inadvertent production does not effect a waiver will be effective against a claim of waiver asserted by a third party. Precisely the same risk is posed by the order envisaged by subdivision (c). Accordingly, it is imperative that litigants following either of these routes also have in place a confidentiality order as a second line of defense against inquisitive third parties. It is equally important that the litigants develop a protocol for, or otherwise instruct, the consultant to minimize the likelihood that the consultant will actually review (as opposed to extract) privileged material.

Subdivision (d). Subdivision (d) sets forth a pair of alternative procedures for the parties to consider with respect to the review of the data once the data have been extracted. Subdivision (d)(i) states that traditional approach, in which the extracted data are furnished to the producing party, who then conducts a review for responsiveness and privilege, and makes production of the data together with a privilege log. Subdivision (d)(ii) identifies an unconventional approach that some parties prefer for financial reasons, as where there is an enormous amount of electronic data, little of it is likely to be either responsive or privileged, and little of that will fall in both categories. Under the (d)(ii) approach, the requesting party first reviews the data for responsiveness and provides to the producing party all data in which it is interested. The producing party then determines if any of the data in question are privileged. If so, the requesting party may not maintain copies of the privileged material unless and until a court sustains its objections to the claim of privilege. This procedure raises the risk of waiver of privilege identified in the comment to subdivision (b). Accordingly, the text of subdivision (d)(ii)(B) contains substantially the same caution as that set forth in subdivision (b).

Subdivision (e). Subdivision (e) suggests a reasonable precaution — that any IT consultant employed by the parties be required to execute an affidavit confirming that it will keep no copy of any data and will not disclose any data provided other than pursuant to the court's order or parties' agreement.

Subdivision (f). Subdivision (f) provides that, before receiving the data pursuant to subdivision (d)(ii), the requesting party is to execute an affidavit stating that it will keep no copy of data deemed by the producing party to be privileged, subject to final resolution of any dispute by the court. This precaution is appropriate in light of the trust that the producing party reposes in the requesting party under the quick-peek approach captured in subdivisions (b) and (d)(ii).

33. Technological Advances. To the extent that information may be contained or stored in a data compilation in a form other than electronic or paper, it is intended that Standards 29-32 may be consulted with respect to discovery of such information, with appropriate modifications for the difference in storage medium.

2004 Comment

Standard 33 recognizes the impracticability of keeping pace with technological change. New, non-electronic media may emerge for the creation or retention of electronic data. This Standard suggests that Standards 29-32 be consulted with respect to discovery of such data, subject to common sense modifications.

Table of Cases

Index

F

W